Decolonizing Mission Partnerships

American Society of Missiology Monograph Series

Series Editor, James R. Krabill

The ASM Monograph Series provides a forum for publishing quality dissertations and studies in the field of missiology. Collaborating with Pickwick Publications—a division of Wipf and Stock Publishers of Eugene, Oregon—the American Society of Missiology selects high quality dissertations and other monographic studies that offer research materials in mission studies for scholars, mission and church leaders, and the academic community at large. The ASM seeks scholarly work for publication in the series that throws light on issues confronting Christian world mission in its cultural, social, historical, biblical, and theological dimensions.

Missiology is an academic field that brings together scholars whose professional training ranges from doctoral-level preparation in areas such as Scripture, history and sociology of religions, anthropology, theology, international relations, interreligious interchange, mission history, inculturation, and church law. The American Society of Missiology, which sponsors this series, is an ecumenical body drawing members from Independent and Ecumenical Protestant, Catholic, Orthodox, and other traditions. Members of the ASM are united by their commitment to reflect on and do scholarly work relating to both mission history and the present-day mission of the church. The ASM Monograph Series aims to publish works of exceptional merit on specialized topics, with particular attention given to work by younger scholars, the dissemination and publication of which is difficult under the economic pressures of standard publishing models.

Persons seeking information about the ASM or the guidelines for having their dissertations considered for publication in the ASM Monograph Series should consult the Society's website—www.asmweb.org.

Members of the ASM Monograph Committee who approved this book are:

Michael A. Rynkiewich, Professor of Anthropology (retired), Asbury Theological Seminary

Sarita D. Gallagher, Associate Professor of Religion, George Fox University

RECENTLY PUBLISHED IN THE ASM MONOGRAPH SERIES

Rosalia Meza, *Toward a New, Praxis-Oriented Missiology: Rediscovering Paulo Freire's Concept of Conscientizacao and Enhancing Christian Mission as Prophetic Dialogue*

James A. Blumenstock, *Strangers in a Familiar Land: A Phenomenological Study on Marginal Christian Identity*

Decolonizing Mission Partnerships

Evolving Collaboration between United Methodists in North Katanga and the United States of America

TAYLOR WALTERS DENYER

American Society of Missiology Monograph
Series vol. 47

☙PICKWICK *Publications* · Eugene, Oregon

DECOLONIZING MISSION PARTNERSHIPS
Evolving Collaboration between United Methodists in North Katanga and the United States of America

American Society of Missiology Monograph Series 47

Copyright © 2020 Taylor Walters Denyer. All rights reserved. Except for brief quotations in critical publications or reviews, no part of this book may be reproduced in any manner without prior written permission from the publisher. Write: Permissions, Wipf and Stock Publishers, 199 W. 8th Ave., Suite 3, Eugene, OR 97401.

Pickwick Publications
An Imprint of Wipf and Stock Publishers
199 W. 8th Ave., Suite 3
Eugene, OR 97401

www.wipfandstock.com

PAPERBACK ISBN: 978-1-7252-5911-9
HARDCOVER ISBN: 978-1-7252-5912-6
EBOOK ISBN: 978-1-7252-5913-3

Cataloguing-in-Publication data:

Names: Denyer, Taylor Walters, author.

Title: Decolonizing mission partnerships : evolving collaboration between United Methodists in North Katanga and the United States of America / by Taylor Walters Denyer.

Description: Eugene, OR: Pickwick Publications, 2020. | American Society of Missiology Monograph Series 47 | Includes bibliographical references.

Identifiers: ISBN 978-1-7252-5911-9 (paperback) | ISBN 978-1-7252-5912-6 (hardcover) | ISBN 978-1-7252-5913-3 (ebook)

Subjects: LCSH: Methodist Church (U.S.)—Missions. | Missions—Congo (Democratic Republic)—Katanga—History.

Classification: BV3625.C6 D46 2020 (print) | BV3625.C6 (ebook)

Use of 7-point mission praxis matrix image granted by JNJ Kritzinger.

All other images used are in public domain.

05/27/21

Contents

Acknowledgments | vii
Summary and Key Terms | ix
Abbreviations | xi

1. Introduction and Research Overview | 1
2. Theoretical Framework | 31
3. The Historical Cultural Context | 62
4. Methodist Mission Partnerships in Katanga | 80
5. Racism, Violence, and Exploitation | 142
6. Reflections on the Relationship | 172
7. Reflecting Theologically on the Relationship | 267
8. Mission Partners Moving Forward | 330
    Epilogue: When a Missionary Dies | 333

Appendix: Introductory Letter, Consent Form, and Interview Schedule | 335
Bibliography | 339

Acknowledgments

The thesis could not have been accomplished without the many people who supported me along the way.

Thank you to my academic advisor, "Klippies" Kritzinger, for introducing me to authors and ideas I would not have found on my own. Thank you for your words of encouragement and for helping me shape my ideas into a structured work.

Thank you to the other scholars who have helped me in my research and writing process, especially to Pamela Couture, Jeffrey Hoover, David Maxwell, and Rene Sephton for sharing their research on Katanga history with me, including copies of difficult-to-obtain documents. Thank you to Kate Koppy and David Scott for your assistance and advice on the pragmatic aspects of writing and editing this thesis.

Thank you to my husband, who made these years of focused research and writing possible, and thank you to my entire family, especially my father, who died before this thesis' completion, for being my coach and co-conspirator.

Thank you to my past and present bishops, Bishop Ntambo and Bishop Mande, for giving their blessings for me to pursue my research topic, to John Maloba and Joseph Mulongo for helping me strategically identify and locate retired clergy, and to all interview participants for giving of your time and trusting me with your memories and your words of wisdom. *Wafwa ko sana.*

Summary and Key Terms

THIS THESIS ASKS "WHAT would a decolonized partnership look like between North Katangan and American United Methodists?" Guided by the 7-point mission praxis matrix developed in the missiology department at the University of South Africa, it explores a series of subquestions. First, the terms "mission," "partnership," and "decolonize" are defined, and literature applicable to these concepts is discussed. In chapter 3, the historical relational power structures and culture of the Luba and Lunda Kingdoms are summarized. Chapter 4 provides a historical overview of American and North Katangan United Methodist (UM) collaborations and describes the dominant relational dynamics and mission models of each time period. This chapter draws heavily from memoirs, reports, and articles published by United Methodist agencies. Chapter 5 explores the psycho-affective dimension of these interactions, focusing on identifying issues of guilt, shame, grief, trauma, and racial biases at play. Chapter 6 documents the responses to in-depth interviews with North Katangan UMs and American collaborators about their memories and beliefs about a twenty-year period (approx. 1994–2014), during which a shift took place in the how North Katangan (DR Congo) church leaders viewed their own capacities relative to those of the American United Methodists they encountered. The final section compares the theological reflections of interview participants, explores the ways in which Methodist doctrine and praxis can be used in furthering the decolonization and healing process through the partnerships, and explores pathways forward. The interviews conducted reveal areas of tension in the partnership, differing missiologies (e.g., *mission as outreach* vs. *mission as relationship*), and visions of the future of the partnership. The responses show that the partnership is currently on a trajectory towards decolonization, but

Summary and Key Terms

that more needs to be done in the areas of healing and self-awareness—both on the individual and collective level.

KEY TERMS:

Christian mission; partnership; The United Methodist Church; North Katanga; patronage; mission as partnership; decolonization; Luba culture; trauma recovery; racism; savior complex

Abbreviations

ACGD	Africa Church Growth and Development Initiative
CEM	Congo Evangelistic Mission, a Pentecostal organization formed in 1919
EMC	Evangelical Missions Council
FDI	Foreign Direct Investment
GBGM	General Board of Global Ministries (of The United Methodist Church)
GBOD	General Board of Discipleship (of The United Methodist Church)
GCAH	General Commission on Archives and History
GCORR	General Commission on Religion and Race
LGBTQ	Lesbian Gay Bisexual Transgendered Queer
MEC	Methodist Episcopal Church
NWO	New World Outlook
POC	Person of Color
UM	United Methodist
UMC	United Methodist Church
UMCOM	United Methodist Communications
UMCOR	United Methodist Committee on Relief
UMN	United Methodist News
UMNS	United Methodist News Service

1

Introduction and Research Overview

1.1 INTRODUCTION

IN 2018, THE UNITED Methodist Church's (UMC) North Katanga Conference celebrated the fiftieth anniversary of its official creation. The history of Methodism in Katanga, DR Congo, dates back further still. In 2010, The UMC's North Katanga and South Congo Episcopal Areas observed one hundred years of Methodism in the region with a grand ceremony in Lubumbashi[1] and a commemorative book[2] with submissions by both American and Congolese members.

Methodism in Katanga began as a collaboration between American missionaries and Katangan evangelists. Its start is usually marked by the arrival dates of Helen Emily [Chapman] Rasmussen Springer and Rev. John McKendree Springer. Upon hearing of the Springers' presence in the region, Congolese Methodists such as Kayeka Changand[3] and Kaluwashi returned home from Angola (where Methodist mission stations already existed) to collaborate with the Springers in hopes of spreading Methodism

---

1. While the celebratory ceremonies were large-scale, with several bishops and dignitaries in attendance, the centennial was not mentioned in the main United Methodist news outlets (headquartered in the United States of America). Some details of the event are discussed in the missionary blog post: Persons and Persons, "July News Centennial."

2. Hoover et al., *L'Église Méthodiste-Unie au Katanga*. This book focuses heavily on the history of the South Congo Episcopal Area due to a lack of submissions from the North Katanga Area.

3. In July 2018, North Katanga celebrated its fiftieth anniversary as a conference. Descendants of Changand, Kaluwashi, and other significant Congolese Methodist evangelists were in attendance and given opportunities to speak about them. Their oral histories about Changand and Kaluwashi affirmed the published histories.

1

into Katanga.⁴ Historian, professor, and American United Methodist (UM) missionary⁵ Jeffrey Hoover stresses that these Methodist missions in Katanga "operated on the ground largely through indigenous evangelists and catechists," but he notes that "*indigenous* is also a misleading term for many of their African co-workers, a very cosmopolitan group."⁶ That is, the original "indigenous" Methodist evangelists were predominately well-travelled in comparison to those in the communities they were serving. They would have been viewed as returnees, having spent years of their lives living in other countries.

Through the memoirs of John Springer,⁷ the official minutes of the denomination's Congo Mission Conference,⁸ the research and writings of Jeffrey Hoover,⁹ the oral histories of second-generation American UM missionaries such as Lori Persons and John Enright as well as other missionary memoirs and biographies,¹⁰ much can be said about the early days of Methodism in Katanga as told from the vantage point of American missionaries. The United Methodist Archives and History Center, located at Drew University in Madison, New Jersey, is a repository of many historical photos and other missionary artifacts of Methodism in Katanga. A handful of UM Congolese historians from the South Congo Episcopal Area, with its relative wealth and easier access to computers and printing presses, have also written on the history of Methodism in the region,¹¹ and a number of student papers are on file in paper format at the library at The UMC's Katanga Methodist University in Mulungwishi, DR Congo. That said, there remains a dearth of published writings and recorded oral histories on the history of Methodism in North Katanga as told from the perspective of North Katangans.

   4. Hoover, "Sipilingas," 74.
   5. Whenever I write "American [United] Methodist" or "Congolese/Katangan [United] Methodist," it is to note the nationality of the individuals, not to imply that these are separate institutions. For the sake of brevity in writing, "America/American" in this thesis refers to the United States of America and citizens of that country. I regret there is no practical alternative term since all people from North, Central, and South America are Americans.
   6. Hoover, "Sipilingas," 74.
   7. Springer, *Pioneering in the Congo*.
   8. A number of the early meeting reports are on file at Yale University's library; I obtained scanned copies.
   9. E.g., Hoover, "Sipilingas"; "Big Men"; "La construction de la Wallace Memorial Church."
   10. E.g., Riendeau, *Deep Gladness*.
   11. E.g., Nkonge, *Examination*; Ngandu, *Contextual Evangelism*. Unfortunately, I did not find copies of these theses until April 2019, after my thesis submission.

The relationship between American Methodist missionaries in Katanga and Congolese Methodist leadership has always been complex. The dynamics of this relationship have evolved over the decades—from a colonial mission model, to a nominal partnership, to something yet to be defined and still emerging. This study explores these changes, compares the different points of view on aspects of this relationship, and looks to see what global trends and mission conversations are impacting its trajectory. While the history of The UMC's South Congo Conference is discussed in the context of the events leading up to the founding of its North Katanga Conference in 1968, this study is focused on the dynamics between the North Katanga Conference leadership and American UMs who have been involved in mission initiatives there.

"Decolonizing Mission Partnerships" was chosen as the title of this study because it seeks to examine a twenty-year period (approx. 1994–2014) during which, according to the assertions of nearly all North Katangans interviewed, a shift took place in terms of a decolonization of how North Katangan church leaders viewed their own capacities relative to those of the American United Methodists they encountered. In the early 1990s, a new eruption of deadly political violence, including pillages, began in the North Katanga region. Foreign missionaries began leaving in waves, with the last holdouts being forced to evacuate in 1998. When the American missionaries and much of the funding for mission station projects in North Katanga left, North Katangans stepped up into full church leadership in terms of identifying mission agendas and contributing to The UMC on the denominational level and in ministry settings in the United States.[12] It was during this period without foreign missionaries that North Katanga began reporting record growth such that it became and remains the largest (in terms of official membership numbers) conference in The UMC.

---

12. A strong argument could be made for an earlier tipping point in the South Congo United Methodist Episcopal Area. A number of interviewees who have lived in Lubumbashi (a major city where the South Congo Area's main headquarters are located) noted that, in contrast to North Katanga, The UMC's South Congo Conference owns profitable businesses, self-funds major construction projects, and runs numerous programs without seeking external assistance. While the causal factors and the dates of the turning point in South Congo are outside of the limits of this study, the fact that there are many Congolese United Methodists in Lubumbashi who have well-paid jobs, successful businesses, and opportunities to travel seem to be the obvious differences between the two areas to consider. The bishop of South Congo (Bishop Katembo) during this time period also had a noticeably different approach than Bishop Ntambo when it came to making efforts to request funds from Americans and, based on talk among missionaries and my anecdotal observations, was slow to show hospitality to Americans until/unless they earned his respect. The causes and results of this approach are a quandary worth noting but beyond this study.

4   Decolonizing Mission Partnerships

As is discussed in this study, the eruption of war/violence in Katanga, the evacuation of foreigners, the arrival of cell phones and internet, the coming-of-age of the first generation[13] of North Katangans to earn advanced degrees and travel and serve internationally, the increase in UM membership in Africa and decrease in America, and the escalation of denominational fights over social issues[14] all converged to create a new context where North Katangan[15] and American UMs began to view and interact with each other differently.[16]

1.2 STUDY LOCATION

While North Katangan church leaders are increasingly traveling in recent years and serving in other countries such as the United States of America (USA), the majority of the history and narratives discussed in this thesis take place within the boundaries of The UMC's North Katanga Conference. For the sake of clarity, shown below is a map delineating The UMC's episcopal areas in DR Congo and the bishops who led them in 2016.[17] The North Katanga and Tanganyika Conferences are shown in the section of the map labeled Bishop Ntambo. Bishop Ntambo was the United Methodist bishop over North Katanga, Tanganyika and Tanzania from 1996 until his official retirement in 2016.[18] The area labeled Bishop Katembo[19] (retired) delineates

---

13. By "first" I am referring to the first wave of significant numbers of church leaders earning masters and doctorates and traveling internationally. There were a few who had the opportunity to study abroad in the past (including a few who immigrated to the USA), but it was not until the past twenty years that these numbers became significant.

14. Voting delegate spots at the UM General (legislative) Conference are determined by membership size of a conference. North Katanga's reported membership numbers increased during this period, resulting in both courtship (for votes) and resentment by American UMs who saw that North Katanga and other African conferences now had the determining votes on controversial denominational stances on social issues.

15. It was during this period that North Katanga became its own United Methodist Episcopal area. Since South Congo and North Katanga are operating out of distinct contexts (South Congo is more urban and has wealthier members), my focus is on North Katanga, which is also the conference of my church membership.

16. This statement refers to general trends in behavior. There are examples of individual North Katangans and Americans who made this shift in thinking long before this period.

17. I created this image by drawing lines on the map found on Wikimedia Commons: "DRCongo Provinces Named." Boundaries drawn by me according to illustration in Lovell, *100th Anniversary*, 30.

18. While officially retired in 2016, he served as acting bishop until the election of Bishop Mande in March 2017.

19. Bishop Katembo was elected bishop in 1980 and officially retired in 2016. His successor was elected in 2017. For portions of his episcopacy, he also oversaw the North

the boundaries of the South Congo episcopal area within the DR Congo.[20] A number of the towns and communities mentioned in chapters 3 and 4 are located in the South Congo episcopal area.

1.3 RESEARCH QUESTION

This study seeks to answer the central research question: "What would a decolonized partnership look like between North Katangan and American United Methodists?" Guided by the 7-point mission praxis matrix developed in the missiology department at the University of South Africa, I explored the following sub-questions:[21]

Katanga area.

20. Just as the North Katanga Episcopal Area created a new conference in Tanzania, the South Congo Episcopal Area spread into Zambia, especially after many missionaries and Congolese were displaced there during the violence in Congo in the late 1990s.

21. Some research projects take their starting point in a problem statement or hypothesis, but mine is driven and structured by a central research question out of which flows a set of sub-questions. The answering of the central question is made possible by addressing the sub-questions. It is this set of questions that gives coherence and

1.3.1 What are the macro-level missiological conversations that this study should be viewed through? How are mission, partnership, and (de)colonization understood in the context of this research?

1.3.2 What are the African cultural, economic, and political patterns that have been prevalent in Katanga before, during, and after the active United Methodist missionary presence?

1.3.3 How did The UMC arrive, spread, and develop in North Katanga? What narratives have been told about this history?

1.3.4 What psychological impact has Katanga's history of colonization and violence had on the people of the region? What unhealed traumas do Americans bring into the relationship? How has this affected the partnership between US and Katangan Methodists?

1.3.5 What are the main issues and assertions that arise when North Katangan and American United Methodists reflect upon the recent (past two decades) developments in their partnerships?

1.3.6 How do participants in the partnership theologically interpret this relationship and what are the dominant missiological models at play? What theological resources are there in the Methodist (and specifically the United Methodist) tradition that can be reclaimed/mobilized/activated to foster a decolonizing partnership? How can our understanding of Scripture and atonement help in healing unhealthy aspects of these relationships?

1.3.7 What contribution can this study make to global missiological discussions on decolonizing partnerships?

1.4 OBJECTIVES AND RELEVANCE OF THE STUDY

The primary academic objective of this study is to bring together a number of scholarly conversations (decolonialism, Third Wave mission, partnerships, racism, etc.) and demonstrate how relational dynamics of boundary-crossing collaborations between church leaders can be better understood by analyzing them through the lens of these conversations.

Beyond its potential for increasing the fruitfulness of future collaborations between North Katangan and American UMs, this study could help The UMC and other denominations better reflect upon the history of colonial mindsets and structures in their mission models and the state of their

---

integrity to the study, since it holds it together as an organic whole. See section 1.12 for more on how these seven questions relate to the mission praxis matrix.

current mission collaborations and identify opportunities for ways forward in developing more meaningful partnerships in the ongoing service of God's mission together.

1.5 LIMITATIONS OF THE STUDY

The recorded interviews conducted for this study asked only about knowledge and perceptions of North Katangan-American interactions in The UMC since the 1990s. This was the period when North Katanga went from having several foreign missionaries to having none. It is also, as I document in this thesis, when a number of other significant shifts occurred that impacted how North Katangans view themselves and interact with the world outside their borders (war, cell phones, internet, scholarships to study abroad, etc.) as well as when American United Methodists began communicating in new ways (e-mail, websites, social media) with each other and their international partners.

While my research included reading the majority of accessible published documents on the history of Methodism in Katanga, this thesis does not attempt to discuss or analyze the entire history of the relationship between American and Katangan Methodists, nor does it attempt to document the history of the ministries of The UMC's North Katanga Conference.[22] The interviews I conducted specifically asked the interviewees to focus on the 1990s until the time of the interview (although some interviewees chose to also speak about their memories of earlier decades, asserting that this was necessary to put their comments in a larger historical context). In addition, this study avoids reporting on specific scandals, accusations against living individuals, or other matters that could rekindle conflicts.

This study looks specifically at the perceptions of North Katanga UMC church leaders and American UMs who have had significant interactions with them. While this can shed light on other relationships, it cannot be used to generalize the current state of relational dynamics in other UM conferences—even neighboring conferences, such as Tanganyika and South Congo, which have different economic contexts—or North Katanga's relationship with Methodist mission organizations in Europe. It focuses on church ministry collaboration dynamics as opposed to other possible interactions, such as sexual/romantic or the complexities of person-to-person friendships across cultural and socio-economic lines.

---

22. I have been unable to locate a comprehensive study on the history of the ministries of The UMC's North Katanga Conference and have concluded that such a document does not exist. I do, however, discuss in chapter 4 portions of that history.

One challenge to my attempts at analysis of the relational dynamics and where they are headed is the role I and my family members have played in North Katanga partnerships this past quarter-century. This became increasingly complicated when, while in the midst of writing this thesis, the newly elected bishop of North Katanga (who knew about my research) appointed me as his assistant tasked with strategic partnership and engagement. To avoid the problems of chasing my own tail and/or making predictions without disclosing sensitive information I now hold due to my appointment, my original plans of using the final part of the thesis to predict and/or critique strategies for the next stage of North Katanga's partnerships have been truncated to conversations about the values and beliefs that have become the foundation of my strategy recommendations.

1.6 STATE OF THE RESEARCH

In the process of my research, I consulted several publications that influenced both the focus of my study and the way in which I analyzed the interview data I collected.

My inquiries into information specific to the history of the relationship between The UMC in the USA and North Katanga led me to conclude that few published documents exist on the subject,[23] and no formal study has been done—especially not on the shifts that have occurred over the past two decades. My findings on recent history were limited to a few pages about DR Congo in *From Missions to Mission: The History of Mission of The United Methodist Church, 1968–2000*,[24] a biography of an American UM missionary couple who left Katanga in the 1990s,[25] Bob Walters's memoir on his thoughts and observations on The UMC's missional work in Katanga over the past twenty five years,[26] and a recently published creative non-fiction novel, *We Are Not All Victims: Local Peacebuilding in the Democratic Republic of Congo*,[27] which focuses on North Katangan leadership during the war that started in the late 1990s. In addition, I searched the digital archives of the United Methodist News Service and New World Outlook (the publication of The UMC's General Board of

---

23. I consulted with faculty at universities in Katanga, staff of The UMC's General Board of Global Ministries and the United Methodist Archives and History Center, North Katangan colleagues, and former American missionaries to Katanga. I also searched online databases of publications via UNISA's library.

24. Harman, *From Missions to Mission*.

25. Riendeau, *Deep Gladness*.

26. Walters, *Last Missionary*.

27. Couture, *We Are Not All Victims*.

Global Ministries) and entered key information from each article I found about DR Congo/Katanga into spreadsheet form in order to examine the content, frequency and semantics of these stories. This helped in terms of establishing the dates of significant events, noting which events were/ weren't covered in the denomination's news outlets, as well as looking for trends in the way in which the stories were told (e.g., Who had agency in the story? Was the language that of charity?).

In attempts to acquire more written accounts of The UMC's North Katanga conference's history, I reached out to each North Katangan United Methodist I knew of who had written a paper or thesis on the topic. Unfortunately, most felt that their writings were not ready for distribution. Due to this lack of publicly available documented accounts of the history of The UMC in North Katanga told by North Katangans, I was very tempted to ask each North Katangan I interviewed to recount all they could remember about the history of Methodism in the region. However, I was wisely advised to limit the focus of my recorded interviews to a more manageable period of time.

In terms of the socio-political history of the Katanga region, there are many publications in English that provide the macro-level backdrop, but most books and articles focus on political/military figures and/or the history of violence in DR Congo.[28] There have also been—on a much more limited scale—ethnographic studies focusing on the culture and traditional political structures of the people groups of the North Katanga region, the most famous being Placide Tempels's *Bantu Philosophy*.[29] Mutombo Nkulu-N'Sengha, a native of Katanga now on faculty at California State University, is currently writing a (not-yet-published) response to Tempels's famous work. His paper "Bumuntu Memory and Authentic Personhood: An African Art of Becoming Humane"[30] touches upon some of the issues that his book plans to address.

Other studies include Anne Wilson's *Long Distance Trade and the Luba Lumami Empire*,[31] which looks at the impact of foreign traders on the Luba empire; Mary Nooter Robert's *The King is a Woman: Shaping Power in Luba Royal Arts*,[32] in which she explores the ambiguities of gender in royal power hierarchies and art (including the role of the Mwadi, a woman in whom

28. E.g., Stearns, *Dancing in the Glory of Monsters*; Hochschild, *King Leopold's Ghost*; Nzongol-Ntalaja, *Congo*.
29. Tempels, *Bantu Philosophy*.
30. Mutombo, "Bumuntu Memory."
31. Wilson, "Long Distance Trade."
32. Nooter Roberts, "King is a Woman."

a dead king's spirit dwells);³³ Thomas Reefe's book *The Rainbow and the Kings*,³⁴ a study on the history of the Luba Empire until the late 1800s, which details the origin stories of the Luba people as well as documents political power structures and how decisions of transfer of power were made; and David Maxwell's paper "The Soul of the Luba: W. F. P. Burton, Missionary Ethnography and Belgian Colonial Science,"³⁵ which provides another layer of insights with his exploration of how the early missionaries in Katanga (especially William Burton) were passionate about ethnographic studies despite their intentions to drastically change local beliefs and practices.

A significant number of Congolese and francophone scholars have written on DR Congo's history.³⁶ This thesis leans heavily on the writings (in English) of George Nzongol-Ntalaja and Mutombo Nkulu-N'Sengha for a Congolese perspective on the region's political and cultural history. While reaching out to those currently on faculty in history departments at major universities in DR Congo would have created richer discussions in the history chapters, in order to maintain a manageable scope of research, this thesis seeks only to provide a broad-brush historical backdrop for those readers unfamiliar with DR Congo's history.

In terms of the recent socio-political history of The UMC in America and The UMC's agencies with headquarters in America, much of my knowledge comes from being active in UMC politics on both local and national levels since my youth. My knowledge of the early history of Methodism in America is built upon books from my seminary studies, such as Fredrick A. Norwood's *The Story of American Methodism*.³⁷ In addition, The UMC's General Board of Global Ministries' *United Methodist History of Mission* book series has expanded and corroborated this knowledge—especially Robert J. Harman's *From Missions to Mission: The History of the Mission of The United Methodist Church, 1968–2000*³⁸ and Charles Cole's *Christian Mission in the Third Millennium*.³⁹

This study has also been informed by cross-cultural communication courses and seminars I have taken and literature on understanding

---

33. According to Nooter Roberts's research, the last Mwadi died in the mid-1980s. Nooter Roberts, "King is a Woman," 79.

34. Reefe, *Rainbow and the Kings*.

35. Maxwell, "Soul of the Luba."

36. E.g., Professors Elikia Mbokolo, Léon de Saint Moulin, Kimena, Vincent Mulago, Bimbwenyi, Buetubuela, Mushila, Munduku, Robert N'Kwim, Tshibangu Tshishiku, and Cardinal Malula.

37. Norwood, *Story of American Methodism*.

38. Harman, *From Missions to Mission*.

39. Cole, *Christian Mission*.

American culture—especially social critiques relating to structural racism and blind spots, White privilege,[40] and the Savior Complex.[41] I also turned to literature on (de)colonialism, which I discuss in chapters 2 and 5. Some may wonder why I put such emphasis on texts from the mid-twentieth century. My reasons are twofold: (1) The social critiques from the period of political decolonization of Africa remain relevant and should be brought back into today's conversations about full decolonization. (2) There is a dearth of recently published books and theses explicitly addressing the interplay of racist (neo)colonial dynamics, cross-cultural church partnerships, and what has been labeled Third Wave mission trends. This study seeks to step into that gap.

This thesis touches upon the fact that the growing number of Congolese delegates to The UMC's quadrennial General Conference has impacted the outcome of votes on church policies on divisive social issues. This impact has led to growing resentment among some American UMs towards African UMs as well as accusations of Americans attempting to treat African General Conference[42] delegates as pawns in a political war. Because this thesis explores possible paths forward for American-North Katangan relationships and because several interviewees mentioned their anxieties surrounding the possibility of a denominational split or restructuring over the question of homosexuality and other issues, the question of the future of the denomination and its possible impact on these relationships is explored. My personal views on the issue have been impacted by my own experiences within the denomination, readings of official United Methodist New Service articles, published reports such as *Methodism at Risk: A Wake-up Call*,[43] which documents the schismatic political forces at play, and the reports/commentaries of United Methodist pastor and *Hacking Christianity*[44] blogger Jeremy Smith.

---

40. Style guides debate whether the words "White" and "Black" should always be capitalized when referring to a socially defined people group. While I have been of two minds on this question, my decision to use White and Black in this thesis was influenced by the arguments made in Lori Tharps's *New York Times* opinion piece, "The Case for Black With a Capital B." Later in this thesis, I apply the same reasoning to my decision to capitalize *Mzungu* and *Bazungu*.

41. My understanding of the "Savior Complex" was influenced heavily by Teju Cole's Atlantic article, "White Savior Industrial Complex."

42. As in the case of when I write "African/Congolese United Methodist," "African General Conference delegate" identifies the origin of the individuals, not that there is (yet) such a thing as an African [Methodist] General Conference.

43. Howell, *Methodism at Risk*.

44. Smith, "Hacking Christianity."

I predict that some sort of major structural change will happen in The UMC within the next four years. In fact, a significant rift occurred during the course of my writing this thesis, when in July 2016 The UMC's Western Jurisdiction elected the denomination's first openly homosexual (and married) bishop, directly violating The UMC's Book of Discipline policies.[45] That same year, the Wesleyan Covenant Association,[46] a voluntary network of socially and theologically conservative congregations with its own shared programs (legally set up in such a way to suggest preparation for a split), held its first official gathering. The February 2019 Special Session of The UMC's General Conference,[47] which I attended, further demonstrated that The UMC has reached a breaking point, yet it is still unclear what the end result of these political/legal battles will be.

There are a growing number of mainstream books and articles that point to problems with the relationships between communities that were once "the missionizers" and the "mission recipients." Some, such as Dambisa Moyo's bestseller *Dead Aid*,[48] speak to the international development community and focus on the negative economic impact of sending aid to countries in Africa. Others, such as the Instagram site Barbie Savior[49] and the Norwegian Students' and Academics' International Assistance Fund's "Radi-Aid Awards,"[50] use satire to raise awareness of patronizing attitudes many Westerners[51] have when approaching do-gooding efforts in Africa and other previously colonized regions of the world. The term "White Savior Complex" has gained traction in online blogs since Teju Cole's viral Twitter post and later article "White Savior Industrial Complex."[52]

In American churches, a handful of similarly-themed books have recently become bestsellers in their demographic market. These include Steve Corbett's *When Helping Hurts: How to Alleviate Poverty Without Hurting the Poor and Yourself*; Robert Lupton's *Toxic Charity: How Churches and Charities Hurt Those They Help and How to Reverse It*; Bryant

---

45. Gilbert, "Western Jurisdiction."
46. "Wesleyan Covenant Association."
47. See Dias, "'We Are Not Going Anywhere.'"
48. Moyo, *Dead Aid*.
49. Worrall, "Barbie Savior."
50. "Radi-Aid Awards."
51. I occasionally use the terms "Western" and "Westerners" in this thesis for lack of better words, recognizing that the terms are highly problematic. When I use them, I am speaking in generalities about people from the wealthier parts of Western Europe and the dominant culture of places their near relatives currently inhabit (such as Canada, the USA, Australia, etc.).
52. Cole, "White Savior Industrial Complex."

Myers's *Walking With the Poor: Principles and Practices of Transformational Development*; and David Livermore's *Serving with Eyes Wide Open: Doing Short-Term Missions with Cultural Intelligence*.[53] Profiting from this trend are books such as Randolph Richards and Branson O'Brien's *Misreading Scripture with Western Eyes: Removing Cultural Blinders to Better Understand the Bible* and Mary Lederleitner's *Cross-Cultural Partnerships: Navigating the Complexities of Money and Mission*.[54] All of the mass-market accessible (i.e., writing not using a heavy amount of academic jargon) publications such as these, however, function as introductory texts for the issues they discuss. That is, their main contribution is to help readers begin to recognize and articulate that the Western Church's do-gooding efforts are based on problematic assumptions. They do little, though, to further the scholarly discourse on the subject.

As will be discussed in more detail in the next chapter, within the academic community there exists (although, in my opinion, still insufficiently) conversations on postcolonial/neocolonial critiques (including power dynamics) of dominant church practices and theology,[55] decoloniality, questioning the meaning of "partnership,"[56] heightened awareness of institutional racism,[57] awareness that forms of "assistance" (especially financial) can be problematic and even harmful,[58] questioning the effectiveness of the popular "mission trip" model,[59] the experience of encountering the other/ending alienation,[60] and the liminal cross-cultural experiences and contributions of the emerging diaspora.[61] What I found lacking in the academic writings were attempts to weave these conversations together: that is, to examine current trends in mission models/mindsets through the lens of

53. E.g., Corbett, *When Helping Hurts*; Lupton, *Toxic Charity*; Myers, *Walking With the Poor;* Livermore, *Serving with Eyes Wide Open*.

54. E.g., Richards and O'Brien, *Misreading Scripture*; Lederleitner, *Cross-Cultural Partnerships*.

55. E.g., Rieger, "Theology and Mission"; Dube, *Postcolonial Feminist; Other Ways of Reading;* Nhiwatiwa, *Preaching in the African Context;* Kurewa, *Preaching and Cultural Identity;* Uzukwu, *Listening Church;* Ingleby, *Beyond Empire*.

56. E.g., Knutson, "Partnership in Mission"; Barnes, "Partnership in Christian Mission."

57. E.g., Harman, *From Missions to Mission;* Thiong'o, *Decolonizing the Mind*.

58. E.g., Moyo, *Dead Aid*.

59. E.g., Howell, *Short-Term Mission*; Friesen, "Long-Term Impact of Short-Term Missions"; Banister, "Rethinking the $3,000 Mission Trip."

60. E.g., Wells, "Rethinking Service"; Kritzinger, "Faith to Faith."

61. E.g., Wan, *Diaspora Missiology*; Kritzinger, "Interreligious Dialogue"; Adichie, *Americanah*; Ault, *African Christianity Rising*; Bouma-Prediger and Walsh, *Beyond Homelessness*.

postcolonial criticism. The examples I did find of this usually were written over thirty years ago. As I attempt to demonstrate in this thesis, such conversations are still relevant and must be revived if we are to have any chance of truly decolonizing our mission models.

In addition to these overarching themes, in my later chapters I examine theological conversations coming from the Methodist tradition: the most important of these being the Wesleyan understanding of grace (including questions of atonement, reconciliation with creation, sanctification, etc.).[62] I then explore how these theological concepts can be used to shed light on our understanding of mission partnerships and help us to discern next steps.

1.7 RESEARCH FRAMEWORK

When identifying one's research framework, it is standard to start by examining what assumptions the research will make about the nature of reality (i.e., the ontological perspective). Some authors, like Sotirios Sarantakos, argue that there are just two ontologies: realist vs. constructionist, but he acknowledges that other labeling systems exist, such as idealism as an ontology for qualitative research.[63] Jennifer Mason lists many ontological elements that can be used to describe the nature of the phenomena or social reality that one investigates,[64] and J. N. J. Kritzinger observes that "most Christian theologians . . . have a theistic and realist ontology in some 'hard' sense of these two terms."[65]

As a Christian researcher, I consider myself a theist and a realist (believing in a reality that is "out there") as well as missional and relational.[66] By Sarantakos's theoretical construction, a realist ontology requires an empiricist epistemology and a quantitative methodology, but that construction does not work in the context of the other ontological elements of my approach. While empiricism assumes that knowledge comes through our five classical senses, Christianity proclaims that reality is beyond what we can perceive and that things are not always as they appear to be. That said, I am not constructionist in my epistemology either, since pure constructivism

---

62. E.g., Wesley, "Scriptural Way of Salvation"; Whitworth, "Missio Dei and the Means of Grace."

63. Sarantakos, *Social Research*, 28–31.

64. Mason, *Qualitative Researching*, 2.

65. Kritzinger, unpublished paper. Excerpts included in UNISA's DTH Missiology research module packet.

66. In the sense described by J. N. J. Kritzinger in the unpublished paper quoted in UNISA's research module packet.

rejects the idea of absolute truths. I believe, however, that most absolute truths can only be understood metaphorically or glimpsed, as others have expressed, through the examination of many fingers pointing towards them from differing vantage points.

Critical realism offers an alternative epistemological framework to Sarantakos's limiting dichotomy. Espoused by NT Wright and numerous other scholars, critical realism "is *relational* and *intersubjective*, so that knowing, understanding, and sense-making take place not only in conversation with a text, a society, or a culture but also within an interpretive community."[67] Since my research focuses on the nature of the changing relationship between United Methodists in the USA and Katanga, I have laid side by side the opinions and experiences of many individuals and subgroups in attempts for the entire community to gain a more complete picture of the state of that dynamic. Thus, a qualitative research method was required.

As Paul Leedy emphasizes in *Practical Research*, "research is not mere information gathering"; it is an endeavor to solve a problem.[68] The goal, or teleology, of my research is to assist these two groups in their discernment of what the Spirit of God is doing in the relationship between them and to point in the direction of possible next steps.

1.8 RESEARCH DESIGN

I used a qualitative design for my research, guided by the Mission Praxis Matrix, which is the preferred analytical tool of UNISA's missiology department.

1.8.1 Qualitative Research

The data I collected in research (both interviews and published documents) does not consist of sufficient sample sizes for statistical (quantitative) analysis techniques to be useful tools. While I can say things such as "the majority of articles found" or "the general consensus among Congolese participants is," my research goal was not to acquire quantifiable/measurable proof of the levels of beliefs and change; I believe the topic to be too complex and subjective to be studied in this way.

Instead, I found that a qualitative research approach was better suited to my goal of documenting differing perspectives on relational dynamics. In doing so, I reconfirmed my belief that the North Katanga-American partnership

---

67. Kritzinger, *Tutorial Letter*, 23.
68. Leedy and Ormrod, *Practical Research*, 2–4.

is much like the Indian fable about an elephant examined by blind persons:[69] each person describes a different aspect of the full reality of what they are perceiving, which can lead each to myopic conclusions. As Paul Leedy and Jeanne Ellis Ormrod explain in *Practical Research: Planning and Design*, qualitative research methods can be used to achieve the following goals:

> *Description:* They can reveal the nature of certain situations, settings, processes, relationships, systems of people.
>
> *Interpretation:* They enable a researcher to (a) gain new insights about a particular phenomenon, (b) develop new concepts or theoretical perspectives about the phenomenon, and/or (c) discover the problems that exist within the phenomenon.
>
> *Verification:* They allow a researcher to test the validity of certain assumptions, claims, theories, or generalizations within real-world contexts.
>
> *Evaluation:* They provide a means through which a researcher can judge the effectiveness of particular policies, practices, or innovations.[70]

The above goals match what this study seeks to accomplish. Leedy and Ormrod note "that one of the limitations of this style of research is that it cannot be used to prove causal relationships." While this means that I will not be able to definitively say, for example, that the evacuation of the foreign missionaries caused the North Katanga church leaders to become stronger and more self-confident leaders, I can say that this is a narrative that has been embraced by a number of key North Katanga leaders and that they believe that these mental shifts have influenced decisions and interactions with Americans. For the purposes of this study, the views of the various church leaders (i.e., what they believe to be true) *are* the realities that I am dealing with.

1.8.2 The Praxis Matrix

The 7-point mission praxis matrix developed J. N. J. Kritzinger has the following shape:[71]

---

69. For one version of the fable, see Backstein, *Blind Men and the Elephant*.
70. Leedy and Ormrod, *Practical Research*, 134–35.
71. Kritzinger and Saayman, *David J. Bosch*, 4 (image used with permission).

Introduction and Research Overview   17

Guided by this matrix, the following sets of questions informed and propelled my interviews:[72]

Discernment for action: What have been the mission activities done in relationship between North Katangans and Americans since the mid-1990s? What initiatives are currently underway and what others are envisioned? What have been the underlying goals of each of these activities? What processes have been used to create and lead these activities?

Agency: Who are the decision-makers/power-holders in terms of joint mission initiatives between North Katanga and the USA? Who were/are the USA missionaries who came to the Congo? What were/are the features of their theology, social position, ideology, etc.? Who has been left out of the decision-making process? What power does each group have in initiating mission work without the other? What changes have occurred in these areas since the mid 1990s? What patterns of relating can be discerned between American and North Katangan partners?

Contextual understanding: How do the agents understand the cultural, socio-political, economic and religious context of their mission? What were the "problems" that they addressed and prioritized in their mission (possible examples: poverty, unbelief, violence, ancestor beliefs and rituals, illiteracy, tribalism, ministerial training, etc.)?

Ecclesial scrutiny: How do the partners understand the nature and purpose of the church on the local, regional, and international levels? What are the various thoughts on issues of authority and ownership on each of the

---

72. These questions are heavily paraphrased/adapted from the description of the seven points of the praxis matrix as found in Kritzinger and Saayman, *David J. Bosch*, 4–6. I have also changed (with the blessing of Kritzinger) the sequence of the seven dimensions.

three aforementioned levels of the church? Are there significant differences in their views of the church's role in society?

Interpreting the tradition: What scriptural passages and theological themes do the agents identify when discussing their mission relationship? How do the previously-discussed themes (their understanding of identity, context, history) influence their theological understanding of their mission?

Reflexivity: Do the agents reflect upon these above-mentioned themes in an integrated way (for example, are there issues of inconsistent logic/rationalization and/or cognitive dissonance)? Do they learn from their experiences and modify their behaviors due to their reflections? Can they articulate complexities, pitfalls and shadow sides of their work? Can they identity their own self-interests and biases? How do the agents articulate (if they do) their reflections and critiques on the history and changes that have occurred in their mission relationship? Are they aware of and have they thought about academic critiques that could be made of their history? What do they think of the concept of a missionary moratorium?

Spirituality: Where is the Holy Spirit in this mission relationship, and how is it experienced/called-upon? Is the Spirit of God experienced/ understood as being the primary agent in this relationship? Are there any significant differences between the spiritualities of the American and Katangan partners?

I have used this praxis matrix to analyze the views expressed by the participants in the interviews. What emerged in that process of analysis was the profiles of a number of different forms of encountering praxis, both from the side of the American and the Katangan participants. This allowed me to draw up a typology of encountering praxis with categories that characterize the matrix from both sides of the encounter. In framing these types of encounter, I drew on postcolonial critiques, commentaries on partnerships, isolation, liminality, cross-cultural interactions, and decoloniality.

This, in turn, provided a basis for in-depth theological reflection, from within the Wesleyan/Methodist tradition, on possible ways to decolonize these particular forms of encountering praxis. In this regard, Methodist understandings of grace, sanctification, atonement, discipleship, and relational polity have been central. My overarching interest lies in the question of how to build mutually positive relationships between Christian communities in formerly colonized/"missionized" places and Christian communities of formerly colonizing/"missionizing" places. The rapidly changing dynamic of the manner in which United Methodists in the USA and Katanga, DR Congo, collaborate in mission provides an example of this process in action. The interview responses of Americans and North Katangans are treated as separate vantage points to be compared, recognizing that one could take this a step further and subdivide the interviews by types of responses and/or demographics. Comparing Mission Practice Matrices of Americans and North Katangans is an especially useful method in that it serves as a way to compare different facets of the differing perspectives such that together they form a holistic picture of each group's perceived reality.

1.9 RESEARCH METHODOLOGY

The data for this thesis was generated in two ways: through consulting literature and through interviews.

1.9.1 *Literature*

In 1.6 above, I indicated the main sources that I consulted for this thesis in order to reflect on academic/theological conversations on neocolonialism, decoloniality, partnership, missionary moratorium, grace, alienation, and related themes.

1.9.2 *Interviews*

The second research method of this study has been in-depth, semi-structured interviews. I took a strategic sampling of twenty-five individuals for official interviews (of which only one participant chose to remain fully anonymous and not have an audio recording made of his/her responses)—after which point I concluded I had reached data saturation in terms of distinct points of view I was hearing as responses to the questions posed. A few potential participants explicitly or passively declined to be interviewed, and a few others I had considered asking to participate I did not contact after learning they had recently declined to be interviewed for a separate research project due to their reluctance to stir up painful and bitter memories and/or to make public their thoughts about North Katanga. Some of the pain and bitterness I have observed on the American (and European) side stem from disappointment when time and money-intensive initiatives have failed; disillusionment when Katangan leaders and those put into management positions have not performed as expected (especially when their behaviors were perceived as being corrupt/selfish); fear of retribution for speaking candidly about their frustrations; feelings of angst and betrayal when a missionary has been treated as *persona non grata* (at times by Katangans, at times by other powerful figures in the denomination, and at times by both) when they question or object to the *status quo*; and what could arguably be labeled Post-Traumatic Stress Syndrome for those who witnessed or experienced violence while in Congo.

The participants were all asked nearly identical open-ended questions, with some variations occurring based on their responses. Interview lengths varied from thirty to ninety minutes per participant. All the participants comfortably spoke French and/or English, and each made his/her own choice as to which language to speak during the interview.

Most interviews were conducted with only myself and the participant in the room. In two cases, participants (a husband/wife and two colleagues who work closely together) chose to be interviewed together. In two other cases, Rev. Maloba, a participant who had already been interviewed, was in the room because he had guided me to the homes of these retired elders and requested to hear what they had to say. In those two interviews, additional recordings were made of the follow-up questions Maloba asked out of his own curiosity after the main interviews were completed.

All the recorded interviews were transcribed and analyzed to identify themes and insights. The importance of my having recorded and transcribed the interviews—and not, instead, taking notes while listening—must be stressed. To my surprise, on a number of occasions, there were profound differences between what I had heard participants say (both American and Congolese) while recording and what I realized they had said once I examined the transcripts. There was more content in the conversations than I initially realized. I found important observations concealed in comments said with a shrug and sharp critiques slipped inside of words of praise. I do not know how much self-awareness was involved in participants downplaying or masking their criticisms, requiring one to at times read between the lines. Such an exploration is left for future research.

In addition to formal interviews, I incorporated information gained from written correspondence and conversations with others who have knowledge of this topic. This included North Katangan expatriates, missionary historians, others doing academic research in the region, and French and Swiss United Methodists who either served as missionaries in North Katanga or have been involved in projects there via The UMC's France-Swiss-North Africa Conference's mission board, Connexio[73] (still known in North Katanga as "The Swiss [Mission] Board").

This study also involved locating and documenting in spreadsheet format news stories about the Katanga region in the *United Methodist News Service* (1991–2015) and *New World Outlook* (1970s–1991), the official publication of The UMC's General Board of Global Ministries. I also spoke to the current editors of the United Methodist News Service (UMNS) and New World Outlook and asked them about their knowledge and thoughts

---

73. "Connexio."

on the changes that have occurred over the years in the way news stories about North Katanga are told. In entering denominational-level news stories about Katanga into a spreadsheet format, I created columns that took note of variables such as who wrote the story, who was mentioned by name (e.g., Just the Americans or the Katangans as well?), and who was described as having agency (especially in the semantics of the headline). I began with the hypothesis that by documenting and analyzing the articles in this way, I would be able to find quantifiable evidence that attitudes and behaviors have shifted in The UMC over the past quarter-century when it comes to mission partnerships. What I found was that measuring a change in attitudes and behaviors via this approach was difficult. I could not find a linear progression, nor could I find a tipping point. Instead, I found a mess of data points suggesting that some leaders within The UMC recognized the underlying problems within mission partnerships decades ago, and others still do not. One could argue that a quantifiable shift in the type of stories told about Katanga occurred beginning in 2005, but since this is when I and my father began proactively feeding stories and interviews to the UMNS, I am not certain how to analyze results created by my own insertion into the subject being studied. While beyond the scope of this study, it would be interesting to see if different results would be found by looking at the news stories from other regions of the denomination—especially since the United Methodist Board of Communications (UMCOM) began an initiative in 2004 to train and equip communicators (that is, church news reporters) in conferences outside of the USA.[74]

The interviews adopted a narrative approach.[75] The questions I posed in the interviews mirrored the analytical lens of the praxis matrix, with its seven dimensions concentrated into three groups of questions, as indicated below. These are not word-for-word questions but rather the interview schedule that I used, in line with the practice of semi-structured interviewing.

Actions and Agency: What mission initiatives involving North Katanga and the USA has the person been involved in (particularly since the 1990s, but background context is also good to know)? What was done? Who else was involved? How was the work and the decision-making power

---

74. This UMCOM initiative included North Katanga but has thus far (2005–2017) had disappointing results due to reasons related to the dynamics/pressures which determined who was chosen to be trained, who had access to communications equipment, and who had authority to report news stories.

75. I specify this approach in contrast to the other possibilities mentioned by Mason, such as psychoanalytic or ethnographic. See Mason, *Qualitative Researching*, 54–59.

distributed (Who decided what was to be done? Who contributed resources? Who did the hands-on work? Who supervised?) What other mission initiatives were going on at that time?

Context, Scrutiny and Reflexivity: What was the local context of the initiatives discussed? What was going on at the time socially/politically? Looking back, what wise choices or mistakes were made? What has been learned? What has been gained/lost over time in this relationship? What have we failed to learn? If you were teaching a class on the history of the mission relationship between North Katangan and American United Methodists, what social critiques would you make? What are the things that the other agents do not understand about this mission context that you wish you could help them understand? What would you like to see change?

Theological Reflection and Spirituality: Where is the Spirit of God in all of this? What Scripture passages or beliefs about God have inspired or sustained the mission initiatives over time? Where is the Spirit leading?

Most of the interviews were done face to face, while a few others were conducted via Skype. The majority of the Congolese participants were interviewed in July 2015 over a two-week period. The majority of American interviews were conducted in January 2016 during a visit to the USA. In addition to Congolese and American participants, there was one Zimbabwean who was interviewed because of his current position at United Methodist Communications (UMCOM), headquartered in Nashville, Tennessee, as well as his visits to North Katanga and his cross-cultural experiences within The UMC, and one German who lives in the USA and works for a denominational-level agency of The UMC.

In contrast to probability sampling, my selections were purposive; those twenty-five selected for interview were chosen because they were key witnesses to certain events and/or were representatives of certain demographics. There were some aspects of snowballing and theoretical sampling in that some of my participants were chosen because previous interviewees identified them as important voices in the conversation.[76] I stopped seeking additional participants once I concluded that I had collected sufficient samples of all the main points of view on the topics raised. I also made certain to interview North Katanga leaders who had a strong chance of becoming the next bishop (election was in March 2017), since their perspectives would impact any mission partnerships going forward.

The demographic categories I identified were:

---

76. Based on the description of sampling methods in chapter 7 of Sarantakos, *Social Research*.

Katangan United Methodist clergy currently serving in the USA or elsewhere abroad with frequent interactions with American UMs.

American friends of North Katanga: Subdivided into three categories: American UMs who have served as a missionary, visitor, or fundraiser to Katanga since 1994.

North Katangan church leaders who worked alongside/as assistants to American missionaries in the 1990s. (While some interviewees spoke about American-Congolese relationships pre-1990s, the focus was on the 1990s–2015.)

Congolese UM missionaries (North Katangan UMs receiving their salaries from the UM mission board, which is headquartered in the USA with mostly American staff and funding sources) and Congolese who frequently travel to the United States or regularly interact with American United Methodists.

A fifth category of North Katangan church leaders—those with virtually no interactions with Americans—was considered, but due to the large number of General Conference delegate spots allotted to North Katanga and the recent uptick of UMC general agency visits, nearly all UM North Katangans with notable leadership roles had had some exposure to American UMs.

1.10 ETHICAL CONSIDERATIONS

Before conducting the interview component of my research, I received clearance from the ethics review committee of the Department of Christian Spirituality, Church History, and Missiology at the University of South Africa (UNISA), including the approval of the informed consent form I used. Before interviewing each person, I explained the purpose of my research, their rights as participants, and obtained consent to have their remarks recorded and/or included in the thesis. Each was presented a copy of the consent form to sign, and translations were provided to those who could not read English. All but one participant agreed to the use of a recording device. Most gave full consent for me to use and save all their remarks for this study and future research. A few (mostly non-Congolese) stipulated verbally during their interview that specific remarks were to be used only if readers would be unable to identify/suspect them as my source. For this reason, I have decided to not include a complete list of the participants' names and am treating the original recordings and full transcripts as confidential documents only to be released upon request after redactions and additional written permissions are obtained.

When doing the interviews, I asked people to recall a period of their past that, for some, contained painful memories. I recognized the risk of rekindling emotions about unresolved past inter-personal conflicts or trauma (i.e., witnessing or experiencing acts of violence). I was therefore careful both in my selection process (avoiding interviewing anyone who was not emotionally healthy enough to discuss the past)[77] as well as framing questions in such a way that did not cast blame nor request the casting of blame onto any person or group. I consulted with respected North Katangan UMC clergy about my research ideas and was encouraged by them to do the interviews. I also spoke with Bishop Ntambo, the bishop of the North Katanga Episcopal area during the time that the interviews were conducted. He not only explicitly gave his blessing for me to conduct my research in his conference but also agreed to be a participant.

For both strategic and ethical reasons, the interviews did not attempt to do an in-depth probe of any specific mission project or station or to uncover crimes, corruption, or scandals in the past or present. It did not involve requesting financial records or do data analysis of financial flows between North Katanga and the United States, even though a look at the shifts (both in quantity and source) of financial flows would in itself say much about the shifts in the nature of the relationship.[78] The history of the relationship was told from multiple perspectives, and I as researcher did not attempt to select the "correct" version of history. Instead, the purpose of my study was to document the differing perspectives of the dynamics of the encounters between US and Katangan United Methodist leaders.

1.11 PERSONAL STANCE/JOURNEY

Although I had never heard the word *missiology* until 2007, I became passionate about the study of mission at the age of fifteen (1995) when I accompanied my father on a trip to Katanga. He had been invited by the United Methodist bishop of the region, but our bedrooms and food were provided by American missionaries. While I did not have the vocabulary to analyze my experience, I returned home with a sense that there was something dysfunctional about my denomination's mission/missionary system. With youthful ego and naïveté, I resolved to learn everything I could about the causes and solutions to humanity's problems and then teach my church a new mission paradigm. Thus began my long journey.

77. Based on the assessment of Congolese colleagues.

78. In North Katanga, inquiries into financial records are often heard as accusations of wrongdoing, and speaking about such matters has historically been viewed as betrayal. This issue is especially sensitive because a scandal involving accusations of misdirection of funds (and a failed official audit) in The UMC's East Africa conference resulted in an extended freeze of financial flows. See Caldwell, "Court Defers East Africa Financial Dispute"; Hahn, "Agency Urges Withholding Funds from East Africa."

The BA/MA in International Development (2002) that I earned laid my foundational knowledge of the dynamics and history of socio-economic divisions in the world, and later my MDiv (2009) provided the vocabulary for theological reflection on these issues. However, the writings that have most influenced how I critique mission models and formulate new ones have been ones I have discovered independently or through my father, the late Rev. Dr. Robert "Bob" Walters. Walters, a United Methodist pastor, became involved in partnerships in Katanga in the early 1990s and eventually served as an official missionary in North Katanga. His DMin in Practical Theology research involved engaging in theological conversations with North Katangan UM leaders. Walters was the primary visionary behind the creation of the NGO Friendly Planet Missiology, and the two memoirs he wrote are missiological reflections on his time in Katanga. While my father and I did not always agree on certain aspects of missiological praxis (e.g., he stressed the importance of maintaining an emotional detachment in order to be an effective non-anxious presence in a community, whereas I believe that a natural result of building genuine cross-cultural friendships is reacting with emotions such joy, sorrow, or anger when a friend shares about joys, sorrows, or injustices faced), he laid the groundwork for my understanding of mission and the legacies of missionary activity in North Katanga. I fully recognize that I give what he taught and wrote an extra degree of deference, for I believe my father was a brilliant missiologist. It is impossible for me to fully detangle myself from his influence on my thinking, nor do I want to. Instead, I build upon those foundations.

Missiology, in its broadest sense, can be understood as the study of the Mission of God and what God is calling individuals and groups to do. It involves discernment and self-critique—a willingness to confess that at times humans confuse God's will with their own, and a willingness to learn and start again. Since God's calls to care for God's creation are numerous (some are called specifically to prison ministry; others to environmental protection; still others to public health), so, too, are the dimensions of missiology.

I began my missiological journey with the question "What does God want me (and others in my socio-economic demographic) to do in response to poverty and suffering in the world?" I concentrated primarily on situations where the majority of the population in a community survives on a subsistence level. This exploration led to a question that left me, a xenophile, in paralyzed despair: "Is it ever appropriate for an outsider of higher socio-economic status to enter into a community with the goal of helping?"[79] My father, who was working on his doctoral thesis, *Scripture as a Tool of*

---

79. I provide a response to this question in section 7.3.3.

Community Development, at the time, introduced me to the pedagogy of Paulo Freire and the faith-based community development initiatives that have been built upon it—such as the *Training for Transformation* workbook series and my father's own work in leading Bible studies on passages from Revelation in Katanga. From this, I concluded that one possibility is for an educated outsider to act as a catalyst by reflecting back to the community its frustrations in a way that sparks problem solving activities to begin. In fact, one could argue that God calls all pastors (especially those in an itinerant system like Methodism) and lay leaders to this task. Samuel Wells's book *Improvisation: The Drama of Christian Ethics* introduced me to several invaluable tactics from the field of improvisational theater that I have incorporated into this approach—especially those related to playing with power dynamics, "overaccepting" instead of blocking, and reincorporating the lost. As is discussed in the final sections of chapter 7, by juxtaposing Freirean methods and Wells's writings on Christian praxis, I end this thesis with a missiological understanding of partnership that has taught me that, while my intentions were noble, I began my journey asking questions that came from erroneous assumptions about who is most in need of saving and why we are called to enter into boundary-crossing relationships. By the time I completed this thesis, I had also concluded that the next stage of my journey needs to be focused on a deeper understanding of racism as a political-economic force and how to disrupt power imbalances. Ibram Kendi's book *How to Be an Anti-Racist,*[80] which was published after the completion of my doctoral program, will heavily influence my future writings.

As a Methodist, I discern God's mission for the church through the lens of the teachings of John Wesley. In his classic sermon "The Scripture Way of Salvation," Wesley describes the way in which God's grace leads individuals to salvation. Grace touches people's hearts and makes them aware of their brokenness and need for God before they ask for intervention; grace leads people to turn to God and be justified, and grace continues to work upon their hearts so that they increase in their love for God and God's creation. When this love becomes perfect, they have become sanctified. The final stage of sanctification is not universally taught or emphasized by popular Christianity, which often treats justification as the end goal. This belief that God's grace is in action before we ask for it[81] and that becoming perfect in love (not being saved from Hell) is our ultimate goal influences my missiology on many levels. As Samuel Wells suggests, the underlying mission from

---

80. Kendi, *How to Be an Anti-Racist.*

81. I.e., God is already putting the players into motion for the completion of God's mission before we even hear the call to join the team.

God is to end isolation.⁸² Christians spread the Good News of God's love for humanity by loving humanity while remembering that the hero and mastermind of their mission is God, not them.

This in part, however, begs the starting question: "*How* do Christians express their love of humanity?" Not everyone is called to the same vocation. In discerning their call they must consider their underlying motives, what they hope to accomplish,⁸³ what they are skilled at doing,⁸⁴ whether their actions are requested/wanted, and whether they have researched the undesired side effects of their actions. The Church as an institution must also consider what kind of power dynamics it is reinforcing when it speaks and acts. Economist Dambisa Moyo, for example, argues that aid dollars undermine business development and feed structural corruption; she advocates for foreign direct investment instead.⁸⁵ Theologian Musa Dube asserts that both imperialism and patriarchy must be addressed when interpreting biblical narratives.⁸⁶ For me, some of the fundamental test questions when discerning whether a mission is Spirit-led are: Are these actions strengthening or weakening levels of love and trust between those impacted by it? Are they resulting in stronger community-based leadership? Are we building relationships or bragging rights?

In 2005, at the invitation of Bishop Ntambo, I returned to North Katanga to the remote⁸⁷ town of Kamina as a volunteer, intending to take a humble learner's stance. I soon discovered that option was not available to me. Despite being a newcomer without knowledge of local/regional culture and politics and with barely any useful language skills or job experience, I was appointed director of the conference's community development department. During that time, I did my best to assimilate into the community; I joined a church youth choir, socialized with young adults

---

82. Wells, "Rethinking Service."

83. Theologian Frederick Buechner, in discussing vocation, wrote, "The place God calls you to is the place where your deep gladness and the world's deep hunger meet" (Buechner, *Wishful Thinking*, 119.) I assert that this must be held in tension, though, with the old adage, "When the only tool you have is a hammer, all problems look like a nail."

84. Several articles and blog posts have recently gone viral that critique mission projects for being unhelpful because volunteers are unskilled. The classic example is teams doing such poor construction/painting work that the local community has to start from scratch after the visitors leave. For example, Elliott, "Giving Back."

85. Moyo, *Dead Aid*.

86. Dube, *Postcolonial Feminist*, 23.

87. While historically Kamina had been a major crossroads town, the collapse of both road and rail infrastructure had made the town extremely difficult to reach without a private airplane or spending several days on bad roads.

my own age, and spent most evenings next door entertaining the children at the Methodist home for abandoned[88] children. For me, it was a year of learning many lessons the hard way: of blindly stepping on cross-cultural landmines and of naïvely thinking I could escape the patroness role that had been assigned to me, question/change systems, or improve the living conditions of my newfound friends. It was a discouraging, infuriating, and heartbreaking experience. I did not know when I flew home for a friend's wedding that, due to the political climate, I would not be allowed to return to Kamina for a few years.

I have had the past decade to process those experiences and have made course corrections. Since then, I have returned several times, co-founded an NGO, Friendly Planet Missiology,[89] served two years as a pastor in a township of Lusaka, Zambia, lived two years in Djibouti, and served three years as a pastor of an international United Methodist congregation (with many members from Congo and other parts of sub-Saharan Africa) in Algiers, Algeria. I was ordained an elder in the North Katanga Conference, and, as of 2017, serve as Bishop Mande's[90] (the newly elected bishop of North Katanga) Executive Assistant for Strategic Partnership and Engagement. More than being just an academic exercise, this thesis has been a way for me to explore on a deeper level the missiological questions that have both haunted and driven me as I attempt to answer my personal calling into border-crossing ministries.

1.12 OVERVIEW OF THE FOLLOWING CHAPTERS

In addition to this introductory chapter, the thesis consists of the following chapters:

Chapter 2, "Theoretical Framework: Mission, Partnerships, and Colonization," unpacks the main title of this thesis (*Decolonizing Mission Partnerships*) by exploring the relevant conversations around the topics of mission, partnership, and (de)colonization. In doing so, it places this particular doctoral study into the context of the broader conversation on the complex challenges inherent when formerly colonized people attempt to

---

88. I bristled that the place was referred to as the home for "abandoned" children, but for the community, being abandoned was the problem—not being orphaned. Being an orphan was not unusual; having no extended family members claim you was. This orphanage had been launched only a few years before my arrival in response to the number of unclaimed children in the midst of the flood of displaced persons the town received during the peak of the recent war.

89. "Friendly Planet Missiology."

90. Mande Muyombo, who is also known as "Guy" Mande, chose to officially go by the name Bishop Mande after his election.

collaborate on missional initiatives with those who economically benefited from colonialism (and vice-versa). The chapter addresses the questions posed in subsection 1.3.2 and provides key concepts with which to analyze the discussions that follow.

Chapter 3, "The Historical Cultural Context," moves the conversation from theoretical to a geographic location, the Katanga province of DR Congo. By providing an overview of the historic spiritual beliefs and economic and political traditions of the Luba and Lunda peoples, this chapter answers sub-question 1.3.2 of this research and sets the scene for the rest of the study by describing the concrete situation in which the mission encounters have played themselves out. As such, it is part of the "contextual understanding" dimension of the praxis matrix (see 1.8.2).

Chapter 4, "Methodist Mission Partnerships in Katanga" discusses the history of Methodist mission collaborations in Katanga—especially in the northern half of the province. By creating "snapshots" of the different phases of these interactions, it does not seek to be a comprehensive history but rather to provide an overall impression of trends and transitions from the 1910s to the 2010s as well as critiques that have been made. It addresses both what was being said and done by Methodists in Katanga as well as how these endeavors were portrayed and advertised (i.e., the rhetoric of fundraising efforts) by denominational publications in the USA. By answering sub-question 1.3.3, it lays the groundwork for an in-depth examination (in the next chapter) of the encounters that took place between American and Katangan United Methodist leaders. This chapter represents the "ecclesial scrutiny" dimension of the praxis matrix.

Chapter 5, "Violence, Exploitation, and Racism: The Impact of Collective Traumas on Mission Partnerships," explores research question 1.3.4 by naming and discussing the negative psychological impact of the colonial period and the violence that has flowed from it (e.g., enslavement, pillaging, dehumanization, genocide, etc.). It asserts that while it is not right to call behavioral trends that result from these traumas "culture," these traumas have impacted the perceptions and relationship dynamics between North Katangans and Americans. The chapter also asserts that just as North Katangans as a whole have unresolved trauma, Americans, too, are still reacting to the skeletons in their individual and collective closets.

Chapter 6, "The Interviews," which constitutes the heart of the study, answers research question 1.3.5 by organizing and analyzing the data generated by the interviews about the dynamics of the encounters that took place between American and Katangan Methodist leaders in the period of 1994–2014. By studying the patterns of interaction between the American and Katangan participants, this chapter uncovers not only the problem areas in the relationship but also the positive and hopeful signs within it. Since the whole praxis matrix is used to describe different forms of encounter, this chapter contains multiple dimensions of the matrix.

Chapter 7, "Theological Reflections," addresses question 1.3.6 and represents the dimension of "interpreting the tradition" (or theological reflection) in the praxis matrix. It explores the missiologies that shape the interview participants' understanding of the partnership, values in the Methodist tradition that can be leveraged to decolonize the mission partnership, and other theological frameworks and praxes that are helpful in this process.

Chapter 8, "Mission Partnership Going Forward" is the concluding chapter, in which some suggestions are made about how to implement the theological vision generated in the previous chapter. This chapter represents the dimension of "discernment for action" in the praxis matrix (1.3.7–8).

2

Theoretical Framework: Mission, Partnerships, and Colonization

THIS THESIS WEAVES TOGETHER several academic conversations which need to be examined together for a better understanding of the dynamics at play when people of faith attempt to cross socio-economic and cultural boundaries in order to answer a sense of missional call. More specifically, it looks at the past quarter-century of interactions between North Katangan and American United Methodists. As the primary title of the thesis suggests, an understanding of the evolving conversations around mission, partnerships, and (post/neo/de) colonization are essential in this task. Hence, this chapter focuses on exploring those three topics.

2.1 MISSION

Mission is a term that is so often used in church settings that its meaning is frequently assumed to be simple and clear. As David Bosch demonstrated in his now classic tome *Transforming Mission,* that is not the case. The dominant understanding of mission has evolved since the days of the writing of the Gospels; the church has applied multiple mission paradigms over its history.

Before examining the academic reflections on mission as it is understood by theologians today, I wish to share my observations on how *mission* is understood by the majority of American United Methodists, since this, too, is important when examining the mindsets and motivations of American United Methodists when interacting with North Katangans.

In my youth, growing up in the United States of America, mission was either a euphemism used at church to describe assistance given to poor people who were not part of our social circles (e.g., mission project, mission trip, foreign missions, etc.)[1] or what secret agents and the crew of the Starship Enterprise were sent on. That is, *mission* contained within it the element of boundary crossing (e.g., inferior community, enemy territory, alien peoples) and prestige through accepting risks/sacrifices to help others.

Beginning in the late 1980s, it became popular for businesses and churches to adopt mission statements[2]—public declarations of their organization's primary task. In 1996, The UMC's General Conference chose for the denomination the mission statement "Making Disciples of Jesus Christ." At the 2008 General Conference, the words "for the Transformation of the World" were added to the statement. There was much political arguing that went into this statement's creation; the theological divides in The UMC were evident in the debate, which hinged on the questions: Is the fundamental mission of the Church to make disciples or to transform the world? Are they, like faith and works, two sides of the same coin? For what reason do we make disciples? Is it we or God who do the work of transformation? In what ways do God's mission (*Missio Dei*) and the Church's mission overlap? Can a denomination have a mission that is different than another's or do all Christians have the same mission and we are debating what it is?

In his groundbreaking work *Transforming Mission*,[3] David Bosch traces nearly two thousand years of differing understandings. He not only places in context the way mission has been defined in our lifetime but also makes a strong argument that "the events we have been experiencing at least since World War II and the consequent crisis in Christian mission . . . [are] the result of a fundamental paradigm shift, not only in mission or theology, but in the experience and thinking of the whole world."[4] Bosch argues that we are shifting away from the previously dominant understanding of mission—that of being related to the work of missionaries, which was "intimately associated with the colonial expansion of the Western World."[5]

---

1. Likewise, a *mission speaker* is a guest (often a missionary and often coming on *Mission Sunday*) who tells the congregation about the poverty of people they don't know personally (usually living in a far-away place) and asks for financial contributions to help them. A *mission trip* is when members travel to build/lead/do something *for* them.

2. While I do not have expertise on the history of organizational mission statements, some references I have come across lead me to suspect they began in the early twentieth century. Regardless, there appears to have been a dramatic increase in their adoption in the late 1980s and 1990s in the USA—especially within mainline churches.

3. Bosch, *Transforming Mission*.

4. Bosch, *Transforming Mission*, 4.

5. Bosch, *Transforming Mission*, 1.

While *Transforming Mission* was published over a quarter-century ago, I argue that we are still in the transition period that Bosch describes as emerging; the vestiges of mental paradigms of the colonial missionary period remain and, in some cases, are so buried in the underlying operating system of our mission models that they corrupt everything that has been built upon them.

Bosch discusses the ambiguities and "impurities" in the mixed motives and theological foundations of emerging mission paradigms. He points out that there is much circular reasoning as well as imperialistic/colonial attitudes imbedded in our mission practices and that "an inadequate foundation for mission and ambiguous missionary motives and aims are bound to lead to an unsatisfactory missionary practice."[6]

While he seeks to describe the emerging mission paradigm, he also cautions that we should "never arrogate it to ourselves to delineate mission too sharply and too self-confidently. *Ultimately, mission remains undefinable.*"[7] Thus, while the transformation of our approach to mission is at the heart of this thesis, its functional meaning varies throughout it based on the context of the conversation.

Today, when churches in the USA speak of mission outside the context of mission statements, they are usually talking about what the church is doing for people they perceive as having fewer resources than themselves.[8] The degree to which this involves converting others to Christianity depends both on whether the recipients are perceived as already being Christian[9] and how evangelical the congregation is. In mainline denominations such as The UMC, mission primarily means addressing the symptoms of financial/material poverty. The most popular examples include construction of buildings, donation of items (often second hand), opening pop-up clinics, digging wells, giving away food, and playing with or teaching children (especially orphans). A few of The UMC's general agencies—such as The General Board of Church and Society (GBCS), United Methodist Women, and The General Board of Global Ministries (GBGM)—have a history of trying to build awareness of mission as also addressing systemic injustices. However, as Robert Harman documents in *From Missions to Mission: The History of The United Methodist Church, 1968–2000*,[10] there has been much

---

6. Bosch, *Transforming Mission*, 5.

7. Bosch, *Transforming Mission*, 9 (my emphasis).

8. One way to demonstrate this assertion is to type "mission" in the search feature of The UMC's official website and note the most common ways in which the word is used.

9. Emphasis has shifted to "partnering" with local churches which are already handling the task of evangelization.

10. Harman, *From Missions to Mission*.

pushback in recent history by Methodist evangelicals over whether The UMC's mission board should be focused more on "making disciples" or "transforming the world." In chapter 7, I discuss that such a tension could be analyzed through the lens of *justification* versus *sanctification*.

It is also important to recognize that the polarization over the question of whether mission is primarily about conversion or social welfare has been occurring in The UMC since its formation and has nearly the same demographic dividing lines as several other issues in the denomination and the nation. Thus, while many are convinced that the debates over homosexuality will cause an official split in the denomination in the near future,[11] the two diverging movements within the USA have been struggling with each other over differing understandings of mission for decades.

The longer I spend living on the continent of Africa, the more aware I become of the peculiarities of the litmus test divisions in the beliefs and practices identified with these two diverging United Methodist movements within the USA. Despite assumptions by both the "left" and "right" in The UMC, the average North Katangan UM pastor's beliefs and missional practices do not fit neatly into either group. That is, North Katangan mission praxes do not fit neatly into the American divide between "progressive" and "evangelical/conservative" mission praxes.

In my adopted home conference of North Katanga, the work of peacebuilding, reconciliation, and post-war reconstruction are understood as major parts of the mission God has given the Church. So, too, is the building and managing of schools, clinics, farms, child welfare centers, scouting programs, choirs, sewing co-ops, etc. With the denomination's official foreign missionaries having all left the conference during the violence of the 1990s, North Katanga is a perfect place for exploring emerging forms of mission praxis in a post-colonial context. Doing so, however, requires moving beyond the two dominant mission praxes found in the American churches.

Bosch offers a semantic tool to break out of the dichotomy United Methodism in America has become stuck inside. He proposes "mission as _____." Thus, we can have mission as evangelism[12] as one of many forms of mission (examples: mission as liberation, mission as inculturation, mission as action in hope, mission as witness, etc.). One of the potential drawbacks of Bosch's numerous "mission as" categories—which he himself recognized—is that when mission becomes defined so broadly, nearly everything becomes mission. Hence, the term risks losing having any distinct meaning.

11. E.g., Smith, "Schism"; Andrews, "Methodist Church May Split."
12. Bosch, *Transforming Mission*, 409.

In his paper entitled "Theology and Mission Between Neo- and Post-colonialism," Joerg Rieger proposes a different analytical distinction model: *mission as outreach, mission as relationship,* and *mission as inreach.*[13] These distinctions I believe to be quite useful when reflecting on postcolonial mission initiatives.

2.1.1 Mission as Outreach

Mission as outreach, Rieger notes, is currently the dominant mission paradigm, and it is growing in popularity.[14] Examples Rieger cites of the mission as outreach paradigm include soup kitchens, medical assistance to the poor, monological teaching and preaching efforts (that is, the missionary speaks while the missionized are expected to take a listening/learning stance), and mission teams which go on mission trips to volunteer. One could easily argue that both the dominant evangelical and progressive mission approaches in America fall under the umbrella of *mission as outreach.*

2.1.1.1 Outreach: Short-term Missionaries and Mission Trips

While the concept and practice of missionaries living extended periods of their lives serving as ambassadors of Christ in foreign lands is old, the practice in mainline denominations of what is often called short-term missions is relatively recent and is due in part to the advent of faster and more affordable means of transportation emerging in the mid-twentieth century. In 1949, the Methodist Episcopal Church (forbearer of The UMC) launched a program for recent college graduates to serve for a limited period in support roles to fulltime missionaries. Other denominations launched similar programs. It was during this time period that mainline missionary efforts shifted away "from evangelism as the driving force of missions, adopting a more humanitarian focus for missionary work."[15] In 1961, the USA government created its own humanitarian version of these such programs aimed at young adults: the Peace Corps. It was also during this same time period that the idea that college students should use their spring breaks as a chance to travel (especially to vacation in warmer climates) became popular.[16]

---

13. Rieger, "Theology and Mission," 201–27.
14. Rieger, "Theology and Mission," 212.
15. Howell, *Short-Term Mission,* §726. Note that the Latter-Day Saints had practiced temporary missionary service since 1830, and the Mennonites and American Friends started similar programs in the 1920s.
16. Howell, *Short-Term Mission,* §744.

The idea of volunteering for a short period of time either overseas or domestically in an impoverished area grew in popularity over the second half of the twentieth century. In addition to volunteering for a year or two, the idea of spending vacation days (i.e., one or two weeks) volunteering also gained traction. By the 1990s and 2000s, summer youth mission trips had grown into an "enormous phenomenon."[17]

Joerg Rieger quotes a 2002 report from a United Methodist youth group in Texas as an example of the kind of narrative that often accompanies such mission trips:

> The eyes and hearts of our youth group and the adults who went along were opened to the desperate needs of other people. What this youth group learned and saw was appalling! . . . This year they are planning to make a . . . video that will show the conditions that these people . . . have to live in. It is our hope that our North Texas Conference will see these desperate needs and help us continue to do something about them. . . . We can't do everything, but we can all do something to make a difference.[18]

2.1.1.2 Outreach: Critiques

While Rieger sees the outreach programs movement as preferable to churches taking a self-centered position, he notes the ways in which it is problematic. His first criticism is that it is a one-sided approach: "Like the missionaries in colonial times, the volunteers engaged in outreach projects too easily project their own ideas and values on other people."[19] He notes that work done in these initiatives is usually one-sided. That is, with the missionized being receivers and the missionaries (in the broader sense of the word—including volunteers both long and short-term) doing all of the giving.[20] Rieger points out the power imbalance in these interactions caused in large part by the "uneven distribution of wealth of the neocolonialist system."[21] He furthermore asserts that the neocolonial system, which is discussed in more detail later in this chapter, is not threatened by the mission as outreach model. Tending to the needs of the victims of a neocolonial system does little to nothing to

---

17. Howell, *Short-Term Mission*, §888.

18. Letter of a United Methodist youth group of the North Texas Conference, August 5, 2002, as quoted in Rieger, "Theology and Mission," 212–13.

19. Rieger, "Theology and Mission," 213.

20. A strong argument can also be made that this receiving/giving flow is an illusion; often the missionized give more than they receive in these interactions in a manner that echoes old patterns of exploitation.

21. Rieger, "Theology and Mission," 213.

dismantle it; in fact, "mission as outreach performs a much-needed service to the system. As long as we are preoccupied with helping others—with all the temptations of trying to shape them in our own neocolonial image and make then conform to our world—we will not raise nosy questions about ourselves."[22] I would add to this that the outreach model creates distorted thinking on both sides: it assists in the perpetuation of poverty by relieving just enough suffering to reinforce the myth that has been accepted by both the "givers" and "receivers" that the solution to suffering comes from this sort of approach. As Bob Walters put it, "The problem is that the system works just enough to keep the hope alive."[23]

As Rieger and many other critics of the outreach mission have recognized "What is missing in the mission as outreach model is the ability to learn from the other in ways that lead to self-knowledge."[24] That is, despite the claims by mission trips returnees that they have learned and gained much from their experience, what they typically report to have learned fits a common narrative they had been exposed to prior to traveling—a narrative that does not challenge systems or any of their earlier assumptions. Anthropologist Brian Howell's 2012 book *Short-Term Mission; An Ethnography of Christian Travel Narrative and Experience* documents the findings from his research on the narrative patterns that emerge from American Christians reporting on their short-term mission[25] trip experiences.[26] While Howell was teaching at a Christian college, he began to notice a strong pattern in the narrative frameworks mission trip returnees told that did not seem to variate despite the numerous different countries returnees has visited. Howell notes some of the most common elements of these narratives: the trip was life-changing, often involving a moment of epiphany and a "gratitude for a relatively affluent life."[27] Through his research, he attempts to demonstrate how these narrative frameworks emerge from a specific context (dominant cultural assumptions) and simultaneously provide a way for returnees to make meaning of their experiences and block their ability to understand them.

---

22. Rieger, "Theology and Mission," 215.
23. Walters, *Last Missionary*, 50.
24. Rieger, "Theology and Mission," 214.
25. While I find the term "short-term mission" problematic for multiple reasons, it is used in this sense to describe a trip billed as a mission-trip that lasts the duration of a typical American vacation (e.g., over the spring school holiday).
26. Since Howell has a Methodist background, many of his examples come from mission trips organized by United Methodists.
27. Howell, *Short-Term Mission*, §142.

A personalist missionary narrative serves a positive function to link these travels to a theological and spiritual understanding that the travelers and their supporters recognize and affirm, while obscuring aspects of the very things many of my team members wanted to understand: poverty, inequality, and cultural difference. By framing the encounter as primarily interpersonal, a service to "the poor," as well as having a theological motive of "sharing the gospel," the guiding narratives through which our team experienced these travels made it *more* difficult to see the structural, historical, and cultural forces at work.[28]

Howell examines the way in which these narratives frame *mission as pilgrimage*[29] as well as *mission as economic aid*.[30] He believes that it is possible to redeem short-term mission trips, and he echoes the sentiments of David Livermore (*Serving with Eyes Wide Open*),[31] assistant bishop David Zac Niringiye,[32] and many other scholars I have encountered in my research in arguing that this redemption would require a shift away from doing and towards listening. Howell adds that part of the shift to listening should include guided research and reflection among participants on the structural issues at play in the socio-economic conditions of the people who are the targets of their outreach efforts.

In his 2004 doctorate thesis, *The Long-Term Impact of Short-Term Missions on the Beliefs, Attitudes, and Behaviors of Young Adults,* Randall Gary Friesen found that despite the vast majority of the mission trip volunteers who participated in his study reporting that these trips had a dramatic positive impact on their lives, "the post-trip regression in participants' beliefs, attitudes, and behavior one year after returning from the mission experience was also significant."[33] Like Howell, Friesen concludes that for short-term mission trips to truly have a transformative impact on the behaviors and worldview of volunteers, much more effort needs to be invested in re-entry debriefings and follow-up.

Jonathan Ingleby, in his book *Beyond Empire: Postcolonialism & Mission in a Global Context,* also has a number of critiques of the mission trip phenomenon, which he compares to Christian tourism. Ingleby writes that "the new missionary remains the privileged outsider, the voyeur Westerner, the

---

28. Howell, *Short-Term Mission*, §199.
29. Howell, *Short-Term Mission*, §543.
30. Howell, *Short-Term Mission*, §638.
31. Howell, *Short-Term Mission*, §2200.
32. Howell, *Short-Term Mission*, §2237.
33. Friesen, "Long-Term Impact of Short-Term Missions," 4.

representative of a superior civilization. There is no need to struggle with the difficult and humbling task of learning languages and culture. There is some raising of awareness ('I never realized how these people lived') but little recognition that *their* poverty is mostly *our* fault."[34] Ingleby views these trips as part of the bigger quick-fix attitude of new imperialism: "Is short term mission little more than another way of expressing the ephemerality of our globalized postmodern culture where we no longer invest in long term relationships and have a pick-and-mix attitude to cultural experience?"[35]

The research of Howell and Friesen along with anecdotal reports of many other scholars, such as Ingleby, suggest that *mission as outreach,* while providing a positive experience for volunteers in the short-term, does little if anything in the long-term in regards to transforming their behaviors and views—nor does it change the underlying system that perpetuates the problems in the visited countries which they wish to alleviate. The only exceptions to this are when these outreach initiatives are coupled with guided listening, research, and discussions about the structural issues at play and these conversations and relationships continue long after the initial outreach activity has been completed.

As touched upon early in this subsection, the one-sidedness of the *mission as outreach* model creates an "us" and "them" dichotomy between "givers" and "receivers"—the receivers having little if any agency in the interactions and not necessarily benefitting from them. This lack of agency is the predictable result of framing the goal as "us" helping "them." In *Beyond the White Noise: Mission in a Multicultural World,* Tom Montgomery-Fate writes about the motivations for economically privileged people to want to help those living in poverty.

> Though there are many others, here are six very basic motivations: (1) guilt; (2) a desire to control, manipulate, and gain power; (3) pity; (4) a desire to proselytize or "save" non-Christians; (5) a desire to "fix things"; (6) a humanitarian and/or faith-based desire for socioeconomic justice. All of these can overlap and may occur on personal or institutional levels. And all are part of the history of cross-cultural mission.[36]

All of these motivations—with the occasional exception of the sixth—feed into what is called the *Savior Complex,* a belief that one has special abilities (e.g., intellect) making her or him capable of rescuing "others" in need and that s/he has a moral imperative to use them. By

---

34. Ingleby, *Beyond Empire,* 170.
35. Ingleby, *Beyond Empire,* 171.
36. Montgomery-Fate, *Beyond the White Noise,* 136.

doing so, one alleviates feelings of guilt for living comfortably while others suffer without disrupting the underlying belief that one is a morally and intellectually superior person. This issue will be revisited in this chapter's discussion on neocolonialism.

Many who have served in the trenches of the *mission as outreach* model have been increasingly questioning its fruitfulness. Books such as Robert Lupton's *Toxic Charity* and Brian Fikkert and Steve Corbett's *When Helping Hurts* have become mainstream bestsellers. Jamie Wright's 2017 memoir *The Very Worst Missionary* is being promoted by the biggest names in progressive, White, female Christian authors in the USA (e.g., Glennon Doyle and Rachel Held Evans).[37] This suggests that critiques of the outreach model are no longer simply the minority report; the minority is growing and possibly approaching a tipping point.

Lupton's 2015 follow-up book *Charity Detox: What Charity Would Look Like if We Cared About Results* takes an even more damning stance towards popular mission outreach initiatives. In it, he speaks of the "power of the entrenched paradigm" and writes "if we intend to move the poverty needle here and in under-developed countries, we must increase our level of self-interest. Mission trips, teaching seminars, and service projects will not get the job done. Even economic assistance—microloans, infrastructure improvements, well-digging projects—as important as they may be, do not create wealth. Only profitable businesses do that."[38]

For Lupton, who has dedicated most of his life in charity outreach ministries, the hard truth must be acknowledged: the charity ministry paradigm tends to disempower those it seeks to help and does not bring about the long-term structural solutions of economic prosperity. He writes that if churches were serious about addressing poverty, they would "put forth a mission call for MBAs rather than MDivs."[39] While Lupton continues by providing examples of business ventures that have brought large numbers of people out of extreme poverty, one of his implicit assumptions is that this is a discussion about business people (and MBA programs) that view the prosperity of employees and communities as their primary goal. This goal, however, is not shared by everyone in the business world.

Critiques of the lack of fruitfulness of attempts to address poverty and suffering are not new. One noteworthy example is Monsignor Ivan Illich's controversial address to the Conference on Inter-American Student Projects made in 1968. Entitled "To Hell with Good Intentions," Illich's speech

37. Wright, *Very Worst Missionary.*
38. Lupton, *Charity Detox,* 36.
39. Lupton. *Charity Detox,* 44.

asserted, "You will not help anybody by your good intentions. There is an Irish saying that the road to hell is paved with good intentions; this sums up the same theological insight."[40] Among his withering criticisms of those from the USA seeking to volunteer in economically struggling parts of Latin America, Illich argues that there is insufficient ground for genuine meetings to occur: "You cannot even meet the majority which you pretend to serve in Latin America. . . . You can only dialogue with those like you—Latin American imitations of the North American middle class. There is no way for you to really meet with the underprivileged since there is no common ground whatsoever for you to meet on."[41]

For those not dissuaded by his scolding, he offers one possible route:

> If you insist on working with the poor, if this is your vocation, then at least work among the poor who can tell you to go to hell. It is incredibly unfair for you to impose yourselves on a village where you are so linguistically deaf and dumb that you don't even understand what you are doing or what people think of you. And it is profoundly damaging to yourselves when you define something that you want to do as "good," a "sacrifice," and "help."[42]

Illich urges would-be volunteers to renounce using the power advantage they have in such relationships and to come to terms with their own powerlessness to do the good they wish to do. "Come to [visit]. Come to study," he says. "But do not come to help."[43]

2.1.2 Mission as Relationship

The question of how to build genuine interactions across cultural and economic boundaries—that is, ones where an economically disadvantaged person has the freedom to tell a wealthy interloper to go to hell—is difficult but necessary to explore.

Rieger puts forth *mission as relationship* as an alternative to the *mission as outreach* paradigm. In the relationship approach, the focus is on mutuality and collaboration. He sees this as both an antidote to the problems of one-sided interactions as well as to the cynical conclusion that others are better off if we got "off their backs." "Mission as relationship recognizes that we are all connected and must, therefore, not leave people to themselves."[44]

---

40. Illich, "To Hell with Good Intentions."
41. Illich, "To Hell with Good Intentions."
42. Illich, "To Hell with Good Intentions."
43. Illich, "To Hell with Good Intentions."
44. Rieger, "Theology and Mission," 215.

Rieger warns that as we begin to talk about mission relationships as two-way streets, we must be careful to examine what exactly both sides have to gain in the interactions. He asks, "Is this 'mission in reverse,' a relationship that allows for a two-way street, or is it yet another way to exploit the resources of others for our own purposes—just like neocolonialism still depends on 'raw materials'? . . . While being enriched is certainly an important part of a relationship, the metaphor has undertones of economic gain that are not unfamiliar in neocolonialism."[45]

Rieger provides examples of how Euro-Americans at times have appropriated the cultural heritage of others in a way that is exploitative instead of mutually enriching. That is not to say that Rieger thinks it is impossible to build mutually beneficial relationships but rather that it is difficult due to the asymmetry of power. The challenges of engaging in mission as relationship in a healthy way is explored more in-depth later in this chapter in the discussion on partnership and mutuality in mission.

2.1.3 Mission as Inreach

Reflecting on the problematic aspects of *mission as outreach* and *mission as relationship*, Rieger posits "What if the most important thing in mission . . . is not what we are doing but what God is doing?"[46] Rieger suggests a mental shift, a "reminder of the fact that mission does not start with ourselves. Mission starts with God's mission."[47] He notes John Wesley's writings on the means of grace—that "works of mercy" are one of these means. Rieger reminds us that "God is the first missionary, and all of us are recipients. . . . Even our acts of mission and solidarity . . . function as means of grace, as channels through which God's grace comes back in our lives. As we encounter the other in mission—and only then—do we become recipients of God's power"[48]

Rieger argues that a shift to this mindset decolonizes attitudes by removing from the equation a sense of control and authority by anyone other than God. Such a mental shift, however, is easier said than done. Mission as inreach requires deep introspection. It requires us to recognize our interconnectedness. It requires recognition of how the current economic system benefits some (cheap clothing, produce, etc.) while oppressing others. It requires acknowledging the hard truth about our role in the system. It also requires us to recognize our prejudices—our assumptions

---

45. Rieger, "Theology and Mission," 216.
46. Rieger, "Theology and Mission," 219.
47. Rieger, "Theology and Mission," 220.
48. Rieger, "Theology and Mission," 220.

of superiority. Rieger notes, for example, recent conversations about "mission in reverse"—where people from formerly colonized nations come to places like Europe and North American for evangelism purposes. The assumption is often that this new generation of missionaries are echoes of missionaries of the past—parroting a primitive faith. Rieger rejects this condescending view.

Rieger sees mission as inreach as the antidote to neocolonialism by removing our blindness to it: "By not addressing the political and economic dynamics of neocolonialism, theology and the churches are not asserting their independence (as we sometimes believe) but forego resistance and are more and more pulled into their force field. In this situation, we need mission as inreach in order to inform us about where we are and about the invisible 'principalities and powers' that use even the most well-meaning efforts at mission for their own purposes."[49] As will be addressed later in this chapter, the historic tendency for American and European mission structures to not address these issues is why the language of *mission as partnership* has often rung hollow and hypocritical.

2.1.4 *Mission as Listening and Prophetic Dialogue*

The ideas of "mission as listening" and "mission as prophetic dialogue" are intertwined. One cannot listen deeply without it leading to prophetic conversations, and one cannot engage in a prophetic dialogue without having first listened deeply.

Once the hard work of listening, introspection, and personal repentance has been done, there must be a call to community/structural repentance. This task of serving as a catalyst and guide to decolonizing mental and structural paradigms merits its own category: that of mission as prophecy, or, as Stephen B. Bevans and Roger Schoeder call it, "prophetic dialogue," which they assert is "the phrase that best summarizes a theology of mission for today."[50] Bevans and Schoeder write:

> Mission is dialogue. It takes people where they are; it is open to their traditions and culture and experience; it recognizes the validity of their own religious existence and the integrity of their own religious ends. But it is *prophetic* dialogue because it calls people beyond; it calls people to conversation; it calls people to deeper and fuller truth that can only be found in communion with dialogue's trinitarian ground.[51]

---

49. Rieger, "Theology and Mission," 222.
50. Bevans and Schoeder, *Constants in Context*, §9432.
51. Bevans and Schoeder, *Constants in Context*, §6783.

Bevans and Schoeder have identified a number of types of conversations that call people into missional interactions. These include Witness and Proclamation as Prophetic Dialogue;[52] Liturgy, Prayer, and Contemplation as Prophetic Dialogue;[53] Justice, Peace, and the Integrity of Creation as Prophetic Dialogue;[54] Interreligious Dialogue as Prophetic Dialogue;[55] Inculturation as Prophetic Dialogue;[56] and Reconciliation as Prophetic Dialogue.[57] Thus, in their framework, all true forms of mission could be labeled as a form of prophetic dialogue. I, however, would like to highlight the conversational mission of the prophet him/herself as described by Walter Brueggemann.

In *The Prophetic Imagination,* Brueggemann writes that "the task of prophetic ministry is to hold together criticism and energizing. . . . Liberals are good at criticism but often have no word of promise to speak."[58] Brueggemann's writings emphasize the importance of prophetic voices addressing community issues. His assertions remind us that a sound definition of mission must involve the element of hope.

Brueggemann describes the prophet as someone who pays attention, someone with a deep awareness of the reality of the situation such that she or he is capable of identifying both the current trajectory and appropriate course corrections. Thus, I find that the literature on deep listening nests nicely within a discussion of Brueggemann's understanding of the role of prophecy.

The concept of *mission as listening* is not a new idea, but it has generally remained underappreciated and disregarded—the assumption of superior intellect has led countless to falsely believe that they have seen and heard enough to understand a community/situation. In Tom Montgomery-Fate's book *Beyond the White Noise: Mission in a Multicultural World,* he raises the vision of mission as cross-cultural listening and reminds us not all missionaries were/are listening. Montgomery-Fate notes that "patience is essential to the listening methodology. Without patience . . . we may continue to hear only white noise."[59] In using the term *white noise,* he means the dictionary definition of the term[60] while at the same time alluding to the problem of

---

52. Bevans and Schoeder, *Constants in Context,* §8361.
53. Bevans and Schoeder, *Constants in Context,* §8612.
54. Bevans and Schoeder, *Constants in Context,* §8797.
55. Bevans and Schoeder, *Constants in Context,* §9018.
56. Bevans and Schoeder, *Constants in Context,* §9196.
57. Bevans and Schoeder, *Constants in Context,* §9290.
58. Brueggemann, *Prophetic Imagination,* 4.
59. Montgomery-Fate, *Beyond the White Noise,* 147.
60. *White noise* is described by the *Merriam-Webster Dictionary* as a "mixture of

how White/colonial perspectives block our ability to hear anything other than (neo)colonial preconceived notions. Montgomery-Fate cites other thinkers who have written about the importance of a listening orientation. He affirms that we should "listen without ceasing" and that listening "is key to the idea of co-mission across cultures."[61]

An eloquent description of how to engage in mission as listening is found in Bob Walters's memoir/manifesto *The Last Missionary*:

> Step one, listen. You listen, then you listen some more. When you think you know something, stop yourself from speaking and listen some more. Listen until what you thought you know is no longer what you know. Listen until you know nothing at all. Let everything you thought you knew fade into nothingness. Listen with your whole body and soul. . . . Don't talk. Listen. . . .
>
> Step one will take months, years . . . [It is] common in a patronage system that all parties have bought into a story that explains their problems that only serves to reinforce those problems. The listener has to get to the other side of this story.[62]

Walters identifies deep listening as the first essential step in the mission model he has embraced. This model has its roots in the community development frameworks of Brazilian pedagogue Paulo Freire, was further developed in Zimbabwe by Anne Hope and Salley Timmel in the workbook series *Training for Transformation*, and introduced to Walters via a global health training developed by David Hilton (former United Methodist missionary doctor). In it, the outsider/missionary does have a beneficial role to play: that as the one who listens to and then reflects back to the community the issues with which it is wrestling. The job of the missionary is not to bring solutions (that would be counter-productive) but rather to encourage the community to reflect deeply and claim ownership of their own problem-solving abilities.

Walters argues that the mistake missionaries, mission teams, and others with intentions to be helpful tend to make is that they fail to listen deeply enough in their rush to solve surface-level problems. They lack the patience to wait until the conversations move beyond the rote responses—until new transformative/paradigm-shifting realizations occur. Hence, the overwhelming failure rate of mission projects—even those that are envisioned as partnerships that seek the input and engagement of local communities.

---

sound waves," "a constant background noise; especially: one that drowns out other sounds," or "a meaningless or distracting commotion."

61. Montgomery-Fate, *Beyond the White Noise*, 13.
62. Walters, *Last Missionary*, 47.

While the Freirian-inspired missionary model has its differences from Brueggemann's prophetic model, both have at their starting point the requirement of listening deeply in order to recognize what is going on beneath the surface. As tempting as it may be to assume that what we see and hear is the complete truth, if we wish to gain a better understanding of the dynamics at play, we must recognize that there is much more going on than is evident. James C. Scott in *Domination and the Arts of Resistance: Hidden Transcripts* writes that, with few exceptions, "the greater the disparity in power between dominant and subordinate and the more arbitrarily it is exercised, the more the public transcript of subordinates will take on a stereotyped, ritualistic cast."[63] That is, the greater the power gap between people, the less likely the person(s) with less relative power will be fully candid when speaking with the more powerful person(s). Instead, the subordinate person will create a protective mask/script for these interactions. "The public transcript is, to put it crudely, the self-portrait of the dominant elites as they would have themselves seen."[64] Because the elites are not trusted, the less powerful will also hide anything that could invoke the rage of the elite and/or risk having negative socio-economic consequences.

I have witnessed on numerous occasions these kinds of scripted interactions between North Katangan United Methodists and Americans whose financial support was being sought. Each group of Americans brought to Kamina is greeted by the same choir, receives the same tour and speeches, and the same farewell party. Efforts are made to mask anything that could betray the image/narrative North Katangan church leaders wish to portray. I began thinking of partner visits like these as "curtain tours"—an allusion to the classic story of The Wizard of Oz where the wizard's true self was hidden behind a curtain.

Another image often used to explain the problems that arise in cross-cultural conversations is the iceberg model.[65] There are numerous varia-

---

63. Scott, *Domination and the Arts of Resistance*, 3.

64. Scott, *Domination and the Arts of Resistance*, 18.

65. In trying to identify the original creator of the iceberg model, I found competing claims for authorship and, despite extensive attempts, could not verify any of them. Many slide presentations cite Edward T. Hall's book *Beyond Culture*, which was first published in 1976. While the assertions in his book can be used to argue that much of cross-cultural interactions occur below the surface of the other's awareness, I found no reason to credit Hall as the creator of this model. Another popular claim is that "The Iceberg Model of Workplace Dynamics" was developed by Stanley N. Herman of TRW Systems in 1970, but I found no way to verify that assertion either. The AIESEC, the world's largest non-profit youth-run organization, credits former MIT professor Edgar Schein as the iceberg model creator in one of its presentations but, again, my search to verify that hit a dead end.

Theoretical Framework: Mission, Partnerships, and Colonization

tions of the iceberg model found in books and presentation slides; what is constant between them is the image of one or two icebergs submerged under the water—with only a small tip visible above the waterline. The premise is that, like icebergs, the majority of the realities of a person or community (e.g., etiquette norms, unverbalized assumptions, values, etc.) cannot be immediately seen by someone from a different culture and/or lived experience. That is, most of what happens in such encounters occurs below the metaphorical surface. When misunderstandings and conflicts arise, this is usually due to an underwater collision of these icebergs. Hence, any mission initiative that assumes that what is visible is the full reality of an encounter is destined for failure.

2.2 PARTNERSHIP, MISMEETING, AND MUTUALITY IN MISSION

The term "partnership in mission," while conceptually a very good thing, is fraught with negative connotations due to the history of it being used in unhealthy ways. As Philip Knutson explains in his 1998 doctoral thesis, *Partnership in Mission: Mismeeting in Jesus' Name*, "partnership in mission and equal partners is a relatively new concept."[66] It is also easier said than accomplished: "The experience of Africans of mutual partnership with their European and American partners has not always been a humanizing or empowering one."[67] The reasons for this are complex.

Knutson begins his extensive discussion on the history of the modern mission partnership concept by echoing the question posed by James Scherer in *Gospel, Church, and Kingdom*: "Is genuine partnership really possible between churches of unequal strength, resources, and historical background?"[68] Knutson responds with a yes-and-no answer. Inspired by Zygmunt Bauman's writings about reclaiming the "arcane art of mismeeting,"[69] Knutson argues that "all meetings are mismeetings."[70] Knutson's definition of mismeeting "does *not* mean the absence or failure of a meeting but stresses the asymmetry, open-endedness, and complex nature of every meeting."[71] In describing partnerships in mission as mismeetings in Jesus' name, Knutson also challenges "the frequently stated goal or purpose of partnership as that of

66. Knutson, "Partnership in Mission," 20.
67. Knutson, "Partnership in Mission," 56.
68. Scherer, *Gospel, Church, and Kingdom*, 33.
69. Bauman, *Postmodern Ethics*, 159. See also Knutson, "Partnership in Mission," xii.
70. Knutson, "Partnership in Mission," xii.
71. Knutson, "Partnership in Mission," xii.

overcoming differences."[72] Instead, he speaks of Christian mismeeting including three perspectives: "the past, present, and future."[73] He poetically writes, "As we meet for the first time, in the present, it becomes evident that we have already met and yet still have to meet."[74]

One method Knutson uses to trace the history of the partnership in mission concept is to examine the key conversations that took place in the major ecumenical missionary conferences in the twentieth century. According to Knutson, the 1910 conference in Edinburgh marks the emergence of the usage of term "partners." In the book *Postcolonial Mission: Power and Partnership in World Christianity*, Desmond van der Water (former general secretary of the Council for World Mission), however, points to the 1928 International Missionary Council meeting in Jerusalem as the first time "partnership" was used "within the global ecumenical community context."[75] Knutson and Water both note that at the 1947 conference in Whitby, the discussions shifted more to the idea of older and younger churches collaborating as "Partners in Obedience," and Water notes that the 1947 conference also marks the formal beginning of the phrase *partnership in mission*. In 1952 in Willingen and 1958 in Achimota, there was an attempt made to move beyond the partnership model that was loaded with problematic sending/receiving and older/younger church language. This was also when the concept of *Missio Dei*—the idea that mission does not belong to us; we are participating in God's Mission—began to gain traction. In 1963 in Mexico City, there was yet again a shift in rhetoric. There, participants affirmed that the missionary movement involved all Christians—that one should no longer think in terms of sending versus receiving churches. This affirmation coincided with the rise of the call for a missionary moratorium—that is, that Western churches should stop sending missionaries to the historically receiving regions so that the younger churches could have a chance to grow independently. It must not be overlooked that all these movements within the church happened concurrently with the independence movements of many colonized countries. James Scherer describes the rising sentiment of sending home the foreign missionaries in his 1964 publication *Missionary Go Home!*[76] By the early 1970s, the calls for a moratorium became a hot conversation topic in world missionary conferences, such as the one in

---

72. Knutson, "Partnership in Mission," xiv.
73. Knutson, "Partnership in Mission," xii.
74. Knutson, "Partnership in Mission," xv.
75. Water, "Council for World Mission," 33.
76. Scherer, *Missionary Go Home!*

Bangkok in 1972–1973 and at the All-Africa Conference of Churches, held in Lusaka in 1974.

In Johannes Verkuyl's 1975 book, *Contemporary Missiology: An Introduction*, he writes that he believes the calls for a moratorium were so controversial partly because they were misrepresented in conversations:

> The pressure was not for smashing relationships but rather for revising them. In the discussions and deliberations the term "moratorium" was bandied about, especially by the Africans. The term itself is . . . most unfortunate, for it connotes the idea of complete cessation of relationships. But those who used it meant something quite different by it. They meant that churches in Africa should temporarily suspend relations with those in Europe and America in order to set their own house in order and then begin anew to build different patterns of relationships.[77]

That said, even the idea of a temporary separation for the purposes of reuniting as equals challenged the dominant power balances and savior narratives of Western churches. Verkuyl reflects upon the conversations at the 1963 Mexico City conference and addresses the paternalistic attitudes that impact mission partnerships. In doing so, he also addresses the complex and sensitive issues of wealthy churches providing assistance to financially poorer churches. According to Verkuyl, in the opening address to the committee meeting of the Division of World Mission and Evangelism of the World Council of Churches, Dr. Philip Potter said, "There is something demonic about a powerful rich sending agency negotiating with poor people and poor agencies. How can there be real 'partnership' between poor and rich? Partnership was a nice word which we fell into the habit of using, but now we have become afraid of using it because we know what it all came down to in practice."[78]

The 1970s and 1980s were marked by a widening gap in political and economic power in the world. These issues were discussed heavily in the 1973 and 1980 mission conferences in Bangkok and Melbourne respectively. This led to increasing conversations about the sharing/redistributing of resources between churches (1987 in El Escorial, 1989 in San Antonio, 1991 in Canberra). It is also when, as Knutson notes, the term *koinonia* (the ecumenical sharing of resources) became popular. Van

---

77. Verkuyl, *Contemporary Missiology*, 334.

78. Verkuyl, *Contemporary Missiology*, 320. Unfortunately, Verkuyl does not cite a published document for the Potter quote and my attempts to find a transcript for this speech only produced two doctoral papers, both of which cited Verkuyl as their source.

der Water writes that at the 1987 meeting in El Escorial sponsored by the World Council of Churches,

> the understanding of ecclesiastical and ecumenical partnership was more comprehensively and clearly articulated. One of the important outcomes of the El Escorial consultation was the adoption of a set of Guidelines for the Ecumenical Sharing of Resources by the ecumenical organizations and churches that participated in the event. . . . At the core of this model was a commitment to partnership in which all the member churches shared equal power and full ownership of the mission enterprise.[79]

These abovementioned guidelines stated (as summarized by Water):

> All parties to be accorded the dignity and respect by which they would be recognized and regarded as equal partners
>
> Mutual trust, mutual affirmation, and mutual accountability to characterize the processes of engagement by parties concerned
>
> A shared commitment to a global value system based on social and economic justice, peace, and the integrity of creation
>
> The engagement in partnership relationships from the perspectives of a holistic understanding of mission
>
> The voice, needs, and concerns of oppressed, marginalized, and excluded groups to be heard and to be allowed to influence and shape decisions about policy, practice, and priorities in the use and deployment of resources
>
> That the spirit and principles of ecumenical sharing be promoted at all levels of church life, namely national, regional, and international.[80]

In the early 1980s, the term *mutuality in mission* was introduced to The UMC's discourse.[81] Its General Board of Global Ministries (GBGM) had published a booklet called *Mutuality in Mission*[82] in 2001 and slowly began to shift its rhetoric from "partnership in mission" to "mutuality in mission." While an admirable idea, functionally, it was an exchange of labels in an attempt to shift hearts and minds to decolonialized paradigms of partnership by removing a word that had become tainted by its problematic

---

79. Water, "Council for World Mission," 34.
80. Water, "Council for World Mission," 38.
81. The earliest mention of "mutuality in mission" I could find in Methodist publications was an article from 1984, Lerrigo, "Mutuality in Mission."
82. Dharmaraj and Dharmaraj, *Mutuality in Mission*.

history. The results of this effort have been mixed. Based on my anecdotal observations and stories I have been told, it seems that instead of leaving behind neocolonial behaviors by replacing old terms with fresh vocabulary, mutuality has also become a tainted word—like changing the sign on the restaurant without changing the chef or the menu. That is, some American congregations and conferences have changed their rhetoric while their attitudes and behaviors remain the same.[83]

As Eugene Stockwell suggested in a 1987 editorial in the *International Review of Mission*, "Mission organization structures, like secular bodies, are notoriously difficult to change for the simple reason that major changes threaten existing power relations."[84] In chapter 4, I discuss more on GBGM's efforts to promote healthier paradigms of partnership/mutuality within The UMC.

In *Friendship at the Margins: Discovering Mutuality in Service and Mission*, Christopher Heuertz and Christine Pohl write on the concept of mutuality in mission and how such a goal can be reached when befriending marginalized persons. While acknowledging in depth the challenges inherent in building healthy relationships across socio-economic divides, they argue that seeking mutuality—authentic friendship—is essential to Christian praxis. Without the element of friendship, our actions turn people into objects.

> When communities have been saturated with missional activity but the good news has not been embodied in a consistent presence of love and concern, folks know that they have been target of one more program. And most of us resent being "target," no matter how well intentioned the effort might be.[85]

The question of how to create true mutuality in mission partnerships echoes throughout this thesis and is especially re-explored through a theological lens in chapter 7.

2.3 (NEO/POST/DE)COLONIALISM

In her essay "Partnership in Mission: An Appraisal of the Partnership of Women and Men," Isabel Apawo Phiri asserts that "the question of partnership in mission, when approached from a post-colonial perspective,

---

83. I am reluctant to provide specific examples for fear of needlessly damaging relationships.

84. Water, "Council for World Mission," 39 (Water summarizing Stockwell's editorial).

85. Heuertz and Pohl, *Friendship at the Margins*, 73.

shows that it is an issue of social justice."[86] What, then, is a post-colonial perspective? To explore that, we first need to understand *colonialism* and its perspective.

In his writings, David Bosch argued that "since the sixteenth century, if one said 'mission,' one in a sense also said 'colonialism,'" and that "modern missions originated in the context of modern Western colonialism."[87] While the words colonialism and colonial can refer to a formal political situation between countries and lands considered to be their territories, they can also be used to describe other aspects of that type of power dynamic. Madina Tlostanova and Walter Mignolo explain:

> The term "colonial" has a specific meaning in decolonial thinking. It refers not to the Roman Empire's understanding of a colony as a polity built or ruled by imperial order but to the modern meaning of "colonial" as a "conquered and managed territory" linked to the process of European "colonization," grounded in destroying the existing social order and imposing one responding to the needs and habitus of the conquerors.[88]

Colonialism is tied closely to the idea of manifest destiny. David Bosch writes:

> The Western missionary enterprise of the . . . [Enlightenment period] proceeded not only from the assumption of the superiority of Western culture over all other cultures, but also from the conviction that God, in his providence, had chosen the Western nations, because of their unique qualities, to be the standard-bearers of his cause even to the uttermost ends of the world. This conviction [was] commonly referred to as the notion of "manifest destiny."[89]

While colonialism is commonly thought of in terms of official political control of one country over another, colonialism can also be understood as a mental model as well as a socio-economic power dynamic that has outlived the historical colonial period. As Jean-Paul Sartre points out, "The idea of privilege is at the heart of the colonial relationship. . . . Even the poorest colonizer thought himself to be . . . superior to the colonized."[90] In the same vein, assumptions of moral and intellectual superiority of the

---

86. Phiri, "Partnership in Mission," 77.
87. Bosch, *Transforming Mission*, 303.
88. Tlostanova and Mignolo, *Learning to Unlearn*, 17.
89. Bosch, *Transforming Mission*, 298.
90. Sartre, "Introduction," xii.

colonizer are at the heart of the colonial model—both in terms of structures and individual mindsets. In chapters 4 and 6, I identify where these colonial assumptions can still be observed at play in the relationship dynamics between American and North Katangan United Methodists both through the way in which news stories about Methodism in Congo are told and through the comments made by both American and North Katangan United Methodists in the transcripts of my interviews with them.

Sartre and numerous other writers have observed that these colonial assumptions of superiority are not only harmful to those considered inferior—they are also harmful to the psyche of the colonizer. Sartre writes, "If colonization destroys the colonized, it also rots the colonizer."[91]

Achille Mbembe goes deeper into this idea:

> The colonial relationship is based on the distinction between the wild animal and the domestic animal. Colonization as an enterprise of domination includes at least three factors: the appropriation of the animal (the native) by the human (the colonist); the familiarization of man (the colonist) and the animal (the native); and the utilization of the animal (the native) by the human (the colonist). One may think such a process was as arbitrary as it was one-dimensional, but that would be to forget that neither the colonist nor the colonized people emerge from this circle unharmed.[92]

Sathianathan Clarke, a professor at Wesley Theological Seminary in Washington, DC, describes the colonizer as "strangled within this heavy machine, which dehumanizes all the participants in its system."[93] Robert J. C. Young echoes this issue in the preface of Jean Paul Sartre's classic *Colonialism and Neocolonialism*: "Caught up in that system, transformed into an oppressor or torturer, the colonizing subject also finds himself in a condition of ontological ambivalence: 'both the organizer and the victim' as Fanon put it 'of a system that has choked him and reduces him to silence.'"[94]

In his 1957 groundbreaking work *The Colonizer and the Colonized*, Albert Memmi examines the psychological and sociological impact of these power dynamics both on the colonized and the colonizer. In it, he describes a system inside of which all actors are trapped. He argues, for example, that the idea that one could be a colonial but not a colonizer is a myth: "A colonial is a benevolent European who does not have the colonizer's attitude toward

---

91. Sartre, "Introduction," xvii.
92. Mbembe, *On the Postcolony*, 236–37.
93. Clarke, "Postcolonial Voices."
94. Young, "Sartre," xii.

the colonized. All right! Let's say right away ... a colonial so defined does not exist, for all Europeans in the colonies are privileged."[95]

This observation that within a society with a colonial power dynamic no individual can escape from being either the colonizer or the colonized (or both, as Jean-Paul Sartre describes himself in the forward to Memmi's book) highlights one of the major blindspots of the majority of American United Methodists engaged in cross-socio-economic mission. When Americans enter into contexts where a colonial dynamic still dominates, they do not have the option to operate outside of this system. Willingly or not, they step into the position of the colonizer—with all the advantages and problems that come with it. As long as they are blind to this reality, there is no hope of deconstructing it.

While Memmi rejects the myth that it is possible to be a colonial instead of a colonizer, he writes with the spirit of compassion when he goes into depth about the plight of the colonizer who is aware of her/his situation and wishes to reject it: "If he wants to help the colonized, it is exactly because their destiny does concern him, because his destiny and theirs are intertwined and matter to one another, because he hopes to go on living in the colony."[96] In addition, Memmi explores the internalized colonial assumptions and angst in the minds of the colonized themselves: "Love of the colonizer is subtended by a complex of feelings from shame to self-hate."[97] This type of complex angst of the North Katangans (colonized) as well as angst of some of the Americans (colonizers) was evident in the transcripts of the individuals I interviewed in my research. Again, I argue that these assumptions and structures built upon them must be faced directly and proactively deconstructed for there to be any realistic hope for a future that has broken free of the forces of colonialism. As Clarke asserts:

> The whole matter of internal colonizations cannot be ignored in a re-membering of the past with assistance from the present. This historical remembering of internally drastic forms of colonialism cannot be erased for the sake of uniting in order to ward off forces of external colonialism. There may be more than one demon of colonization that needs to be named, confronted, and disbanded in any historical context.[98]

In other words, any attempts at moving forward together without first facing our demons of the past *and* recognizing that those demons are more

---

95. Memmi, *Colonizer and the Colonized*, 10.
96. Memmi, *Colonizer and the Colonized*, 36.
97. Memmi, *Colonizer and the Colonized*, 121.
98. Clarke, "Postcolonial Voices."

than just memories—they live on via neocolonial forces—would be folly. In addition, we should not be so naive to think that there is only one issue—one demon—to be exorcised; there are many manifestations of and layers to the colonial baggage we carry.

Because the colonial legacy is complex, multiple prefixes have been attached to the word in attempts to better articulate these issues:

2.3.1 *Postcolonial*

Postcolonial is often understood—especially by Americans—as the period that began after the end of the colonial period. However, it can also be used to describe the colonial period itself (that is, what happened post the beginning of colonialism). In *Postcolonial Feminist Interpretations of the Bible*, Musa Dube writes that "the word *postcolonial* has been coined to describe the modern history of imperialism, beginning with the process of colonialism, through the struggles for political independence, the attainment of independence, and to the contemporary neocolonialist realities. This definition emphasizes the connection and continuity between the past and the present, between the colonizer and the colonized."[99]

Postcolonialism, writes Sathianathan Clarke, "is deliberately ambiguous. It includes both a historically narrow and trans-historically broad dimension into its disciplinary focus and scope."[100] Thus, *postcolonial* as a descriptive label of context, theology, critiques, etc. is so wide as to be at times hard to define precisely. Clarke describes postcolonialism as one "option to understand and cultivate the worldview of historically dominated peoples and to represent their particular tack on matters concerning God-world-human with a view toward advancing their welfare."[101] That is, whenever a representative of an historically dominated people expresses their point of view on a matter out of the context of having been dominated, theirs is a postcolonial point of view. More specifically, as Clarke explains, "the trauma and the tragedy of western colonialism, as it drastically and collectively affected the people of the world, are at the heart of postcolonial studies."[102] In other words, postcolonial discussions are discussions about the impact of the lingering trauma of colonialism. In addition to this, "postcolonialism implies the banding together of all human collective who are affected by various kinds of domination and who seek to resist and overcome such

---

99. Dube, *Postcolonial Feminist*, 15.
100. Clarke, "Postcolonial Voices."
101. Clarke, "Postcolonial Voices."
102. Clarke, "Postcolonial Voices."

colonizing strategies and structures."[103] More than just a mark of a period of history (such as Victorian literature), postcolonial writings are about the shared struggles of dominated peoples. Postcolonialism, asserts Clarke, "has extended the future of global discourse of emancipation."[104]

2.3.2 Neocolonial

Neocolonial is the term used when the emphasis is on describing ways in which the colonial assumptions and structures have manifested during the period after the official end of the colonial period. It especially focuses on new manifestations. In this thesis, I focus on neocolonialism as it exists within the church—particularly in the relationship and power dynamics between American and North Katangan United Methodists.

In his paper entitled "Theology and Mission Between Neo- and Postcolonialism," Joerg Rieger writes that "talk about neocolonialism serves as a reminder that, even in a postcolonial age, colonial mentalities have not disappeared; many have simply been pushed underground and have adapted in other ways, frequently taking more vicious shapes than ever before."[105] Rieger goes on to provide examples of how colonial paradigms and structures have manifested in the mission approaches of North American churches after the colonial period:

> The end of blatant ecclesial and colonial self-centeredness does not end self-centeredness as such. A neocolonialist bent appears already in these early postcolonial missions. The end of formal colonial structures does not signify the end of colonial intellectual attitudes, reflected now for instance in the belief in the "manifest destiny" of the missionaries and their nations, led by the US, to shape the globe in their own image. Neither does the end of the formal colonial structures signify the end of economic dependencies, reflected now in the growing capitalist networks that mainly benefit one side.[106]

Lest one accuse Rieger of exaggeration in his assertions that the idea of *manifest destiny* was held strongly by the American missionary movement, one simply has to dust off The Methodist Church's mission promotional materials of the mid-twentieth century to be reminded that the imagery

---

103. Clarke, "Postcolonial Voices."
104. Clarke, "Postcolonial Voices."
105. Rieger, "Theology and Mission," 207–8.
106. Rieger, "Theology and Mission," 208–9.

and language of crusading and conquest into other lands was used and portrayed as a divine moral imperative.[107]

As Rieger points out, the support of globalization and neocolonialism go hand in hand. He criticizes the viewpoint that globalization (i.e., the spread of "free markets" and cultural values) is a "benevolent strand of neocolonialism."[108] Rather than being benevolent, it is at its roots about economic and thus political domination of other nations. While neocolonialism may be less overt than colonialism, it is still based on the assumption that "we" know better and that we are the ones with the authority to make decisions for others.

One of the best critiques of the view of globalization as a benevolent manifestation of neocolonialism is found in Benjamin Barber's now-famous, prophetic article, published in *The Atlantic* in 1992, titled "Jihad vs McWorld." In it, he wrote that "the planet is falling precipitantly apart *AND* coming reluctantly together at the very same moment."[109] On one hand, he notes an increasing struggle (jihad) against the globalizing forces that are trying to homogenize the world; it is a struggle to maintain a sense of local identity and community, but it comes at the price of parochialism, is "grounded in exclusion," and leads to violence against outsiders to maintain solidarity. On the other, there are the forces of globalization—of multinational companies dominating world markets. He refers to these forces as McWorld in a nod to the ubiquity of the McDonalds restaurant chain throughout the world. While McWorld may be appealing in its seeming way of unifying the world, it comes "at the cost of independence, community, and identity," and its mechanisms do not care about human rights or including all in the benefits of the economic profits. Barber asserts, "Neither McWorld nor Jihad is remotely democratic in impulse. Neither needs democracy; neither promotes democracy." While he does not explicitly state it in his article, what Barber is writing about is the underbelly of neocolonial economic structures and the predictable reaction to them.

Rieger notes that one reason why Americans tend to be blind to their neocolonial assumptions is that, despite its belief in *manifest destiny*, the United States of America was never officially a colonial power.[110] Neocolonial power structures tend to be less visible than colonial structures because of the way they operate (e.g., stock markets, international corporations,

107. I will discuss this further in chapter 4.
108. Rieger, "Theology and Mission," 209.
109. Barber, "Jihad vs McWorld."

110. This is, of course, ignoring all the unofficial ways in which the United States acted as a colonial power in taking over the lands of the first-peoples of the Americas and using its military and economic power to dominate other nations/"protectorates."

clandestine finances of guerilla groups, etc.). Thus, I assert that as a nation and as members of The UMC, Americans have yet to truly examine and repent of our past behaviors. It is this lack of authentic repentance (that is, wrestling with the demons of racism and assumptions of superiority) that has maintained a fertile environment for this mental virus to flourish.

Digging deeper into the roots of this blind spot, Rieger notes that "colonial Christianity failed to question colonialism, mostly because it operated under the tacit assumption that the colonial enterprise was the Christian enterprise. Contemporary Christianity, by comparison, is even less able to question neocolonialism, mostly because we are unaware of its existence on a grand scale and how it shapes our mission."[111] Yet, both in colonial and neocolonial times, there has always existed the issue of power and authority resting in the hands of the missionary. While this power was more overt in the past, it still exists—and based on my readings and observations over the years, both those with and without this power are on some level aware of this dynamic. What most disturbs me is when neither side questions whether one side is truly intellectually and morally superior. As Rieger notes:

> Mission is now shaped by these neocolonial realities, whose dark side is often overlooked. Economic networks distribute power unevenly . . . and issues of multiculturalism or "inculturation" often do not challenge cultural power. . . . If mission and theology fail to develop an awareness of these developments and some insight into the close relation between authority and power, we will end up, once again, on the side of the powers that be, escaping colonialist traps only to be caught in the neocolonialist ones.[112]

More concretely, neocolonialism in mission models manifests as *mission as outreach*. It is not unusual for American churches to even officially label their missional activities as "outreach ministries." As discussed earlier in this chapter, mission as outreach ranges from everything from organizing soup kitchens and clothing drives for the poor living in close proximity to a congregation to *mission trips* composed of *mission teams* to help needy people in other parts of the country or world through providing free labor (painting, building, teaching, etc.) in economically struggling communities. To emphasize, these sort of mission programs are typically built on underlying assumptions of "us" and "them," with the

---

111. Rieger, "Theology and Mission," 210.
112. Rieger, "Theology and Mission," 211.

"us" being narratively framed as the hero who goes to help the morally and/or intellectually weaker "them."

This sort of (neo)colonial hero narrative which commonly manifests itself today is often referred to as the *Savior Complex*. The term Savior Complex in relation to mission projects has gained traction in recent years since Teju Cole's explosively controversial viral Twitter post and later article "White Savior Industrial Complex." Cole writes:

> One song we hear too often is the one in which Africa serves as a backdrop for white fantasies of conquest and heroism. From the colonial project to *Out of Africa* to *The Constant Gardener* and Kony 2012, Africa has provided a space onto which white egos can conveniently be projected. It is a liberated space in which the usual rules do not apply: a nobody from America or Europe can go to Africa and become a godlike savior or, at the very least, have his or her emotional needs satisfied. Many have done it under the banner of "making a difference."[113]

The Savior Complex is about an inner desire to affirm one's importance, that is, one's superior status in the world by seeking to play the role of rescuer of people perceived as lacking the intellectual or moral maturity to fix their own problems. The vanity of this mindset has been mocked by a handful of groups. For example, the Instagram site "Barbie Savior"[114] and the Norwegian Students' and Academics' International Assistance Fund's "Rusty Radiator" Awards[115] have gained large followings for their parodies of stereotypical foolish and racist things said by those who have bought into the foreign savior narratives. The annual Rusty Radiator and Golden Radiator awards highlight both the worst and best ad campaigns of charity/development organizations. The goal is to push people and organizations to shift the dominant language and approaches to relating to and assisting those in need.

To emphasize, the savior mentality is not benign. It is more than simply a glory-seeking impulse of certain individuals that is fed through engaging in charity work. It is more than even failing to recognize the larger system at play that creates these differentials of wealth and power and one's own role in it. As Cole asserts, it is a system itself: The White Savior Industrial Complex.

---

113. Cole, "White Savior Industrial Complex."
114. Worrall, "Barbie Savior."
115. "Radi-Aid; Africa for Norway."

> What innocent heroes don't always understand is that they play a useful role for people who have much more cynical motives. The White Savior Industrial Complex is a valve for releasing the unbearable pressures that build in a system built on pillage. We can participate in the economic destruction of Haiti over long years, but when the earthquake strikes it feels good to send ten dollars each to the rescue fund. I have no opposition, in principle, to such donations (I frequently make them myself), but we must do such things only with awareness of what else is involved. If we are going to interfere in the lives of others, a little due diligence is a minimum requirement.[116]

What, then, is a repentant "savior" to do if she or he feels a deep desire to be helpful? Cole responds to similar question by writing, "It begins, I believe, with some humility with regards to the people in those places. It begins with some respect for the agency of the people of Uganda in their own lives. A great deal of work had been done, and continues to be done, by Ugandans to improve their own country, and ignorant comments (I've seen many) about how 'we have to save them because they can't save themselves' can't change that fact."[117]

Becoming aware of the dynamics of neocolonialism and everyone's role in it and then consciously attempting to dismantle this system is a decolonizing action.

2.3.3 Decolonial

Decolonial is the term used when the emphasis is on the deconstructing of colonial assumptions and structures. Decolonialism recognizes the continued presence of (neo)colonialism in our world and seeks to actively dismantle it. As Kuam-Hsing Chen writes in "The Decolonization Question":

> If decolonialism, at the historical juncture, no longer simply means the struggle for national independence but a struggle to abolish any form of colonization, then postcolonial/cultural studies has to recognize that (1) structurally, neo-colonialism, neoimperialism, and globalization are the continuity and extension of colonialism (in the wider sense of the word, meaning any structure of domination); (2) colonialism is not yet a legacy, as mainstream postcolonial studies would have it, but still a lively operator in any geocolonial site. . . . That is to say,

---

116. Cole, "White Savior Industrial Complex."
117. Cole, "White Savior Industrial Complex."

colonialism, engineered by the apparatus of capitalism, still covers the entire globe.[118]

The need, then, is to publicly name all of the manifestations of colonization and to strategically dismantle them—that is, to decolonize them. In his book *Decolonizing the Mind: The Politics of Language in African Literature*, Ngũgĩ wa Thiong'o reflects upon ways in which African minds have been colonized. He writes, "The biggest weapon wielded and actually daily unleashed by imperialism against that collective defiance is the cultural bomb. The effect of the cultural bomb is to annihilate a people's belief in their names, in their languages, in the environment, in their heritage of struggle, in their unity, in their capacities, and ultimately in themselves."[119]

Thiong'o writes about how colonial powers created a formal education system where European languages, stories, and traditions were highly valued while African languages, stories, and traditions were looked down upon and in many instances even banned. He asserts that "we have to coldly and consciously look at what imperialism has been doing to us and to our view of ourselves in the universe."[120] Thiong'o encourages Africans to reject the narrative that to be worthy of esteem one must try to become as European as possible. He calls African writers to write books and plays in their mother tongues, and he writes about the political persecution he faced for doing so.

While *Decolonizing the Mind* was first published in 1981, Thiong'o's assertions remain relevant, especially in the context of this thesis, which examines the psychological aspects of (neo)colonialism and the decolonizing process. In this thesis' title, I chose to use *decolonizing* as the active verb in order to emphasize that the decolonization of the relationship dynamics between American and North Katangan United Methodists requires conscious dismantling of both assumptions about authority and superiority and the structures used for interactions and collaboration. It is not enough to attempt to use healthier mission models; we must face and exorcise the demons in our minds and systems.

---

118. Chen, "Decolonization Question," 28–29.
119. Thiong'o, *Decolonizing the Mind*, 2.
120. Thiong'o, *Decolonizing the Mind*, 88.

3

The Historical Cultural Context

3.1 THE LUBA AND LUNDA EMPIRES

THE RELATIONSHIP DYNAMICS BETWEEN the people of Katanga and the foreign missionaries who entered into their territory cannot be fully understood without an exploration of the pre-existing power structures and protocols within the Katangan empires as well as how the leaders of the Lunda and Luba people viewed these new arrivals. While this thesis' overarching research question of relational dynamics between American and North Katangan United Methodists extends beyond the Katangan setting, the early interactions were nearly entirely Americans in Katanga and not vice-versa. Thus, this chapter examines the initial primary setting of these relationships.

The North Katanga conference of The UMC is primary Luba territory, while southern Katanga is the home of the Lunda empire. This chapter thus focuses more on the Luba people of North Katanga but also discusses the Lunda kingdom since that was the entry point for Methodism in Katanga as well as the region where most of North Katanga's pastors continue to go for their theological studies.

The Luba empire flourished from 500 AD to 1900 AD. It continues to survive today, albeit splintered and weakened by the period of Belgian colonial rule (1880–1960).[1] It is currently divided into six Luba kingdoms, with its chiefs recognized by the DR Congo government as having territorial ruling rights.[2]

The Lunda empire can be traced back to the fifteenth century AD; by 1650, the Lunda king had "established trade routes from his capital to

1. Mutombo, "Baluba," 97.
2. Mutombo, "Baluba," 97.

the Atlantic coast and initiated direct contact with European traders eager for slaves and forest products."[3] While the Lunda and Luba are distinct empires speaking different languages, it was not uncommon for Lunda royalty to marry descendants of Luba kings in order to build alliances. Today, marriages between the two groups are common—especially since the cities with the most profitable job prospects are mostly in areas overseen by Lunda chiefs.[4]

The Lunda king is called the Mwant Yav. Beneath the Mwant Yav are regional governors and local land chiefs. The Lunda Mwant Yavs welcomed John and Helen Springer, the first foreign Methodist missionaries in their territory,[5] and continued to welcome other Methodist missionaries over the years. Gina Riendeau writes, "Although Catholic missionaries had been in the area for quite some time, the Mwant Yav appreciated the Methodist practice of learning the local Lunda language and sending teachers and doctors into areas needing ministry."[6] John Springer described the Mwant Yav as a hardworking monarch and judge. Despite welcoming the contributions of the Methodist missionaries, it was not until E. Stanley Jones brought a Christian Ashram to lead an Ashram-style camp meeting (attended by Methodist missionaries Ken and Lorraine Enright and many others) that the Mwant Yav publicly declared himself a Christian.[7]

With the notable exception of the recent writings of Mutombo Nkulu-N'Sengha, most of what has been researched and published about the Luba people has been done by missionaries and other foreigners. In the early 1970s, American Thomas Reefe did his doctoral research (revised and published as a book in 1981) on the history of the Luba empire. Reefe was fascinated by the history of this empire, and since the last published research on the Luba's history had been in 1936 (and in French), he felt an imperative to delve into the subject. In his writings, he quotes American missionaries such as United Methodist Jeffrey Hoover. In fact, Reefe based himself in the town of Kamina, the current headquarters of The UMC's North Katanga Conference, during the year he spent interviewing Luba elders about their people's history. Reefe

---

3. Bortolot, "Kingdoms of the Savanna."

4. While the DR Congo is now officially a democracy with elected governors and government officials, the traditional chiefs, such as those of the Luba and the Lunda people, still retain elements of control. To obtain a piece of land to build upon, for example, one must first go to the local land chief for permission.

5. Technically Helen and her first husband, William Rasmussen, came to Congo nearly fifteen years prior to this, but their time there was extremely short due to ill health. Rasmussen died in 1895.

6. Riendeau, *Deep Gladness*, §698.

7. Riendeau, *Deep Gladness*, §726.

expresses gratitude to the expatriates in Kamina who helped his family there, including UM missionaries Everett and Vera Woodcock.

The Luba empire is located primarily on grasslands, and, in contrast to the Lunda Empire, its location in the middle of central Africa isolated it somewhat, shielding it from the direct impact of the slave and ivory trade until the 1870s and 1880s, when, according to Reefe, "integration into the forward edges of the expanding frontiers of international trade tore the Empire apart."[8] In terms of economic history, the Luba are traditionally "patrilineal subsistence farmers who practice . . . slash-and-burn agriculture."[9] When the missionaries arrived in Katanga, subsistence farming as well as hunting and fishing (in communities along the river) continued to be the primary way in which households supported themselves. The Luba also were historically known for their advanced iron forging techniques, with well-crafted axes and spears becoming symbols of political power.[10] Examples of these intricate Luba iron works can be found on display in art museums around the world, including the Metropolitan Museum of Art in New York.

In the eighteenth and nineteenth centuries, the Luba Empire was a "large-scale dynastic state, and its fame was such that groups far beyond its frontiers evidently felt compelled to claim a putative Luba ancestry."[11] Art historian Alexander Bortolot writes, "The Luba empire's expansion was due to its development of a form of government that was durable enough to withstand the disruptions of succession disputes and flexible enough to incorporate foreign leaders and governments."[12] Their governing model, based on the "twin principles of sacred kingship (*balopwe*) and rule by council,"[13] was adopted by the Lunda and spread into what is now Angola and parts of Zambia.

John Enright, a pastor who grew up as the son of American Methodist missionaries in Katanga and who then became a Methodist missionary in Katanga himself,[14] spoke to me about the continued importance of the Luba chiefs into the twentieth and twenty-first century:

---

8. Reefe, *Rainbow and the Kings*, 3.
9. Reefe, *Rainbow and the Kings*, 3.
10. Bortolot, "Kingdoms of the Savanna."
11. Reefe, *Rainbow and the Kings*, xiv.
12. Bortolot, "Kingdoms of the Savanna."
13. Bortolot, "Kingdoms of the Savanna."
14. Enright left Katanga in the 1990s and lived in Zambia until his death in 2017.

> Lubaland ... tends to hold on very tightly to the traditions; the three paramount chiefs of the Lubas and then all the traditional land chiefs have truly ancient traditional values that sort of run parallel to the established government and in fact are much more powerful and older than the kinds of governments that came and went. Obviously, the government of Mobutu [Mobutu Sese Seko] was at the top, but Mobutu had multiple regimes and governors and sort of sub-regimes that came and went.[15] —*John Enright*

The Luba people's hierarchical system of grand chiefs and regional chiefs and overseers was built upon a model of governance which involved the paying of tributes and redistribution of resources to the different parts of the empire as well as a shared spiritual understanding that Catholic missionary Placide Tempels (who served among the Luba people in the early to mid-twentieth century) named the "vital force."[16] Reefe elaborates:

> An important theme of Luba history is the development of ideologies, insignia, and institutions which were exported to clients on the distant periphery and which enabled the king and his kinsmen to claim a degree of loyalty from them. The Empire emerged among people possessing a homogeneous religious culture. The Luba and their neighbors venerated their ancestors, for it was the ancestors who gave each person his vital life force. Some spirits became associated with human collectivities or enjoyed reputations that extended over whole regions, and these spirits entered the pantheon of the most famous Luba ancestral deities.... Cooptation of elements of this religious system by the royal dynasty and its agents represents an important ideological breakthrough in the early history of the Empire. Tribute exchange between patron and client was the most fundamental expression of political loyalty.[17]

3.1.1 Empire Boundary Maps

The two maps below show the scale and boundaries of the Lunda and Luba empires.

---

15. John Enright, interview with the author, January 6, 2016.
16. Tempels, *Bantu Philosophy*, 44.
17. Tempels, *Bantu Philosophy*, 5.

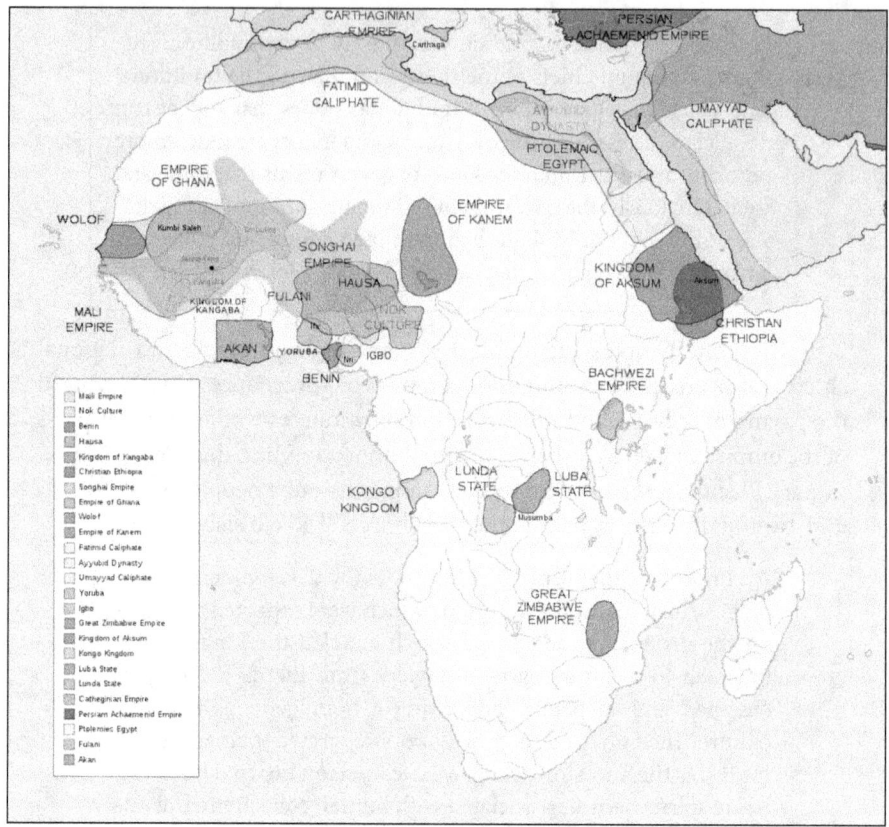

18. Israel, "African Civilizations Map."

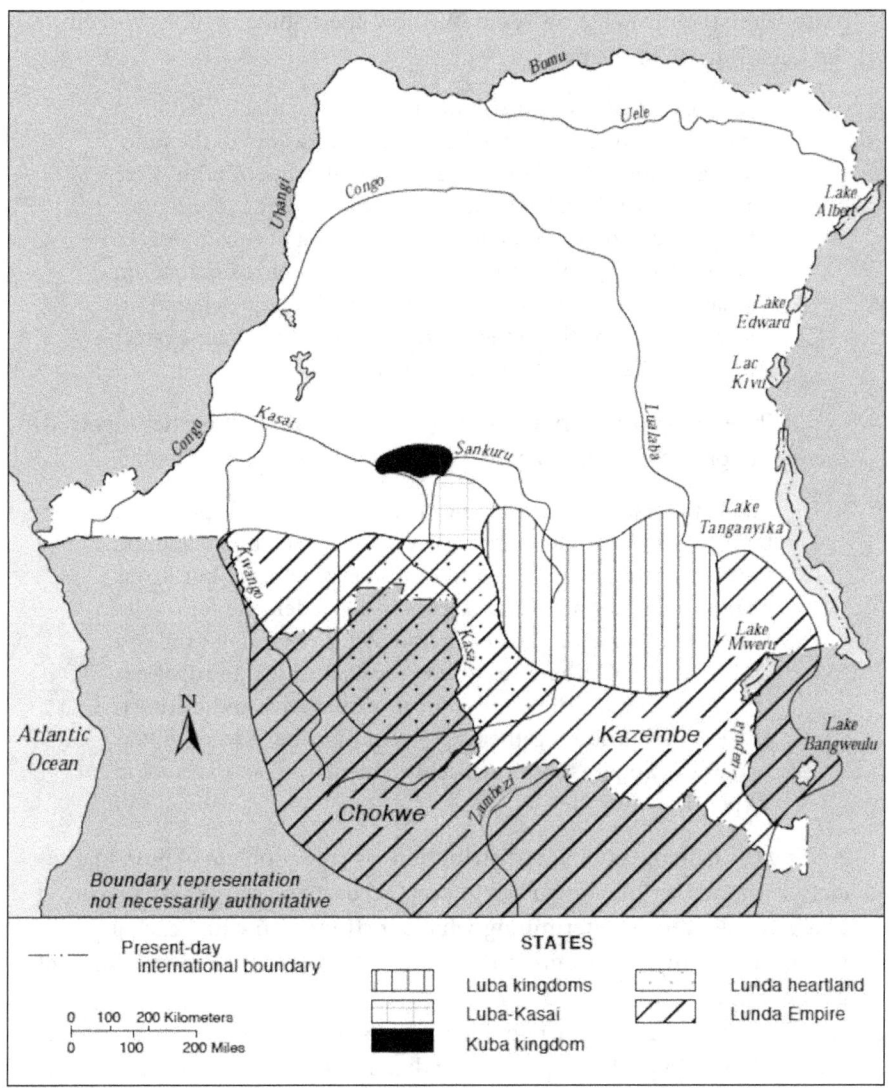

19

3.1.2 Paying Tribute/Understanding Patronage

One practice of the Luba empire that still exists today is the paying of tributes. That is, the giving of gifts to leaders with the expectation of assistance/protection in return. Tributes are an integral part of the Luba

---

19. "Lunda Empire."

patronage system. Reefe writes about how the tribute system worked in the Luba Empire in the past:

> The Luba Empire was a tribute-monger. . . . Manipulation of reciprocity and control of redistribution were keys to the functioning of the tribute system. The king and his subjects were mutually dependent. Reciprocity was expressed by a subordinate giving tribute to a superior and receiving a gift of equal value. In central Africa a royal court was a major nexus of redistribution, for hard-to-get items produced in areas with unique natural resources were brought to the court and given to tribute-bearers from areas that did not possess those resources.[20]

While, in theory, a tribute system is beneficial to all parties involved, there were problems in the way in which tributes were redistributed:

> The royal court became a major consumer of goods produced by the villagers of the southern savanna, considerably draining the redistributive capacity of the tribute system . . . but it was nearby villagers who bore the brunt of court demand for staples [perishable foods]. . . . Court personnel thrived upon the size and diversity of tribute, and they travelled widely to supervise tribute collection. The erection of an exploitative and territorially extensive tribute-gathering system must be judged both as one of the Empire's historical achievements and as a symbol of its political life.[21]

Adding to challenges of fair redistribution was the problem of how, in a society without a written language, to keep accurate records of gifts received and given as well as determining what constituted an equal exchange. As the size of the royal court grew, the more imbalanced the redistribution of gifts became.

In section 6.1.1, I return to this conversation on the practice of patronage and how it impacted the relational dynamics between North Katangans and American missionaries.

3.1.3 *The Luba Chieftaincy System*

A number of European and American anthropologists and historians have written about the political power structure of Luba Empire. North Katanga's new bishop, Mande Muyombo, believes that they and many missionaries failed to understand and appreciate key aspects of the chieftaincy, and that

---

20. Reefe, *Rainbow and the Kings*, 5.
21. Reefe, *Rainbow and the Kings*, 6.

the Luba's traditional chieftaincy system has advantages over Western versions of democracy. For example, the chieftancy system seeks consensus building instead of majority rule. In a phone interview with me a year before his election as bishop, Mande said:

> If you study the chieftaincy concept, this is what you will learn. The chief is not a dictator. Traditionally, the chief speaks on behalf of the council. There is a lot of consensus building in the chieftaincy system. In this debate about democracy, dialogue, and so forth, people are now realizing that, well, maybe for Africa we need to go back to looking at the positive things of the chieftainship. The colonial powers looked at chieftaincy as a trap, so over the years it has been abused, misused, and I have to say some of the chiefs abused it.
>
> Chiefs who abused power did not last long because the essential provisions require that a chief, before making any decisions, will conduct extensive consultations. And, in those consultations he or she has to seek not the will of the majority, which is the principle of democracy—but the chief has to seek a consensus by giving a listening to the minority. . . . Again, this is something that some missionaries and colonial powers did not understand about the notion of chieftaincy. It was looked at in a very negative dictatorial way.
>
> The chief is not a dictator. A traditional chief is required to abide by the will of the council. That's why the council—if you look at the traditional role—in some of these communities the council can dismiss a chief if the chief starts undermining the wisdom of the council. So, how do we then use that consensus building in the church sector? You will find that The United Methodist Church with the Roberts Rules of Order—it is a very democratic space, where most of the time it is the will of the majority. One of the credits of adapting the Book of Discipline to some of the contexts in Central Conferences is that—especially in Africa—there have been a lot of opportunities for dialogue and consensus building on the key issues. Whenever the will of the majority has been used, it has left the minority to deal with a lot of things.[22] —*Mande Muyombo*

Mutombo Nkulu-N'Sengha also highlights the positive aspects of traditional Luba leadership models, such as the ability to check abuses of power:

22. Mande Muyombo, interview with the author, January 2016.

> Power was never personal; it was exercised by a body of several people. The Baluba understood that the power of the King should be limited and controlled to guarantee the welfare of the people. Thus, the Luba empire was governed by an oral constitution based on the will of the ancestors. . . . A powerful religious lodge, the Bambudye, acted as an effective check on the behavior of the King and even had the power to execute him in the case of excessive abuse of power. It was assumed that the King must obey the mandate of heaven by governing according to the will of the ancestors. These ideals of genuine personhood and good government had their foundation in the spiritual values inculcated by Luba religion.[23]

These ideals of the Luba chieftaincy system are expressed in the origin story of their government. The story contrasts the characters of their first two emperors: Nkyongolo Mwamba, the "red king," was a drunken and cruel tyrant. He was without self-control or manners, even eating in public. In contrast, Ilunga Mbidi Kiuwe had beautiful black skin and was known as the "civilized prince." He had self-control and good manners, and he took his meals in private. He was the "admired, caring, and compassionate king,"[24] who serves as the archetype of a wise and just ruler.

Based on these descriptions, instead of being dictatorial or kleptocratic in nature, the traditional form of Luba governance was designed to be a consensus-based and redistributive system.

3.2 THE SPIRIT WORLD AND THE VITAL FORCE

As documented by Placide Tempels, who researched Bantu culture and customs while living among the Luba people in Katanga in the early to mid 1900s, there exists in the dominant Luba worldview a spiritual understanding which he names the *vital force*.[25] This life force can be acquired or lost through various supernatural actions: "In calling upon God, the spirits, or the ancestral spirits, the heathen ask above all, 'give me force.' If one urges them to abandon magical practices, as being contrary to the will of God and therefore evil, one will get the reply, 'wherein are they wicked?' What we brand as magic is, in their eyes, nothing but setting to work natural forces placed at the disposal of man by God to strengthen man's vital energy."[26]

---

23. Mutombo, "Baluba," 99.
24. Mutombo, "Baluba," 99.
25. Tempels, *Bantu Philosophy*, 44.
26. Tempels, *Bantu Philosophy*, 45.

Tempels asserts that understanding this concept of life force is crucial to understanding Bantu philosophy. He writes, "Where we [Europeans] see concrete beings, they see concrete forces."[27] He discusses how the regularly used Kiluba exclamation, "*wafwa ko!*" is an allusion to this concept of spiritual force. Tempels writes that this is an expression of sympathy, which is commonly mistranslated as "you are dying" but is better translated as "your vital force is lowered."[28] The words "*wafwa ko*" and the appropriate response (which differs depending on if one is male or female) were the first things I learned to say in Kiluba because they are used so often. While Tempels describes it as an expression of sympathy, in my many travels in North Katanga, I have found that it is used in the expressing of many emotions to another person (to express joy at someone's arrival, gratitude for a gift, congratulations on an accomplishment, condolences for a loss or disappointment, etc.). Over the years, I had asked a number of Luba friends on its literal meaning, but they were unable to articulate a translation or an etymological origin. After pushing the question, my Luba colleague UM pastor Joseph Mulongo searched for an answer and found one from UM pastor Banza Nkulu Wandulu who responded that it comes from the verb *kufwa* (to die). He explained that when used as an expression of gratitude and congratulations, it is an acknowledgement that the other person made a sacrifice to reach this result.[29]

It is difficult for me as an outsider to measure any changes that may be occurring in the strength of the beliefs Tempels described—especially due to my sample bias and a reluctance (embarrassment?) among my contacts to acknowledge to me that certain beliefs and practices still exist. Anecdotally, it appears that some practices and beliefs which were transmitted through stories are disappearing. For example, in the past, the name of a Luba newborn was discerned through dreams and visions. The name of the child indicated which ancestor's spirit had been in some nominal manner reincarnated in her or him.[30] This is also why the Luba do not have a system of family names (that is, a shared last name).[31] My North Katangan colleagues today frequently name their children after living people (including foreign missionaries) they wish to honor or simply choose names they like. French and English names are popular, and increasingly Katangans who

27. Tempels, *Bantu Philosophy*, 52.
28. Tempels, *Bantu Philosophy*, 47.
29. Joseph Mulongo, correspondence with the author, May 23, 2017.
30. The fact that many children could be given the name of the same ancestor was not seen as an issue.
31. Munza, *Letter to Africa*, 10.

travel internationally are creating family/last names to reduce confusion when traveling internationally. When I have inquired about the history or symbolism behind certain Luba names, I generally find that the books and articles written by Europeans and Americans about Luba history contain much more about such subjects than the average North Katangan knows. The same is true when I have asked to be told Luba legends and folktales by friends in their twenties and thirties. I do not know if this is the result of fewer Luba knowing Luba history or if such things have always been held as the secret sacred knowledge of an elite few.

American Methodist missionary John Enright, who grew up in Katanga, asserts that Western foreigners tend to be blind to the continued dominance of the belief in spiritual forces among people in Katanga:

> It is a very slow-moving, evolving society, and so the radical changes that took place post-1960s had an appearance of modernity . . . but in fact it was just an appearance. The underlying worldview, which is the spirit world, ancestors, the traditional religion and values, remained—for the most part—very much intact and as they were. So, 1990 would be, for me, simply a continuation of what John Springer would have encountered. . . .
>
> For me, [the above-mentioned dynamic] was always at play. I thought of it as a coat of whitewash. A kind of a veneer of western sensibility which worked. One of the diagnostic questions you get in a room of White people and Black people is, "How many of you believe that witches fly at night using the spirits of children as fuel?" Of course, all the White missionaries think that is complete rubbish, whereas . . . Congolese in the room would say "obviously that happens all the time; that is normal." . . . Everybody thinks they are sitting on the same planet, having the same worldview and the same understandings, when in fact we are not on the same planet. We are living in two very different worlds and really not a whole lot of communication between the worlds.[32] —*John Enright*

I asked Joseph Mulongo, a United Methodist District Superintendent who is Luba and has spent his whole life based in Katanga, what he thought of Enright's assertion about the belief in flying witches. I expected him to say that such beliefs were limited to certain villages and/or increasingly dismissed as superstition by those with higher levels of education. Instead, he replied:

---

32. John Enright, interview with the author, January 6, 2016.

> I will respond according to what I have heard, as I have not experienced the issue. Yes, he is correct. It is said that witches fly at night using children's blood as fuel. Most of the people in North Katanga believe that people who practice witchcraft are capable of flying. In the Luba tribe, it is not everyone who practices witchcraft who is capable of flying. Some can fly—especially women (*Mfwityi*). Others do not fly but can stop the witch from flying. I have seen so many people, including pastors, believing that witches are killers of innocent people. Every sickness or plague in the village is interpreted as caused by the witch. They believe in fétiche as a source of power. Before all this, I think it is important to know how someone becomes a witch! The witchcraft can be given through food (any food given by a witch). To confirm it, or to be admitted in their world, you have to offer a member of the family for confirmation. Or it can be a family "gift." (I mean a family that is known as witch family.) Many people believe these things. The faith in this comes from educated people, even from those who did not go to school.[33]

Traditional beliefs about the spirit world and the ability to manipulate spirits to gain supernatural powers for good and evil were not displaced by the arrival of Christianity in Katanga (nor were they displaced by Christianity's arrival in Europe). Instead, they were incorporated into the beliefs, and it appears the majority of North Katangan Methodists continue to believe them.

3.2.1 *Spirits, the Gates of Life and Death, and the Impact of these Views*

In 2005, I was given transit lodging/hospitality by a Luba traveling companion's uncle, the now-deceased UM pastor Kasongo Munza. Munza and Enright lived as neighbors at a mission station in Zambia at that time. I spent time at both their houses during those few days and was fascinated by how the two men told me very different versions of the same events and relational issues in North Katanga. I regret that I did not come equipped to record those conversations. I remember Enright speaking much about the Luba belief in spirits and witchcraft and that he asserted that he had himself been accused of cavorting with magical beings in the river and of having special powers. Enright was markedly cynical about missionary efforts in North Katanga. Munza, while himself admittedly living in a type of

33. Joseph Mulongo, correspondence with the author, June 1, 2017.

exile,³⁴ dismissed much of Enright's version of events in North Katanga as like listening to someone describe their former spouse after a bitter divorce. Munza would then offer explanations of the origins of relational conflicts between North Katangans and missionaries that were more in-line with American sensibilities (that is, citing actions and motivations that did not involve spirits or curses).³⁵

Munza wrote the short book *A Letter to Africa About Africa* that same year, which was published posthumously. In it, he identifies and critiques the "traditional African worldview." The son of a Luba chief, Munza had been carefully instructed by his father about their ancestral beliefs and the importance of remembering them. At the same time, his father decided to send him to the "White man's school" in order to "learn what [he] needed in order to make it in the world."³⁶ In Munza's book, he describes the worldview his father taught him as cyclical in nature: a person enters the spirit world through the gate that is death and enters back into the physical world through the gate that is the mother's womb.³⁷ According to Munza, because the womb and death are gates, many taboos and traditions exist around them (e.g., pregnancies hidden until a ceremony which is done in the fourth month, sterility believed to be due to a closed gate, seeking visions and diviners to identify which ancestral spirit is coming back in a newborn, etc.). In this belief system, the ancestral spiritual beings possess "omnipotence, omnipresence, and omniscience" and are "the sources of everything good or evil that happens in the physical sphere."³⁸

Munza makes a distinction between good and evil mediums that assist in the intercommunication between the physical and spiritual spheres. The good ones he calls diviners (*bilumbu* or *ba bwanavidye*), healers (*bangaga*), and priests (*bitobo*). The evil ones are witches (*bamfwishi*) who use their ability to communicate with evil spirits in order to harm other people.³⁹ It is vital that harmony be maintained between the living and dead. This is

---

34. While Munza had received Bishop Ntambo's blessing to relocate to Zambia and serve there, a major motivating piece of this relocation was the political tensions/accusations that existed because Munza was perceived by many as a someone worthy of being bishop and thus a threat to the episcopacy. As documented in Reefe's book, historically rivals for the Luba chieftainship were assassinated until only one champion (the new chief) remained.

35. I say this as a generalization, as the belief in ghosts, psychics, witchcraft and the practice of Voodoo exists in the USA but is dismissed in academia and mainstream media.

36. Munza, *Letter to Africa*, 7.

37. Munza, *Letter to Africa*, 7–8.

38. Munza, *Letter to Africa*, 10–11.

39. Munza, *Letter to Africa*, 11.

done by protecting the honor of family members (both living and dead), sharing possessions communally, standing in solidarity by helping others with any needs, and preserving ancestral heritage (including traditions, power status, and land).[40]

Munza continues his letter by identifying the problems that come from these views. He sees them as an obstacle to progress and economic development and cites a Kiluba proverb that translates to "This is how we received it; as we received it is how we have to leave it."[41] He sees the idea that everything—including illness—is caused by spiritual beings (and/or witchcraft) as rejecting the benefits of modern science and medicine. He also sees this as a method of avoiding taking responsibilities for one's own actions (i.e., "Everything bad that happens to me, happens either because someone bewitched me, or because the spirits predestined it"[42]). According to Munza, this sense of fatalism has resulted in people believing that success in life comes through the use of fetishes as opposed to hard work.[43]

Munza identifies the belief in the sacredness of ancestral lands (specifically, the obligation to remain in possession of it) to have become the cause of conflicts and genocide on account of the impact colonialism had on changing territory maps and displacing people. In addition, the value of sharing with others has become twisted into what in America would be labeled as nepotism.

This sharing has been expanded to mean power or benefits if one has any social or political position. It involves much more than sharing food or goods or taking care of family. It means that if you have the office of President or Bishop or District Superintendent or Pastor you must fill the key positions around you with family members or tribal members. Churches and conferences only want fellow tribesmen or family members to have power. Qualifications and ability and character are non-issues in this matter.[44] For these reasons, Munza is dismissive of democratic elections that are held in Africa. He refers to these democracies as "tribocracies."[45]

Munza dedicates a chapter of his book to the topic of cannibalism, which he himself calls a "huge secret" in Luba society. The idea of cannibalism still existing is shocking to most Americans, but it is a reality in

40. Munza, *Letter to Africa*, 11.
41. Munza, *Letter to Africa*, 13.
42. Munza, *Letter to Africa*, 13.
43. Munza, *Letter to Africa*, 14.
44. Munza, *Letter to Africa*, 15.
45. Munza, *Letter to Africa*, 15. Note that Munza's book makes many sweeping generalizations about Africa. His lived experiences in Africa, however, were primarily limited to Katanga and, in his final years, northern Zambia.

North Katanga—especially during times of war. Cannibalism, as Munza explains, is not about a desperate act motivated by threat of starvation. It is about the transfer of supernatural power—one's life force. Animals, domestic and wild, can also be ritually sacrificed to obtain power, but human sacrifices are believed to bring more power—especially those of children (who are full of life) and high-ranking individuals. Once sacrificed, they are eaten and/or turned into fetishes. As Bishop Ntambo has recounted on numerous occasions, when the feared Mai-Mai[46] warlord Chinja-Chinja appeared at his door to participate in peace talks, he was wearing fetishes, including the genitalia of many of his victims.[47] Although Ntambo was afraid, this was not his first encounter with someone who practiced ritual cannibalism. Ntambo has often noted in public that his own grandfather was a witchdoctor who practiced cannibalism, and that he would have been trained by his grandfather to also become a witchdoctor had Ntambo not converted to Christianity.

According to Munza, the practice of cannibalism and making fetishes from ritual sacrifices is believed by many to grant "invincibility, invisibility, invulnerability, luck, success in business, winning an election, winning a soccer match, winning your spouse, winning the favor of your boss." Munza asserts that this practice is found among all social classes—even highly educated politicians and church leaders. Munza estimates that 80 percent of people from the communities he knows practice fetish, and about 10 percent of this 80 percent practice cannibalism.[48]

3.2.2 Bumuntu and Dignity in Luba Society

The concept of *Bumuntu* (known as *Ubuntu* in southern Africa) is key to understanding Luba self-understanding. It "means the quintessence of personhood."[49] *Bumuntu* is about one's virtue and ethics. "The distinctive characteristic of *Bumuntu* is the feeling of humanity toward our fellow human beings. . . . *Bumuntu* is defined in terms of hospitality and solidarity."[50]

---

46. The Mai-Mai are known for their particularly terrifying acts of violence when they attack, including eating their victims. The name Mai-Mai translates to Water-Water, a reference to the belief that bullets pass through them like water, leaving them unharmed.

47. I have heard Bishop Ntambo recount his meeting with Chinja Chinja several times. Versions of the story (based on interviews with Bishop Ntambo and others involved) are found in at least two books. See Robert, *Joy to the World*, 141–45; Couture, *We Are Not All Victims*, chapter 6.

48. Munza, *Letter to Africa*, 55.

49. Mutombo, "Bumuntu," 142.

50. Mutombo, "Bumuntu," 143.

Bumuntu in its purest form is about understanding one's interconnectedness with one's community and desiring prosperity for one's neighbors. A person who embodies these values "does not feel threatened that others are good or successful. She or he celebrates cooperation over competition."[51]

Mutombo Nkulu-N'Sengha, a Luba, born and raised in DR Congo, and now-tenured professor at California State University, is the co-founder of the Bumuntu Peace Institute.[52] He writes the following:

> The core of the Luba religion is the notion of *Bumuntu* (authentic or genuine personhood) embodied in the concept of *mucima muyampe* (good heart) and *buleme* (dignity, self-respect). *Bumuntu* stands as the goal of human existence and the *sine qua non* condition for genuine governance and genuine religiosity. Thus, religion played a crucial role in defining the Luba vision of good governance and "civilized life." This notion of nobility of heart is enshrined in the creation myth of the glorious phase of Luba empire when *Buluba* (Lubahood) became a label of quality.[53]

In his essay "Bumuntu Memory and Authentic Personhood: An African Art of Becoming Humane," Mutombo Nkulu-N'Sengha discusses in detail what is required to be considered a genuine human. In doing so, he highlights the importance of maintaining one's dignity by following the ethical guidelines imbedded in the concepts of *Bumuntu*:

> There are three fundamental concepts—*Muntu, Kintu*, and *Bumuntu*—involved in the definition of a human being in the African context. In Kiluba language, a human being (man or woman) is referred to as a *Muntu*. . . . *Muntu* is not an ethical concept but a generic term for every human being. . . . The word "Kintu" refers to things, and to human being who have lost their dignity. All over Africa, we find a clear distinction between genuine humans and bad ones. Thus, to the fundamental existential question, "What is a human being?" Africans respond: *Bumuntu*.[54]

Bishop Mande discusses how the concepts of *Bumuntu* and dignity are in a way synonymous in Luba society, and that dignity is lost when one does

---

51. Mutombo, "Bumuntu," 143.
52. See "Bumuntu Peace Institute."
53. Mutombo, "Baluba," 98.
54. Mutombo, "Bumuntu Memory," 306.

not take care of others. He also notes that when mission partnerships are experienced as undermining dignity, they are rejected:

> One thing that a Luba person values is the notion of dignity. You can be an administrator in the government, you can have all the money that you have, and a Luba person can tell you, "You don't feed me." A Luba person is a very proud person. That is why when you cross the line of the Luba, they've been known as warriors. They fight for their dignity. The concept of dignity in the Luba culture is known as *Bumuntu*. A Luba person values their dignity—the *Bumuntu*. If a mission relationship affects the dignity of the people, they will be the last ones to accept [it]. So that, from an anthropological/cultural concept that is also relevant in the theological and biblical understanding, the notion of Bumuntu—dignity—is paramount among the Luba people. So we encourage partners that they are dealing with a culture that values dignity.[55] —*Mande Muyombo*

In Kiluba (the Luba language), the word *Muntu* (pl. *Bantu*) refers to a human being; "*Kintu* refers to things and to human beings who have lost their dignity."[56] In this way, there is a clear linguistic distinction between those considered real humans and those who are not. To lose one's dignity is to lose one's personhood.

Over the past two decades of interacting with Luba friends and colleagues, I myself have observed that the desire to not lose face in one's family or community is indeed a strong motivator, but the ideals of cooperation and solidarity are tainted by jealousy and suspicion. Beyond announcements of graduations, my Luba friends are generally reticent to share their joys or misfortune publicly (including on social media). When asked, each have explained to me that they fear attracting the wrath of jealous peers or the cruel gossip of those who seek their downfall. Stories of sabotage and intrigue—including even fears and accusations of assassinations within the church—are common. I do not altogether blame this toxic dynamic on traditional Luba culture. Instead, I recognize this as a common phenomenon that occurs in communities—including those in the USA—that have been traumatized by violence and/or struggle to survive in the context of extreme poverty.

---

55. Mande Muyombo, interview with the author, January 2016.
56. Mutombo, "Bumuntu," 143.

3.3 CLOSING REMARKS

The Luba Empire is among the most famous and influential African kingdoms. Not only do some scholars believe the Baluba people to be one of the protobantu groups, "Luba philosophy and religious thought played a crucial role in the development of African philosophy and the Negritude Movement in the twentieth century."[57] It is vital that the strengths of this heritage not be forgotten when we reflect upon the trauma the Baluba in Katanga have experienced since the colonial period and the current social dysfunctions (e.g., cycles of violence, extreme poverty, distrust, etc.) they face. As such, references to the strengths discussed in this chapter can be found in chapter 5, which focuses on the impact of the traumas the communities in Katanga have endured.

---

57. Mutombo, "Baluba," 97.

4

Methodist Mission Partnerships in Katanga

A Historical Overview

To UNDERSTAND THE CURRENT relationship dynamics between American and North Katangan United Methodists, it is necessary to put any comments made about this into the context of the history of the relationship. While the interviews I conducted focus on the past quarter-century, this chapter provides a discussion of the history of the relationship as well as the events and rhetoric that were fueling the Methodist missionary efforts in Congo at that time. Since an exhaustive history of Methodist mission partnerships in the Katanga region is beyond the scope of this thesis, this chapter highlights historical information that can shed light on the later discussions of what was said in the interviews I conducted. For the sake of brevity, it leaves out many things. It does not attempt to mention every significant actor or missional initiative in Katanga over the past century. It does not include a discussion of the history of Methodist missionaries and initiatives coming from Europe, especially Switzerland, or the history of the interactions between Methodists and missionaries of other denominations. It also does not explore how the relational dynamics in the mission initiatives in western areas of Congo sponsored by the Methodist Episcopal Church South[1] compared to those in Katanga, which were sponsored by

---

1. The Methodist Episcopal Church South was created in 1844 in the denomination's schism over the issue of slavery in the USA (the southern church supported slavery). The two halves reunited in 1939 to form The Methodist Church, although some southern congregations rejected the reunion and formed the Southern Methodist Church that same year. The United Methodist Church was formed in 1968 with The Methodist Church's merger with the Evangelical United Brethren Church. Pre-reunification of the denomination, the MEC had its mission stations in Katanga, whereas the

those of the Methodist Episcopal Church (MEC). The chapter touches upon major political events outside the church—especially those in Congo—but only insofar as identifying issues heavily impacting church leaders in Congo and their American collaborators.

The primary function of this chapter is to anchor the analytical discussions in future chapters in a specific location with a specific relational history. Thus, while the chapter does contain some analytical commentary, its main purpose is to provide a historical context to the responses given by interview participants. While some may question why events from over one hundred years are important for a conversation about relationship dynamics over the past twenty-five years, these historical relationships not only set the tone and trajectory for future relationships, the stories of these early encounters and collaborations are very much alive in the consciousness of many North Katangan church leaders. This awareness of the past was evident at North Katanga's Jubilee ceremony in July 2018, where the descendants of early Congolese evangelists such as Kaluashi and Changand were invited to come forward and share testimonies that had been passed down to them, and the names and photographs of all past bishops over the region (starting with John Springer) were presented and given a moment of honor.

4.1 THE FOUNDERS

The Methodist movement in Katanga can be traced back over 110 years. The first ordained Methodist pastor to establish a mission station in Katanga was the American missionary John McKendree Springer and his wife, Helen Emily Rasmussen Springer.[2] They had previously been serving as missionaries at Old Mutare[3] in Southern Rhodesia (Zimbabwe). From the very beginning, American missionaries and Congolese Methodist leaders

---

MEC South had its missionaries in western Congo. See also "History of The United Methodist Church in Africa."

2. Helen first came as a missionary to Congo in 1891 with her husband, William Rasmussen, but left within six months due to malaria. They returned to Africa in 1894 with a son, but William and their son died soon after. Helen then went to Southern Rhodesia in 1901, where she was a groundbreaker in many respects. She is credited for translating Scriptures and hymns into Shona and founding Methodist girl's education there. She married John Springer in 1905, and together they walked across what is now Zambia into Katanga to open more mission stations. See "Springer, Helen Emily [Chapman] Rasmussen."

3. The Old Mutare (Old Umtali) mission station is now home to the United Methodist-founded Africa University (AU). North Katanga's previous bishop, Ntambo Nkulu, served as Chancellor of AU and North Katanga's newly-elected bishop, Mande Muyombo, is a graduate of AU. Several of North Katanga's clergy have graduated from AU over the past twelve years; two of them have served on faculty there.

collaborated for the growth of the church in Katanga. A few of the most famous early Congolese Methodist evangelists were Kayeka Changand,[4] Kaluwashi,[5] and Kayeka Mutembo—all of whom returned home from Angola (where many Congolese had been held captive) upon hearing of the Springers' arrival.[6]

While there is a dearth of written records about the early days of Methodism in Katanga from the Katangan perspective, memoirs and other documents do tell us about the founding Congolese evangelists from the missionary point of view. The evangelist Kayeka Changand was the first person John Springer discussed in his 1916 memoir *Pioneering in the Congo*. Springer described Changand as a "tall, lean Lunda" and guessed him to be between thirty-five and forty years old. He was captured as a boy and sold as an enslaved worker to an Angolan who lived near a school run by the MEC's mission agency. Changand was given permission to attend the school, and while there he became a Christian and began to pray for missionaries to be sent to the Lunda people. He married a young Christian woman who was also enslaved, and together they had four children, whom they named Sarah, Rachel, Esther, and Moses. With the support of his congregation, Changand began formulating a plan to become a missionary to his people back in Congo. He made a business deal with the man who "owned"[7] him, leaving behind his wife and children as collateral as he traveled east as a caravan leader, trading in rubber and other goods in order to return with sufficient wealth to purchase his freedom and resettle his family in the region of his birth. It was during this trip that he first sought out Springer, told him of his passion to find a missionary for his people, and the two agreed to work together to establish a new mission station among the Lunda.[8]

Cambridge professor David Maxwell has written about the main actors in this early period and the motivations at play. Maxwell researched the archives at the Methodist University in Mulungwishi (MUM), DR

---

4. Hoover, "Sipilingas," 74. Joseph Mulongo, friend of one of Kayeka's grandsons, insisted in a message written to me on February 15, 2018, that since Kayeka was of the Rund tribe, the proper spelling of his name is "Kayek Tshangand." However, all published documents I have found (including the official program of North Katanga's Jubilee celebration in July 2018) use the spelling "Kayeka Changand." I have decided to use "Kayeka Changand" for future ease of name searches by researchers.

5. Hoover, "Sipilingas," 80.

6. In the 1910s there was a wave of formerly enslaved people traveling from Angola back to their homelands in Congo following the government in Angola's abolishment of slavery. For more about this, see Maxwell, "Freed Slaves," 80.

7. Their business arrangement was made during the time period where slavery in Angola was officially illegal yet still practiced.

8. Springer, *Pioneering in the Congo*, 1–5.

Congo, and interviewed professors there as well as David Changand, the grandson of Kayeka Changand. Maxwell obtained a rare copy of a report by John Springer and quotes it in his paper "Freed Slaves, Missionaries, and Respectability: The Expansion of the Christian Frontier from Angola to Belgian Congo."[9] Springer wrote that "an interesting item in Kayeka's testimony in prayer meetings was how he had felt the similarity between himself and Joseph, who had been sold into slavery in a far country, and that God had designed Joseph to be the deliverer of his people, so he, Kayeka, had felt that he had been taken into slavery that he might bring back spiritual deliverance to the Alunda."[10]

According to Maxwell, Kayeka Changand's identification with biblical stories of slavery and deliverance was common among the Congolese Christians returning home. It is not coincidental that Changand named his son Moses: "The Exodus narrative was appropriated by the returnees and sustained them as they journeyed home and faced hunger, illness, random violence, and the corruption of colonial officials."[11] The narratives also helped shape their self-understanding and sense of purpose as evangelists to their people and "[enabled] them to envision an alternative future."[12]

When Changand returned to Springer after settling his affairs in Angola, he brought with him Kaluwashi, a Luba evangelist, who had settled near a MEC mission station in Angola after working as a porter for a caravan of rubber traders. Springer writes that when Changand had arrived back in Angola, "the news soon spread that he was to return to his country, as now there was a missionary there to father and protect him."[13] Thus, a collection of Baluba communities in Angola held a meeting and appointed Kaluwashi to accompany Changand and Springer in order to report back the feasibility of the exiled Luba peoples returning to their homelands. They also paid a carrier named Mbundu to help transport Kaluwashi's steamer chair, an item which was "commonly used in Christian homes in Angola."[14] Such chairs were used for preaching since sitting on the ground was viewed as demeaning.

Upon the mission caravan reaching Kaluwashi's former home in Katanga and meeting his relatives there, large crowds gathered to hear Kaluwashi speak, to the point that Kaluwashi's voice became hoarse from

9. Maxwell, "Freed Slaves," 89.
10. Springer, "Work in Lunda," discussed in Maxwell, "Freed Slaves," 89.
11. Maxwell, "Freed Slaves," 89.
12. Maxwell, "Freed Slaves," 88.
13. Springer, *Pioneering in the Congo*, 5–6.
14. Springer, *Pioneering in the Congo*, 6.

preaching. Springer learned that Kaluwashi was a skilled mason and subsequently hired him to build the Springers a brick house at their new mission station. With this money, Kaluwashi returned to Angola to report back to the Luba there and to bring his wife and children back with him to Congo.[15] He also later built a house in Mwanza for the British missionary William Burton.[16]

Maxwell writes about how Kaluwashi's passion for evangelism made such a strong impression on the Springers that he managed to persuade them to assist him and other returnees in founding a mission station and schools amongst the Luba in Kabongo[17] despite the location's vast distance from the nearest MEC mission station, hundreds of miles south in the Lunda region. Kaluwashi's relationship with the American Methodist missionaries in Kabongo and other parts quickly soured and fractured, however, due to reasons that will soon be discussed.

The third of the most famous early Congolese Methodist evangelists was Kayeka Mutembo. The son of a chief among the Lunda peoples, he had been kidnapped by slave traders and taken to Angola as a boy. In Angola, he and other Congolese converted to Christianity at an MEC American Board mission station.[18] Mutembo prayed fervently for the Methodist Church to send missionaries to Katanga; he believed the arrival of the Springers was God's answer to that prayer. In 1914,[19] working alongside American Methodist missionaries Arthur Lewis Piper, a medical doctor, and his wife Maude Piper, Mutembo organized approximately three hundred Congolese emancipated from slavery in Angola to return home to Congo, forming the Methodist mission colony in Kapanga.[20] This medical-focused mission station became what is now known as Samuteb Hospital. The Pipers served approximately forty years in Kapanga.[21] Mutembo lived well into the 1950s, and he and his

15. Springer, *Pioneering in the Congo*, 7.

16. Burton was the first field director of the Congo Evangelistic Mission (CEM), which was a Pentecostal organization formed in 1919. He served in Congo for many years along with his wife, Hattie, who worked primarily among women and children.

17. Kabongo remains an important site of missional activities in the North Katanga Conference; there is currently both a Methodist hospital and university there.

18. Kurewa, *African Pilgrimage on Evangelism*, 95.

19. Not coincidentally, 1914 was also the year in which King Albert of Belgium granted the Methodist Episcopal Church legal status in the Belgian Congo, which gave the church the ability to purchase land and operate openly as a denomination. Thus, in the following years, there were increased efforts to raise mission funds and recruit missionaries for mission stations in Katanga.

20. Kapanga is not within the North Katanga Episcopal Area, but those administrative borders did not exist during those days.

21. House, "House Notes."

family members worked collaboratively with the American missionaries who arrived in Katanga in the following decades, including the Enrights.[22]

4.1.1 Tensions in Founding Mission Partnerships

Maxwell writes about the multi-layered motivations of the Christian returnees to Congo during these early years. He emphasizes their deep desire for dignity, respectability, and high social status (in contrast to what they experienced while enslaved) as well as the tensions this created both between them and the communities they were returning to and the foreign missionaries. Having gained new marketable skills and exposure to the outside world during their years in Angola, the returnees saw themselves as more modern than those in their ancestral villages:

> This [group of formerly enslaved people] was reliant upon missionaries for patronage, protection, employment, and connection with the wider world. Yet their relationship with missionaries was intense and often fractious. . . . The Congolese returnees, working mostly as evangelists and pastors, considered themselves civilized and cultivated respectability to assert their status. Respectability is a highly mutable ideology that takes local forms, involving codes of conduct and physical markers that are continually renegotiated. It is usually asserted against some notional threatening "other" who is variously defined as rough, backward, ignorant, inferior, and generally immoral. It is also often motivated by a desire for social mobility and public recognition.[23]

I assert that the returnees found themselves in one of the classic plights faced by any person who returns home after extended exposure to a foreign culture: s/he becomes a neither-nor, forced to reside permanently in a liminal social position, no longer fully belonging to the community of one's birth yet not claimed by the place that transformed her/him. Adding to this dynamic is one of the most common self-defense mechanisms of people responding to the psychological shock of returning home—to interact with others in a way which is generally perceived as putting on an air of superiority.[24] Returnees often rejected living under the authority

---

22. Riendeau, *Deep Gladness*, §36. See also this book for a photo of Kayeka.

23. Maxwell, "Freed Slaves," 84, 83.

24. Much has been written on this kind of experience and the re-entry shock that occurs when attempting to re-negotiate one's place when returning home. See esp. Pollock and Reken, *Third Culture Kids*. Unfortunately, there is insufficient space for that exploration in this thesis. Comparisons could be made between the early Congolese

of traditional chiefs and instead "chose to reside at mission stations or subsequently in their own Christian villages."[25] It must not be forgotten that the majority of the founding Congolese Methodist evangelists and pastors would also have still been dealing with the psychological trauma of their period of enslavement.

Despite the early collaborations between the Congolese and American missionaries, there were deep tensions—especially when it came to matters of respect and authority. Maxwell writes that Wesley Miller, the first permanent Methodist missionary at Kabongo, had little respect for Kaluwashi and the other returnee evangelists he encountered. He viewed them as "uppity" and a "worthless crew."[26] Miller criticized Kaluwashi for agitating the Congolese Christians and for perpetually behaving like he had a grudge against someone.[27] Kaluwashi and the returnee-evangelist Saul (who had "deserted his post" in attempts to win back his wife, who had left him for a White man) relocated to Mwanza. They were both banned from speaking in meetings and labeled as back-sliders.[28] Later, Kaluwashi took two additional wives[29] and completely broke ties with MEC missionaries. After two of his three wives passed years later, he began unofficially collaborating with the CEM.[30]

In the April 1919 report to the MEC's Congo Mission Conference, Roger Guptill, who briefly served with his wife in Kabongo 1917–1918, notes the warm welcome they received from the Luba chief and community upon arrival and that the chief built a large school for the mission station despite the chief's aunt's protests that his mother had come to her in a dream

---

evangelist returnees and what is currently happening when North Katangans return after having earned degrees in other countries. This in itself would make a good topic for future research.

25. Maxwell, "Freed Slaves," 93.
26. Maxwell, "Freed Slaves," 98.
27. Maxwell, "Freed Slaves," 99.
28. Maxwell, "Freed Slaves," 98.
29. Polygamy was and is commonly practiced in Katanga. As was taught to me, polygamy as it is practiced in Katanga is more about the ideal household structure for economic survival than it is about sex. It takes multiple women in a household to accomplish all the work assigned to females that must be done each day. In single-spouse households, one still sees multiple women (younger sisters, cousins, etc.) living with the couple in order to help the wife manage the domestic tasks. While I do not explore this issue here, the ban on polygamy in the Methodist Church remains a hotly debated topic in the North Katanga Conference. For example, there remains the question of the morality of requiring someone in a polygamous marriage to divorce a spouse in order to join the church or become a leader in it.
30. Maxwell, "Freed Slaves," 101.

saying she would die upon the completion of the construction project.[31] While Guptill framed his report about Kabongo with optimism, other missionaries had harsh words. John Springer described the people of Kabongo to be the "purest Luba," "the rawest heathen," and a "considerable number of cannibals,"[32] and Miller wrote the following about his observations while serving in Kabongo: "When one occasionally sees with clearer vision than usual the degradation of the Luba people, the prospect becomes oppressive. Politically, intellectually, social, morally, and religiously, the Luba cult is opposite to and inimical to Christianity. The Baluba have had very little intercourse with White men; consequently, their points of view are as far removed from ours as the ends of the earth."[33]

Read through modern eyes, Miller's April 1919 report to the Congo Mission Conference is alarming in the level at which he expresses contempt towards the population he has been appointed to serve. He writes at length about the Luba people being "filthy,"[34] "drunken," and "lazy," and he asserts that "virtue and chastity are almost unheard of among Luba women."[35] It is little surprise that there developed an animosity between Congolese evangelists in Kabongo and the MEC missionaries (via Miller) and that a number of Congolese Methodists chose to relocate.

I do not know if Miller was normally of such bitter, condescending disposition or if his writings could be partly attributed to the irritable post-honeymoon phase that is common among people experiencing intense culture shock; such a question would make an interesting, albeit difficult to research, paper. Roger Guptill's official remarks five months later, in the September 1919 Congo Mission Conference report, suggest that Miller's American colleagues were alarmed by Miller's report. Guptill opens his comments about the Kabongo mission station describing it as one of the "choice spots of Central Africa" and then transitions into "Brother Miller's" difficulties, pointing out that Miller is a new missionary "placed in a new mission and practically left to work out his salvation with fear and trembling. In his report he will tell you about the fears and trembles, no doubt. He has been continually in our prayers and God has blessed him."[36] Miller's September 1919 report has a notable shift in

31. *Journal of the Second and Third Sessions*, 66.
32. *Journal of the Second and Third Sessions*, 56.
33. *Journal of the Second and Third Sessions*, 77.
34. *Journal of the Second and Third Sessions*, 80.
35. *Journal of the Second and Third Sessions*, 81.

36. *Journal of the Second and Third Sessions*, 108–9. While one must read between the lines, I do not think that communication styles have changed so much in one hundred years that this American Methodist cannot recognize that Guptill was using

tone from his previous. He refrains from harsh complaints, asserting that "relations with the chief Kabongo and with the people of the vicinity are cordial" and that they have recovered from the "wholesale defection" of mission teachers that was mentioned in his spring report.[37]

While difficult to prove definitively, I see the above as evidence that among the American missionaries were those making efforts to push their American colleagues to take a less overtly condescending and hostile stance towards Congolese. I also believe that it was not coincidental that the September 1919 report contains explicit guidelines on how "our missionaries" are expected to relate to each other, to missionaries of other societies, and to "the natives." According to these guidelines, other missionaries should be treated "with courtesy and due regard to their devotion [to Christ]" and natives should be treated as younger brothers, with the goal of mentoring them and gradually giving them as much responsibility as they can bear.[38] In the journals of the Congo Mission Conference in the late 1920s and early 1930s, the Congolese Christians are consistently referred to as our "native brethren" and, while still none are officers of the conference and none give reports that are included in these journals, a handful are listed as members of subcommittees in attendance, serving in appointments, and on the ordination track.[39]

In Springer's 1916 memoir, his writings discuss in depth the difficulties he and his wife faced in their initial years in Congo (examples he gave include finding carriers for their belongings, developing serious illnesses, avoiding cannibals, etc.). Springer's descriptions of the Congolese, while progressive relative to the dominant narratives of his day, are condescending to today's ears (e.g., references to "heathens" and "natives"). He writes much about slave traders, rubber processing factories, witchcraft, and conflicts with local and paramount chiefs. He takes it as a given that, upon baptism, a Congolese person should acquire a "Christian" (that is, Western European) name. When Springer does praise Congolese leaders, it is with a patronizing tone[40] and an implication that he sees such virtues to be the ex-

---

church-speak to diplomatically communicate that Miller's struggles in Kabongo were more about his own inexperience and inner demons than the problems in Kabongo itself.

37. *Journal of the Second and Third Sessions*, 137.
38. *Journal of the Second and Third Sessions*, 113–14.
39. *Congo Mission Conference of the Methodist Episcopal Church.*
40. For example, Kayeka Changand, already a successful evangelist and trade caravan leader who was approximately in his late thirties, is described by Springer as a "humble slave boy." Springer continues, "I have come to understand that it was because this faithful pray-er who was two thousand miles away on the other side of the

ception rather than the norm. While the Springers' motives were honorable, their accomplishments significant, and their willingness to risk their lives to share their faith a testament to their concern for the Congolese people, the attitudes expressed in John Springer's writings are inarguably colonial. It is clear from Springer's memoir that the couple saw themselves as morally and intellectually superior to the Congolese they encountered.

David Maxwell reflects on the complexities of these types of relationships:

> As actors in a colonial setting, missionaries often manifested a somewhat schizophrenic attitude towards Africans, seeking at once to preserve the past, promote economic change, and protect them from the worst effects of modernity. At times, freed slaves' notions of respectability, which fused Christian ideals with older African notions of rank and honor, conflicted with missionary conceptions of respectability, particularly with regard to gender norms. The former slaves' sophistication in diet, deportment, and dress ran counter to the demands of Christian humility, and their own evangelical initiatives conflicted with loyalty to new missionary patrons. Moreover, their rejection of the uncivilized "other" ran counter to the demands of Christian fellowship. And while they were indebted to missionaries for patronage and support, the trauma of enslavement coupled with missionary racism and paternalism produced what missionaries described as a "nameless grudge" against authority.[41]

In his analysis on the source of this "nameless grudge," Maxwell includes a mention of the memoirs of Hettie H. Burton (married to William Burton), noting that she attributed this grudge to be the result of the extreme cruelty the returnees had experienced in their lifetimes. She had observed among the women she worked with (many of whom were widows and returnees) signs of deep emotional scars[42] left by horrors they had experienced and witnessed. She wrote about how these women had seen others being burned alive and killed in other torturous ways and that she felt she had to be careful to not startle them for fear of once again retriggering these memories of abduction, slaughter and slavery.[43] As I readdress in chapter 5, I do not believe one can overstate the impact the trauma of colonial occupation,

---

continent was holding on to God in child-like faith for his own Lunda people in their unrelieved heathen darkness" (Springer, *Pioneering in the Congo*, 4–5).

41. Maxwell, "Freed Slaves," 80.

42. The reactions H. Burton describes seeing would today be labeled Post Traumatic Stress Syndrome.

43. Maxwell, "Freed Slaves," 99. See also Burton, *My Black Daughters*, 76–78.

forced labor, and the acts of genocide inflicted upon the Luba and Lunda people had on both the individual and collective psyche of the early as well as current Congolese Methodists.

4.1.2 Rhetoric and Motivations of Methodist Missionary Campaigns

A Centenary Survey of Methodist Episcopal Missions, published in 1919, helps us place the arrival of American MEC missionaries in Congo in the context of the mission priorities of American Methodism during that time. The vest pocket edition of this book describes there being three "battle fronts" for the Church in Africa: North Africa, which was labeled as "Mohammedan," "Christian" South Africa, and the "pagan" Central Africa. The report's author expresses alarm over the spread of Islam in Africa: "The Mohammedan gain is so rapid that unless great haste is made to teach the Gospel of Jesus Christ, pagan Africa will surely become Mohammedan."[44] The report later states: "The Mohammedan advance in Africa is the largest missionary world problem confronting the whole Church at the beginning of the twentieth century," says Bishop Joseph C. Hartzell. "Our most immediate and insistent duty is to give the gospel to Africa's millions, thus saving them from the Moslem faith, and the continent for Christ."[45] The report goes on to describe the missionary efforts the denomination was making in different parts of Africa:

> In the midst of the Belgian Congo there is a rapidly developing industrial mission which is surrounding that center with eighty primary schools. Training in agriculture, carpentry, and brickmaking supplements and extends evangelistic work. Fertilizers are supplanting fetishes in making crops grow. The supreme demand of the hour is to throw across Central Africa, from the western to the eastern coast, a line of mission stations to occupy vacant areas and stop the advancing Mohammedan wave.[46]

The 1919 report also included the still-popular mission catalog system, with listings of what one's financial contributions could sponsor (e.g., $25/year for a child's school fees, $60/year for a "native" nurse's salary, $600/year for an American nurse's salary, $500 for a motorcycle, etc.). The catalog listings show that the fundraising goals included salaries for both Africans and Americans in ministry postings, construction projects (churches,

---

44. *Centenary Survey of Methodist Episcopal Missions,* 14.
45. *Centenary Survey of Methodist Episcopal Missions,* 15.
46. *Centenary Survey of Methodist Episcopal Missions,* 16–17.

parsonages, schools, and hospitals), the equipping of schools and hospitals, Bible distribution, and motorcycles. For $5,000, one could "equip the only printing press among a whole race."[47]

While this thesis does not attempt to identify the complex personal motivations of each of the American Methodist missionaries who served in Katanga, it is important to note that the aforementioned report makes it clear that the fear of Islam spreading throughout the African continent was a significant motivator used in the fundraising campaigns in the USA for the Methodist mission stations in Congo during this period and that military metaphors were used in describing the strategies being used.

4.2 Mid-Twentieth-Century Mission Partnerships

The arrival of the "pioneer" missionaries soon led to a swell of foreign missionary activity in Katanga and the creation of several mission stations, including schools and hospitals, in both Lunda and Luba areas. A comprehensive overview of even just the American Methodists who arrived and all their activities during this time would take a tome in itself. Instead, the following section provides a snapshot of the nature of the collaborative initiatives which were happening between Congolese and American Methodist missionaries in the early to mid-twentieth century.

4.2.1 Political Context

The late 1950s and 1960s were a time of heightened political turmoil in Congo. There was widespread, political-related deadly violence and the displacement of thousands of expats (a number of whom were killed)[48] in the wake of the declaration of Congo's (renamed Zaire) independence as well as the failed secession attempt of Katanga and the interventions of foreign nations (Belgium and the USA[49] included) in attempts to retain control of Congo's vast natural resources.[50] The foreign Methodist missionaries

---

47. *Centenary Survey of Methodist Episcopal Missions*, 21.

48. The most famous of such incidents in Katanga occurred in 1964 and is often referred to as the Stanleyville massacre. E.g., Garrison, "28 More White Hostages Found Slain."

49. In August 1960, US President Eisenhower authorized America's collusion in the assassination of Congo's Prime Minister, Patrice Lumumba. The USA in collaboration with the UN was also complicit in stopping the Katanga secession attempts. See Nzongola-Ntalaja, *Congo*, 272–73. For an extensive discussion on how the USA was complicit in the perpetuation of kleptocratic rule in Congo, see Kelly, *America's Tyrant*.

50. Such resources include uranium, which is necessary for creating nuclear weapons. The USA supported Mobutu because he was seen as a strategic ally in the Cold War. In exchange, Mobutu allowed the USA to build large military bases (neighboring

weathered the storm, albeit with some losses and occasional temporary evacuations.[51] One of the missionaries lost during this period was American Methodist pilot Burleigh Law Jr., who was shot dead on the runway of Wembo Nyama mission station by a rebel guard in August of 1964.[52]

While this thesis does not have space to go into the complex history of the political struggles and battles in Congo, it is worth noting that many of the graduates of these MEC schools in Katanga went on to become significant political figures, such as Moise Tshombe. After Congo gained its independence in 1960, Tshombe led the rebellion of the Katanga region against the government in Kinshasha and has been implicated in playing a role in the death of Congo's Prime Minister, Patrice Lumumba. Tshombe went into exile in 1963 and died in Algeria in 1969. Tshombe was well known by the missionaries in Katanga, having come from one of the prominent families in Sandoa. In fact, his parents paid for the construction of the Methodist church building (sanctuary) at the Sandoa mission station where the Enright family served from 1956 to 1966, after leaving Mulungwishi.[53]

4.2.2 Mid-Century Missionaries: Missionary Dynasties

The story of American Methodists in Katanga cannot be told without discussing at least one of the Methodist missionary family dynasties in the region: the Enrights[54] and their cousins, the Vances. In 2011, Gina Riendeau began interviewing eighty-seven-year-old Lorraine Enright, and from these conversations she published *A Deep Gladness: Stories from the Lives of Ken and Lorraine Enright*. With Newell Booth's blessing—the (American) Methodist Bishop of Congo—Lorraine and her husband, Ken Enright, arrived as missionaries to Katanga in 1950 after one year of missionary training by the Methodist mission board in addition to a year of French language study in Brussels, Belgium.[55] From 1950 to 1956, they served at the Mulungwishi

---

Angola was communist) and extract uranium.

51. Missionary numbers were significant until the opening of the 1990s, when eruptions of violence triggered the start of what may prove to be the final large-scale exodus of foreign missionaries in Congo.

52. Navarro, "Flying Methodists of Zaire," 16.

53. Riendeau, *Deep Gladness*, §698.

54. The Enrights have been involved in ministries with the Luba and Lunda Methodists for three generations—with a fourth generation (Ken and Lorraine's great-grandchildren) currently growing up in Zambia. One could even make the argument that they are now at five generations since Lorraine's mother eventually moved in with them and was buried at the mission station at Luena.

55. Since Congo was still under Belgian rule at the time, competency in French was necessary to conduct any official business. French was also (and remains) the language

mission station alongside Doris and Woody Bartlett. Ken was named District Missionary (akin to District Superintendent) and taught at the local high school, while Lorraine taught at the Women's School. During this time, they also were required to learn Swahili. When Lorraine and Ken left Mulungwishi to serve deeper in the interior, administration of the women's school was turned over to local leadership.

When describing the historical context of 1950s Katanga, Riendeau writes:

> The Methodist Church was a thriving denomination before the mid-century missionaries arrived. . . . Early Methodist missionaries arriving at the turn of the nineteenth and twentieth centuries had good success establishing churches and schools. But it was their own initiative and passion for God that spurred the Congolese churches and their need for pastors. When Ken and Lorraine arrived in Congo in 1950, they entered a country of actively growing churches, many without pastors, and many Congolese wanting and needing to be trained to lead congregations. The seminary at Mulungwishi was a response to this obvious need.[56]

In the years following World War II and into the 1980s, the number of American Methodist missionaries serving in the Katanga region grew considerably (albeit with interruptions during periods of violence), and their names and projects are too numerous to list in full. Since the Enrights and Vances are the names of American Methodist missionaries[57] that were most often mentioned by the North Katangans I interviewed when they spoke of their personal early memories of Methodist missionaries, I have focused on their stories—both via Riendeau's book and via recorded interviews I conducted with John Enright and Ken Vance—when examining the history of the relational dynamics. One cannot easily put definitive, descriptive labels on the relationship dynamics between the members of these families and Katangan church leaders. There are too many individual personalities at play, spanning too many years/generations of interactions.

Ken and Lorraine Enright made an effort to learn local languages, the culture(s) of the region, and to integrate themselves into Katangan society.

---

of instruction in secondary schools.

56. Riendeau, *Deep Gladness*, §496.

57. There were also missionaries, albeit not as many, being sent by the mission board of the France-Swiss conference of The UMC. My research did not focus on their stories, although my anecdotal observations suggest that there was a different—arguably healthier—dynamic in that relationship.

They received some of their Katangan culture training from Joab Mulela, a Congolese pastor and "one of the early Christian pioneers in the Congo and vigorous in his seventies,"[58] who would sit in the Enright's front room and teach as they listened. When Lorraine organized and led women's conferences in Sandoa, it was decided that the missionary women would sleep in the same place as the Katangan women—on grass mats inside a circular grass fence. Considering the state of the civil rights movement in America during the 1950s (with segregated schools, drinking fountains, hotels, etc.), this was a bold decision. Many missionaries of that period (especially those from certain other denominations)—and up until more recent history—would not have done the same. For example, (American) United Methodist Bob Walters recalls in his memoir a memory from 1996, where he was invited for tea at the home of an elderly long-serving British Brethren missionary doctor in the village of Kasaji. Walters was shocked at the non-subtle way the doctor spoke condescendingly about the Congolese, and he was disturbed even more so when he realized that his friend Ntambo (now retired Bishop Ntambo) had been required to wait outside the house for Walters.[59] When I asked North Katanga UMC's oldest living pastor, Kabila wa Kubangimayo, about overt racism displayed by American missionaries of the past, he denied this being a significant issue among the Methodist missionaries, but he pointed his finger at missionaries from other denominations, especially the Pentecostals and the British Brethren, who are locally known as the Garenganze after the location of their first mission station in the region:

> A Black person could enter into the house of an American [Methodist] missionary, they could share a meal together, whereas with the Garenganzes and the Pentecostals, that was difficult. Like I told you about my father, during the time he worked for the Belgians at the Garenganzes' place, it was impossible for a [Congolese] pastor of a church there to enter into a missionary's house or eat with them, but the Methodists were different. A [Congolese] pastor could arrive at an American [Methodist] missionary's house, and the [missionary] would ask him to come in and ask him if he wanted a drink . . . So for the [Methodist] church of North Katanga with its missionaries, . . . there was only maybe small problems between individuals.[60] —*Kabila wa Kubangimayo*

58. Riendeau, *Deep Gladness*, §98.

59. Walters, *Last Missionary*, 82.

60. Kabila wa Kubangimayo, interview with the author, Lubumbashi, DR Congo, July 22, 2015. Original: "Un noir peut entrer dans la maison d'un missionnaire américain, on peut partager le repas ensemble, tandis que pour le Garenganze et les

Thus, while critiquing the attitudes and behaviors of the Methodist missionaries such as the Enrights during this time period, I recognize that, in comparison to their colleagues from some of the other denominations and their communities back home, the bulk of these missionaries were making a conscious decision to reject racism in all forms that were not in their blind spots. For example, Ken and Lorraine Enright's eldest son, Kenneth Nelson Enright, recalls he and his brother John joining their father and their Lunda and Luba friends on hunting parties in the bush. He writes that "around campfires in hunting camps, there were no racial or cultural divides. And it was here we came to know well the Africans with whom we hunted. We learned to admire their skills and their character." His father's hunting adventures and skill with a rifle became well-known and "established his name and reputation. He was soon admired and respected. This hunting background helped him greatly in the conflicts and wars that came later. More importantly, he started to fully understand Africans."[61] Riendeau writes: "Ken became known for being a prodigious worker. He immersed himself fully into Luba culture and was embraced wholly by those with whom he worked. . . . He understood the meaning of his calling and threw himself fully into sharing the teachings of Christ. 'I was having so much fun, such fun, teaching the young ladies at Sandoa,' remembered Lorraine, 'and then the war came and upset the fruit basket.'"[62]

With the violence, chaos, and upheaval following the country's struggle for independence in 1960, Methodist missionaries were evacuated from Congo. The Enrights returned to the USA, officially on their second furlough. Ken used this time to train to become a pilot, a skill he used upon their return to Katanga the next year. With the exceptions of scheduled furloughs, Ken and Lorraine remained as missionaries in Katanga (serving in Sandoa, Lake Kafakumba, Lubumbashi, Kolwezi, and Manono) until their retirement in 1987. Even in retirement, they split their time between Florida and Congo (and later Zambia). Their son John followed in their footsteps, serving in North Katanga until the United Methodist General

---

Pentecôtistes, c'était difficile. Comme je vous avais dit au sujet de mon papa, au temps où il travaillait avec les belges, chez les Garenganze, un pasteur d'une église lui est impossible de rentrer dans la maison d'un missionnaire ou bien pour manger ensemble, mais pour les méthodistes, c'était pratique; un pasteur peut arriver chez un missionnaire américain, on lui dit approchez, et on lui demande; qu'est-ce que vous voulez boire et on vous donne, tandis que pour d'autres missionnaires, d'autres communautés, c'était très difficile mais pour les méthodistes. Donc pour l'église du nord Katanga avec les missionnaires, ce problème-là jusqu'à là dans la conception, il ya peut être un petit problème entre les individus."

61. Nelson Enright, "Foreword," §98.
62. Riendeau, *Deep Gladness*, §879.

Board of Global Ministry (GBGM) ordered all their missionaries to evacuate in 1998 due to the violence and political instability at that time. John and Kendra Enright, Ken and Debbie Vance (also serving in North Katanga), and their families relocated to northern Zambia, where much of the family remains today—including children, grandchildren, and John's sister, Elinda (Enright) Stuery, and her husband, Nate.

4.2.3 *Mulungwishi Mission Station*

By the mid-century, a number of Methodist mission stations had been established in Katanga. Mulungwishi,[63] one of the legacies of the Springers' work, is arguably the most significant. Located northwest of the city of Likasi, today it serves as the primary pastor training center for both the South Congo and North Katanga United Methodist Episcopal Areas. This station, which was founded by John Springer in 1918 as an education center, is now a fully accredited university. As of 2006, "all the [living] United Methodist Church bishops in the Congo and most of the superintendents in Katanga province [were] graduates of the seminary."[64]

In 1951, American UM missionaries Elwood "Woody" Bartlett and Maurice Persons officially launched the theological seminary at Mulungwishi with the help of fellow American UM missionary David Enright.[65] "The seminary stemmed from Springer Institute, founded in 1910 as Fox Bible School, which trained teacher-catechists. In 1976 the school became the Kimbulu Kayeka Seminary, with a three-year university seminary program. In 1985 the seminary became the FMT [Faculté Méthodiste de Théologie] with an additional two-year graduate level program."[66] In keeping with the times, the seminary now offers computer and internet training and requires seminarians to submit their papers typed.

The Mulungwishi center, which has housing for students, their spouses, and their children, also includes the Doris Bartlett[67] Women's School, a

---

63. While Mulungwishi is technically in South Congo Episcopal Area—not North Katanga—it has had a significant impact on North Katangan UM leadership, and the American missionaries who have served there over the years have greatly influenced the nature of American-North Katangan mission relationships.

64. Persons and Persons, "Seminary."

65. My various written sources only explicitly name the male missionaries as the actors in this effort. I suspect their wives who were serving there also played a key role, but that is merely my conjecture.

66. Persons and Persons, "Seminary."

67. Doris was married to Woody Bartlett and served at the Mulungwishi mission station with him.

training program for clergy wives.[68] The women's program includes classes aimed at helping wives have income-generating activities as well as to serve as role models in their congregations and broader communities. Included in the women's training are lessons in Bible and church history, child rearing, health and hygiene, baking, sewing, and other home-economics skills.[69] The multitude of ripple-effects created over the years by this women's training program should not be underestimated. It is, for example, why one can find bread baked in the town of Kabongo (646 kilometers north of Likasi) that tastes exactly like the breadsticks served at the American chain restaurant Olive Garden.

During his forty years at Mulungwishi, Woody Barlett advocated vocally for Black leadership in the church in Congo. During his missionary days, however, this was not a popular point of view among the foreign Christian communities in Congo. According to Walters, "the Methodists were the minority voice on this issue. When a national council of Protestant churches was formed [in Congo], [Barlett] was the Methodist delegate. The reserve delegate was Black. [Barlett] feigned sickness in order to excuse himself and seat the reserve. That was not taken well by the heads of the other denominations, all White."[70]

Bartlett was a trailblazer when it came to pushing for the Africanization of the Methodist Church in Katanga.[71] When asked about Barlett's progressive views on evangelism and church leadership, his son-in-law David Persons notes that Bartlett helped to create Mulungwishi with the vision of working himself out of a job by training Congolese pastors to take over. "He encouraged Frederick Kanjundu to come up with the communion service done with African Music," and the distinctive religious imagery in "the church at Mulungwishi is [due to] his encouragement to Congolese artists to portray Christ as they saw Him. The result is a church filled with windows by Kafusha Laban showing Christ as an African." When the bishop appointed a Congolese scholar-pastor to replace Bartlett as head of the seminary, Bartlett gladly accepted working under him.[72]

The Bartletts' daughter Lori Persons, along with her husband David, son of aforementioned Maurice Persons, followed in their parents' footsteps and served most of their adult lives as the official missionaries at Mulungwishi:

---

68. There are a small but growing number of Congolese UM pastors who are women, but with rare exception they are also married to UM pastors.

69. Persons and Persons, "Women's School."

70. Walters, *Last Missionary*, 13.

71. Hartzler, "Zaire After 21 Years," 15.

72. David Persons, email with the author, February 24, 2018.

David as Dean of the Mulungwishi Theological Seminary (FMT) at The University of Katanga at Mulungwishi, and Lori as director of the Doris Bartlett Women's School. Although recently retired, the couple still spends much of their year volunteering at Mulungwishi and living in their house there. Among their many activities, they have served as a public relations/fundraising bridge between the school and American donors.

I have visited Lori and David a number of times over the years. Without disclosing the details of the off-the-record conversations we have had and the words of wisdom they have offered me, I would say that they are what global nomads now refer to as Third Culture Kids (TCK). TCKs, as described so well in David C Pollock and Ruth van Reken's modern classic *Third Culture Kids: The Experience of Growing Up Among Worlds*,[73] are people whose formative years are spent in a cross-cultural setting such that in their way of seeing and interacting with the world, they are neither fully aligned with their parents' home culture nor do they entirely fit within the culture(s) where they grew up. Instead, they live in a liminal space such that they connect most easily with other TCKs. That is not to say that all children of missionaries inhabit the same liminal space, for this, I believe, requires a person to question assumptions of cultural and intellectual superiority and wrestle with self-identity. Living in the liminal zone does not mean that you fully embrace, are accepted by, or even understand either your adopted or ancestral culture(s). It does mean, however, that you are in a position to see truths (especially when cross-cultural interactions are involved) that neither group can see.

4.2.4 *Episcopal Viewpoints: Methodist Bishops in Central Africa*

In his wave-making 1964 book, *The Unpopular Missionary*, American Methodist Bishop Ralph E. Dodge boldly addressed the problems he saw in the attitudes and behaviors of American Methodist missionaries in Central Africa. Dodge, who became a bishop in 1956, was the first Methodist bishop elected by the denomination's Africa Central Conference—a break from the previous practice of the Methodist bishops serving in Africa being selected and appointed by church leaders living in America. From 1956 to 1968, he served as Methodist bishop over the areas currently known as Angola, Mozambique, Zimbabwe, and the Democratic Republic of the Congo. As previously noted, this was a period of political upheaval, as African nations were struggling to overthrow colonial governments and declare self-rule.

---

73. Pollock and Reken, *Third Culture Kids*.

Dodge, who had completed his doctorate in 1944 on the topic of "Missions and Anthropology: A Program of Anthropological Research for Missionaries Working Among the Bantu Speaking People of Central and Southern Africa," put a lot of thought into the interplay between colonial governments and White missionaries. He begins his 1964 book's first chapter, "Colonialism," by quoting scathing statements he has heard made by African youth within the Church: "'Many of the churches of the country are agents of government in the oppression of the African people.' . . . 'There is always conflict between a missionary and an African Christian; the latter wants both Christianity and freedom from colonial powers. There are some missionaries who support colonial power.' . . . 'The Christian missionaries accommodated themselves to the psychology of the colonizers.'"[74]

Dodge argues that if this "swelling chorus" is not taken seriously and changes are not rapidly made, the church in Africa will be destroyed. He notes three main reactions made by the current church leadership upon hearing such criticisms. There are those who only hear the threats of violence imbedded in the critiques, and thus they conclude "that the people of Africa have been led away from the church by various evil influences."[75] They denounce the attitudes of the African young people of the 1960s as unnatural (blaming communism and/or nationalism for corrupting minds), and they long for the olden days when the "White man's message" was embraced. The second group, while recognizing some of the past mistakes of the church, believe that overall its missiology is sound. They dismiss criticisms directed at the church as simply the predictable rhetoric of times of political upheaval, and thus they make no course corrections. The third group, however, listens attentively to such criticisms in hopes of learning from them and correcting problematic behaviors. Those in this group "realize that the church of Christ is composed of human beings who are subject to error. They acknowledge the place of reformation and in humility carefully consider all criticism against the church, accepting what is valid and opposing and correcting what is false. Only by taking this last position can the church in Africa find a way to become truly effective in meeting the needs of African Christians in the modern world."[76]

Dodge relates to criticism as a healthy thing and gently speaks to missionaries who feel unfairly attacked—their mistakes receiving more attention than their merits. He reminds them: "One should never forget that the church of Christ in Africa will not be built by foreign missionaries. It will be built by

---

74. Dodge, *Unpopular Missionary*, 17.
75. Dodge, *Unpopular Missionary*, 17.
76. Dodge, *Unpopular Missionary*, 18.

Christ. The church in Africa will come into its own on that day when African Christians are a body under Christ rather than under a foreign Board of Missions or even under the World Council of Churches."[77]

Dodge pulls few punches as he then continues to fill the bulk of his book with examples of White missionaries behaving in racist, colonial, and/or shameful ways. One example involves a visit he had taken to a Methodist primary school in the town in Katanga that is now known as Lubumbashi. Dodge had asked the pupils about the career goals, and a couple of them responded with ambitious dreams: one wanted to become a pilot, the other a doctor. The European headmaster was quick to admonish these responses, stately firmly, "In the Congo we do not have native doctors."[78]

Dodge also addresses the issue of missionaries generally being lumped into the same categories as the rest of the colonizers by the local population, with only a few managing to earn the trust and respect of the communities where they serve to have been deemed worthy of the label "White African."[79] In the next breath, he writes about the dearth of Black and other American missionaries not of western European descent, especially Black American men. He recognizes that this is in part due to the refusal of some colonial authorities (esp. in Belgian colonies) to grant residency permits to Black American missionaries, but asserts that the missionary community in general has been reluctant to diversify their ranks: "White missionaries . . . have at times been reluctant to receive non-White colleagues, partly because of the discrimination which Negroes would have to suffer and partly because of the embarrassment which they might cause their colleagues in a segregated society."[80]

Perhaps Dodge was trying to generate an excuse that did not involve a direct accusation of racism on the part of the missionaries and missionary-sending societies, but I disagree with his conjecture. Yes, perhaps the preference to only recruit White American missionaries was not the result of a conscious form of racism, but I find laughable the idea that a dark-skinned American missionary serving in Central Africa in the 1960s would have been subject to more discrimination and social snubs than she or he faced back home. Yes, the reluctance was partly due to fears of discomfort and embarrassment, but I believe that the underlying reluctance was due to the discomfort of the White church leaders, not the Black ones. The presence of dark skinned American Methodist missionaries would have

---

77. Dodge, *Unpopular Missionary*, 18.
78. Dodge, *Unpopular Missionary*, 20.
79. Dodge, *Unpopular Missionary*, 21.
80. Dodge, *Unpopular Missionary*, 21.

metaphorically held a mirror up to the White missionaries' blind spots, forcing them to wrestle more deeply with how they define "us" and "them" within their circles of friendship.[81]

All that said, Dodge also provides examples in his book of missionaries taking stands against manifestations of racism that were headline issues of that era: integration of public and private spaces, including non-discriminatory practices by stores. He writes of a missionary vocally refusing to shop in a store that insisted that African customers use the back window to make purchases (and the store's policy changed in the aftermath of the protest). He praises those—both foreign missionary and local church leader—who have persevered in their integration efforts despite the backlash they experienced. He also notes that colonists and Europeans rarely interact with Africans who have university degrees, and thus they fail to realize that those Africans "may be their superior in knowledge and culture."[82]

Dodge's many critiques of the status quo build up to the final section of his book, which looks to a way forward. He fittingly titles one of these chapters "Relinquish the Reins," where he argues the necessity of immediately transferring the oversight and administrative authority of the church in Africa to African leaders. He calls out sham gestures; for example, when a committee is nominally chaired by Africans while the power behind the chair remains European.

As Dodge discusses in his later memoir, *The Revolutionary Bishop*, the reaction to his abovementioned book—especially to him telling White church leaders to recognize the inevitability of "the approaching rebellion and to train nationals for administrative positions"—was so explosive that the government of Rhodesia immediately expelled him and his wife from the country.[83] Dodge reflects that what added to their grief about their expulsion was that "two areas of moral support which we greatly needed at this time were, to my knowledge, completely lacking. Never once did we hear from the Council of Bishops of my own church, nor from the Board of Missions."[84]

---

81. While socially progressive for their contexts, the missionaries still operated in many ways like a closed social club. For example, Bob Walters recounted to me that even into the late 1990s, the foreign Methodist missionaries operated on one ham radio frequency while their Congolese Methodist counterparts used another. When vital information needed to be communicated, the groups were literally talking on different wavelengths. When the 1998 evacuation began, GBGM called Walters's wife in Indiana asking if she knew his location because the missionaries did not. Had they tried searching through Congolese Methodist leadership communication networks, they would have quickly located him.

82. Dodge, *Unpopular Missionary*, 107.

83. Dodge, *Revolutionary Bishop*, 153–55.

84. Dodge, *Revolutionary Bishop*, 157.

In Dickson A. Mungazi's book *In the Footsteps of the Masters: Desmond M. Tutu and Abel T. Muzorewa*, Mungazi dedicates an entire chapter to examining the legacy of Bishop Dodge, who preceded Bishop Abel T. Muzorewa as the head of the Methodist Church in Zimbabwe. Mungazi also traces the trajectory of the episcopal leadership lineage of the Methodist Church in Zimbabwe, starting with Joseph Hartzell, who was elected bishop and appointed to Africa in May 1896. Hartzell, who was followed by Eben Johnson, retired in 1916. In 1918 Hartzell lamented, "Africa has suffered from many evils. Slave trade and exploitation by the White man have through many years preyed upon the life of Africa and have left its population reduced and uncertain about the future."[85] Serving as bishop until 1936, Johnson's term focused on the building of Methodist institutions with the goal of providing holistic education to the African population. His successor, the previously discussed John Springer, is credited by Mungazi for greatly expanding these initiatives in Africa, especially in the area of fundraising. Mungazi writes, "The Methodist Church aroused in Africans a new level of thinking and a collective consciousness that educational endeavors would make it possible for them to progress in the future and so enable them to make a visible contribution to the development of the country."[86] Springer was succeeded by Newell Booth, who was succeed by Dodge in 1956.

Referring to all the aforementioned American bishops, Mungazi writes,

> Believing in both the importance of their assignment and what they clearly saw to be the potential of the African to function effectively in the future and in the context of the white man's culture, they all pursued their objective with vigor and dedication. Even though conditions of the times demanded otherwise, their sensitivity to African opposition of anything that represented the white man's culture would later prove to be the hallmark of Methodist Church commitment to the African struggle for selfhood. Slowly but steadily, the Africans began to build a viable basis of mutual respect.[87]

Dodge's commitment to his belief that Africans should be leading the church in Africa can be seen in many ways, including in the bishops who succeeded him: in what was then called the Rhodesia conference, this was Abel Muzorewa, who was also the prime minister of the short-lived Zimbabwe Rhodesia.

85. Mungazi, *In the Footsteps of the Masters*, 40.
86. Mungazi, *In the Footsteps of the Masters*, 40.
87. Mungazi, *In the Footsteps of the Masters*, 41.

Bishop Muzorewa's opinion of the mid-century American Methodist missionaries in Zimbabwe was overall a positive one. In a private letter written to Marshall Murphree,[88] the son of American Methodist missionaries Dr. and Mrs. Lois Murphree and at the time professor of Race Relations at the University of Rhodesia, Muzorewa writes of his deep appreciation for the Murphree's ministries—especially the leadership role played by Lois Murphree, who helped organize the Methodist women's movement, worked alongside her husband to develop the first formal theological and Christian Education program in the Methodist Church in Zimbabwe, and helped develop the hymnody of the conference alongside Rev. Greeley and Rev. Kapenzi. Lois Murphree taught Muzorewa while he was a student at Old Umtali mission station's Theological College. The Murphrees also adopted two Zimbabwean orphans, one of which became Muzorewa's wife. Muzorewa's letter provides an example of how some American Methodist missionaries during this period (including some of those in Congo) made a proactive effort to become part of the community where they served—even adopting local orphaned children—and that a family-dynamic was created in their relationship with some local church leaders.

4.2.5 Mid-Twentieth-Century Mission Motivations in the Methodist Church in America

In 1944, (American) Methodist Bishop G. Bromley Oxnam launched the Crusade for Christ, with a goal of raising twenty-five million US dollars over four years in order to finance evangelism campaigns and relief efforts related to the humanitarian crises caused by World War II. The fundraising campaign raised two million dollars more than the original goal, and "an unprecedented 1.6 million new members join[ed] the Methodist Church in one year."[89]

As Gina Riendeau explains, the period post-World War II marked a change in the Methodist Church in America's relationship with overseas mission:

> The Methodist Church had experienced very lean years during the Great Depression and World War II. Work that had been started earlier by pioneering missionaries in Congo John (later a bishop) and Helen Springer, had been cut back or turned over to African leadership. Many of the earliest missionaries were

---

88. Muzorewa, "Letter to Marshall Murphree." I inherited a copy of this letter because Lois Murphree was my paternal grandmother's first cousin.

89. "Timeline: 60 Years of Sharing."

104   Decolonizing Mission Partnerships

unable to tolerate the conditions in Congo—malaria and tropical illnesses took many lives; others returned to the United States because of chronic medical conditions or schooling for their children. After World War II, however, interest in Methodist work in Congo was renewed—along with new drugs to prevent and treat the diseases encountered there.[90]

In 1948, three years after the end of World War II, the Methodist Church in America[91] launched a new program: The Advance for Christ and His Church. Now known simply as The Advance, it continues to be the primary method endorsed by the denomination to financially support mission initiatives. I have inherited a rare surviving copy of *The Christian Advocate's* (at the time, the Methodist Church's weekly newspaper) February 17, 1949, issue, which was dedicated to promoting The Advance. The cover itself speaks volumes of the missiology of that time:

---

90. Riendeau, *Deep Gladness*, §368.

91. Again, whenever "America," "American," "Congo," "Congolese," etc. is used in conjunction with the word "Methodist" or "United Methodist," it is to specify a subgroup—not to imply separate denominations.

The theme from the cover, "From Crusade to Conquest," continues in an article found inside. Written by Harold Mohn, the then executive director for The Advance, the article opens by stating that Christian love and mercy required the church to launch the Crusade for Christ, and "Now we have to have an Advance for Christ and His Church, because 'Man's Disorder and God's Design' make that forward step imperative."[92] Mohn continues:

> For every question there is an adequate answer. Those who have the answer are divinely called to give it. The Advance is Methodism's answer not only to the physical needs of humanity but to its hunger for righteousness in the midst of spiritual destitution.
>
> "Nothing but a total Christianity will have any power to combat mass paganism and materialism," as reported at Amsterdam last summer. The "dark places among heathen races," to which we have so long referred, is now general because darkness encompasses the whole earth, including America and Europe.
>
> The Advance is Methodism's part of God's design for dealing with worldwide human disorder. This is an advance not for numbers nor for power, but for Christ's conquest of the whole world in a day when nothing less can save it.[93]

The theme of disorder versus God's design was inspired by the report of the opening assembly of the World Council of Churches (WCC) in Amsterdam in 1948 and the nine-hundred-page book WCC concurrently published, *Man's Disorder and God's Design*, which was sent for free to all Methodist pastors in America and was promoted heavily in the Feb 17, 1949, issue of *The Christian Advocate*.

Also in 1949, the denomination "launched a program for recent college graduates ... emphasizing development work, medical service and missionary support roles."[94] Similar to the government initiative that American President John F. Kennedy launched, this program predated the Peace Corps by twelve years.

At the March 1948 General Conference of The Methodist Church, the Advance Fund program was presented and acted upon[95] as part of the overall plan for Christ and His Church. This large campaign set the missiological views and rhetoric for Methodists in America. Included in this was the introduction of the concept of "second mile giving," expressed visually in the following illustration:[96]

---

92. The Methodist Episcopal Church, *Christian Advocate*, 5.
93. The Methodist Episcopal Church, *Christian Advocate*, 5.
94. Howell, *Short Term Mission*, §726.
95. *Journal of the 1948 General Conference*, 331.
96. The Methodist Episcopal Church, *Christian Advocate*, 5.

Methodist Mission Partnerships in Katanga 107

It is crystal-clear already! Our world's great need and our Methodism's great heart make the Advance for Christ our second-mile step . . .

The "second-mile giving" concept continues to be used by The UMC today.[97] The implied message is that financial support of mission initiatives is something one does after fulfilling tithe obligations; it is going over-and-above the old expectations to help address the problems of the world. Thus, unlike apportionment dollars (that is, the financial contribution each congregation is obligated to send to their conference headquarters to be used to cover the general operations of the denominations), Advance projects were funded through designated giving. Still today, "projects authorized for giving through The Advance receive designated funds from churches and conferences directly."[98]

At the 1952 General Conference,[99] the concept of "Special Conference Partnerships" was officially established, the Advance program was renewed for another quadrennium, and in what appears to have been a response to local vs global mission debates, a provision was added that

97. "About The Advance."
98. "About The Advance."
99. In The UMC, General Conferences are quadrennial meetings. Thus, the 1948 session was directly followed by the 1952 session.

"10 percent of funds raised would go to conference-initiated projects in the United States."[100]

At the next General Conference in 1956, The Advance officially became a permanent program of The Methodist Church. Additional regulations were created related to the collection and distribution of funds. Apart from minor restructuring of the oversight committees and the advancements in technology creating new communication and contribution methods (e.g., online listings of Advance projects, online donation options), little has officially changed since then in how the Advance operates. As will be discussed in chapter 6 in the interview with retired Bishop Ntambo, the most significant change that has occurred over the last quarter-century in how The Advance functions in North Katanga is that before it was the missionaries applying and fundraising for Advance projects; now it is the bishop and those he appoints.

At the 1960 session of General Conference, Newell S. Booth, at the time bishop of the Congo, spoke of the dream of a development initiative for Congolese youth. The proposal was accepted, and a denomination-wide fundraising campaign was launched for it. Upon receiving this news, Bishop Ralph Dodge requested the fund be for all of Africa. This request was also accepted, and nearly one million US dollars were raised. A significant portion of these funds were used for post-secondary education opportunities for African leaders in the Methodist Church.[101]

4.3 THE 1970s–1980s

The following section primarily explores the macro-level dynamics at play in the missiological conflicts in The UMC in the 1970s and 1980s as well as what was being reported to American United Methodists at that time about the church in Katanga. An understanding of the origins of the conflicts discussed in this section is key to later discussions on the current political situation in The UMC—in particular, proposals and predictions of schism and questions on the impact that will have on The UMC in North Katanga. By explaining how GBGM's changes in the 1970s were attempts to reject neocolonial behaviors and honor the spirit of the calls for a missionary moratorium by giving priority-setting agency to church leaders in areas that have historically been recipients of paternalist mission models, this section challenges the dominant narrative that the traditionalist movement within The UMC is the clear side for North Katanga and other parts of Africa to

---

100. "About The Advance."
101. Dodge, *Revolutionary Bishop*, 138.

choose to align itself with (in contrast to the progressive branch) when the denomination's restructuring/divorce occurs.

4.3.1 Reforms in the Board of Missions

With the merger of the Methodist Episcopal Church and Evangelical United Brethren (EUB) in 1968, the 1970s were a transition period as denominational agencies and staffing were overhauled, creating a window of opportunity to think strategically and critically about what sort of denomination this new UMC should be. The newly restructured Board of Missions "engaged in a painful process of listening to representatives of constituencies that were violated by policies and practices reflecting the sins of prejudice, paternalism, exclusion, and indifference."[102] Influenced by the discourse of the Civil Rights Movement and Women's Rights Movement in the USA as well as liberation and postcolonial theology, the Board proactively strove to root out institutional racism and reform its hiring practices and (neo)colonial behaviors. In 1969, African Americans staged a sit-in at the Board offices demanding reforms.[103] Among the priorities presented to the Board of Missions in the Black Staff Task Force Proposal was the "retraining of Board missionaries to understand the trends in the Black revolution."[104]

Also in 1969, the USA began drafting young adult male civilians into fighting in the Vietnam War. This intensified the anti-war movements of the 1960s and pushed a considerable number of United Methodist conscientious objectors to enroll in theological studies and/or volunteer for relief, development, or other forms of missionary service with the Board—especially since clergy, seminarians, and those in missionary programs were draft-exempt.[105] Considering the wave of youth-led social protests in the 1960s, I believe it no coincidence that youth and young adults within The UMC were vocal and articulate in their calls for change at the Board. A youth task force was created, and the position paper it presented was scathing, "charging the church with 'complicity' in the forces of colonialism, racism, and oppression."[106] Among the paper's numerous accusations and calls for change was the demand to give local church leaders control of mission funds:

They called for decision making over the use of funds to be devolved to local control, especially to those organizations that represent poor and

---

102. Harman, *From Missions to Mission*, 2.
103. Harman, *From Missions to Mission*, 10.
104. Harman, *From Missions to Mission*, 11.
105. Harman, *From Missions to Mission*, 36. See also "Clergy: Should Ministers be Draft-Exempt?"
106. Harman, *From Missions to Mission*, 15.

oppressed peoples' legitimate claims for self-determination. "Supremacist assumptions" of the missionary movement were to be reviewed and the impact upon other religions and cultures addressed. Duplicity was alleged in the fact that, while the church accepted reparations from governments that seized church properties and resources in acts of war, it refused to consider restitution for damages cause by its own racism.[107]

Robert Harman writes that in the lead up to the 1968 merger and in light of the calls for a "missionary moratorium" and the decolonization of church relationships, three options were offered to Methodist church bodies seeking more self-determination: "(1) Autonomy, or structural independence from The UMC; (2) united churches, or mergers of Methodist bodies with other local churches, which then could request autonomy from the General Conference; and (3) central conference status, remaining within the organizational structure of The UMC. Autonomous and united church could seek an "affiliated" status with The UMC."[108]

Responding the Harman's list of the above-mentioned options, David Scott, Director of Mission Theology at GBGM, notes that The Commission on the Status on Methodism Overseas considered at least two more possibilities at its 1966 meeting in Green Lake, WI: "The creation of some sort of 'international Methodist church' and the creation of larger regional bodies that went beyond the extent and powers of the central conferences. For a variety of reasons, while those options were presented to GC1968, they were not further explored."[109]

Nearly all of the Methodist churches in Latin America and Asia chose the option of becoming autonomous institutions. The churches in Africa and Europe, however, chose to remain in a central conference structure, and a major factor in this decision was the fear of decreased financial assistance from The UMC if they chose full autonomy.[110] In 1974 African UMC bishops made a statement in consultation with The UMC's Board of Global Ministries.[111] In it they affirmed the Central Conference relationship and

107. Harman, *From Missions to Mission*, 17.
108. Harman, *From Missions to Mission*, 21.
109. David Scott, correspondence with the author.
110. The EUB church in Sierra Leone initially chose autonomy, but in 1972 chose to join The UMC's West Africa Central Conference. Note also that we are only talking about churches originating from missionary efforts of the EUB or MEC; thus, other autonomous Methodist denominations, such as the Methodist Church in Britain, are excluded from this conversation. See Harman, *From Missions to Mission*, 22–23.
111. The UMC's Board of Missions became the Board of Global Ministries in 1972. Later, it became known as the General Board of Global Ministries (GBGM). See Harman, *From Missions to Mission*, 25. Until recently, when Methodists in Katanga referred to "The Board" or "New York," it was implied that they meant GBGM.

their desire to become more self-sufficient in their ministries. They also asserted the following:

> We do not want to foster paternalism and we resent being called "product." We now want to produce as well in order to minimize or end the humiliation of being wretched beggars and burdens on the World Division. When we strive toward relative selfhood of the churches in Africa, we will be able to serve the church with dignity, integrity, and self-response and thereby achieve true partnership in mission. . . . We ask that the African Churches be allowed larger freedom to plan and implement their own indigenous leadership in cooperation with persons in mission, that they use personnel and financial resources to their best judgement and adopt and implement policies without hindrance.[112]

That same year, the All Africa Conference of Churches called for a missionary moratorium. Even before that, leaders within the Methodist Church had been debating the wisdom of foreign missionaries remaining at mission stations. In 1968, Bishop Lloyd Wicke, president of the United Methodist Board of Missions, spoke to the Board about this. In his report he mentioned Methodist missionaries in Latin America choosing to return home in order to allow indigenous leadership to fully take over and referred to the assertions of another Methodist missionary that foreign missionaries in the Philippines had overstayed their welcome and had become more harmful than helpful to the local church.[113] While acknowledging the problems created by foreign missionaries, Wicke took an empathetic stance towards them:

> The missionary is a "caught" person in many ways, seeking freedom for the friend yet not knowing how to free himself. He is impaled between the expectations of the sending agency and its constituency and the demands made upon him by those to whom he is sent. . . . The older absolutes which provided clear beacons for his predecessors are fading and the newer ones too often appear as institutional relativities or authoritarian irrelevancies.[114]

Without calling for a full missionary moratorium, Wicke urged the Board to do deep soul searching and seek to develop alternative approaches,

---

112. "Report of the Africa Bishops Consultation," 484.
113. Harman, *From Missions to Mission*, 86.
114. "President's Report," 153.

including taking a more active role in domestic poverty and justice issues. Throughout the 1970s, the Board continued to wrestle with the challenge of addressing racist and paternalistic attitudes and behaviors both within its structure and its staff. Efforts were made to retrain staff, especially career missionaries. Methodist mission historian Robert Harman writes that, unfortunately, "such efforts were only short-term in duration and were often insufficiently reinforced in places of assignment."[115] In the conclusion of his chapter on changes that occurred in The UMC's mission agency in the 1970s, Harman concludes that the mission board "cannot be accused of sitting out a revolution." That said, "neither the leaders of the forces of change nor the reactionary forces within the church found the changes initiated by GBGM to be satisfactory."[116]

Included in the changes during this period were decisions about how best to strategically spend the Board's financial resources. Spending was shifted away from maintaining a large number of foreign missionaries in the field to funding the stated priorities of grassroots leaders. The Board still faced criticism from the progressive wing of the church for not doing enough to address racism and injustice in the world, but it also faced an outcry from the evangelicals for reducing the number of traditional missionary assignments and focusing more on alternatives such as sending technical specialists as requested by national church leaders. Harman writes: "The evangelical critics of the Board saw this situation as a major retrenchment, especially from the work of evangelism and church growth that they insisted was far from over. Influential critics, including former missionary personnel, formed an ad hoc Evangelical Missions Council (EMC) to air their concerns more effectively."[117]

The EMC, launched in 1974 by Good News (an association of socially and theologically conservative United Methodists) quickly became the unofficial conservative Board of Missions in The UMC and a powerful caucus pushing back against the Board's attempts at changing its mission models. Good News continues to be a vocal critic of GBGM. In a 2017 article in *Good News Magazine* entitled "The Integrity of Missions," Riley Case writes about this history from their point of view. He notes that from 1976 to 1986 the executive secretary of EMC traveled around the USA holding mission conferences for EMC while simultaneously holding dialogues to "discuss ministry and theology with United Methodism's missions bureaucracy.

---

115. Harman, *From Missions to Mission*, 42.
116. Harman, *From Missions to Mission*, 46.
117. Harman, *From Missions to Mission*, 87.

The talks proved to be fruitless, but the call to missions message was being spread."[118]

4.3.1.1 PUSHBACK

The 1980s in the USA saw the rapid expansion of political power of what is referred to as the "Religious Right."[119] The public faces of these movements were mostly charismatic televangelists who preached a mix of prosperity gospel, faith healings, dogmatic fundamentalism, male household leadership, and social conservatism. During this time, the USA's interests in influencing politics in Latin America and the surge of evangelical efforts there were notably intertwined. This period also saw the rise of faith-based charity organizations running television commercials that focused on images of abject child poverty and portrayed Americans as having the ability to save these children through nominal donations, such as the cost of a daily can of soda or cup of coffee.[120] It was into this context that in 1984 the EMC created The Mission Society for United Methodists "because of a widely perceived movement of the General Board of Global Ministries (GBGM) away from ministry that has a specific objective of helping people come to faith in Jesus Christ."[121] Riley Case supports this assertion by claiming that in 1968 there were 1,650 United Methodist missionaries serving outside the USA, but by the early 1980s there were barely 500, with those numbers continuing to decline.[122]

For conservative evangelicals in The UMC, the Board had become a place of "inflexible progressivism." From their perspective, many Methodist

---

118. Case, "Integrity of Missions."

119. Randall Balmer, a professor at Dartmouth College, argues in "The Real Origins of the Religious Right" that while the dominant narrative is that the movement came in response to the 1973 Supreme Court ruling to legalize abortion, it actually began earlier as a racist backlash response to the desegregation of schools. Fundamentalist Christian universities, such as Bob Jones, heavily resisted racial integration. In her *Washington Post* piece "How Abortion Became a Political Litmus Test," Sarah Kliff shows that throughout the 1970s there was no correlation between Americans' political affiliation and their views on abortion. These divisions did not emerge until the 1980s. Many historians have also challenged the origin narratives of the Religious Right, including arguing that the anti-abortion movement was strategically created with political motives. See Balmer, "Real Origins of the Religious Right"; Kliff, "How Abortion Became a Political Litmus Test."

120. The most iconic of these were the Christian Children's Fund's commercials narrated by their spokeswoman, actress Sally Struthers. See also Haller, "Africa's Sick and Hungry."

121. Case, "Integrity of Missions."

122. Case, "Integrity of Missions."

seminaries "became centers of criticism for those who stressed a 'personal' rather than a 'social' gospel." The Board of Missions had shifted from a focus on saving lost souls to "missions without salvation."[123] In the May–June 1983 issue of *Good News*, the magazine's associate editor ran a twenty-page article entitled "Missions Derailed: A Special Report on the UM General Board of Global Ministries."[124] The chief accusation in that report was that the Board was neglecting its primary convert-making task and instead "concentrating on saving the world through 'liberation theology' and other political solutions."[125] The report also claimed that GBGM underreported how much of its spending was on overhead and administrative positions in its New York headquarters. The report pushed for a change in the Board's charter to include a focus on personal conversions, a reduction of the operations budget for headquarters, staffing changes, and a reduction/ban on contributions to certain organizations deemed by the author to be too radical.[126] GBGM was, and continues to be to this day, trapped in a no-win situation. Despite acquiescing to many of the demands from conservative leaders, it continues to be publicly criticized by conservative groups, which actively promote rival mission programs.[127]

Jeremy Smith, ordained UMC elder and author of the blog *Hacking Christianity* makes the following assertions when tracing the origins of the conservative movement within The UMC:

> The 1980s were an explosion of traditionalist efforts to operate *parallel denominational resources without oversight or accountability*. Through the Mission Society (1984 parallel to the General Board of Global Missions), Bristol House Books (1987 parallel to Abingdon), and the RENEW network (1989 tiny parallel to UM Women), traditionalists created a parallel structure that provided books, women's fellowship, and missionaries for congregations to support outside of United Methodist oversight, accountability, or connectional leadership. The parallel entities in the 1980s gave the narrative that they were to support the persecuted, downtrodden conservative minority. But looking back, that simply wasn't the case.[128]

---

123. Case, "Integrity of Missions."

124. Robb, "Missions Derailed." See also Anderson, "Conservatives in the 10-Million Member."

125. Robb, "Missions Derailed."

126. Anderson, "Conservatives in the 10-Million Member."

127. E.g., Boyette, "WCA Launches Mission Fund."

128. Smith, "UMC Schismatics are Now in Plain View."

Smith laments that by claiming minority/persecuted status, the conservative leaders in The UMC were able to intimidate the "moderate majority" into inaction about social justice issues while at the same time playing the victim card in their publications. This, he asserts, led to, among other things, "a Church that was silent in the face of the AIDS epidemic.... The 1980s taught us that silent, moderate Methodists could be intimidated into believing perspectives that didn't stand the test of time, leading to harm and death." Smith argues that the conservative groups that were paralyzing The UMC in the 1980s are the same groups that are fueling and planning schism today.

4.3.2 Through America's Eyes: New World Outlook

While Methodist missionary memoirs and meeting minutes about Katanga are relatively easy to obtain from the colonial period of the 1900s, after the 1970s they become rarer and harder to acquire. The digital archives of The UMC's mission magazine *New World Outlook* (*NWO*) are, however, publicly available and can provide insight into what the average highly-active United Methodist in the USA was (and was not) reading about mission initiatives in Congo (then Zaire). Thus, this next section of this chapter focuses on what I found by examining all its mentions of Katanga from the 1970s to the recent present.

The *NWO* serves as a record of the shifts in rhetoric, behaviors, and priorities in terms of mission in the denomination over the years. It is important to note that the *NWO* was viewed by many of its supporters and detractors as having a progressive bias. From 1911 to 1965 (under its previous name), the position of magazine editor was always shared by two people, one male and one female,[129] and from 1940 to 1964, half of every issue was "devoted to the Women's Society of Christian Service, a forerunner of United Methodist Women. In 1964, mission operations were reorganized and the magazine given a single editor, Arthur J. Moore Jr."[130] The previous female editor, Dorothy McConnell, became the head of the newly formed Women's Division, which went on to create its own mission magazine, *response*.[131] George Daniel, a Black American, joined the *NWO* alongside Moore at some point in the 1960s.[132] According to a source[133] I contacted,

129. Kemper, "How Mission Sustains the Church."

130. Kemper, "How Mission Sustains the Church."

131. The "r" in the name of the magazine *response* is deliberately lower-case. Unfortunately, I was unable to obtain access to its archives.

132. I found inconsistencies in my sources on his exact years there.

133. Anonymous phone interview with the author. Source formerly worked at NWO office.

between 1968 and 1970, the magazine lost approximately half its subscribers; the primary reason being cited as political fallout related to the creation of The UMC in 1968 and its restructured mission agency. Over the years, the magazine's operational budget drastically shrank until it became a staff of one. The magazine officially ended in 2018.

From the 1970s until the advent of accessible internet in the USA, most of the information UM Americans received about the church in Congo came either through the *NWO*, *response*, or directly via missionaries themselves—through their personal newsletters or speaking engagements during furloughs. Using keyword search functions, I created a spreadsheet of every discussion of Congo/Zaire in the *NWO* in the 1970s and 1980s. I found surprisingly few articles in my search, with some years having no mention at all. I also made note of the headlines, subject matter, and the way in which the subject is described in order to be able to document any possible shift in semantics.

In 1972, there was a brief mention of the election of Bishop Fama Onema; two years later, there is a full flattering article about the great work of Bishop Onema and the complexities of his job.[134] Later in 1974 is a story written by American missionaries in Kinshasa about a Spirit-filled ecumenical movement and miraculous healings. There are no mentions the next two years, but it is worth noting that in December 1975 under the headline "Mission Memo: Moratorium" there is the following statement:

> The United Church of Christ's Board for World Ministries will set no moratorium on overseas missionaries, according to Dr. David M. Stowe, executive vice president of the agency, which supports three hundred professionals in forty countries. In an address to the board's Fall meeting, Dr. Stowe responded to suggestions that American and Western European churches consider a missionary moratorium to insure the indigenous development of Christianity in Africa, Asia and Latin America. The issue he said is not of closing down mission, but of making it even more effective by genuine partnership with churches everywhere, each carrying primary responsibility for mission in its own situation.[135]

The next mention of Zaire is in June 1977: a full-length article about the exemplary ecumenical evangelism work being by Rev. Museba Kasangami,

---

134. Onema, who was ordained deacon by Bishop Booth, earned a BA in philosophy and sociology in the USA and then returned to Congo. He was ordained an elder by Bishop Shungu. See "Bishop Fama Onema."

135. "Mission Memo: Moratorium," 3.

especially in Kapanga and Lubumbashi.[136] In the combined July-August 1977 edition, the Mission Memo page reports violence in the Shaba (another name for Katanga) region of Zaire and its impact on UMC missionaries: Dr. Glen Eschtruth was killed by Zairian soldiers who accused him of concealing ham radios,[137] and Missionaries Frank Anderson and Carton Maughlin were reported missing but escaped to Angola and then returned to the USA. The obituary for Dr. Eschtruth noted that he and his wife had served since 1961 and had been named [local] chiefs in the Lunda tribe. Dr. Eschtruth had established a ham radio network between the mission stations and supervised the medical ministries at Samuteb.[138] The following month, *NWO* contained a brief memo stating that Zaire's president Mobutu had arrested several government officials and that the paramount chief of the Lunda (a United Methodist and brother of deceased Katanga independence leader Moise Tshombe) had been charged with treason.[139] In December of that same year, *NWO* wrote that a "Zairian Christian" had written to evacuated missionaries Warren and Lois Jackson that "conditions are deplorable—that the soldiers who restored security also looted and destroyed everything they found, leaving the population without food, clothing, medicine, transportation, or merchandise."[140] The following July, *NWO* ran an article about the harrowing, near-death experiences UMC missionaries (the Amstutzs and the Enrights) faced attempting to evacuate from Kolwezi.[141] Rev. Ken Enright expressed criticism towards the American government for their role in the political crisis. The *NWO* reiterated that despite accusations, neither Ken nor the other UMC missionaries "knowingly engage in CIA intelligence gathering activities."[142]

In 1979, Zaire received a large amount of coverage in *NWO*. One mission memo reports that the town of Kolwezi is rebounding from the "invasion from Angola," which left approximately one thousand of its residents dead, and that the UM congregations there are rapidly growing. It also notes

---

136. "Zaire: African Evangelism," 42.

137. I have been told by many sources that American missionaries were frequently accused by soldiers of being enemy spies. Dr. Eschtruth was one of a number of Methodist missionaries killed or nearly killed by soldiers/rebels in Congo over the years.

138. "Mission Memo: Zaire" (July/August 1977), 3; "Dr. Glen Eschtruth Slain in Zaire," 50.

139. "Mission Memo: Zaire" (September 1977), 3.

140. "Mission Memo: Zaire" (December 1977), 6.

141. Their very narrow escape from soldiers in Kolwezi is also recounted in Riendeau's book.

142. "Mission Memo: Zaire" (July/August 1978), 4; "UM Missionary Tells of Trial in Kolwezi," 43.

that "some 80,000 refugees have returned from Angola and are dependent upon church and UN assistance. In Angola, the Methodist Church is supporting three pastors who work with Shaba refugees in that nation."[143] Two months later, *NWO* ran a feature article "A Panorama of Church Development, Vitality, and Growth in Zaire, Africa." In it is the following assertion:

> Twenty years ago there was pronounced dependency on the western missionary, relative to church program development, administrative leadership and local church outreach. Today, after sixty-five years of missionary presence providing training, counsel and commitment, the change is impressive. Church leaders carry out their responsibilities with ability, resourcefulness and dedication. They have assumed leadership while the missionary, who is still needed and welcomed with open arms, fills a supporting role of undergirding and supporting the church.[144]

In that same *NWO* issue, there is a brief mission memo about the Church of Christ in Zaire (CCZ), an umbrella association of protestant churches (including The UMC) in Zaire, which was celebrating one hundred years of protestant churches being in Zaire.[145] Later that year, a Mission Memo reports that missionary pilot Stan Ridgway (age 29) and a Peace Corps volunteer were seriously injured and "an African woman was killed" when Ridgway crash landed in Kasaji after discovering damage to the runway by rain storms too late. Other unnamed passengers were injured. Wife Linda Ridgway was not on the flight.[146]

In 1981, *NWO* contains a brief mention of a cholera outbreak and that one (unnamed) UM pastor in Shaba died from it as well as one-sentence stating the creation of a third conference (that is, episcopal area) in Zaire and the election of Kayinda Katembo as its bishop.[147] In 1982, it runs a long

---

143. "Mission Memo: Zaire" (January 1979), 3.

144. Brinton, "Panorama of Church Development," 22. Howard Brinton was the first Methodist missionary to serve in Kolwezi. He was raised in Congo in a missionary family and returned from 1946 to 1996 as a missionary in his own right. At the time of writing the 1979 article, he was the executive secretary in the Cultivation section of the Education and Cultivation division of The UMC's Board of Global Ministries. The narratives told in this article show Brinton as someone with deep respect for Congolese church leaders; he makes them three-dimensional heroes of the stories, with individual names and specific accomplishments and challenges.

145. "Mission Memo: Zaire" (March 1979), 6.

146. "Mission Memo: Zaire" (May 1979), 3.

147. "Mission Memo: Zaire" (January 1981), 1; "World Division," 14.

article, "Zaire After 21 Years," written by Omar Lee Hartzler.[148] Hartzler's piece includes a discussion of the creation of the North Shaba (later renamed North Katanga) Conference:

> Immediately after independence, the Southern Zaire Conference sponsored an exploratory mission by its Luba pastors and laymen into their homeland in North Shaba, which had been effectively abandoned by other missionaries because of war. As a result of their visit, a coordinated and determined effort to occupy the North Shaba with Methodist-style broad ministries was undertaken almost exclusively by African leadership.... A new annual conference was organized, and by 1980 it had grown to dimensions which justified its having its own bishop, Ngoy Kimba Wakadilo.[149]

Hartzler writes about the "Africanization of the Gospel," which includes more than selecting Africans for top leadership positions but also "utilizing all of the resources of African culture to express the faith in terms that are genuinely African," such as the creation of church music, liturgy, and images that reflect local sensibilities.[150] Hatzler also expresses his "deepest appreciation" for the "courage and faith" of those in Zaire who "make the personal sacrifice to serve the Mission of God as pastors, teachers, doctors, nurses, farmers, chaplains, home-makers, administrators, and bishops."[151] He rejoices that some of his friends and former students have obtained prestigious jobs, remained faithful to the church, and resisted temptations to abuse their positions for personal gain, but he laments that some have succumbed to the temptation.[152]

These comments he sets in the context of a detailed discussion of the problems in Zaire's government—corruption, inefficiencies, and "mismanagement by an incompetent centralized administration." These problems resulted in a crisis in the school system such that a public uproar in 1976 led to churches like the United Methodists once again being allowed to manage schools (but did not receive sufficient government funds to cover expenses).[153] He talks also about the challenges faced by Methodist medical centers (e.g., hard to acquire medicines, salary interruptions) and

---

148. Hartzler was a former missionary in Zaire and at the time of writing the article (1982), the Executive Secretary in the Africa Office of GBGM.
149. Hartzler, "Zaire After 21 Years," 14.
150. Hartzler, "Zaire After 21 Years," 14–15.
151. Hartzler, "Zaire After 21 Years," 18.
152. Hartzler, "Zaire After 21 Years," 18.
153. Hartzler, "Zaire After 21 Years," 16.

notes that there has been a substantial reduction in the number of foreign Methodist missionary doctors and nurses while at the same time there have been efforts made to expand rural and urban health centers. Hartzler reports on Zaire's collapsing infrastructure (roads, hospitals, etc.), inflation, and urban blight and writes that Zaireans report that "the conditions of rural life are worse than they were in the pre-colonial era more than a hundred years ago."[154] All of these issues he blames on corruption and mismanagement on all levels of the government.

Later in 1982, *NWO* published a few photos of the Kimbanguists, a church native to Zaire. The following year, it ran "Zaire: How Poverty in the Midst of Plenty Challenges United States Policy."[155] This piece was highly critical of Zaire's president, Mobutu Sese Seko, as well as American and Israeli political involvement. The next mention of Zaire wasn't until May 1985 with a brief report, entitled "Missionary Injured," of a plane accident in Luena, which seriously injured Lorraine Enright and killed an "African," Mbuya, who worked for John Enright.[156] This was followed that September with a piece about the missionary-run aviation ministry, Wings of the Morning. The article was primarily about Ken and Lorraine Enright, and it mentioned that in 1985 the program had an eighteen-member crew, "a full third of fifty UMC missionaries" in the nation. These consisted of nine male pilots and their wives, who acted as ground controllers.[157] The relatively lengthy article went into detail on the various ways the aviation program had benefited the church and region, including flying in crates of medicines during the 1981 cholera epidemic. It also included references to and quotes from other missionaries in the aviation program, including noting the killings of pilots Burleigh Law in 1964 and Stanley Ridgway in 1984.[158] I believe it is worth noting, however, that the article did not interview any Katangan church leaders or mention local leadership outside of a closing mention that Bishop Onema Fama had created a scholarship program so that Zairian Methodists could train to become pilot-mechanics. More telling of the article author's blindspot/bias was when he wrote that "Wings of the Morning has had its share of crashes, fortunately none of them fatal," yet two paragraphs later stated that an "African passenger" was killed earlier that year

---

154. Hartzler, "Zaire After 21 Years," 17.
155. Jackson, "Zaire," 8–11.
156. "Missionary Injured," 6.
157. Navarro, "Flying Methodists of Zaire," 14.

158. Navarro, "Flying Methodists of Zaire," 16. Law was shot by a rebel guard on the runway. Ridgway was shot in Moba for refusing to fly a Zairian general who was attempting to commandeer the Methodist plane.

during a forced landing of a flight Ken Enright piloted.[159] 1987 contained two brief mentions of work in Zaire, noting that the Zairian government had requested The UMC take back over school and health programs and that efforts were being made particularly in the area of vaccinations, including the acquisition of solar-powered refrigerators to allow vaccines to be taken to areas lacking electricity.[160] There were no more discussions of Zaire in *NWO* until 1989, when "Mission is More Than a Two-Way Street" mentions a Zairian serving as a missionary in Algeria.[161]

The coverage of Zaire by The UMC's main mission news magazine in the 1970s and 1980s was almost entirely driven by the reports of Americans who had experience as GBGM missionaries there. This, as will be shown in the next sections, was true until nearly the present day. The reasons for the dearth of Zairian/Congolese voices in the articles are complex and include pragmatic (lack of infrastructure for easy communication via phones and letters) and relational issues (lack knowledge of who to contact), but the rarity of American missionaries submitting stories featuring Congolese church leaders and/or seeking out and translating reports written by Congolese leaders does suggest that missionaries tended to treat their Congolese colleagues as objects of ministry instead of peers capable of telling their own stories to denominational news outlets. While the missionaries themselves might have reacted with shock and offense had they been openly accused of racist mission praxis, the neocolonial assumptions that Congolese lives and stories are of significantly lesser value is at play in the stories missionaries chose to tell and those they ignored.

The previously mentioned 1985 article "The Flying Methodists of Zaire" highlights the degree to which Congolese church leaders were rendered invisible in the denomination's news media; not even their deaths were counted in the same way. What is even more striking to me is that its author, Nelson A. Navarro, was not American himself but a Filipino journalist who was living in New York as a political exile from the Marcos regime and was covering "the international social development programs of The United Methodist Church"[162] during that time. This shows that this journalist from a colonized country had also internalized colonial beliefs such that he, too, could only see the American missionaries as fully human actors with lives and perspectives worthy of note.

159. Navarro, "Flying Methodists of Zaire," 16

160. Sano and Billings, "World Program Division," 9; Ammons and Murdock, "Health and Welfare Ministries," 31–32.

161. "Mission Is More Than a Two-Way Street," 9.

162. "Nelson Navarro Memoir to Launch."

4.4 THE 1990s

The 1990s were a pivotal period in the history of The UMC's North Katanga Conference—one which will be revisited in later chapters via the reflections of the interviewees. The following subsections attempt to sketch a historical backdrop for those discussions.

4.4.1 Politics and Violence in Zaire/Congo

This thesis cannot adequately recount the complex politics of the violence in Katanga in the 1990s. For that, I defer to the writings of Georges Nzongola-Ntalaja and other political historians. It is key for the reader to know that in 1991 political tensions were escalating, and that in September to October 1991 Zairian soldiers (who had not been receiving their salaries) began a deadly looting spree in communities across the country. A second wave of looting led by soldiers occurred in January 1993 amidst the increasingly volatile power struggles in Kinshasa. This second wave included the assassination of the French ambassador to Zaire and hundreds of other murders in Kinshasa.[163] In both of these instances, United Methodist mission stations were destroyed, the homes of many church leaders were ransacked, and foreign missionaries were evacuated.[164] Few of the evacuated missionaries returned to Katanga after these harrowing and disheartening events.

In 1994, the genocide in Rwanda spilled over into Zaire, with over one million Rwandans fleeing across the border into Katanga.[165] In October 1996, Rwandan troops entered Zaire under the auspices of dismantling Hutu rebel fighter cells in Kivu. That same month, the AFDL (Alliance of Democratic Forces for the Liberation of Congo) was established with Laurent-Désiré Kabila as its head, and they began their military campaign to overthrow Mobutu. In response, GBGM began ordering its missionaries to evacuate, with the last remaining foreign missionaries leaving in March 1997. In May 1997, with the support of Uganda and Rwanda, the AFDL took over Kinshasa, and Kabila declared himself the president of the renamed Democratic Republic of the Congo.[166] In 1998, war re-erupted as Kabila's refusal to comply with demands of Rwanda and Uganda enraged the two countries, who had their troops stage rebellions in Congo. Angola and Zimbabwe aligned with Kabila and sent their troops in to push them back. Local

---

163. Nzongola-Ntalaja, *Congo*, 275.
164. See "Missionaries Safe in Wave of Looting in Zaire"; "Missionaries Leave Zaire"; "Homes of Zaire Bishops, Missionaries Looted."
165. Nzongola-Ntalaja, *Congo*, 275.
166. Nzongola-Ntalaja, *Congo*, 276.

militias were also formed, initially to defend their villages from the waves of attacks by foreign soldiers, but eventually many of them—like the infamously brutal Mai-Mai—began looting, raping, and butchering their own people, including clergy, and forcing children to join their ranks.[167] And yet, as Rev. Mwilambwe, Superintendent of North Katanga UMC's Ankoro District reported in 2006, "most of those who joined the Mai-Mai groups were Christians and children of our church members."[168] This added further layers of complexity to The UMC's peace-building efforts.

The cast of characters and political intrigue was extremely complicated in the late 1990s and into the 2000s. The result was that communities and infrastructures were decimated, millions of civilians were killed and countless more left traumatized and with severe, untreated medical issues. It was into this context that the leaders of The UMC's North Katanga Conference entered into a period of a *de facto* missionary moratorium. How they responded to this situation and how it impacted the way they saw themselves and interacted with their American counterparts is one of the primary questions explored in the interviews I conducted.

4.4.2 *United Methodist News Service Coverage; 1990s*

By the late 1990s, stories published in *The United Methodist News Service* (UMNS), the denomination's official news distribution agency, had a broader readership than the *New World Outlook* magazine—partly because their articles are frequently re-published in regional UMC newspapers and newsletters. This became especially true as email distribution systems and e-news systems became widespread in the USA. While I was not able to access its deep archives, I was able to search its digitized records going back to 1991. The following is a summary of the stories about Zaire/Congo published in the UMNS in the 1990s.

There were a number of mentions of Zaire in UMNS in 1991. In May, an article entitled "Make Noise—Bishop Asks United Methodists in Zaire" was about Bishop Katembo encouraging church members to speak out about conditions in Zaire despite the potential repercussions of criticizing the government. "We must do something. . . . If we just keep quiet, things will not change."[169] In June, "Church in Zaire Reported Thriving" stated that

---

167. Bishop "Guy" Mande Muyombo wrote a number of theological reflections on this subject while doing his university studies, including Mande [Muyombo], "Theological Responses," 27–35.

168. Muyombo, "Theological Responses," 28.

169. McAnally, "Make Noise—Bishop Asks United Methodists in Zaire." This article quotes an interview with Katembo in a United Methodist TV program called *Catch the*

despite the stagnant economy, The UMC in Zaire was healthy and growing: "Church membership now numbers nearly half a million in Zaire, with the only limitations on growth being personnel and funding, according to the Rev. Julius Jefferson, a staff member of the Board of Global Ministries World Division. 'They can't train people fast enough,' he said."[170]

September and October 1991 included reports of extensive looting and the evacuation of all forty-three UMC missionaries in Zaire.[171] October included an advertisement for a special feature on Zaire ("the political upheaval . . . and its related stories of corruption and violence") via The UMC's television program, *Catch the Spirit*, scheduled to air twice in November on multiple cable channels.[172] In November, UMNS reported that The UMC's Council of Bishops had made an official statement expressing concern for the political strife in Zaire,[173] and in December they reported acute food shortages in the southern part of the country: "Bishop Katembo Kainda told the denomination's Board of Global Ministries November 19 in a telephone call that most stores in Lubumbashi have been looted and burned. Most church property has escaped damage, he said."[174]

In 1992, there was more talk of politics. In March, UMNS reported on a solidarity march held in the USA to condemn the violence in Zaire (especially the killing of demonstrators in Congo the previous month) and demand that President Bush ask Zaire's President Mobutu Sese-Seko to step down.[175] The next month, UMNS reported that GBGM's directors also vocally urged Bush to cut ties with Mobutu.[176] A few months later, UMNS wrote that the political crisis was an opportunity for the church in Zaire: "People attempting 'to find help in moments of extreme difficulty' are 'turning to the church (because) nothing else works,' said Elaine Crowder during the denomination's annual conference for missionaries on home assignment, retiring missionaries and mission interns. Elaine and Doug Crowder, who have served in Zaire since 1958 but were evacuated in 1991 in the face of violent uprisings, are returning there in late August."[177]

Spirit. I was unable to acquire a copy of that program.

170. "Church in Zaire Reported Thriving."

171. "Missionaries Safe in Wave of Looting in Zaire"; "Missionaries Leave Zaire."

172. "Upheaval in Zaire Featured on TV Series." I was unable to obtain a copy of the program discussed in the article.

173. "International Strife Addressed by Bishops."

174. "Food Shortages Reported in Zaire."

175. "March Opposes Zaire Violence."

176. "United States Urged to Cut Ties with Zaire."

177. "Oppression Seen as Opening Doors for Church."

That autumn only included three mentions of Zaire, and all pertaining to a slander lawsuit between a GBGM missionary and his supervisor in regards to insinuations of responsibility for a deadly civil disturbance in Luena, Katanga.[178] The lawsuit was later dropped, and the missionary Lowell Wertz and his wife Claudia both resigned from GBGM.[179]

In 1993 there were only two mentions of Zaire: February reported the looting by disgruntled soldiers of the homes of Bishop Onema and Bishop Wakadilo as well as missionaries, with Wakadilo's location unknown and missionaries evacuated.[180] In April, the GBGM directors released a letter calling for President Clinton to respond to the "rapidly deteriorating situation in Zaire."[181] The next mention was not until sixteen months later.

In August 1994, UMNS reported that GBGM's director, Bishop Felton May, planned to visit refugee camps in Zaire and in an open letter urges President Clinton to seek additional volunteer medical personnel as well as other relief and reconstruction aid and "congressional reassessment of US foreign policies affecting central and southern Africa."[182] Later that month they reported on what the delegation found in that visit:

> Members of a United Methodist delegation have expressed shock and horror at what they saw during a recent five-day, fact-finding tour of refugee camps in Zaire and Burundi.... The tour coincided with the launch of a ten-year, fifty million US dollar Bishops' Appeal and campaign to increase support for United Methodist churches and mission work throughout Africa. The first United Methodist medical team to be sent to refugee camps in Zaire is expected to arrive August 28. Mission executives estimate that as many as eight hundred volunteers will be dispatched within the next year.[183]

Four stories about Zaire were distributed in September 1994—all pertaining to the waves of medical teams dispatched to refugee camps in Zaire. The focus of these reports was on what the American teams are

---

178. "News in Brief" (September 11, 1992); "News in Brief" (October 2, 1992); "News in Brief" (October 30, 1992).

179. After their split from GBGM, they relocated to Kigoma, Tanzania, where they continue to run Joy in the Harvest Ministries, working closely with the Tanganyika and Tanzania Conferences in which Lowell remains an ordained elder in good standing. Thus, polity-wise, they report to the bishop of the North Katanga Episcopal Area. Lowell and Claudia were both raised in Africa as missionary kids.

180. "Homes of Zaire Bishops, Missionaries Looted."

181. "Board Addresses Mid-East, Africa Concerns."

182. "Bishop Asks for Medical Teams to Africa."

183. "Delegation Visits African Refugee Camps."

doing, although the September 16 article included a discussion of local church members assisting refugees in Uvira, Bukavu, and Goma and that some doctors working at the camps were refugees of the conflict themselves. There was mention of The United Methodist Committee on Relief (UMCOR)'s substantial involvement in various relief efforts there.[184] Two more follow-up articles in December and the following month wrote of additional Americans going to serve in the refugee camps.[185]

In December 1994, the UMNS briefly reported the death of Bishop Ngoy Kimba Wakadilo of the North Shaba (Katanga) Area. Wakadilo, who had been bishop since 1976, died in Nyembo Mpungo of a heart attack.[186]

Zaire received eight mentions by the UMNS in 1995, six of which were about various relief efforts to Rwandans in the refugee camps—including the withdrawal in September of much of the relief staff due to escalating violence.[187] The two others were about the commissioning of new American missionaries in the region, including two couples assigned to North Shaba (the Woodwards and the Groves).[188]

Of the eleven UMNS stories in 1996 on Zaire, ten were on the relief work and/or conditions in the refugee camps—including reports of violence escalating again, destruction of UMC property and foreign aid workers evacuating. November contained a report of Bishop Felton May urging the American government to convene a peace summit. There was one mention in 1996 of Zairean UM leadership.[189]

The ten UMNS stories on Zaire in 1997 focused mostly on the evacuation of missionaries and the political situation there.[190] February contained the first passing mention I found of Ntambo, who was identified as the bishop of North Shaba. March mentioned a lay leader from Kananga being chosen as a delegate to the British Methodist Conference. A May 1997 issue stated that some missionaries had returned to Lubumbashi, Likasi, Mulungwishi,

---

184. "First Medical Team Goes"; "African United Methodists Strengthen Refugee Work"; "United Methodists Dispatch Second Team to Zaire"; "Refugee Work Exhilarating but Hard."

185. "Church World Service Sends United Methodists to Rwanda"; "United Methodist Teams Work in Zaire Refugee Camps."

186. "News in Brief" (December 16, 1994).

187. See "News in Brief" from the UMNS for January 16, February 10, June 16, September 1, September 8, and December 1, 1995.

188. See "News in Brief" from the UMNS for April 28 and December 8, 1995.

189. See "News in Brief" from the UMNS for February 2, May 10, September 27, October 25, November 1, November 8, November 15, November 22, and December 13, 1996.

190. See "News in Brief" from the UMNS for February 14, February 21, March 14, March 28, May 16, May 19, May 23, September 12, and November 14, 1997.

Methodist Mission Partnerships in Katanga   127

and Kananga after waiting out the violence in Zambia. Also in May, we found what appears to be the first time Bishop Ntambo is interviewed by UMNS. He said he agreed "100 percent" with Bishop Onema's assertion that the "church is alive" in Zaire and that the overthrow of Mobutu Sese Seko would not hurt the church.[191] In September, there was a report that the new DR Congo government was receptive to consultations from UMC leaders, and that all three UMC bishops in DR Congo viewed Kabila's government as progress.[192] November reported that most UMC missionaries were now returning to their assignments in Congo; the extended version of the report noted that the three bishops said conditions had greatly improved and were now stable—with the exception of the Great Lakes region.[193]

There were no stories during the calm of mid-1997 until mid-1998. The next report, in August 1998, was of the "rebel uprising" fighting the Kabila government and the missionaries once again evacuating.[194] The next month contained an announcement that Nkemba and Mbwizu Ndjungu, Congolese missionaries serving in Senegal, lost their young daughter, Tontine, in a tragic accident. This story is noteworthy in that it was the first example I have found of a denominational publication reporting a significant event in the life of a Congolese UMC leader as well as one of the rare mentions of Congolese leaders serving The UMC outside of Congo.[195] In the fall of 1998, there was one mention of some missionaries returning to Congo, and an "emotional plea" from Bishop Ntambo and other bishops for the American government to intervene:

> Responding to an emotional plea from colleagues in Africa, United Methodist bishops are calling on President Clinton and the US government "to intervene . . . now" to bring an end to regional conflicts ravaging central and southern Africa. "We beg you, in the name of Jesus, bring peace to Africa," said Bishop Nkulu Ntanda Ntambo, living in exile from his assigned North Katanga Area in the Congo. "Africa needs peace. We want the church to be peacemakers." The conflicts have been responsible for thousands of refugees, displaced persons and deaths, the bishops said in their call for action November 5.[196]

This was the last mention of Congo in the UMNS until April 2000.

191. Bloom, "Zairian Bishops Express Confidence."
192. "Bishops in Congo See Progress There."
193. Bloom, "Most Missionaries Return to Congo."
194. "Missionaries Move out of Congo as Fighting Rages."
195. "News in Brief" (September 11, 1998).
196. "US Should Act Immediately to End Wars in Africa."

Stepping back and looking at these news stories as a whole, what strikes me is not so much what was reported but what was not. If someone wanted to learn about The UMC in North Katanga during this period by reading denominational news articles, s/he would know that the 1990s were full of violent political turmoil and that UMCOR and American teams were working to help refugees. Little, however, could be learned about the ministries of Congolese United Methodists in North Katanga or the names or thoughts of Methodists serving in the region other than bishops and American missionaries. While neocolonial/racial bias is a factor in the absence of Congolese voices from these stories, on a pragmatic level there was also the problem UMNS staff faced of having limited ways of obtaining information other than through the handful of people (e.g., American missionaries, visiting mission teams, and bishops) with the means to go to Congo and communicate (via telephone, USA postal mail, and later email) with the UMNS office. What we do begin seeing is hints of the growing capacity of Congolese bishops (who had traveled to the USA for Council of Bishops meetings and such and had begun speaking directly with American reporters) to communicate directly with Americans in the USA. The story about Congolese missionaries losing a child also suggests that it was the factor of being a missionary (who thus has a direct line of communication with GBGM) that determined whether one's story was told more than it was about being an American vs Congolese. The following survey of *NWO* in the 1990s paints a similar picture.

4.4.3 New World Outlook: 1990s

The 1990s archives of the *NWO* magazine paint a similar picture to that of the UMNS stories, albeit with more details. The majority of the mentions of Zaire/Congo during this period were about missionary evacuations, violence, and/or the refugee camps near the Rwandan border. There were a few exceptions to this which merit highlighting. In May 1994, *NWO* published a special *Geographical Mission Study Issue: African Churches Speak*. Its lead article was by a Zairian, Lahi Luhahi, who was at the time serving as a UM missionary in Kenya.[197] In the piece, Luhahi addresses what he described as a common belief among Africans that all Americans are rich and that mission funds sent by Americans are "extra money that Americans

---

197. This is a rare example of a pre-2010s article written by a Zairian in a UMC publication. The dearth of articles by Zairians/Congolese and other Africans did not begin to be proactively addressed by the United Methodist Communications agency until 2005, and the fruits of their effort did not begin to emerge until nearly a decade after that.

didn't have any use for."[198] Luhahi's views on this were first challenged by the Rev. Dr. Shaumba Teneya Wembo, a UMC leader in Zaire who traveled to the USA in the 1950s to visit congregations and returned home with stories of the financial struggles and sacrifices he witnessed among members of The UMC communities he encountered. This and Luhahi's later experiences led him to wrestle with questions about "how rich we Africans think we need to be before we can significantly engage in mission work."[199] He asserted that the emerging African middle class should also engage in funding mission work. He gave the example of his congregation in Kinshasa supporting the salaries of pastors serving in non-Methodist regions of the conference—an initiative launched in the late 1980s that was succeeding until the economic crisis in 1991.

Luhahi celebrated that in Africa "more and more annual conferences wish to take a more active part in mission work and mission sending," and he noted that the faith and resources to do so exist locally. That said, he observed a lack of "skills to organize and manage the mission enterprise. . . . Until very recently, Africans didn't know how the mission enterprise was managed. We enjoyed the fruits of the mission but had not experienced the pain and the joy it takes to make it happen. The challenges awaiting The United Methodist Church in Africa in the twenty-first century will require the full participation of Africans in mission outreach."[200]

Luhahi pointed out one of these major challenges on the horizon: the rate of membership growth was outpacing the denomination's capacity to provide needed services, such as regular visits to each congregation from an ordained pastor. He stated that without Africans organizing to address these issues, inroads already made may be negated. While appreciating the support provided by Americans and Europeans over the years, he said we "have to review our priorities in Africa in a way that enables African churches to contribute more to the mission work done in Africa." One major piece of this would be for the development of profit-generating projects. He pointed to the many commercially successful businesses run by the Catholic Church in Zaire: "Such activities are not new to our United Methodist Church in Africa. What would be new would be to run them as money-making activities for the church." Instead of investing in a scattering of small projects, he believed that regional initiatives, such as The UMC's Africa University (Old Mutare, Zimbabwe), have the best chance for long-lasting success.[201]

198. Luhahi, "Africa," 4.
199. Luhahi, "Africa," 5.
200. Luhahi, "Africa," 5.
201. Luhahi, "Africa," 6.

In the same *NWO* issue as the Luhahi article was an article on the Africa Church Growth and Development (ACGD) initiative of The UMC, which was launched in 1980. The article focused on efforts to empower and equip African United Methodists to be stronger leaders and administrators in the church. While the article was about work on the continent in general, it noted that "rampant inflation has caused Zaire to reduce its giving [to the church growth fund] to only a token amount, despite Herculean efforts to raise its share."[202] It also mentioned that the United Methodist Committee on Relief (UMCOR) had given grants to ACGD to address humanitarian crises such as those in Liberia and Zaire.[203]

Also in the *African Churches Speak* special edition were country profiles. Much of the section on Zaire read similarly to what one would expect to find in an encyclopedia entry: general population statistics, history, etc. It stated the country's newly reformed currency had devalued by 98 percent, that unpaid soldiers were on a rampage, and the crisis was impacting all of Central Africa. The profile also briefly summarized the history of The UMC presence in the country and made special mention of the origins of the North Shaba (now North Katanga) conference: "After Zaire gained independence in 1960, Methodists living in the northern part of the seceding Katanga Province challenged the church to expand there despite the civil war. So successful were the efforts of the evangelists, pastors, and teachers sent to the new district in northern Katanga that it was made the North Shaba Provisional Annual Conference in 1968 and a full annual conference in 1970. An episcopal area since 1980, it is headed by Bishop Ngoy Kimba Wakadilo."[204]

Under the subheading "Mission in Zaire," the profile gave statistics showing a dramatic increase in the number of UMC clergy, members, and preaching points in the country from 1988 to 1992. It also noted that The UMC in Zaire was operating "schools, theological seminaries, literacy programs, technical training centers, hospitals and clinics, and agricultural extension work" as well as an aviation ministry and the sending of local evangelists/missionaries into Tanzania and Zambia: "The North Shaba Annual Conference has established churches in Kigoma, Tanzania, and hopes to plant the seeds for congregations through the area. Zaire's three indigenous bishops have been guiding one of the fastest-growing churches in the world.

---

202. Adkins, "Heirs of God in Mission," 8.
203. Adkins, "Heirs of God in Mission," 10.
204. "United Methodist Church Structure," 26–27.

They need the prayers of all United Methodists to carry them through the political and economic crises that threaten Zaire and its people today."[205]

Another article of note was the 1997 profile piece on Daniel Mulunda Ngoy,[206] a second-generation United Methodist pastor from North Shaba. Ngoy was described as being "committed to ministries of peace and reconciliation among youth in situations of conflict throughout Africa" and holding an MA in Theology and International Peace. In the interview with him he spoke of the death of his infant nephew due to a general strike paralyzing Kinshasa and his plans to return to Zaire to push for political change.[207]

In 1997, a brief mission memo reported that Laurent Kabila had replaced President Mobutu and that a number of names had changed in the process, including the country (now DR Congo) and UMC conferences (North Shaba became North Katanga, Southern Zaire became South Congo; the conferences in Bishop Onema's area became West Congo, Upper Congo, Northeast Congo and Central Congo).[208]

In 1998, there was a cluster of articles written by American missionaries serving in Congo—one about progress on a cooperative agriculture initiative launched by Paul and Roxanne Webster and two about being a missionary child/family in Lubumbashi.[209] The latter articles gave this reader the impression that the family members had minimal interactions with Congolese outside of those working as domestic servants in their house. Also in 1998 were two mentions of Congolese GBGM missionaries Nkemba and Mbwizu Ndjungu serving in Senegal; the first report noted their arrival in Dakar; the second the drowning death of their young daughter.[210] In 1999 there was only one significant mention of Congo, and that was a discussion of John and Helen Springer as pioneers in expanding Methodist mission work.[211]

The *NWO* articles in the 1990s support the assertion I made in the previous section: the rarity of Congolese voices in denominational news outlets over the years cannot be explained as simply being due to colonial

---

205. "United Methodist Church Structure," 27.

206. Ngoy has since become a powerful politician. After being expelled from The UMC in a controversial decision by his bishop (Ngoy appealed to The UMC's Judicial Council, but later withdrew his appeal), Ngoy formed his own Methodist Church in DR Congo.

207. Wilkinson, "Panel of Witnesses," 15.

208. "Mission Memo: Changes in Congo," 19.

209. See Webster and Webster, "Improving Agriculture and Family Health"; Gipe, "Adventures of a Missionary Kid in Africa"; Gipe and Gipe, "Christmas in Congo."

210. "United Methodist Church in Senegal," 27; "Mission Memos: Deaths."

211. Robert, "History Lessons for Methodism in Mission," 7.

reporting practices at *NWO* and *UMNS*. It has had much to do with the challenges of UMC news outlets in directly contacting Congolese church leaders and vice-versa. That said, the hanging question remains: Why did so few American missionaries leverage their ability to submit articles in order to create opportunities for Congolese Methodists to share their stories on a denominational level? I suggest that the absence of articles/reports written by Congolese Methodists during the 1970s–1990s is indicative of the relationship dynamics that existed between American missionaries and Congolese church leaders. By retaining control of the power to report the stories to the broader church, the missionaries were also retaining control of relationships and financial flows, hence assuring the continuance of their position in the community as provider who must be appeased/respected by following his/her rules. I am not saying that these were necessarily conscious decisions, but I am asserting that, when accessing relationship dynamics, the question of who controls how a community's stories are told to the rest of the world is significant.

4.5 THE 2000S–2015:

In January 2001, DR Congo's President Laurent Kabila was assassinated by one of his bodyguards, and his son, Joseph Kabila, took over as the country's new president. With violence in the Congo still raging and the looting[212] (especially of Coltan, a mineral required in the production of compact electronics such as cell phones, tablets, and laptops) and the death toll mounting, major American news networks slowly began to take interest in covering the story. An exposé on the Congo crisis was scheduled to air in the USA in mid-September 2001. The attacks on the World Trade Center buildings and the Pentagon on September 11, 2001, however, took over the news cycle such that the vast majority of Americans I have spoken with to this day remain ignorant of the international war in Congo and the role the global demand for minerals such as Coltan had in funding it.

In a 2009 report for the International Relations and Security Network, Edoardo Totolo noted:

> The demand for Coltan by western industries reached its peak at the end of 2000 when new technologies started being used for mobile phones and other electronic devices. According to Toward Freedom's John Lasker, high market prices were mainly related to the mass production of Sony Playstation 2 combined with a global shortage of supplies. Correspondingly, the price

---

212. See UN Security Council, "Report of the Panel of Experts."

for Coltan rose dramatically: from 30 USD per pound in 1999 to 380 USD per pound in December 2000.

High market prices provoked the so-called Coltan Fever. Entire communities in the eastern DRC became involved in Coltan mining; students dropped out of schools; farmers and shepherds left their lands and livestock in favor of artisanal mining activities.[213]

Totolo continued by discussing how the various armed forces in eastern Congo profited off the looting of minerals and cites the UN's 2001 report that over one hundred western corporations had been complicit in the funding of armed groups in Congo via the purchasing of "dirty" Coltan. As Bob Walters often asserted in my conversations with him, the commanders of the various armed groups fighting in Congo did not really care whether or not they "won" the war; they preferred anarchy and a terrified population, since the violence was not primarily fueled by tribalism or philosophical/political ideological differences—it was about plundering fortunes.

While it is impossible to adequately summarize all important events and players during this period, the website of the BBC news network has a timeline that marks Congo's key events, and I direct those in search of a better understanding of the macro-politics to it.[214] Major chronology markers include the international peace talks and peace accords signed between groups in 2002, a new constitution adopted in 2005, the first free election held in four decades in 2006, a peace pact signed between government and rebel militia leaders in 2008, including General Laurent Nkunda (despite this pact, Nkunda continues violent clashes in the east), second elections held in 2011, another peace pact signed in 2013, Katanga's former governor Moise Katumbi expressing intentions to run for president and then being forced to flee the country in 2016, and elections being delayed and tentatively scheduled for December 2018. Despite the numerous peace accords, during the entire time there have been struggles for control, assassinations of rivals and waves of extreme violence—especially near the Rwanda/Uganda borders.

4.5.1 *The UMC North Katanga Response*

Since the final mass evacuation of American UMC missionaries in 1998, North Katanga has not had a single American UMC missionary serving in its conference.[215] Thus, the end of the 1990s and the start of the 2000s

213. Totolo, "Coltan and Conflict in the DRC."
214. "Democratic Republic of Congo Profile-Timeline."
215. A handful of Americans have come for short periods of time as volunteers (such

marked the beginning of a period when local church leadership could no longer turn to missionaries to raise funds for initiatives nor were there missionaries managing/controlling any initiatives. In the book *We Are Not All Victims: Local Peacebuilding in the Democratic Republic of Congo,* seminary professor Pamela Couture documents the experiences and peace-building efforts of The UMC's Bishop Ntambo and others during this turning point. Ntambo, who was elected bishop in 1996, began his episcopacy at the pivotal moment in time where Kabila's army was marching across the country to overthrow Mobutu, regional violence was escalating, and foreign missionaries were about to depart en masse. As Couture documents, he made conscious decisions to recruit and appoint promising Congolese leaders to key conference positions that had historically been filled by foreign missionaries.[216] As the violence heightened, so too did the humanitarian crisis and displacement of communities. Instead of ordering an evacuation, Ntambo decided to continue to appoint Katangan clergy and church members (such as doctors and teachers) to crisis zones, including establishing a chaplain and agriculture (i.e., food security) program to the Kamina military base, with hopes of preventing a repeat of the military pillages of the early 1990s. He also used his charismatic personality and preaching skills to forge direct friendships between him and leaders of church agencies, conferences and congregations in the USA and Europe.[217] This helped in raising funds for relief supplies (especially via UMCOR) and the building of schools, clinics, parsonages, churches, and an orphanage in the midst of chaos and political uncertainty. Bishop Ntambo also forged pastoral relationships with traditional leaders, government overseers, soldiers, and heads of rival factions, and he encouraged his clergy to do the same. His reputation as a peacebuilder was why the governor of Katanga asked Ntambo to host a peace conference of Mai-Mai (a notoriously brutal militia) leaders at his house in Kamina in 2004, which included bringing the Mai Mai warlord Chinja-Chinja to the negotiating table.[218] His success in these efforts is partly why, when elections came in 2007, Ntambo was nominated and elected by his province as senator in the Congo's Parliament.[219] In 2010, the Tanenbaum Center in New York City awarded Ntambo the Peacemaker in Action award

as Bob Walters), but no American working as an official GBGM missionary has lived in North Katanga for the past twenty years. 2017 marked the first foreign GBGM missionary (a Zimbabwean agronomist) to be appointed to North Katanga since the 1990s.

216. See Couture, *We Are Not All Victims,* esp. 31–32.

217. See Couture, *We Are Not All Victims,* esp. 153.

218. See Couture, *We Are Not All Victims,* 275–309, for a detailed account of this conference and the dynamics at play.

219. "Meet the Peacemakers."

for his courageous and effective work of building and sustaining peace in his region.²²⁰ And in 2013 the DR Congo government awarded him the highest civilian prize for public service, the Order of the Leopard.²²¹ Over the years, Bishop Ntambo invited many groups of visitors to North Katanga (mostly staying in Kamina) but after the missionary evacuation of 1998, he did not request GBGM to send a full-time foreign missionary to North Katanga or Tanganyika.²²² Ntambo officially retired as bishop in 2016 and was replaced by Bishop Mande Muyombo in 2017. The initiatives and changes occurring under Bishop Mande's leadership are beyond the limits of this thesis. That said, since I have been appointed Bishop Mande's Executive Assistant for Strategic Partnerships and Engagement, the conclusions and suggestions made in this study are already influencing choices being made.

4.5.2 UMNS Coverage 2000s+

With home internet connections becoming common in much of the USA in the late 1990s, a shift occurred in how United Methodists received denominational news. Subscriptions to printed magazines such as *NWO* dropped, while readership of UMNS reports (with the advent of e-news and social media) increased dramatically. Thus, for this thirteen-year period, I focused on documenting UMNS articles.

In researching the digital archives of UMNS, there was a hole (2000–2002) in the publicly accessible documents due, I suspect, in part to the technological changes in the way in which UMNS stories were created and saved during this period. The transition to email and web-based articles also appears to have impacted the length, content, and frequency of stories published in the 2000s and beyond. While my data samples were limited to just stories about Congo—and thus too small to draw blanket conclusions using quantitative analysis—I became convinced from the many days I spent

---

220. "Celebrating Bishop Ntambo." Bob Walters and Pamela Couture traveled to New York to attend the Tanenbaum award ceremony for Bishop Ntambo. Afterwards Walters remarked to me his disappointment and frustration that no UM bishops or representatives from church agencies were there despite GBGM's office's close proximity to the event location. The UMNS did not publish a story about a UM bishop winning the award despite it being highly prestigious.

221. "Meet the Peacemakers."

222. This statement could be debated by citing nuanced exceptions (none of which resulted in a full-time salaried foreign GBGM missionary living within the borders of North Katanga), but the fact that Ntambo did not actively seek to repopulate his area with American or European missionaries but instead requested salary support from GBGM for Congolese persons to fill roles historically done by Americans or Europeans is an important change, which I assert has helped shift relationship/power dynamics on the leadership levels of the conference.

searching through these archives that over the past decade (2008–2018),[223] and especially the past few years, a significant shift has occurred in how and how often UMNS covers stories about UM conferences outside of the USA. From both my observations and conversations with UMNS staff, this change came from deliberate efforts. Assigning causality to these efforts is complicated by the fact that for the past thirteen years I have been a vocal advocate within The UMC—and especially in conversation with UMNS reporters—for such changes, and thus I do not know to what degree my activism influenced these trends and/or how much my and their evolving views were influenced by greater trends. In order to not chase a moving target and because there has recently been a dramatic increase of UMNS stories about Congo (due in part to UMCOM funding communicator positions in various conferences, including North Katanga, with a recently added requirement to submit news stories in the contract),[224] I chose to only spreadsheet articles up until when my formal research began in 2013.

From 2003 to 2013 I found over 220 UMNS stories that discussed Congo either directly or in passing (for example: including Congo in the list of where delegates at a meeting were from). Of those, 50 stories included mention of North Katanga or a church leader from North Katanga. The topics of the 50 are listed in the table below.

NUMBER	TOPIC
12	News stories in which Bishop Ntambo was involved and/or made comments that do not inform the reader about The UMC in North Katanga itself (e.g., serving as interim bishop in Nigeria, acting in his capacity as Africa University's chancellor, preaching at General Conference, general political situation in DR Congo)
6	Reports of various events with mentions of someone from North Katanga attending it, including an article about the increase in "Non-US" delegates to General Conference and a story about protests from bishops about visas being denied to many General Conference delegates.

---

223. One of the main assertions in *New York Times*-journalist Thomas L. Friedman's book *Thank You for Being Late: An Optimist's Guide to Thriving in the Age of Accelerations* is that 2007 was a turning-point year for many technologies, including computing and online media. See Friedman, *Thank You for Being Late*, 19–35.

224. UMCOM's effort to have trained and equipped communicators in all UMC conferences was launched in 2005. It had a rocky start, with some bishops initially selecting individuals who lacked the minimal skills and passions to be trained as reporters, but by 2017 significant changes could easily be noticed in terms of the quality and quantity of stories published by UMNS submitted by reporters from Central Conferences, such as DR Congo.

NUMBER	TOPIC
3	UMCOM communication technology initiatives being implemented in various places, including North Katanga
4	Funds for medical/health initiatives (mosquito nets, medicines, clinic, HIV program) being given to North Katanga through multiple sources.
1	Brief profile of Beatrice Musambu, an Africa University graduate from the North Katanga Episcopal Area in a piece about Africa U. graduates that year.
2	Articles about a volunteer American missionary (me) serving in Kamina
1	Article about Joseph Mulongo (North Katanga) and Bob Walters (Indiana) biking around North Katanga together visiting communities. Discusses what they saw in those communities.[225]
1	2012 article about an Oklahoma congregation distributing bibles in Congo. Article opens with: "The word of God is reaching poor and illiterate people in the Democratic Republic of the Congo in several ways, thanks to the generosity of a United Methodist congregation in Tulsa, OK."[226] (Note: The distribution was in Tenke, North Katanga, although the article not does specify either of these details.)
1	2008 article about a Sunday School class in Arkansas raising funds for a well to be dug in Kamina.
1	2010 story about the Katuba congregation in Kamina, North Katanga welcoming Bishop Bledsoe to preach at their worship service. (Note in this story the congregation is described as the subject instead of passive recipient)
4	Stories about Arkansas Tech students raising funds for construction at Kamina University as well as visiting Kamina (2005/2006).
4	Stories pertaining to the aviation ministry: two focused on US conferences raising funds and two on the aviation program itself, piloted by Gaston Ntambo.
1	2004 a story about American pastor, Jon Mac, serving as president (i.e., lead fundraiser) of Kamina Methodist University
1	2009 photo-essay about problems in Congo and UMW financially supporting locally-led projects there. Includes photos taken in Kamina, North Katanga.
1	2010 announcement of remapping conference boundaries, including North Katanga.

---

225. For details, see Gilbert, "Pastors Bike through Congo to Bring Hope."
226. Schutz, "Oklahoma Church Sends Bibles to Congo."

NUMBER	TOPIC
1	2013 global hunger report includes mention of successful introduction of moringa tree and soybean farming in Kamina (UMCOR project) as nutritious alternatives to cassava.
1	2004 quote from Kasap Owan Tshibang, a General Conference delegate from North Katanga about not wanting to get drawn into debates about homosexuality
1	2004 story specifically about Bishop Ntambo's peace-building work.
1	2003 story about The UMC Council of Bishop's Hope for the Children of Africa initiative, which began in 1998. In it, Ntambo celebrates that with these funds North Katanga has built five new schools (one primary, two secondary, and three colleges, built with five hundred thousand USD). Ntambo also speaks of 2,000 bikes and 243 cows distributed thanks to additional funds given by annual conferences.[227]
1	2010 story on Bishop Ntambo's success in reducing malaria-carrying mosquito population in Kamina by mobilizing community to dig drainage canals.
1	2007 story on Bishop Ntambo being elected a senator. Includes discussion of his peace-negotiation work in Katanga in 2004.

Comparing these UMNS stories to those of previous decades, one sees that Bishop Ntambo received dramatically more news coverage than his episcopal predecessors. This I credit to changing times and to Ntambo's charismatic personality and the efforts he made to build personal relationships across the denomination. There was also a notable increase in the number of North Katangans reported to have attended denominational meetings. This too I credit to a combination of Ntambo's efforts as well as the advent of free email platforms (such as Gmail) and the arrival of cell phones in North Katanga, which allowed agencies in the USA to more easily communicate directly and in real time with church leaders in Congo. The third trend I would like to point out is the number of stories about specific initiatives in North Katanga, with their funding sources being outside of the traditional Advance/GBGM system. While these stories tended to be framed as Americans (the givers/heroes) raising money for projects (the North Katangan leadership as silent recipients), it still was a shift away from missionaries raising and distributing funds via the Advance to direct links between American bishops/congregations/individuals and North Katanga's bishop.[228] Thus, the stories from 2000–2013 are primarily the story of Bishop Ntambo's efforts to

---

227. Tanton, "Bishops' Appeal Changes Lives in Africa."

228. This trend is also noted by Bishop Ntambo in the interview he gave for this research.

develop direct relationships with church agencies, congregations, and individuals in pursuit of funds for his various initiatives.

Yet even with Bishop Ntambo's efforts to claim agency over the narratives about North Katanga, there was a major story missing in the media reports—perhaps partly because it was a gradual event: the story of North Katanga becoming officially the largest conference (in terms of members) in The UMC during the period of Ntambo's episcopacy. The growth not only meant a rapid increase in the number of clergy and preaching points in the conference, it was meant the North Katanga gained a staggering number of delegate spots to General Conference sessions in the USA. For the upcoming 2020 General Conference, for example, North Katanga is allotted fifty delegates while conferences in the USA have between two and twenty-two spots.[229] This, as touched upon in other parts of the thesis, means that those trying to influence the votes at General Conferences see the North Katanga delegation as a strategic group to befriend.

4.6 OFF THE RECORD: LOOKING BACK AND BEYOND

By stepping back and taking a sweeping view of what all these published documents—personal memoirs, formal histories, and news coverage—can tell us about the history of relationship dynamics between American and North Katangan Methodist over the decades, it is easy to recognize that (neo)colonial realities and assumptions have created barriers to building a partnership of equals. This is seen not so much in the stories told but in the stories/voices that are absent from the archives. Similar things could be said of other important pieces of the puzzle that are missing from the published accounts, such as an absence of discussions about conflicts between Katangan church leaders (power struggles, differences in ministry priorities, accusations of wrongdoing, etc.), what Katangans were doing in ministry apart from foreign partnerships, and what they thought about the foreign missionaries serving in their area.

Between reading memoirs of former missionaries to North Katanga and having informal conversations with missionaries and Katangans over the years, I know that there were often conflicts between missionaries and local leadership. It would be easy to dismiss such conflicts as having to do with colonial attitudes or cultural biases, but the truth is messier. Conflicts weren't always a clean Congolese versus American issue. Often Americans would become triangulated into a conflict, where less powerful church leaders would come to them complaining about the actions of a higher ranked church leader. Such conflicts tended to involve accusations of the misappropriation of funds/resources, nepotism, or some other misconduct that

---

229. "2020 General Conference Delegate Distribution."

negatively impacted others. Neither Americans nor North Katangans can be lumped together when it comes to personalities or behaviors. There have been the proverbial saints and sinners on both sides.

While I have avoided recounting scandals and individual interpersonal conflicts in order to not needlessly reignite pain and anger, I believe it would be dishonest to not at least recognize that a major falling out occurred between Bishop Ntambo and a number of American missionaries who had served in North Katanga. The most impactful fallout was between Ntambo and John Enright. There are competing versions of what happened, but the two had been good friends and collaborators in ministry in their younger days. Not long after the bishop's election, though, things turned sour to the point that Enright would tell anyone who would listen to not trust Ntambo. The congregations that had financially supported the ministries in North Katanga previously managed by the Enrights and the Vances turned their backs on Ntambo and shifted their energies and funds to mission stations in Zambia and elsewhere.

While the official story is that continued political instability was the reason GBGM stopped sending foreign missionaries to North Katanga after the last evacuation, the truth is more complex. Bishop Ntambo did not advocate for any to be sent, and thus there were no foreign United Methodist missionaries living in North Katanga during nearly the entire span of his two decades as acting bishop. While, as will be discussed in the next chapter, this *de facto* missionary moratorium created space for church leaders to fully take charge and challenge internalized messages that Congolese were not capable of successfully leading the church themselves, it also removed the system of control that had previously existed between bishops and representatives of the denomination who could not easily be intimidated into silence (i.e., foreign missionaries).

While the practice of using foreign missionaries to check the power of bishops is (neo)colonial, the abrupt ending of this dynamic created a period where it was now the bishop who essentially held absolute power (control of communication, bank accounts, job appointments, modes of rapid transport, etc.) in the conference. This led to accusations of abuse (e.g., nepotism, conference resources and money not being used for their designated purposes, etc.) and played a significant role in the breakdown of trust and cross-cultural relationship building, especially over the past two decades. Addressing this breakdown of trust is an essential component in any strategic plan to build a healthy mission partnership in the coming years.

We can also see from the survey of news stories since the 1970s that a shift did indeed occur in the years since the last evacuation of missionaries from North Katanga. No longer are missionaries controlling the telling of the stories. That said, there remains an element of the neocolonial Savior Complex in many of the stories. For example, one finds statements such as: "The word of God is reaching poor and illiterate people in the Democratic Republic of the Congo in several ways, thanks to the generosity of a United Methodist congregation in Tulsa, OK."[230]

As I consider such stories through the lens of my observations of Bishop Ntambo over the twenty-five-plus years I have known him, I would argue that, in a sense, he played into and leveraged such savior complexes as a fundraising strategy. When big or potential donors would come to visit North Katanga, they were flown into Kamina and received a carefully scripted welcome befitting saviors or celebrities. A choir would sing as they exited the plane, children would present them bouquets of flowers, and a long line of clergy and church officials would be there to shake their hands. They would receive an official guided tour of projects needing funding, opportunities to teach and/or preach to large crowds, and a party on the final evening featuring two choirs and a traditional dance troupe on loan from the Catholics' cultural center plus a formal speech by the bishop about how wonderful they were along with a public presentation of gifts of new outfits, malachite jewelry, and copper tableaus along with an explanation of how the image on that tableau was a metaphor for something the bishop wanted to honor about that specific person. Ntambo had a gift for making American donors feel like heroes and accomplices in his grand vision for peace and prosperity in North Katanga. Instead of the missionaries, now he controlled the shaping of the narrative. And as he was fond of reminding his clergy in the presence of Americans, when the bishop declares something (even when it is a joking claim to have prepared a meal someone else has clearly cooked), everyone is to respond "Amen."

This chapter created a sketch of the history of the relationship dynamics between North Katangan and American Methodists, and in the process it showed that elements of (neo)colonialism have been and remain present in the partnership. In the next chapter, I explore some of the collective psychological traumas that have created barriers to healthy partnerships between North Katangan and American United Methodists, and include in this a deeper look at the issues of neocolonialism/racism as well as the impact of violence and (internalized) racism and shame avoidance behaviors. In chapter 6, I then layer upon these discussions the key talking points that emerged from my formal interviews on the subject of the (changing) dynamics of this partnership. Together, they form a three-dimensional picture of the nature of the partnership over the past quarter-century.

230. Schutz, "Oklahoma Church Sends Bibles to Congo."

5

Racism, Violence, and Exploitation

The Impact of Collective Trauma on Mission Partnerships

> "No movement you are part of will be any healthier than you are." —Nanci Luna Jiménez[1]

> "Let's call culture anything that is benign or spiritual or connected. And let's call anything that demeans and devalues human beings oppression. Let's separate the two. Because if we don't, then in order to not be oppressed it begins to feel, for many of us, that we have to lose our culture." —Lillian Roybal Rose[2]

CULTURE, IN THE CONTEXT of speaking about human communities, is a notoriously difficult word to define. As scholar Mahadev Apte has noted: "Despite a century of efforts to define culture adequately, there was in the early 1990s no agreement among anthropologists regarding its nature."[3] Nor does that debate seem to have approached resolution today. While difficult to pin down, it is heavily used and, as Joshua Rothman noted in *The New Yorker*, with increasingly negative connotations (e.g., rape culture, celebrity culture).[4] That said, most academic programs I have found promote definitions similar the one used by the USA's Peace Corps: "Culture is a system

---

1. Nanci Luna Jiménez, conversation with the author, March 19, 2017. (Jiménez cited her mentor Lillian Roybal Rose as well as Shelly Brown in the origins of this assertion.)
2. Rose, "Healing from Racism," 17.
3. Apte, "Language in Sociocultural Context."
4. Rothman, "Meaning of 'Culture.'"

of beliefs, values, and assumptions about life that guide behavior and are shared by a group of people. It includes customs, language, and material artifacts. These are transmitted from generation to generation, rarely with explicit instructions."[5] The problem with using this definition, however, is that beliefs and traditions that facilitate the well-being of the community are lumped together with beliefs and practices that came about through trauma experienced by a community and that, while passed down from generation to generation, fuel cycles of violence and oppression. Thus, when exploring interpersonal relations between two groups of people, I want to make a distinction between shared beliefs and practices that bind a community together in a mutually beneficial way and the psychological wounds, scars and oppressions present in these communities. The identification of collective psychological disorders and unprocessed anger and grief as "culture" is not only disrespectful to the community being discussed, it creates unnecessary barriers to healing and fruitful relationships. For these reasons, I am giving discussions on community trauma their own separate chapter instead of weaving them into the previous sections.

The history of violence and exploitation over multiple generations in DR Congo has been documented by numerous historians and journalists: from the horrors and brutality of the early days of colonial rule—most famously detailed in the book *King Leopold's Ghost*—to the kleptocracy and strategic neglect of infrastructure and impoverishment of the people (in order to maintain control) by Mobutu Sese Seko over nearly three decades, to the conflict that erupted at the end of the twentieth century and became commonly known as Africa's World War. Due to this history of violence and oppression, there are no North Katangans alive who remember a time of peace, stability, and prosperity in their homeland. The psychological impact of this cannot be overstated.

Beyond post-traumatic stress, unprocessed grief, economies of scarcity, the normalization of violence, hatred, internalized racism, the resistance to reintegrating those who have committed brutal acts (including child soldiers) back into society and the church, paranoia and shortage of social capital (that is, networks of trust), there lies fatigue and a profound sense of futility and abandonment. As Bob Walters notes, "In our deep listening in remote districts the number one pain that we heard was the feeling of abandonment—of not being connected."[6] This, I believe, applies both to a disconnect to the outside world and to one's own history.

5. "Defining Culture."
6. Bob Walters, interview with the author, January 11, 2016.

Advantages Americans often take for granted, such as the ability to keep cherished material objects indefinitely (accumulating wealth and possessions over time), do not exist in North Katanga. When North Katangans visit my parents' home in the USA, the thing they invariably marvel about is that the home is mostly furnished and decorated with family heirlooms, some of which date to the 1800s, and they express sadness that they do not possess old objects or photos—neither from their past nor from their ancestors. All had been abandoned during times of crisis, ruined by storms/exposure to the elements and/or stolen. This factors into the way North Katangans tend to make decisions—be it purchasing objects, saving money, launching a new business, or collaborating with others.

This chapter names and explores the most significant psychological traumas that impact the interactions between North Katangans and Americans. The identification of these traumas is essential to understanding the dynamics at play in the encounters between North Katangan and American Methodists, and it greatly informs the lens through which the reader is to process the interview responses found in chapter 6.

5.1 VIOLENCE AND EXPLOITATION

Both the USA and North Katanga have legacies of violence and exploitation. The USA's economy and infrastructure were built upon the backs of enslaved Africans and political/economic refugees on land taken from the continent's first nations, who were systematically displaced and murdered at genocidal levels. It has built the largest military in the world[7] and has engaged in numerous wars and battles over its history, leaving generations of veterans and their families with inadequate assistance in dealing with the resultant physical and mental health issues. Mass shootings, hate crimes, and violence disproportionately committed against POCs by persons in positions of authority are commonplace. Thus, talk of the legacy of violence and exploitation as an issue impacting North Katangans but not Americans would be complicit in the whitewashing of America's history. That said, neither should we equate the impact of this violence on the American United Methodists involved in collaborations in North Katanga to the violence (and fear of future violence) experienced by church leaders in North Katanga. While in one sense trauma is trauma, there are differences in how it impacts those who have personally been on the receiving end of violence and those who observed or participated in it. As discussed more below, North Katanga has suffered generations of the most extreme forms of violence and exploitation

---

7. Bender, "Ranked."

of its human and natural material resources. This has created a general ethos of distrust, vengeance, and dehumanization of others.

5.1.1 Recent Violence in North Katanga

It has often been said that the DR Congo—especially Katanga—has been cursed by its wealth. Katanga is one of the wealthiest regions of the world in terms of its natural resources, yet the financial gains from these resources are held by only a few whilst the vast majority of Katangans themselves live in extreme poverty and insecurity due to the cycles of violence triggered by struggles for control of these resources (e.g., Coltan, gold, uranium, copper, diamonds, etc.).

As discussed in section 4.4.1, the arrival of the 1990s marked the beginning of the end for DR Congo's (then Zaire) kleptocratic ruler who had named himself Mobutu Sese Seko, which means "the all-powerful warrior who, because of his endurance and inflexible will to win, will go from conquest to conquest leaving fire in his wake." Under Mobutu's rule, government employees (administrators, teachers, police, soldiers, etc.) were rarely paid and the country's infrastructure was deliberately neglected. Leveraging the power of one's position to obtain money/resources from others was a common survival strategy. One memorable example was the 1991 pillage in Kamina (the headquarters of the North Katanga Conference) and other locations; government soldiers looted the communities, and it is thought that Mobutu himself was behind it as a method to appease his frustrated troops and to keep the population (especially Katanga, which had previously fought for its independence) so focused on surviving the day that they wouldn't have the ability to mount an organized rebellion against him.

Mobutu's strategy might have worked longer if it had not been for the 1994 genocide that erupted in the neighboring Rwanda and spilled over into eastern Congo, sparking a chain of events that led to his overthrow and the deadly chaos that has been called Africa's World War. Towns and villages in Katanga were looted and burned—sometimes multiple times over. The death toll has been difficult to calculate, but it was in the millions.

Outside of a discussion of the work Katangan United Methodist leaders did in striving to build peace (which has been researched and documented by Pamela Couture),[8] the details of the war are beyond the scope of this thesis. What is key in terms of this discussion is to take note of the levels of violence and feelings of powerlessness among the population and how traumatic experiences of violence tends to be self-perpetuating in that they can manifest as rage, lashing out against others, especially the most

8. Couture, *We Are Not All Victims*.

vulnerable. Internalized oppression/violence is one of the struggles North Katangan leadership faces.

5.1.2 Distrust, Sabotage, and Curses

One of the manifestations of internalized oppression in North Katanga is a deep fear of sabotage and murder (through natural or supernatural means) by peers. Over the years, I have heard numerous reports of such incidents occurring, even in times of relative peace. One example of this is the precautions Bishop Ntambo takes to avoid poisoning. While in the USA, he eats and drinks whatever is served to him without hesitation. In Katanga, however, I have observed that he will only eat food prepared by vetted people, and he will only drink beverages opened in his presence or prepared by those in his inner circles of trust.

The belief that one can be sabotaged or killed through supernatural acts (i.e., curses) heightens this general paranoia. One such manifestation of distrust is the impulse to avenge the death of family members—even when their deaths are determined by medical professionals to have been accidental or caused by disease or other health problems. Much like the infamous witch trials in America in the late 1600s, people in Katanga can be accused of (and then ostracized or even killed for) putting curses on other people. For example, in 2016, Rev. Dr. Boniface Kabongo, a major contender for becoming the next UM bishop of North Katanga, suddenly fell ill in Kamina during a meeting of district superintendents with Bishop Ntambo. He was taken by the UM airplane for treatment in Lubumbashi, but he died soon after. Medical examiners identified the cause of death as natural (heart/stroke related), but, as has been explained to me by multiple Congolese colleagues, all untimely deaths are seen as having a spiritual cause behind them. News of Kabongo's death was met with rage. A UM church in Kamina was burned down in revenge, and many church leaders feared the possible consequences of being accused of having caused his death through witchcraft.

Paranoia, unprocessed grief, and rage also lead to persecution of the most vulnerable innocents. As Rev. Ilunga Mwepu Dikonzo asserts in his doctorate research proposal,[9] pastoral counseling is greatly needed to address the tendency of grieving families to blame and persecute the widow or widower of their deceased family member. As has been reported by orphanages in some parts of DR Congo, it is also not uncommon in some areas for families to throw out a child from their home, accusing him or her of causing maladies through demonic supernatural forces.

---

9. Ilunga Dikonzo Mwepu, correspondence with the author, May 14, 2018.

This atmosphere of distrust also impacts American–North Katanga interactions, as I learned the hard way in 2005, when Bishop Ntambo appointed me head of the conference's development department. Questions asked in pure curiosity or for writing basic reports (e.g., "How many cattle do we currently have at our conference's farm?") are often heard as accusations (i.e., "I suspect you have stolen cattle."). Similarly, as Bishop Ntambo warned me then, asking "Why?" questions can create tensions—both because "Why?" is not a question average North Katangans have been raised to ask/answer and because, when heard by a fearful person, it is interpreted as an attack.

Lest Americans be tempted to speak condescendingly of North Katangans' beliefs concerning maleficent spiritual powers, it should also be noted that, by my observations, most Americans are fearful of spending the night in an allegedly haunted house, would not purchase a home where a violent death has occurred,[10] and embrace in their daily parlance the concept of spiritual warfare or a universal force—as popularized in the Star Wars film series. While I have never, to my knowledge, met an American who practices cannibalism or ritual sacrifice with the goal of obtaining power from the thing sacrificed, it is important to note that a percentage of Americans practice what we call witchcraft and voodoo, particularly the use of voodoo dolls (a small effigy of the person ones wishes to harm that is stuck with pins or burned). I am aware of at least one American UM clergy (not of African heritage) in a leadership role in the denomination who has used voodoo dolls with the intention to supernaturally chase off colleagues.

I have slowly come to realize that the belief in the existence of the spirit world and the ability of diviners and other ritual specialists to manipulate its powers is strong in North Katanga. This stretches well beyond debates over the efficacy of the methods of traditional healers or the belief—held even by many Americans—that the spirits of deceased family members can still interact with individuals and assist them. As already touched upon, this also manifests at times in deadly ways.

5.1.3 *The Difficulty of Forgiveness and Reintegration*

While not explored in depth in my research, it is also important to name and point to existing studies on the challenges of reintegrating those who have committed heinous acts (such as murder, mutilation, and rape) into North Katanga society and congregations. Pam Couture's previously mentioned creative nonfiction novel *We Are Not All Victims* deals with this topic as well as the doctoral and postgraduate writings of Bishop Mande Muyombo,

10. E.g., Montgomery, "Disclosing Murder or Suicide When Selling a Home."

who has written extensively on the challenges of reintegrating former militia members back into the communities and congregations they had once terrorized.[11] Without such reintegration, peace is not possible. While these studies focus on navigating and transforming the relationship dynamics between Congolese (i.e., forgiveness, reconciliation, reintegration, etc.), they also shed further light on the context of interactions between North Katangans and Americans. The North Katangan leaders who are wrestling with how to rebuild trust and agape love in communities composed of persons who committed what would, in normal circumstances, be considered unforgiveable acts are the same leaders wrestling with how to relate with foreigners. As will be revisited in chapter 7, the theology developed to address the former impacts how to approach the latter.

5.2 RACISM

Racism, as professor David Wellman explains in *Portraits of White Racism*, is both a structure of racial advantage and beliefs that defend this advantage. Wellman argues that racism should thus be analyzed as a "system of exclusion and privilege *and* as a set of culturally acceptable linguistic or ideological constructions that defend one's location in that system."[12] Racism, therefore, is not a synonym for prejudice. As professor Beverly Daniel Tatum asserts, prejudice is a preconceived opinion or judgement which usually comes from ignorance of all the facts.[13] While racism is often described as "prejudice plus power," Tatum argues that such a definition does not adequately communicate the varied manifestations of this power in that it doesn't explicitly name that power as being a system we are all living in regardless of our individual opinions. Hence, many of her White students working with such a definition conclude that since they do not perceive themselves as having power, racism has nothing to do with them.[14] Tatum also notes that, in America, the label "racist" holds emotional power: "For many White people, to be called racist is the ultimate insult"—it feels like being called a "low-life scum."[15] For this reason, the majority of White American United Methodists I have encountered in my life have not chosen to engage in deep exploration of how their assumptions and behaviors support and/or fail to challenge racism. I assert that this lack of exploration and self-examination has, as discussed in chapter 2's section on (neo)

---

11. E.g., Muyombo, "Theological Responses to the Mai-Mai Conflict."
12. Wellman, *Portraits of White Racism*, 25.
13. Tatum, *Why Are All the Black Kids Sitting Together*, 5.
14. Tatum, *Why Are All the Black Kids Sitting Together*, 8.
15. Tatum, *Why Are All the Black Kids Sitting Together*, 10.

colonialism, influenced perceptions and actions (and lack thereof) in regards to their interactions with North Katangans and unknowingly perpetuated manifestations of racism.

The following sections seek to explore racism and how it impacts the abovementioned issues in more detail.

5.2.1 Unexamined Racism: Microaggressions, Racist Acts of Love, and White Fragility

One reason that words and actions stemming from racial biases are, for some, difficult to recognize is they often come from unexamined (unconscious) assumptions of superiority of people who see themselves as morally good. These racist behaviors tend to be cloaked in the veneer of acts of love and generosity (e.g., White Savior Complex) or ambiguous enough for plausible deniability (e.g., microaggressions). When rebuked for their behavior, such individuals can feel their core self-identity under attack and quickly react with strong emotions (i.e., White Fragility).

Derald Wing Sue, a professor of counseling psychology at Columbia University described by *Psychology Today* as a "pioneer in the field of multicultural psychology,"[16] has written extensively on the subject of racial microaggressions, which was first coined in the 1970s by psychiatrist Chester Pierce. Micro-aggressions are actions or words stemming from assumptions of superiority that are insulting and yet subtle so as to be easy to deny if called out. Sue created a flowchart on forms of racial microaggressions that has been cited in multiple publications and is widely available.[17] This chart identifies and defines a number of racial microaggressions, such as microinsults, microassaults, and microinvalidations. While racial microaggressions can be done deliberately, most of what I have witnessed, been told about, and even committed myself in terms of racially biased interactions on an interpersonal level between North Katangan and American United Methodists over the past quarter-century would fall under Sue's categories of unconscious microinsults ("behavioral/verbal remarks or comments that convey, rudeness, insensitivity, and demean a person's racial heritage or identity") or microinvalidations ("verbal comments or behaviors that exclude, negate, or nullify the psychological thoughts, feelings, or experiential reality of a person of color."[18] With many North Katangan leaders still wrestling with their own internalization of racist

---

16. "Derald Wing Sue."
17. Flowchart can be found in Sue et al., "Racial Microaggressions," 278.
18. Sue et al., "Racial Microaggressions," 278.

beliefs and their fear of alienating financial donors, these incidents are rarely pointed out when they occur.

Another blind spot for White Americans is that racism is generally understood as being cruel or unjust to another person because of the color of their skin. Thus, it rarely occurs to well-intentioned White Americans that their actions (or, more often, inactions) contribute to the problem of structural racism or that something they intended as an act of love could be stemming from his/her unexamined assumptions of superiority and be, in fact, demeaning to the recipient.

Frantz Fanon's writings (especially *The Wretched of the Earth* and *Black Skin, White Masks*) were some of the first to examine colonial relational dynamics from a psychologist's point of view. In Fanon's essay on understanding the Black-White relationship, he talks about the White individual being locked in his whiteness[19] and asserts that "an individual who loves Blacks is as 'sick' as someone who abhors them."[20] As Fanon further explores the complexity of Black-White relationships, he shows how even consensual sexual relationships between Blacks and Whites is not proof of a couple overcoming racism between them; instead, he provides examples of such relationships being motivated by complex neuroses and sexual myths: both sides exoticizing the other—either as a path to whiteness (internalized racism/oppression) or as access to a more intense sexual experience (seeing the other as having a more savage/primitive nature).[21]

Increasingly, articles and blog posts about the subconscious racial biases of White people are being written and going viral. Two terms that have gained traction over the past few years are "White Fragility" and "White Tears." Both were coined to express criticism about the typical conversation-stopping reactions of White persons when their privileges or insensitive behaviors are pointed out to them. A few of the numerous noteworthy writings on this topic include "White Fragility: Why It's So Hard to Talk to White People About Racism,"[22] "White Fragility Leads to White Violence: Why Conversations About Race with White People Fall Apart,"[23] and "When White Women Cry: How White Women's Tears Oppress Women of Color."[24] Increasingly, people are engaging in conversations on the internet addressing how the feelings of guilt for being privileged combined with the

---

19. Fanon, *Black Skin, White Masks*, xiii.
20. Fanon, *Black Skin, White Masks*, xii.
21. Fanon, *Black Skin, White Masks*. See esp. chapters 2, 3, and 6.
22. DiAngelo, "White Fragility."
23. Judge, "White Fragility Leads to White Violence."
24. Accapadi, "When White Women Cry."

unconscious assumption of superiority and the desire to see oneself both as important and a good person result in efforts to "save" others done in such a way as to be offensive/shaming to those on the receiving end. Examples include discussions of the previously-mentioned White Savior Industrial Complex[25] and public-awareness via satire, such as the Instagram site Barbie Savior and the Rusty Radiator Awards—a public-awareness campaign launched by the Norwegian Students' and Academics' International Assistance Fund (SAIH) to highlight the racist assumptions of a number of charity programs.[26] Within The UMC, there are efforts being made to raise awareness of these issues. The UMC's General Board of Church and Society, The General Commission of Religion and Race (GCORR), The Women's Division, and the General Board of Global Missions all speak about this. For example, in 2016 GCORR launched a DVD and study guide series called *Vital Conversations on Race, Culture, and Justice*. Its opening session focuses on "Deconstructing White Privilege."[27] Thus, while this problem persists, there are signs of progress.

To my knowledge, none of the American United Methodists who have been involved in mission initiatives in North Katanga since the 1980s consciously believe that light-skinned people are inherently superior to dark-skinned people. However, many who have served believe that the primary task of mission work is to save souls. As J. N. J. Kritzinger has pointed out in our correspondence, such an approach can be functionally racist in that "unsaved" Katangans are viewed as morally and intellectually inferior. And as previously discussed, believing that racism is bad and being completely immune to the smog of racism one has been indoctrinated with since birth are two entirely separate things.

The tangled mental messes to overcome when striving to decolonize the partnership exist on both the subconscious and structural levels. While the issues of racial biases are interconnected with conversations about (neo)colonialism, they go deeper in that they deal with how one relates to one's own identity and how one views oneself in relationship to others. As discussed later in this chapter, the emotionally-charged word *Mzungu* is a perfect example of this.

5.2.2 *The Pain Not Discharged: Americans and Racism*

While North Katangans may find it easy to identify the causes of their collective trauma, Americans—especially White Americans—tend to be

---

25. Cole, "White Savior Industrial Complex."
26. "Radi-Aid Awards."
27. GCORR, *Vital Conversations on Race*.

unaware of the ways in which their actions—in particular, their mission initiatives—are motivated in part by unprocessed emotions of grief and guilt. Nanci Luna Jiménez, an educator who specializes in conversations aimed at helping individuals and groups heal from the effects of oppression, notes in her talks that the USA was built by people who were separated from their homelands and families, and that, as a nation, it has yet to "discharge its pain," including the pain of relocation.[28] It is a society that resists looking back at painful and/or shameful memories. In contrast to countries such as Germany and South Africa, the USA has also failed as a nation to collectively do soul-searching, confession, and repentance of its crimes against humanity. As has been documented by many historians and social scientists (a recent example being the documentary film *13th*,[29] which shows how the USA's prison system and forced labor therein are the result of a legal workaround created to continue the disenfranchisement of minorities—especially Black communities—and continue to receive the economic benefits of slavery), the USA remains a deeply racist country whilst it indoctrinates its school children in the myth of being a meritocracy founded on the belief that "all men [sic] are created equal."

The result of this is that a large number of Americans—especially, but not exclusively, those who are White and who view themselves as middle-class—have not been taught to understand the nuances of racism and structural oppression and their role in the system. And yet, on some level of their consciousness, many recognize their privilege, feel guilty about it, and have a profound urge to exonerate themselves from that guilt by helping those who are less fortunate. I include myself in this group. It was not until my early twenties as a result of a university course on cross-cultural communication that I began to self-identify as White. Before that point, I, like many others, was under the naïve (and privileged) impression that by refusing to acknowledge White as my ethnicity as defined by the society I lived in, proactively seeking out friendships with People of Color (POC),[30] and getting involved in justice and charity initiatives, I could distance myself from the collective sins of White people and therefore be something other than White. This point of view is similar to the previously mentioned myth addressed by Memmi—the fallacy that one could somehow be a colonial without being a colonizer.[31]

28. Nanci Luna Jiménez, conversation with the author, March 19, 2017.

29. DuVernay, *13th*.

30. While People of Color (POC) is problematic in that it treats Whites as not having a color, it is currently one of the least offensive terms in use to talk about all people except those who are viewed as being White.

31. Memmi, *Colonizer and the Colonized*, 10.

"White Guilt" is a term often used when discussing White persons who lament the racist actions of their ancestors and/or the injustices those historically oppressed continue to face. This profound sense of guilt can be a powerful motivator to try to help those who have been wronged (I know that sense of guilt intimately). Ironically, though, guilt (grief + power) itself can be a manifestation of racism in that guilt—in contrast to grief—contains the assumption that the guilty party had the power to prevent what happened. A major breakthrough in my self-examination was when I realized that my savior complex and feelings of guilt both assumed I had a superhuman amount of power. Coming to terms with my limited powers allowed me to both begin a healthier grieving process (i.e., discharging the pain) and identify ways to leverage my privileges for change. Unfortunately, this guilt/grief distinction in the context of understanding White Guilt is one I stumbled upon myself and, to my knowledge, is not widely understood.

While a more in-depth discussion of the pyscho-affective realm of racism in the USA is beyond the scope of this thesis, certain issues are particularly pertinent to understanding the underlying motivations of American United Methodists involved in mission initiatives.

Racism tends to be a taboo topic of conversation in White America. There is so much fear around saying the wrong thing—to be accused of being racist and/or ignorant—that little is said at all. Racism is not part of the curriculum in most schools apart from short units in American History about slavery, segregation, and the Civil Rights Movement. The contributions of people of color are rarely noted outside of Black History or Hispanic Heritage Months, where a short list of exceptional persons are mentioned—this list is so short and predictable that it gives the impression that these are the only POCs who have done anything worth mentioning, and thus in effect reinforces racist assumptions. While the majority of White Americans these days believe that racism is bad (sadly, there remains a significant number of vocal White Supremacists)—such that they react defensively if/when accused of racism—my observations over the years is that most (myself included) have grown up with an incomplete understanding of racism, which has led to their lack of self-awareness of their racist attitudes and behaviors.

Numerous studies have shown that racist beliefs persist in America. For example, an implicit bias test taken by over two million people online has concluded that "most White Americans demonstrate bias against Blacks, even if they're not aware of or able to control it."[32] This bias impacts every aspect of our society; at least sixteen respected studies have

---

32. Mooney, "Across America."

concluded that racism plays a role in how American police treat suspects.[33] In short, the data is overwhelming; racism remains alive and strong in the USA. As Tatum puts it, the assumption of the superiority of Whites is so omnipresent in American society that it is "like smog in the air."[34] From the casting of our television shows to which names move to the top of the resume stack, it impacts us countless ways. Sometimes this smog is hard to see, but everyone breathes it in daily.

5.2.3 Racism in North Katanga[35]

As previously touched upon, the story of King Leopold claiming of Congo for himself and the horrors committed against the Congolese people by those acting on his authority, including genocide, dismemberment, and forced labor, have been well documented. The Rev. Dr. Nelson K. Ngoy (pastor in The UMC's New York Conference, but originally ordained in North Katanga) emphasized in his 2019 paper "Paradigm Shift in Twentieth-Century Mission in Post-Colonial Africa: Rethinking the Future of The United Methodist Church in Light of Emerging Challenges" that King Leopold II had explicitly instructed missionaries serving in the Congo to help Belgium maintain its control over the region by discouraging Congolese from seeking economic prosperity for themselves and by teaching in such a way that undermined competence in anything other than manual labor:

> He instructed them as follows: "Your role as evangelists, pastors in the land of Congo, is to facilitate the interests and benefits of Belgium." He continued, "Your role as pastors is to interpret the Bible in a manner that protects the interests of the metropolitans." He further stated, "Your knowledge of the Bible will help you to find the texts that sanction poverty . . . use in your sermons texts such as blessed are the poor in spirit for theirs is the kingdom of God (Matt 5:3). It is hard for someone who is rich to enter the kingdom of heaven: It is easier for a camel to go through the eye of a needle than for someone who is rich to enter the kingdom of God" (Matt 19:23–24). Leopold instructed the missionaries to teach the local people to be faithful and irrational, to be physically strong, but rationally weak. He clearly

---

33. Makarechi, "What the Data Really Says."
34. Tatum, *Why Are All the Black Kids Sitting Together*, 6.
35. My focus is on White vs. Black racism. I do not explore here the history of certain people groups being given preferential treatment/power by the colonial authorities in central Africa—creating an explosive racist system within itself (such as what created the Hutu/Tutsi conflict).

Racism, Violence, and Exploitation   155

stated, "Teach them to obey, to be physically strong for labor, to forgive but not to retaliate."[36]

Racist policies continued in the region even after Leopold lost his control of it. Under Belgian rule, Congolese persons were legally inferior to White persons and were generally treated as such. Those few Congolese who managed mastery of the French language—despite the many obstacles to gain access to advanced levels of literacy—and European dress and protocols were granted the status of "évolués" (that is, "evolved"), and in 1950 the Belgium Congo government created a "civilized person" identity card available only to Congolese of certain socio-economic status, which would give the possessor permission to eat, enter, or live in otherwise Whites-only places. From 1950 to 1960, "only 217 évolués accepted these cards."[37] Despite the post-independence political rhetoric and policies under Mobutu Sese Seko of *Authenticité* (or Zairianisation), which rejected the vestiges of colonialism and promoted the embrace of uniquely African names, dress, and traditions, the internalized messages of Congolese inferiority lingered. This internalized racism/oppression is explored in greater detail later in this chapter.

As touched upon in chapter 4, missionaries serving in Congo were not immune to racist (neo)colonial beliefs. While my research and observations over the years did not reveal instances in the past quarter-century of American United Methodist missionaries or partners engaging in physically abusive actions towards North Katangans or other words or behaviors associated with racially-based violence and oppression, assumptions of intellectual and/or moral superiority and double-standards in terms of what consists of fair wages and adequate living conditions[38] could be found all the way up to the present day.

> One thing that I saw in some missionaries was that they were the *Mzungu*—the big chief. There was an arrogant attitude "We are superior to you," and it was very blatant, clear and evident even to children. . . . It was an arrogant attitude of "We are here to save these poor people." I think that led to some of the

---

36. Ngoy, "Paradigm Shift" (Ngoy's translation of Leopold's famous speech).

37. Edgerton, *Troubled Heart of Africa*, 179.

38. This in itself is a complex issue deserving of its own thesis. There are numerous stories of Americans attempting to eliminate this double-standard and finding that their efforts created problems they had not foreseen. Unfortunately, there is not space in this thesis to adequately explore the topic of the issues created when some people are paid several times more than what their neighbors and fellow congregants make (a problem that is facing the economy in the USA as well).

> bitterness and resentment from some of the indigenous people.[39]
> —John Enright

These condescending attitudes occur not only in interactions related to American United Methodists' involvement in initiatives in North Katanga but also in the microaggressions and dismissive remarks North Katangans have experienced when claiming their rights as full delegates (with voice and vote) at denominational-level gatherings, especially gathering where polarizing matters are voted upon.

5.2.4 Racism in The UMC

The UMC is not immune to racist assumptions and practices despite its efforts to overcome them. The restructuring that took place in the 1968 merger that formed The UMC included the dissolution of the Central Jurisdiction, which had been created in the 1939 reunification of the MEC, MEC South, and Methodist Protestant Church as a way to segregate Black Methodists into a separate jurisdiction based on skin color, not geographic region (thus ensuring that White congregations would not be appointed Black pastors and that Black leaders could not have supervisory authority over White leaders). To monitor and facilitate these integration efforts The UMC also formed the General Commission on Religion and Race (GCORR) that same year.

Despite the work of GCORR, racial biases continue to be an issue that has yet to be fully overcome in our denomination. At the gathering to mark forty years since the Central Jurisdiction's dissolution, Erin Hawkins, chief executive of GCORR, said, "Many concerns still remain today for African Americans and other people of color" in The UMC. According to Hawkins, they include:

> Equity in compensation between clergy of color and White clergy has not yet been realized;
>
> Annual conference nomination committees still disproportionately recommend lay and clergy leaders of color to serve in ministries related to ethnic and social concerns;
>
> The itinerancy system continues to be a source of much institutional racism within the church; and

---

39. John Enright, interview with the author, January 6, 2016.

Even after forty years of integration, people of color are but one group still seeking full inclusion in the life of the church.[40]

These statements remain true today. In addressing The UMC's North Georgia Annual Conference in 2017, Bishop Sue Haupert-Johnson remarked that she still has to deal with congregations who reject the idea of being appointed an African-American or female pastor.[41]

Over the years, a number of North Katangan UM leaders who have spent time in the USA have approached me to share and try to process their experiences of feeling treated as lesser human beings (instead of colleagues in ministry) during their interactions with American United Methodists—especially in regards to White American UMs active in international mission initiatives. While some of their complaints could be partially dismissed as cultural differences (for example, I was asked by some North Katangans why during their time in the USA for church meetings no one offered to host them in their houses—not even for a meal—that instead they were put in hotels and left to eat in restaurants), others could not.

After the 2008 General Conference, Bishop Ntambo arranged for many of the delegates from his episcopal area to be divided into groups and sent to different partner conferences in the USA for relationship-building and fundraising purposes. One of these groups came to Indiana; my father and I borrowed a van and drove the group from Texas to Indiana and then to multiple communities within Indiana. We arranged for hospitality along the way, sharing meals and lodging arrangements and attempting to balance the pressure to introduce them to potential financial donors with the opportunity their Indiana visit presented for them to take a much-needed vacation (that is, rest from their stressful lives and a chance to strengthen the relationships within the group). I was later told by North Katangan friends that the delegates compared their experiences when they arrived back home. What was striking for them was the differences in levels of hospitality and treatment they received, which they attributed to racism. Some groups felt very disrespected during their time visiting with "partners," some of whom had raised large amounts of money for mission initiatives in North Katanga. This complaint of perceiving racist attitudes by certain United Methodist partners in the USA has come to me from several colleagues, and in regards to a number of interactions. I have heard it from North Katangans, a Black American who was interested in getting involved via a partner conference, and from a well-known White American theologian whose wife was

---

40. White, "Leaders Remember Central Jurisdiction's Dissolution." For more on the Central Jurisdiction, see also Butler, "50 Years on."

41. Shearer, "Bishop Issues Call for Tolerance."

disturbed by what she heard when attending a gathering for those interested in their conference's mission initiatives.[42] The general outcry was especially fierce at the 2008 General Conference, when caucuses within The UMC were accused of trying to manipulate African delegates by buying them expensive gifts such as cell phones and sending them texts about how they should vote on certain issues.[43] I do not believe that the mission partners who I or my sources have observed are fully aware of how their words and actions have been received.

5.3 NORTH KATANGANS AND INTERNALIZED OPPRESSION

The term "internalized oppression" refers to when people who have experienced oppression turn that violence inward by treating each other in the oppressive way they have been treated and by accepting as truth the derogatory beliefs about themselves (aka internalized racism). The late educator Erica Sherover-Marcuse, who specialized in internalized oppression, taught that "when there's an imbalance of power, rage can only vent in two places: against ourselves, and against members of our own group. It can't vent up into those who hold power."[44] The pain of disenfranchisement and injustice tend to manifest as rage. In contrast to outrage, which is a healthy anger, rage is self-destructive. Rage comes from "imbalances of power that never let us attain equilibrium."[45] The cycle of violence and oppression in Katanga (both in terms of physical violence against others and internalization of the belief that Africans are inferior to pale-skinned foreigners) can be better understood by viewing it through this lens.

5.3.1 *Internalized Racism and the Mzungu*

The psychological impact of (neo)colonialism can be seen in the highly loaded word *Mzungu* (plural *Bazungu*[46] or *wazungu*). Although the word

---

42. Due to the sensitively of this issue, I am refraining from naming my sources or the partners they visited.

43. I cannot remember the exact month or year, but around that same timeframe the progressive advocacy group Methodist Federation for Social Action flew me to their main board meeting to offer sensitivity training to its members about healthy methods to build relationships with Congolese delegates and to raise awareness to their own racist attitudes towards African delegates, which were partly fueled by anger over nearly all of them voting against the acceptance of sex-gender marriage and homosexual pastors.

44. Rose, "Healing from Racism," 15.

45. Rose, "Healing from Racism," 15.

46. The Swahili spoken among the Luba people in North Katanga is influenced by the Kiluba language: the plural prefix "wa" often becomes "ba."

wazungu is literally translated from Swahili as "aimless wanderers,"[47] its common functional definition is "White people."[48] The connotations, however, go much deeper, and based on my observations and interviews, American United Methodist *Bazungu* tend to be unaware of these complexities as they step out into this field of emotional landmines.

5.3.1.1 Origin of the Term *Mzungu*

While most interviewees did not mention the origins of the word *Mzungu* when asked about its meaning, a few did. Kabila wa Kubangimayo, the oldest living UM pastor of the North Katanga Conference, recounted the time from his youth when he asked his father about the word *Mzungu*:

> Since my father worked with the Belgians, I asked him the same question. My father told me that the term *Mzungu* is used because you see someone was circulating everywhere—from the swahili word *kuzunguluka*: that means, to go from one place to another. Sometimes it means to be White with a color different from ours. That's what my father told me back in Likasi. I went one day on vacation, and I posed him this question: Why do we call the Belgians, the Greeks, and the Italians [this]—because at our place there were many Greek businessmen. For example, in Malemba Nkulu there were Whites, the Pentecostal missionaries. In Malemba, there were Catholic priests. In Mulongo, there were Garenganzi missionaries.... So, back then I thought about such things. [*Mzungu*] is someone without a fixed location. Just like in our dialect we say "baluba"—a term that means a lost one, he doesn't know where he comes from or where he is going. So that's the way in which I think the term *Mzungu* comes from, but today it means someone of a different color than our own.[49]
> —*Kabila wa Kubangimayo*

---

47. This is found in several sources, including Che-Mponda, "Meaning of the Word *Mzungu*."

48. Nkulu Ntanda Ntambo, interview with the author, July 20, 2015; Joseph Mulongo, interview with the author, July 18, 2015.

49. Kabila wa Kubangimayo, interview with the author, July 22, 2015. Original: "Alors comme mon père travaillait avec les belges, je lui ai posé cette même question, mais mon père m'a dit des choses, le terme Mzungu, parce que vous voyez dans un contrait il y avait peut-être un seul alors qui circulait presque partout, est ce mot Mzungu veut dire kuzunguluka c'est à dire partir d'un endroit a un autre, ça c'est un sens et puis le mot Mzungu, parfois signifier être blanc avec une couleur différentes dès notre. C'est que mon père m'a dit car il a travaillé avec les belges, quand j'étais a Likasi, je suis allé un jour en vacances, je lui est posé cette question; pourquoi nous appelons les belges, les grecs et les italiens parce que chez nous, il y avait beucoups de

5.3.1.2 *Mzungu* and *Tutsi*

In chapter 3, I wrote about the Luba understanding of *Muntu* (person; pl *Bantu*) and that according to Luba linguistics, all people are *Muntu* unless they lose their dignity to the point of becoming *Kintu* (a thing/object). This appears to be true among the Luba people themselves, but, as Bob Walters learned, in the eyes of North Katanga's Bishop Ntambo Nkulu, *Bazungu* are not *Bantu*. Walters tells the story of a conversation he had:

> "Bantu means people," I said to Ntambo. "Are all people Bantu?"
>
> "Most, but not all."
>
> "Am I Bantu?"
>
> "No. You are Tutsi."
>
> That knocked me off the foundation I thought I had established with him. For the previous few years, I had considered Ntambo my best friend . . . Now he tells me that I can never be Bantu. I will always be Tutsi. I will always be an outsider.[50]

Walters goes on to discuss the complicated relationship between the Bantu in Katanga and the Tutsi, a people group who reside primarily in Rwanda, Burundi, Uganda, and eastern borders DR Congo. Despite also speaking what linguists identify as a Bantu language, Tutsi are viewed as untrustworthy outsiders. And yet, they are also perceived as being smarter and more competent.[51] Walters notes that Bishop Ntambo hired Tutsi contractors to rebuild the conference offices, and he identifies this preference for hiring Tutsi managers as a manifestation of the internalized racism/inferiority complex of Luba leaders. Walters writes: "On a macro level, however, this is a clue to the problem of poverty here. There is so little sense of

---

grecs qui étaient commerçants et alors mon père m'a dit cela, je ne sais pas, est ce que c'était vraie ou faux mais a mon avis que peut être la réponse de mon père était exacte . Par exemple au Malemba Nkulu, il y avait des blancs, les missionnaires pentecôtistes. A Malemba, y avait des prêtres catholiques. A y avait que des missionnaires Garenganzi–ils étaient les seules pour évangélisera et puis finalement avec la tendance des Swahili, on parlait des gens comme ça, on parlait toujours de ces blancs qui partaient partout qui aujourd'hui il est ici, demain il est là. Alors ce temps-là on a pensé a cela. C'est quelqu'un qui n'a pas un endroit fixe. C'est comme dans notre dialecte, on nous appelle : Baluba c'est un terme qui signifie un perdu, il ne connait la d'où il vient, il ne connait pas là ou il va, c'est de la que part je sens du terme Mzungo et puis aujourd'hui e la veut dire celui qui a une couleur différente de la nôtre."

50. Walters, *Last Missionary*, 86–87.

51. This view was created by colonials, who chose to offer more educational and promotion opportunities to Tutsis due to them tending to have slightly more European physical features.

self-worth and self-confidence that it is always assumed that an outsider (Tutsi or American) is better, smarter."[52]

5.3.1.3 MZUNGU AS EMOTIONALLY CHARGE WORD

While the word *Mzungu* has gone from meaning any aimless wanderer to the label given to pale skinned persons, it is more than just a synonym for other words that convey skin color or ancestry. *Mzungu* is an emotionally charged word. I stumbled upon a deeper understanding of the emotions connected to this word while conducting research interviews. I initially framed the interview questions using the semantics of "North Katangan" and "American" relations and collaborations. In one of the early interviews, I noticed that the respondent's remarks shifted from flat diplomatic answers to emotionally electric and bold statements after the word *Mzungu* was mentioned and explored. I decided from then on to deliberately ask each respondent about the meaning and significance of *Mzungu* mid-way through the interview. As I hypothesized, there was a noticeable increase in passion and candidness in nearly all the Congolese respondents, but this was not true for the Americans interviewed.

5.3.1.4 RESPONSES FROM NORTH KATANGANS ON THE MEANING OF THE WORD MZUNGU

Every North Katangan I asked about the term *Mzungu* gave responses that echoed the sentiments of the others. Since the colonial period, the *Mzungu* was perceived as having superior intelligence, resources, and competencies. Befriending a *Mzungu* was seen as a path out of poverty—a way to access resources and protection. Yet, at the same time, as former American missionaries have shared, *Bazungu* were distrusted and accused of being exploiters and spies. Below are a few samples of the North Katangan responses from the recorded interviews.

> In the 1960s we thought that *Mzungu* was intelligent, was higher than us, because the education system was not good in Africa. We saw that *Mzungu* was able to do everything . . . and we could not do anything.[53] —*Floribert Mwamba Kora (ordained elder)*
>
> A *Mzungu* is an all-knowing person, having everything. The one who is not *Mzungu* has nothing, knowing nothing. The *Mzungu* will come and equip and give everything to make the Black now

---

52. Walters, *Last Missionary*, 87.
53. Floribert Mwamba Kora, interview with the author, July 14, 2015.

> a person. This was the image of any *Mzungu* that came to Africa. Who created that? Maybe the *Mzungu* him or herself gave that impression to the Black, especially with the colonization. [It was] as if Black was an animal, and we [the colonizers] are going to help you with everything. What you were doing was wrong, your culture, your behavior, your religion and everything was just nothing; let us then create a new person. This was somebody who would be created by the *Mzungu*.
>
> That image has created all the problems. Because the *Mzungu* is coming with everything for the person. . . . Receiving everything, they were also asked to remove everything that they had, so that they started depending completely on the *Mzungu* and working for the Mzungu according to the instruction from the *Mzungu*.[54] —*Nday Bondo (ordained elder and lecturer at Africa University)*
>
> People from my area here thought that *Mzungu* is a very important person in my life. If a *Mzungu* is with me, it is not just for a simple friendship, talking, sharing experiences. A *Mzungu* is there to change my environment . . . like a messiah to change my entire life. So from my observation, people were thinking that if *Mzungu* is there, he is ready do everything for me; I'm unable to do anything; it is only that *Mzungu* who can respond to all my needs.[55] —*Gertrude Mukalay Mwadi (ordained elder and lecturer at Africa University)*

5.3.1.5 Changing Views Among North Katangans

The general consensus among the North Katangans I interviewed[56] is that there has been a change in recent years in how North Katangans view themselves in relation to *Bazungu*. While *Bazungu* are still generally viewed as having access to resources unavailable to those in the rural areas, there is a growing view—which was promoted by Bishop Ntambo in his speeches at annual conferences[57]—that North Katangans are capable of

---

54. Nday Bondo, interview with the author, July 14, 2015.

55. Gertrude Mukalay Mwadi, interview with the author, July 14, 2015.

56. When attempting to draw conclusions from these interviews, it must be kept in mind that all of my interviewees have an above-average level of formal education relative to the local population.

57. Since 2005, I have attended at least four annual conference sessions led by Bishop Ntambo. In all of them, he promoted the message of the capability of North Katangans to accomplish things themselves—be it obtaining MAs and doctorates, launching and managing church programs and construction projects, or raising funds among themselves so as to not be merely "beggars" or "squatters" in abandoned colonial era properties.

the same accomplishments as *Bazungu* (especially in terms of educational levels and project/business management), and that *Bazungu* should be viewed as peers, not superiors.

> Today they are saying no, it is not only *Mzungu* who can respond to all my needs, I can also do something from what I have as a source of money.[58] —Gertrude Mukalay Mwadi
>
> Now things are already changing, you see that *Mzungu* is a partner, is a human being like everybody and with weaknesses and strengths. *Mzungu* is limited even in the way he or she can assist other people. *Mzungu* is just there to help you to understand what you should do, not to replace what you should do. *Mzungu* is there to assist you because it is there, and it is established that yes, we are somehow down, we need somebody who can come and help us to go up. That is the role that *Mzungu* came to teach us because we did not have that church. He came to bring us that church and should teach us what we should do to continue with our church, not the *Mzungu* church, but our church as people who have received that church. So the image also impacted too much on the way we see things in the church and in the way we now we are struggling up to now to understand that we can— how we can—have a good partnership with the *Mzungu*. So the *Mzungu* is not bad, it is good, but the image that the *Mzungu* came with, destroyed a lot of things. . . . I can say that a lot of things have changed.[59] —Nday Bondo
>
> But from this time, people are able to do things on their own without even the presence of *Mzungu*. Because what we know, we could have a responsible for what we want to do and then see where we are going and are coming from. And then see what was difficult on that period and then what is able to be done this time because we are now trying to learn. We have computers as *Mzungu* is doing computers. We need to do research as *Mzungu* is doing. But that part of inferiority thinking we are less than *Mzungu*, that is the dangerous we are looking into our churches because here we have everything with us, but we do not work properly with our things. We need somebody else from outside to come and work on our place. That is the big problem. And maybe when we are getting something, we need to work for other things what we have for other things and then when somebody who is coming to look that things which is selling money for that thing which was not found, and then we are doing other

58. Gertrude Mukalay Mwadi, interview with the author, July 14, 2015.
59. Nday Bondo, interview with the author, July 14, 2015.

> things. That is the major issue. If people can understand their responsibilities, they can take their responsibilities on time. I believe that conflict between the *Bazungu* and the Africans will be less than resolved this issue.[60] —*Floribert Mwamba Kora*

That said, internalized racism remains at all levels of leadership. Just after Christmas 2017, second-generation UM missionary John Enright was killed in a traffic accident near his home in northern Zambia. At his funeral (which was streamed on Facebook), the mayor of Luanshya, Nathan Chanda, gave a eulogy. In it, he recounted a comment Enright had made to him: "When a *Mzungu* has a pie, and there is two or more, they will think about making more pies. But with an African person, they will think about how to eliminate the other person to get the lion's share.' This is the life that we are celebrating today."[61] I was initially unclear how to interpret Chanda's remark. Was his intent to praise or criticize? I asked a few of my North Katangan colleagues who had also watched the funeral, and they replied that Enright had made an accurate observation about African behavior, and that the mayor was a praising his ability to observe and teach. They did not view Enright's comment as offensive but as a challenge to change.

The potential impact of the pie story on the community is not insignificant. As Bishop Katembo (retired, South Congo Episcopal Area) asserted at the funeral, "Three-quarters of the pastors we have in Congo[62] were trained by John Enright."[63] Longtime UM missionary Ken Vance, who worked alongside Enright for many years, noted that Enright had used the pie comment "on many occasions to challenge pastors and leaders to move in a way of love and servanthood," and that Robert Kilembo (clergy and director of the Kafakumba training center, which Enright helped build and lead) had told Vance that Enright had "told him the story over and over to get the point across until [Kilembo] "finally 'understood' the message and the point."[64]

No one I asked about the pie comment expressed to me objections to using it as a teaching illustration. I, however, find it problematic on multiple levels. Any time one states "*Bazungu*" think like this, but "Africans" think like that, one is broad-brushing over the large diversity of thought that exists within these categories. It is factually untrue that all *Bazungu* (let alone all or

60. Floribert Mwamba Kora, interview with the author, July 14, 2015.

61. "Funeral for John Enright," 1:19:00.

62. I believe it was understood that he was referring to United Methodist pastors in the Katanga region, not all pastors in all the country.

63. "Funeral for John Enright," 34:00.

64. Ken Vance, correspondence with the author, September 3, 2018.

Racism, Violence, and Exploitation   165

even the majority of Americans) see resources as unlimited and the metaphorical pie as always expanding. The current political climate in the USA and much of Europe, with the resurgence of angry assertions that immigrants are taking jobs and benefits is a clear example that many *Bazungu* see "the pie" as a scarce resource to guard and not share. By framing the teaching as African behavior versus *Mzungu* behavior (instead of, for example, those who see scarcity versus those who see abundance), (neo)colonial assumptions of intellectual and moral superiority are reinforced, and the implication is that for a Black African to become a better person s/he must act less "African" and more "White."[65] One healthier way to address the behavior of fighting over pies would be to engage in conversations about the psychological impact of the experience of scarcity (e.g., childhood memories of fighting siblings for a desired item, chronic hunger, inability to purchase needed things, etc.)—how it shapes the mind to perceive everything as zero-sum game. The alternative behavior could be framed in theological terms such as abundance and radical acts of love. Acknowledging that even in places like America these struggles can be seen helps to open honest healthy conversations about human problems that break out of the (neo)colonial dichotomies of "good behavior = Mzungu" and "bad/primitive behavior = African." In this way, attitudes and behaviors can be transformed without the unnecessary shame and inner conflict created by the narrative of rejecting African culture for White wisdom.

5.3.1.6 Perceptions of White American UMs

When interviewing Americans, I found a larger range of responses. Those who had spent years working in North Katanga could articulate many of the complexities of what it means to be labeled a *Mzungu*. Those partners from general agencies of The UMC and those who had never been to DR Congo or had only come for brief visits had a limited to non-existent understanding of the views expressed in my interviews with North Katangans, although some sensed that there was more going on than they understood. Below are a few excerpts from the responses:

> [*Mzungu*] felt like a very derogatory term when I was in the Congo. This was last year when I was there and called *Mzungu* as I was traveling in east Congo. I was in a car and the windows were down and there was a young Congolese man who was walking on the sidewalk. He saw me and pointed at me and said

---

65. While outside the scope of this thesis, much more has and could be said on the impact of (neo)colonial teachings which depict bad behaviors as being African and good behaviors as belonging to White culture.

"*Mzungu!*"—just yelled it. Other people said it who didn't know me, so it felt derogatory. But then Bishop Ntambo said it in teasing about the Ebola video that we were able to create and he said "Oh, this is *Mzungu* magic," and he had a broad smile on his face. And I thought maybe, ok, maybe this is White privilege magic. We are able to get something done that may seem out of reach for those living in the Congo.[66] —*Neelley Hicks (ordained deacon serving full-time at United Methodist Communications)*

It is so much like the word "Methodist," that is a word of derision. . . . I refer to myself as *Mzungu*, and they all laugh. I think the tones that go with it from what I've identified is that "these are people from outside," "these are people who have weak stomachs, people who have to be cared for, people who have access to resources, but on the other hand we have to take care of in our culture, people who have to be respected, people who are clueless." There is some Poisonwood Bible stuff going on there. On the other hand, in my experience in the Christian community . . . these are people who we want to engage with, and we will relate to them and we'll check them out . . . and as you ask the right questions and as you win some trust, then Congolese are willing to be very open. So even though you are *Mzungu*, I don't experience it as a word of derision. . . . It means I'm an outsider, a visible minority. . . . Now if it is somebody outside the Methodist community, they may be saying that with deep hostility and criticism, but I don't experience that in relationship with the Christian community.[67] —*Pamela Couture (ordained elder and professor who has researched peacebuilding in Katanga)*

[*Mzungu*] is a word that is coming out of the east coast. The tribes that use the "z," like the Nyanga, Shona, and Swahili, pronounce it "*Mzungu*," and the Bembas and other tribes that do not have the "z" in their vocabulary pronounce it "*Musungu*." And what we were able to do, the Mzungu, was to put into that word incredible energy and connotations. We loaded the word. So, the adjective *Kizungu* means anything that is well done, attractive, properly done, good, etc. The other side of *Mzungu* in the word Muntu. Muntu is a person, but not White person, because a White person is not genetically a human being. They are not really people. They are *Bazungu*. Often I would

---

66. Neelley Hicks, interview with the author, January 11, 2016.
67. Pamela Couture, interview with the author, January 8, 2016.

> be introduced as a *Mzungu* who was actually a muntu. . . . The White people played this game where they tore down, insulted, belittled, ridiculed, and then, in their education system, made sure that everyone who got an education bought into that.
>
> I think of the use of creams for the lightening of skin. You have all of these Black people putting on these extremely toxic creams so that their skin looks attractive. We have all of these beauty aids that allow for your hair to be straight and your skin to be white and the fact that it destroys your liver and kills you eventually—turns your skin cancerous—this is not here nor there. The White people manage to sell a product and the Black people have been brainwashed to think that Black skin is unattractive. So, that would be the baggage I would see connected to the word *Mzungu*.
>
> We loaded the dice, we stacked the deck; we took a neutral word and plugged meaning into it. . . . So, if I were to say to you *nyumba ya kimuntu*, that would be a poor person's mud hut. If I said *nyumba ya kizungu* [a *Mzungu* house] even if a Black person built it, to compliment them, you would say *unajenga kizungu*. So, we really—the White people—did a tremendous disservice. The word is not the problem, but the word is an indicator to a much deeper problem.[68] —*John Enright*

5.4 GRIEF, GUILT, SHAME, AND EMPATHY

While not adequately explored in this thesis, the dynamics of guilt, shame, and grief on mission partnerships is a topic worthy of further research. This section identifies starting points for that discussion.

Much has been said on the topic of "White Guilt" as a motivator. In my personal wrestling with my own feelings of profound guilt, I had a breakthrough when I realized that much of my guilt itself was racist. That is, when one feels guilty about something that did (or did not) happen, there is within this guilt an assumption that one had the power to change the outcome and failed to do so. For me—and I assert for many others as well—guilt can be a way of feeling bad about the suffering of others without relinquishing the narrative of having superior capacities to them (i.e., White Savior). When one accepts the limitedness of one's powers (i.e., acts committed by family or peers, people/communities one could not release from their poverty, etc.), what is left is grief—and grief comes from a place

---

68. John Enright, interview with the author, January 6, 2016.

of vulnerability—a place White American society strives desperately to avoid and rapidly overcome.[69]

While each person's grief is unique, and each grief journey is different, there is a universal aspect to the experience of loss, mourning, and vulnerability. As will be revisited in chapter 7, grieving together can create a path to healing together, which in turn creates a powerful foundation for a healthy partnership.

Transforming false guilt (i.e., guilt which assumes power one does not have) into a recognition of grief can be complicated by another emotion: shame. While guilt and shame are often seen and synonyms, they are two distinct emotions. Guilt contains an assumption of control, whereas shame comes from a deep place of vulnerability. Shame is a form of grief about who one is that lacks a sense of hope that redemption is possible. As researcher Brené Brown explains: "Shame is a focus on self, guilt is a focus on behavior. Shame is, 'I am bad.' Guilt is, 'I did something bad.' How many of you, if you did something that was hurtful to me, would be willing to say, 'I'm sorry. I made a mistake?' How many of you would be willing to say that? Guilt: I'm sorry. I made a mistake. Shame: I'm sorry. I am a mistake."[70] As Brown goes on to explain in her 2012 TED talk, interviews, and audio books, shame is a much more toxic emotion. Guilt can function as a motivator for self-improvement (i.e., I regret that I did something that does not match who I am deep-down; I'll make amends and do better next time). Shame, in contrast, creates a downward spiral (i.e., I screwed up because I'm a screw-up). Shame is born in the belief that one is in some way inadequate—inferior—unacceptable. Shame grows in environments of secrecy, fear and alienation. It is petrified of public opinion (i.e., What would the neighbors think?) and is "highly correlated with addiction, depression, violence, aggression, bullying, suicide, [and] eating disorders."[71]

Both guilt and shame negatively impact the ways in which Americans (more specifically, White Americans) approach mission. Guilt can perpetuate neocolonial/racist/classist *mission as outreach*/savior complexes. Shame about one's privilege leads to inaction and further isolation. As explained by public theologian Christena Cleveland, "So often, privileged people, when invited to participate in the work of justice and equity, end up being paralyzed by defensive shame and a lack of purpose."[72] This combination of

---

69. See also theologian Barbara Brown Taylor's book on how American churches tend to have "solar" theologies—such that they are unable to respond to the spiritual needs of those who are grieving. Brown Taylor, *Learning to Walk in the Dark*.

70. Brown, "Listening to Shame."

71. Brown, "Listening to Shame."

72. Cleveland, "How to Be Last."

shame and disorientation (that is, loss of role/identity) also occurs in the minds of socially privileged people when they are challenged to see marginalized people as leaders in the work. As explained Cleveland's piece:

> The most effective justice and equity work in history has been led by the marginalized. . . . Justice and equity work should be led by the marginalized—by those who have firsthand knowledge of the unjust systems that are in need of dismantling. If the marginalized lead, then the role that privileged people play is a supportive one. However, when privileged people are invited to play a supportive role in justice and equity work, they often feel disoriented, marginalized and role-less. Since they're not "leading," they don't know what to do. Since they don't have a "leadership" role, they don't believe they have a valuable role to play. This disorientation and lack of clarity is further confounded by the shame that privileged people often experience when they realize that it is precisely their "leadership" that has led to the current inequities.[73]

I assert that this shame-filled disorientation that Cleveland describes in the context of racial and gender equity work in the USA also occurs when American Christians wrestle with what decolonizing mission partnerships requires of them—that is, to let go of their self-understanding as the heroes/leaders in relationship. While my interviews did not explore this psycho-affective experiences of American partners attempting to let go of their leadership roles, I believe this topic to be an important one for future interviews.

Both guilt and shame must be overcome to build authentic boundary-crossing partnerships, and North Katangans also wrestle with such psychological issues, especially shame. Brown explains in her 2012 audiobook that when men feel shame for in some way falling short of the dominant concepts of manhood (e.g., acquiring a wife, protecting and providing for their family, etc.), they tend to either shut down (depression, avoidance) or become filled with rage and aggressive behaviors, such as violence.[74] Applying Brown's findings on the psychology of shame, it is predictable that shame would be a common problem in a region where most men are unable to provide sufficient economic support and/or physical protection for their households. While women tend to not manifest shame with rage responses, female feelings of inadequacy often result in social avoidance, depression, and/or actions of cruelty/sabotage to anyone who she has power over or who she views as a threat to her carefully crafted public

---

73. Cleveland, "How to Be Last."
74. Brown, *Men, Women, and Worthiness*.

persona. I have witnessed numerous examples of this phenomenon in both The UMC in the USA and Katanga.

Inferiority complexes (i.e., internalized racism) coupled with poverty, lack of access to schools, and a deep fear of losing face greatly add to the challenge of removing the elements of shame and colonization from mission partnerships—especially when Americans are unaware that these issues are at play. While my interviews for this study did not include direct questions about how shame, guilt, and grief impact partnerships, Walters wrote about shame and mission relationships in Katanga.

Bob Walters, who personally struggled with shame issues, quickly recognized honor and shame as twin motivators for the people and communities he spent time with in North Katanga. He notes that "honor and shame are the primary motivators" in a patronage system[75] and that while the fear of being publicly shamed could be leveraged to persuade someone into action, it could also produce paralysis in a person or community. One example Walters gave of the fear of public shame at play in the partnership is how both Americans and North Katangans crack jokes about meetings and services in North Katanga operating on "Africa Time" (i.e., starting later than officially scheduled). Walters did not believe the excuses given that Africans are more laid back about time; it contradicted his observations. What he saw were not people who did not care about punctuality, but an infrastructure so broken that their efforts were constantly undermined (e.g., transportation problems, long wait times, overwhelmed with responsibilities, exhaustion/sickness, etc.). Thus, he concluded that "Africa Time is a cover for the awkwardness that exists when we Americans try to help Africans. It is an attempt to regain dignity lost, to reframe the embarrassment of need into a cultural explanation, to regain some sense of control."[76] I believe that while joking about "Africa Time" may be a coping strategy to save face (i.e., avoid public shame),[77] it is a highly problematic joke. For example, when a Congolese colleague jokes with me about Africa Time,[78] I see this as an indicator that s/he is trying to save face with me and thus does not (yet) view me as an empathetic friend. With those who do trust me, I am told instead about the series of unfortunate/frustrating events that led to schedules being thrown off or simply "Sorry. It's been one of those days."

75. Walters, *Last Missionary*, viii.

76. Walters, *Last Missionary*, 118.

77. Bishop Ntambo has often said to visiting American partners "You Americans keep time, but we Africans make time" when facing the awkwardness of being behind schedule.

78. Outside of the context of cynical humor about their personal exasperation at how long something is taking. Note also that face-saving excuses and jokes are common in both the USA and Katanga. Even I admit to sometimes blaming traffic for my tardiness when the real reason was, for example, poor planning.

Thus, I believe that for the mission partnership to move beyond our fear of losing face (i.e., shame) in front of each other, we must create a relationship built on empathetic responses, and we need to drop the tired old jokes. This is not to say we should completely stop joking; shared laughter is cathartic and removes shame about frustrating and/or embarrassing situations. In a decolonized partnership, we will joke together better.

As will be returned to in chapter 7, shame's most effective antidote is empathy and connection; when secrecy is replaced with honest, empathetic[79] conversation, shame dissipates. Just as guilt can be transformed into grief that can then be openly mourned, I believe that shame, through the power of affirming community, can be transformed into a named grief/injustice that the community address together.

5.5 IMPLICATIONS

This primary goal of this chapter was to shine a spotlight on what I have identified as the biggest elephant in the room: the fact that neither Americans nor Congolese as a society have effectively faced their inner demons surrounding violence and racialized imbalances of power and perceived value[80] and that this lack of self-awareness and healing impacts the way they view themselves and others, including the unexamined assumptions they make when engaging in missional initiatives together. These assumptions and responses to them permeate our societies so fully and deeply that, once we begin to see them, we realize, as I have begun to, that nearly everything we do is polluted by them. Hence, it was essential that this chapter come before the discussion of the other themes in the interview transcripts, for I am convinced that all of the responses have been impacted by the traumas addressed here.

In the next chapter, I have organized responses to the questions I posed in the recorded interviews into themes based both on the types of answers given and the analytical concepts discussed in this and previous chapters. Large excerpts of interview transcriptions are included in attempts to avoid comments being taken out of context of the conversation. The interview responses are arising from the history and traumas discussed in chapters 3, 4, and especially 5, and thus should be interpreted through those lenses.

---

79. There is a powerful difference between empathetic and sympathetic responses. Expressing sympathy (e.g., "You poor thing") can increase a person's feelings of inadequacy, whereas expressing empathy (e.g., "Gosh, I hate when that happens," "Me too," etc.) makes a person feel not alone.

80. The same can be said of gender-based violence and oppression, but that important topic was mostly omitted from this thesis due to the lack of time and space to do it justice.

6

Reflections on the Relationship

THE PRIMARY GOAL OF this thesis is to achieve a deeper understanding of the dynamics at play in the mission collaborations between North Katangan and American United Methodists so this knowledge can inform attempts to become a truly decolonized partnership. Previous chapters have focused on the state of academic conversations on these topics as well as the historical events and interactions that have led to the current relationship dynamics. This chapter focuses on the responses of those I interviewed and is intended to be read through the lens of the conversations in previous chapters.

Most of interview transcript excerpts included in this and the following chapter are longer than what it typically found in a research report. This is a deliberate choice that comes from the practice of deep listening, a discipline essential to healthy partnerships (see 2.1.4). While I believe I understand what each participant is trying to say, I recognize that there is nuance I may have missed, and I believe that by using short soundbites I also risk putting my words into their mouths. Thus, I have tried within reason to include statements as they occurred as complete thoughts. Doing so also creates the possibility that others may notice things which I did not and can incorporate the richness of these transcripts into their own research and writings.

While I have not made a quantitative analysis of these transcripts my research priority, there were some response patterns that were noteworthy despite the relatively small sample size. All but one interviewee said they saw the collaboration between North Katangans and Americans as a good thing that should be continued.[1] Most North Katangans interviewed strongly sup-

---

1. Among the North Katangans, there was one outlier responder (who did not want to be identified by name) who expressed support of American United Methodists

ported the end of the *de facto* missionary moratorium and the return of fulltime American missionaries to the region, while the Americans tended to be ambivalent about this idea. Nearly all of the North Katangans and many of the Americans articulated areas where misunderstandings and/or frustrations continue to exist.[2]

When people have differing understandings of their duties and place within a relationship, tensions inevitably arise. The interviews I conducted brought to light a number of these differences as well as the dynamics/issues interviewees identified as key in their retelling of the partnership history. This chapter is structured to highlight and discuss the most frequent and most poignant responses I heard in the nearly twenty-four hours of transcribed interviews of twenty-five individuals, seventeen of which are North Katangans (fourteen of those seventeen are/were ordained elders). Respondents were given the choice of speaking in French or English. Remarks that were made in French have been translated by me. Occasionally, remarks made by North Katangans (both in English and French) required minor editing by me to make their intended meaning clear to readers who are not accustomed to how French and English tends to be spoken in Katanga. Four persons requested that all or parts of their responses be included anonymously. Hence, the citation of "anonymous" includes transcriptions and notes from multiple interviews. I also acknowledge that there is an unfortunate gender imbalance, with only five women included in the interview excerpts. This is due to two main factors: (1) the vast majority of persons in formal leadership positions in North Katanga are male, and (2) in both North Katanga and the USA, I found it much harder to find women willing to be recorded for the interviews compared to men. Some women would initially agree but then say they did not have time even when offered the option of answering a written questionnaire instead; others did not want to talk about the subject.[3] Even three of those five who were recorded expressed in the interview doubts that they had anything insightful to say on the subject. My hope is for there to be future research which focuses on the female experiences and perspectives, and my friend and colleague Lana

---

pulling out of North Katanga and asserted that the USA was on the verge of economic collapse due to its support of homosexuality. Interestingly, this person also acknowledged personally receiving large sums of financial support from American UMs.

2. The interview contained specific questions about points of misunderstanding and critiques of both Americans and North Katangans.

3. The subtext I heard for some was that they did not want to revisit and/or speak publicly about the anger or "guilty knowledge" they held about what they had experienced or observed.

Robyne is already in the beginning stages of a doctoral research proposal involving interviewing female church leaders in the Katanga region.

6.1 CONFLICTING EXPECTATIONS

When American United Methodists arrive in North Katanga using the language of being "partners in mission," they are (both as my observations over the years and interview responses indicate) often unaware of the social contracts they are seen by many North Katangans as having implicitly signed. They may think that they are coming as helpers, teachers, allies, or simply curious visitors who will report their experiences to friends back home, but that does not mean that is what is expected of them by those who are receiving them and showing them generous hospitality. There is an economic chasm between them and nearly all North Katanga church leaders which they cannot change, and there is an implicit expectation that they will, like a traditional patron and/or foreign missionary, acquire and distribute material and financial resources to the projects and individuals they favor.

In addition, as previously touched upon, a pale skinned foreign Methodist cannot opt out of being a *Mzungu*;[4] she or he cannot navigate relationships with North Katangans without the assumptions about *Bazungu* coming into play—especially those expectations based on past experiences about *Bazungu* who come specifically to work with the Church. No matter how they see themselves, failing to learn or ignoring the common beliefs and emotions pertaining to missionaries and *Bazungu* does not help decolonize the relationship; it merely sets her or him up for being blindsided by conflict. I say this both as a scholar and as one who once naively held this misconception and suffered the consequences of it. There are barriers to achieving the type of partnership that most American UM volunteers envision. While some of these expectation-based barriers are beginning to diminish (especially among North Katangan church leaders who have lived outside of Congo), they have far from disappeared.

---

4. Anecdotal observations and reports suggest that dark-skinned American United Methodists are not held to the exact same expectations as pale-skinned ones, but the arrival of a dark-skinned American United Methodist in North Katanga has been too rare in the past for me to be able to make any firm assertions about this. Recently, there has been an increase in the number of African-American UMs visiting North Katanga as well as the arrival of a foreign missionary from Zimbabwe. It is too early to make any conclusions about these new relationship dynamics beyond those based purely on anecdotal evidence. In a similar vein, I have noticed that obese Americans who visit North Katanga tend to be assumed by North Katangans (in particular, those who have limited exposure to Western media and culture) to be wealthier than thin ones.

6.1.1 Patronage and Partnership

Based on the responses to interviews, it appears that most Americans currently involved in partnerships with North Katanga do not understand how the patronage system functions within the North Katanga Conference or the implicit social contract they sign (to serve as patron) when they accept gifts from groups and communities there. As discussed in this section, being a good patron is a complex task, and distributing wealth is a major piece of that job.

Bob Walters, who was the first to teach me about patronage and how it functions in Katanga, expressed deep frustration in his interview about the lack of understanding American missionaries have had of patronage and the problems this ignorance has created.

> I was just amazed that missionaries had not even been taught the concepts of something so biblical. If you are going to be a Christian missionary, it is unthinkable not to understand how patronage works. Look at the social-economic setting of first-century Galilee; it is an almost perfect overlay of present-day North Katanga. And to not understand how that works is strategically tragic, but it is also theologically tragic in that here is a case where there is a particular brokenness—a system that is not working—our biblical story is shaped in that same broken system. And the connections are not made.
>
> What you have are Americans coming as missionaries out of a twentieth-century evangelical mission model, arriving to serve in a community that is structured in the same way as first-century Galilee—how they are so ill-prepared and why expectations are not met—not even understanding the simplest elements of a patronage system where honor and shame are the primary motivators and confusing honesty for honor and not getting clear on the differences there. Just fully not understanding what is happening in the community and then trying to push the community into a model that doesn't fit. . . .
>
> On the Congolese side, it is kind of the reverse there. As I watch leadership develop, I do get frustrated—frustrated is too mild of a word—I get frustrated watching the emerging Congolese church leadership buy into American ministry models that don't fit—which wouldn't be so bad if it weren't for the fact that the models that do fit are already there and indigenous—so you don't see enough of the claiming of understandings that the community already has.[5] —*Bob Walters*

---

5. Bob Walters, interview with the author, January 11, 2016.

While perspectives do appear to be changing among North Katanga church leaders, the view of the foreign missionary as bringer of knowledge, money, and resources still persists—especially in areas where economic opportunities are scarce. When an American and/or *Mzungu* offers friendship and/or training but not money or material objects, tensions occur. As one who attempted to live in Kamina on extremely limited financial resources, it was a painful realization that, since I was not publicly distributing money or material resources, many assumed that the few North Katangans who had become my friends and regular companions had acquired wealth from me and were selfishly not sharing. They suffered retaliation and social ostracization because of this. I myself became unpopular because I was perceived as refusing to help people and programs who asked me to be their patroness. Below are excerpts of North Katangans reflecting on this expectation.

> A *Mzungu* is seen as someone with means, who comes to help us. A Congolese thinks that a *Mzungu* always has money—which isn't always the case, but it is our conception. If a *Mzungu* does not help them, they are disappointed. That is the problem. People, seeing a *Mzungu* who doesn't give out money, are unhappy. But, these *Bazungu* are working for the church that has sent them and the church doesn't give enough to accomplish what they should do.[6] —*Mpiana Disudiapasu (retired elder and former conference treasurer)*
>
> You know, it's really a problem because in North Katanga when we see a *Mzungu*, it is like we have the solution to all our problems. . . . But if you don't receive the help you thought you are supposed to have then you create hate, sabotage, and whatever. So, the *Mzungu* in North Katanga was seen as somebody who comes to solve the problem and practically all we see is money. . . . [Yet] money doesn't solve the problem. What solves the problem first is the mind. But when you come that area where we think that is the mind but they think that is the money it gets really complicated sometimes to understand. Because I know that the Americans, in all that they do, they see the sustainability . . . and they create strategies which is really the human resources themselves. They work on . . . money comes after the

---

6. Mpiana Disudiampasu, interview with the author, July 2015. Original: "C'est quelqu'un qui a beaucoup de moyens, qui viennent ici pour nous aider. Un congolais pense qu'un Mzungo a toujours de l'argent mais ce n'est toujours le cas, qui est riche, non, mais ici, c'est notre conception. Si un Mzungu les ne les aident pas ils sont déçus. Et c'est ça le problème. Les gens, voyant un Mzungu, qui ne donne pas de l'argent, ils sont mécontents, mais ces Mzungu sont aux services de l'Église qui les a envoyés el l'Église ne donnent assez de moyen pour accomplir tous ce qu'ils devaient faire."

other stuff. But here, we would appreciate to start with money and then go to the other stuff. So, then, these create a conflict which is based on this difference of culture. And sometimes what the missionaries bring as solution, after they go, it is also hidden; nobody works on that. And what everyone waits on is money, and when there is money, we don't even remember the principles, the basis of all that we learned and how to use that. ... When we see a *Mzungu*, we see money, we see goods, we see all we need. Yet this is not what the *Mzungu* wants. The *Mzungu* wants to work on the human resources, on changing the mind, because if the mind is in a right way, we can start even by very small things that can really prosper and go ahead.[7] —*Shabana Banza (young adult and son of UMC pastor. Has acted as translator for Friendly Planet Missiology tours. Employed as bank teller while volunteering as lay preacher.)*

Bob Walters also spoke in his interview about how foreign missionaries have tended to misunderstand their place in the patronage system in North Katanga. His thoughts on this were best articulated in his memoir:

> There was a time when missionaries were common in the remote districts of the Democratic Republic of the Congo. They were the rescuers in an otherwise oppressive economic system. Their help kept the villagers surviving and gave them hope that someday, their struggle would reach a prosperous end. Missionaries were the link to the outside world. They had real money. They provided jobs. Oh, and yes, they preached the love of God as demonstrated in Jesus Christ to a hungry people in an inhospitable land.
>
> Missionaries were the referees of the constant wrestling for position in a world that is both postcolonial and neocolonial. They buffered the jealousies that fed the village gossip. And for a young person who wanted more out of life, a relationship with the missionary was the way out of the village.
>
> Brave and compassionate, they came to save souls and make life better. They came into a system they could not control and did not understand, a system that could not deliver what it promised. Just as unaware of their function as the people they came to serve, missionaries were the priests of a patronage system that rescued the community from its poverty and, at the

---

7. Horace Shabana Banza, interview with the author, July 11, 2015.

> same time, ensured that the community would never become self-sufficient.
>
> Here's the thing: The missionaries, then and now, think that they are proclaiming a simple and straightforward Gospel message aimed at converting the hearts of natives to Jesus Christ, fully unaware that those to whom they are preaching live in a world more like the world of Jesus than the missionary can ever know. The ones being preached to bring the missionary into their world to play the role of the patron in an economic system that they intuitively understand better than the one preaching. Unwittingly, the missionary reinforces the very problem that the Gospel is meant to remedy.[8]

By making a foreigner the community's patron, the local economy that develops around this patron/client relationship collapses when the foreign patron departs. As will be discussed later in this section, Walters asserts that the Gospel of Jesus Christ frees humans from patronage relationships with each other, and that by playing the role of patron the missionaries were undermining the development of mature disciples.

This expectation that an American United Methodist's job is to bring money and gifts can be better understood by exploring the social obligations in a patronage system, a topic which was touched upon in chapter 3. The practice of presenting gifts to powerful people with the expectation of receiving a difficult-to-obtain resource in return continues to this day in North Katanga and many other parts of the world. Foreign visitors and missionaries, however, do not always understand the unspoken rules in regards to these gifts. As E. Randolph Richards and Brandon J. O'Brien explain, Westerners tend to not understand the way patron/client relationships work and thus are blind to the ways in which they appear. In attempting to explain this in a way their readers can grasp, the authors use the example of the famous American mafia film *The Godfather*. The Godfather—that is, patron—solves his clients' problems with the expectation of reciprocation through "loyalty, public praise, readiness to help the patron (as much as he could), and, most importantly, gratitude."[9] A patron provides protection and connections, but with these come the unspoken understanding that the client will immediately do whatever their patron asks of them—no matter the hardship it brings.

Richards and O'Brien lament that modern Westerners frequently use forensic language when defining patronage: "We describe the relationship

---

8. Walters, *Last Missionary*, 1.
9. Richards and O'Brien, *Misreading Scripture*, 83.

between a patron and a client as contractual, like a business, rather than as familial."[10] Instead, the authors assert, central to this practice of exchanging favors and gifts was the establishing and strengthening of relational ties. They cite Apostle Paul's letter to the Philippians as an example of Paul wrestling with the strings attached to accepting gifts in a patronage society: "To refuse the gift (and thus the offer of friendship) was rude," but "if he accepted the gift [from a congregation and/or church leader], Paul would become the client."[11] Paul's desire to assert himself as self-employed was about having some level of freedom from social obligations which clients and patrons do not have. From Paul's letters, we can infer that it was a difficult struggle for him.

Reflecting upon my own experiences living in North Katanga and consciously resisting becoming a patron (both for naïve missiological reasons and the fact that I had limited resources to give), the choice was not fully mine to make. My failure to play the part implicitly assigned to me by the community—to reciprocate gifts with the amount of money/materials expected from a patron and to refrain from dictating how gifts are used (for example, in my appointment as Community Development Department Director, I asked direct questions about how projects were managed and resources were distributed)—was met with a period of shunning/exile. When Bishop Ntambo finally permitted my return, he proceeded to publicly scold me in front of all the annual conference delegates for not having raised funds for the orphanage since my departure. The reasons I had not sought these funds were my disillusionment with the program and the bishop's refusal to answer my calls and emails. In the eyes of the bishop, however, this was irrelevant. I had returned to North Katanga bringing neither a tribute to publicly honor him nor a large gift to the conference, as were his expectations for me as a foreign "partner."

Albert Memmi touches upon this question of choice over roles within a system when he describes the concept of "the colonial" as a myth: in a colonial system, one is forced into the role of colonizer and/or colonized: neutrality is not an option.[12] Likewise, Walters saw himself as forced in the patron role when he was in North Katanga. He wrote, "One of the comical dynamics of the patronage system is that the patron works for the client."[13] Walters found that he was not in charge of his life: the community told him

---

10. Richards and O'Brien, *Misreading Scripture*, 162.
11. Richards and O'Brien, *Misreading Scripture*, 164–65.
12. Memmi, *Colonizer and the Colonized*, 10.
13. Walters, *Last Missionary*, 49.

what events he had to attend, what speeches he had to hear, and what items/money he was expected to acquire for them.

Although he pointed out the problems with the patronage system, Walters was also quick to note that missionaries and foreign donors are incorrect in labeling requests from those seeking a patron-client relationship as a sign of being stuck in a dependency cycle: "Patronage and dependency are not the same thing. Clients in a patronage system are not lazy. They work hard. But their work is directed toward the patron, not their own progress."[14] He also praised those who leverage the system for the good of the community. He gave the example of the Grand Chief of Sampwe, whom he met in 1998: "Nobody did patronage better than this chief did. He worked his patron, the governor, for what the community needed, and played the patron in the community, passing out resources and his constituents to work on projects. His project now was building a school. I watched as he played the Methodists against the Catholics in an honor/shame game to motivate us to build his dream school. Our [United Methodist] district superintendent was equally skilled in the honor/shame game and got a commitment of forty thousand bricks from the chief. Well played."[15] As Walters's example suggests, patronage can be healthy when its participants leverage it for the redistribution of resources to those who most need them.

A missiologist trained in practical theology, Walters's reflections on patronage in North Katanga have gone through the steps of a praxis cycle. He drew a connection between the patronage system that was at play in the Gospels and the issues faced by Katangans. Walters asserted that the addressing of the issues of the patronage system was central to the teachings of Jesus: "When you sit inside a patronage system, all the kingdom of God sayings make sense."[16] Walters described Jesus' answer to patronage as twofold: (1) "If you are going to have a patron, get a good patron, and God is the only good patron. This is what the *Our Father* . . . is about,"[17] and (2) "You don't need a patron. 'The kingdom of God is within you.' . . . Walk away from the system."[18] Walters went on to share that when he began preaching sermons in North Katanga on the anti-patron theme of "Everything you need, God has already provided," he felt callous saying such things to desperately poor people, yet the feedback he received from the local community leaders hearing these sermons was overwhelmingly positive.

14. Walters, *Last Missionary*, 51.
15. Walters, *Last Missionary*, 52.
16. Walters, *Last Missionary*, 122.
17. Walters, *Last Missionary*, 122.
18. Walters, *Last Missionary*, 122.

On repeated occasions, Walters recounted in conversations that not all Katangan community leaders have related to him as a patron who was expected to bring everything from abroad. Occasionally, he would encounter community leadership that would scold those who presented Walters with a shopping list of requests—especially requests for secondhand items. Instead, they sought to identify what resources could be locally procured/created (for example, choir robes) in order to break the pattern of being the clients of foreign patrons as well as to claim their own community's capacity to create valued objects.

In North Katanga, the system of paying tributes to and receiving gifts from patrons appears to have grafted itself onto the polity of The UMC, with its district superintendents, bishops, and apportionment[19] system. While in the USA conference apportionment formulas are rarely changed (and thus predictable), in North Katanga it has been common in recent years for the bishop or a conference-level committee to announce a new project or event and then inform each district and church affiliated institution (including schools and clinics) how much they are expected to contribute. The distinctions between apportionments, mandatory contributions, and tributes become fuzzy. As president of an organization[20] which is loosely related to the North Katanga Conference, on numerous occasions I have been told (not asked) that our NGO must give a specified amount of money or use of our equipment (e.g., our truck for hauling rocks to a construction site) for projects (e.g., building a cathedral), events (e.g., annual conference, ceremony for the new bishop), and gifts (e.g., retirement gift for the outgoing bishop). Although it is common for districts and institutions to fail to contribute their assigned amount, failure to do so brings public reprimand and the risk of the leaders of these districts and institutions being removed from their jobs. In contrast to The UMC's system in the USA, in North Katanga there is the expectation that the bishop and superintendents will play the role of patron, acquiring resources and distributing them back to the communities they oversee. At each annual conference gathering, there are numerous speeches and formal public presentations to mark who has given what to whom that year, and each official

---

19. In The UMC, "apportionments" are the funds each congregation is expected to send to its conference office to be used to cover conference, regional, and denominational-level programs and positions. Each conference decides the formula used to determine what congregations should contribute. For more, see "How are Local Church Apportionments Figured?"

20. Namely, Friendly Planet Missiology, which has legal status as an independent NGO in DR Congo.

report given begins with a lengthy expression of gratitude, explicitly naming those individuals and groups that provided support.

6.1.1.2 Post-Patronage Relationship

As previously discussed, beliefs and expectations about Western missionaries and *Bazungu* are shifting, and gaining access to wealth locally does appear to hasten this shift to no longer looking at these foreigners primarily as patrons. My anecdotal observations echo comments I heard from North Katangans who have recently spent extended periods of time in the large city of Lubumbashi (South Congo Conference) that the comparatively wealthy South Congo Conference does not look to foreign contributions to solve problems in the way that North Katanga does:

> As North Katangans, we have said that we cannot let go of our American friends. They are always our partners. If we have projects, we send them over there to ask for assistance. But in South Congo, they did not really have to ask for money from over there. They will work little by little until they can solve their problems themselves. But I also know that they did not completely break their relationship; there is still funding coming from the United States. . . . But for us, it's clear. If we send anybody to make the fundraising for even for the university education, for example, for the North Katanga, they say, yes, we remain in partnership with America.[21] —*John Maloba (ordained elder and conference treasurer)*
>
> So, when I come for example in the South Conference [Lubumbashi], here, I don't understand yet, but they don't even talk about the Mzungu very much. . . . When I was in the north I saw the Mzungu everywhere. They would go here, there, in this parish and so on, but since I am here I don't see that regularly, the Mzungu. So I don't understand. I am limited to really

---

21. Mulume wa Umba John Maloba, interview with the author, July 12, 2015. Original: "Nous le Nord Katangan, nous avons dit que, on ne peut pas relâche nous amis, les américains. Ils sont toujours nos partenaires. Si nous avons des projets, nous envoyons là-bas pour demander l'assistance. Mais au Sud Congo, c'est fait que, eux n'ont pas vraiment encore de demander l'argent là-bas. Ils vont travailler petit à petit jusqu'à ce que, ils puisent résoudre leurs problèmes eux-mêmes. Mais ce que je connais aussi ils n'ont pas rompu [?] aussi. Il y a toujours le financement qui vienne des États Unis. Mais, nous, pour nous c'est clair. Si nous envoyons quelqu'un faire le fundraising pour même pour l'enseignement, universitaire, pour, pour exemple, quel que soit un autre projet, pour le Nord Katanga, ils dissent, oui, pour le Nord Katanga nous restons dans le partenariat avec les américains."

> comparing the north to the south.... I mean, what I think in the south is people are to some extent spiritually mature. To sometimes really be by themselves. I see some churches that are being built here just by their members. So, economically this can be also understood because in the south you have so many people with a job, even in the church. But when you come in the north, there are not so many jobs, and the members, most of them are farmers, and others of them are teachers, and their income is not really good to support things like this.[22] —Shabana Banza

My personal observations over the years of the differences between how Bishop Ntambo and Bishop Katembo (recently retired bishop of South Congo) interact with Americans also support the suggestion that South Congo is closer to being post-patronage (at least when it comes to American missionaries/volunteers) than North Katanga. While Bishop Ntambo was known for his charisma and lavish hospitality to American partners (e.g., taking teams out to expensive dinners in Lubumbashi, organizing grand farewell parties with expensive gifts—even to those who just visited a few days—having uniformed choirs greet their plane, etc.) and skill at persuading these partners to fund projects, Bishop Katembo was known to generally keep his distance from American missionaries and visiting teams, rarely making time in his schedule to speak with them. Even after I finally earned his respect, he never asked anything from me but simply expressed appreciation for the way he had observed me interact with Congolese Methodists.

While these differences may be partially attributed to different personalities, I believe they are also two different responses to the post-colonial context—two responses to the question of whether to continue to accept *Bazungu* as patrons. That said, I do not believe they are the only possible responses. Bishop Ntambo's successor, the recently-elected Bishop Mande, is also a charismatic man who actively engages in relationship-building and fundraising among Americans. However, there is a distinct difference in the nature of his friendships with Americans, and I believe this difference has much to do with the fact that Bishop Mande has for the past several years worked and raised his family in cosmopolitan cities in the USA, where he was rapidly advancing in supervisory roles at GBGM. His awareness of the nuances of American cultural expectations and colloquialisms allows him to create a level of rapport with American partners that has been inaccessible to Katangan bishops before him. The full impact of this difference on efforts to decolonize partnership is yet to be seen, but it does raise complex

22. Horace Shabana, Banza, interview with the author, July 11, 2015.

questions about relationship dynamics and whether different social systems can effectively co-exist when there is a bridge person who acts like a voltage transformer between them (e.g., Could the collaborations between Bishop Mande and his American friends be considered a decolonized mission partnership whilst the expectations of much of the membership of the North Katanga Conference remained that of the colonial patronage system?). In his first year as bishop, I have already seen a subtle yet significant difference in the way he frames his conversations with colleagues who he hopes will assist him in raising funds for initiatives in his episcopal area. I would label these new relationships as attempts at collaborating with peers in contrast to attracting new patrons or feeding savior complexes by downplaying the agency of North Katangan leaders in those conversations.[23]

The year before his election to the episcopacy, Mande offered his analysis of the changes he has observed in how North Katangans perceive American *Bazungu*:

> We have stories of some missionaries which were born in the country—some of them adopted the language of the people as their own. I'll give an example: missionaries like the Persons: David, Laurie and their parents or John [Enright] and the parents. These individuals became so much acquainted with the culture that at some point they could be seen as coming from one tribe. John, for instance, speaks better Kiluba than I do. He speaks Runda better than many Lunda people. So that interaction started in a way of breaking the cycle of this *Mzungu* who represented oppression and privilege and power. It became more of somebody with whom we could partner.
>
> And if I now come to 2000. In the 1990s—your dad and yourself—some of you devoted to leave your own families and come and live with the people. And gave the opportunity to folks to realize that if Bob is coming to Africa, if Taylor is coming to Africa, it doesn't mean that they have the money. They don't have the money, but they are coming because they love the people; they feel as one of them.
>
> And again, especially when our brothers and sisters from North Katanga also have an opportunity to come to the US and

---

23. In full disclosure, not long after Bishop Mande's election, he appointed me as his Executive Assistant for Strategic Partnership and Engagement. Thus, he and I have discussed my research on decolonizing mission partnerships, and I am playing an active role in the shaping of the narratives now being used when inviting anglophone conferences and organizations to participate in initiatives in North Katanga and other conferences in his episcopal area.

> witness some of the living conditions of American friends and realize that some of them were not rich as people had thought. They were just coming to serve and be with the people. So, how again, as I said, the word *Mzungu* evolved I think today because of the incarnational aspect, because of the relationship that folks had built. The word *Mzungu* has been transformed to a friend—not somebody who has resources. One of the highlights of North Katanga was when you and George Howard spent significant time with the orphanage. It was tough to see the kids crying when you were leaving. This will be my suggestion that that concept has evolved. But, can we find a replacement [term]? I'm not sure. Maybe a replacement will be "brothers and sisters." Not necessarily *Mzungu* because *Mzungu* can be offensive. *Mzungu* can mean stranger. But I think that the word *Mzungu* has evolved. People are now able to call one another brothers and sisters.[24] —*Mande Muyombo*

As Mande asserts, the practice of a number of American missionaries and partners of doing their best to integrate themselves into North Katangan communities combined with the increased awareness of North Katangan leaders (thanks to new opportunities to travel to the USA) that these partners were not as financially wealthy as had been believed, has shifted perceptions and made possible a more level relational dynamic as siblings in Christ.

6.1.2 *Missionaries as Mercenaries*

Another noteworthy assertion on the subject of conflicting expectations came from my interview with John Enright, who arrived in Katanga in 1950 at six months of age and considered Swahili his first language. While he left North Katanga in the last major missionary evacuation in the late 1990s, he continued to be in full-time ministry with Congolese United Methodists at the center he built in northern Zambia (where he lived until his untimely death in 2017). When asked to discuss the changes he observed over past quarter-century of Methodism in North Katanga, he insisted that the relationship dynamics since the 1990s could not be understood without a deeper historical perspective—especially that of the role of mercenaries:

> Now where do the missionaries fit into this? Well long ago, from the earliest times the paramount chiefs brought in mercenaries. They brought in alien forces that helped them in times of need.

24. Mande Muyombo, interview with the author, January 2016.

> So in the Lunda wars of the late nineteenth century, [foreigners] were brought in from Angola and they had firearms. And they were used as mercenaries to fight against the rebel group—the Lunda group from Sandoa revolted . . . and the mercenaries were brought in. . . . So plugging into the ancient tradition, I'd say that the missionaries were simply the mercenaries. They were the alien forces who came in to help the chief and the tribe in a difficult situation.
>
> In 1990, unbeknownst to the missionaries who did not have a clue about this—I mean, why should they? There was no one to teach them—they were plugging into something that was already there and fit quite nicely into the whole structure. The problem was that in many instances the missionaries didn't understand their place, and their place was to support the chief and to support the status quo. And so the missionaries, I'd say very misguidedly, were coming with Western values, Western understandings, wishing to manipulate the system in a Western way, and this really is not appropriate. It was a mixed bag. They were doing some good things—this, that, and the other—but they are really supposed to be miracle workers. I mean, they are supposed to do astonishing things, and often they were not able to do that. So there was disappointment on the part of the African tradition "You guys aren't living up to your part!" Now it was hard because the White people didn't have a clue what their part was, and the Africans just couldn't work out why on earth these people don't understand what their role is.
>
> So that is how I would see it today where essentially the White missionaries are all gone in North Katanga. There are a few people paid by GBGM, which would be called technically missionaries, but they are from within the culture, so there wouldn't be that kind of tension and sort of misunderstanding. So I think that the role of the alien mercenary helper kind of had its field day and kind of wound down; and today they are virtually all gone. It is kind of how I see it.[25] —*John Enright*

Enright's analysis that American missionaries were expected to function like mercenaries—that is, foreigners who helped the chief maintain power—is a different analogy than missionaries as patrons. In both scenarios, the foreigners are expected to be sources of wealth and status, but I see the key distinction being that in the mercenary comparison the community does not view the foreign missionary as the head patron who

---

25. John Enright, interview with the author, January 6, 2016.

outranks the regional chief and/or bishop. Instead, the foreigner's primary role is to serve the chief by helping him retain the status quo in terms of balances of power. Enright's adamancy about the missionary as mercenary model is probably related to the fact that he witnessed and personally experienced many foreign missionaries becoming *PNGed* (*persona non grata*) for what could easily be interpreted as the offense of questioning the bishop's actions/decisions or those of members of the bishop's family. Once seen as noncompliant/disloyal, their presence was no longer welcomed by the bishop. My personal experience of Bishop Ntambo running hot and cold on me could also be explained through this lens. When I was compliant (that is, making the bishop look good), I was publicly embraced as his beloved daughter. When I expressed concerns or objections about the ways certain church programs were being managed (unbeknownst to me, the managers were often his close relatives), I was labeled a troublemaker and even prohibited from returning for a period of time. The ban was lifted once I was again perceived as someone who could bring desired relationships and prestige (e.g., my new husband's job involved interviewing visa applicants at the geographically nearest USA embassy to North Katanga) and had learned to ask fewer questions.

While the word mercenary contains strong negative associations (e.g., a hired thug/gun), the idea of the expected role of foreign missionaries being to help the bishop successfully implement his/her vision and to relate to the bishop as one who outranks them, is not inherently an unhealthy model. It is, in fact, a decent description of the stance I have chosen to take vis-à-vis my relationship with Bishop Mande. Such a relationship dynamic can function as a corrective measure to the not-so-distant (neo)colonial past when bishops had to beg their missionaries for financial assistance. Relational breakdowns in the past have occurred when American partners and/or foreign missionaries have, rightly or wrongly, openly challenged a bishop to take (or not take) certain actions based on their understanding of morality and/or justice.

6.1.3 *Americans as Political Enemies*

While it rarely was mentioned in the interviews, there have been tensions over the years between North Katangans (more so among non-Methodist North Katangans) and American missionaries because of decades of hostile policies of the Belgium and US governments, which made foreign missionaries viewed as potential enemy collaborators/informants.[26] As touched

---

26. This is not simply about the colonial period but also about the US government's support of Mobutu as well as decisions during the Clinton presidency concerning a

upon in chapter 4, some missionaries lost (or nearly lost) their lives due to such accusations. Bishop Ntambo spoke of this bad blood in his account of the North Katanga Conference's history:

> North Katanga has a bad history between White and Black because during the [time of] independence, the South—known as South Congo today—wanted to be out of Congo. It was a secession.... Belgium didn't want to give independence to Congo. They asked Katanga to be out [of Congo] so they [Belgium] can remain. The Baluba people of North Katanga they wanted Congo united. But this split of ideas between the south and the north brought a lot of hatred.... Many *Bazungu*—which means White people—have fear to go to north, even to do the work, but we received for the first time, it was John Enright who was there. And after John came Lowell Wertz, the Ken Vances, then Enright—the father himself—then Everett Woodcock as a pilot. So we now had a number of *Wazungu*.[27] —Nkulu Ntanda Ntambo

As conference evangelist Guy Nyembo Kinkundulu noted in his response to the question concerning the wisdom of imposing a missionary moratorium, a distinction needs to be made between the anger about actions of the American government and objections to American civilians living in North Katanga:

> Should the Americans be chased out? Yes and no.... People here confuse American politics and American civilians. American civilians like you are not the ones making American government decisions ... those are the politicians. But when we want to react, we take it out on innocent people. We think it's the Americans who are hurting us; it's the Americans who are bothering us. People think that these American [civilians] are CIA agents, but this is not the reality. These are the problems that killed missionaries like Eschtruth, Stan Ridgeway, and [Maoba?] ... They are people who have suffered.... You bring soldiers here.... They kill the missionaries and we lose because of the politics of the United States.... These are situations that we need to think a lot more about and continue to help our people. When the US government does bad things, it is not the fault of

response to Rwanda's invasion of Katanga in the late 1990s. Bishop Ntambo has expressed on numerous occasions his dislike of the Clinton administration; he thought it had much Congolese blood on its hands.

27. Nkulu Ntanda Ntambo, interview with the author, July 20, 2015.

> those here. It's like with Rwanda. When Rwanda was attacking the Congo, people did not want to see Rwandans—especially Tutsis: "It's them who kill us." Some come and kill everyone, the innocents just like [what happened to] certain Congolese in Rwanda who were killed. But those in power are in Kinshasa; those who make decisions are in Kigali. It is the regime and not the population, someone who sings in the church, somebody one who is preacher down there. . . . No, no. The same thing with the American presence in Africa.[28] —*Guy Nyembo Kinkundulu*

6.1.4 Americans as Educators

Many of the fulltime American UM missionaries in Katanga in the 1980s and 1990s focused on education, especially in the area of evangelism. While some of the things they taught appear to have been more (neo)colonial indoctrination (such as assigning Shakespeare's plays to an English class) than the transference of practical knowledge, a number of these missionary-teachers/trainers are remembered with appreciation for what they taught and how they financially supported training efforts, including addressing logistical barriers such as transportation. The loss of the

---

28. Guy Nyembo Kinkundulu, interview with the author, July 15, 2015. Original: "Les américains les chasser, oui et non, oui quand on se met du côté de ceux qui s'oppose contre le système ou encore on a pas besoin d'eux pas les gens du système qui est là lorsque les américains s'opposent surtout ceux qui parlent parce que la population chez nous confond américains et politique et américains et civile, américain civile comme vous là, les décisions américaines c'est pas vous là qui les prenaient, ce sont des politiciens mais quand on veut réagir, on réagit sur des innocents, parce que on pense que ce sont les américains qui nous font souffrir, ce sont les américains qui nous dérangent, les gens pensent que ces américains pour leurs pays ils sont des agents de la CIA, des soupçons, ce ne sont pas des réalités, çà a fait parfois des difficultés qui ont fait tuer même quelques des missionnaires comme—Eschtruth, Stan Ridgeway, . . . Maoba? ont décédés et on avait enterrer la bas, ce sont des gens qui ont souffert, ah bon, vous vous ramenez des militaires ici, on va vous avoir, ici ils viennent, ils abattent les missionnaires et nous nous perdons a cause de la politique des états unis et nous des missionnaires, ce sont des situations pareils que nous devons beaucoup plus réfléchir et continuer a aider notre population. Lorsque le gouvernement américain fait du mal. Ce ne sont ceux qui sont ici. C'est comme avec le Rwanda, quand le Rwanda agressait le Congo, les gens ne voulaient pas voir des rwandais, partout les Tutsies, c'est eux qui nous tuent, certains tous venant on les tous a tuer, innocent, comme certains congolais au Rwanda, on les a tuer, pendant que ceux qui sont au pouvoir sont a Kinshasa, ceux qui prennent des décisions sont a Kigali, c'est le régime et non la population, quelqu'un qui chante a l'église, quelqu'un qui est prédicateur la bas, on pense qu'il est venu pour . . . non, non, la meme chose avec la présence américaine en Afrique, on soupçonne sur certaines situations de paye, parfois ces gens au pouvoir ce payent leurs factures c'est ça."

financial support missionaries gave for education and evangelism work since their departure is especially lamented:

> If today the church has spread, [it was] at the time of Mr. John Enright who worked in evangelization with the Rev. Myombo and Rev. Kabila. At that time the church knew a big growth in North Katanga thanks to their work and their expertise. They gave their money; they opened accounts; they pushed that the church be planted here and there. You speak with evangelists. . . . We have no funds; we have no vehicle; we have to manage, run behind some people to tell them help us, give so many dollars to go evangelize, but we had our own means in the time of Mr. John Enright. . . . It is the vision of the missionaries who wanted the Church to be spread, as it is in response to the mission of Jesus in Matthew 28:19: "Go everywhere." . . . So this mission was to go everywhere—go tell the Good News. That's what he was aiming for, and then it was a positive vision, because it was necessary to announce the good news then, the missionaries, the Church have wanted the blooming, the expansion of the African man, his spiritual fulfillment.
>
> I saw Mr. Everett Woodcock [American missionary], when we were still in the JPC [church youth movement], Mr. Woodcock organized camp meetings. We went into the bush some 80km from Kamina; many people were in the vehicles, a large vehicle organized by Woodcock, to go to pray in the bush. . . . There were the Americans, the Swiss missionaries among others. Mr. Werner Eschler [Swiss missionary], he worked among the young people. He realized a great work, he pushed the young people to have spiritual life, nights of prayer, vigils of prayer, companions of evangelization with Mr. Eschler. The concern of the American Church was to see the Church flourish and also the spiritual, physical, spiritual and intellectual flourishing. Why? [Because] fulfillment is in the Bible; Jesus grew spiritually, morally and even in stature. That's what the American Church saw. The fulfillment of the Black man, intellectually offering him schools and also morally and in his practical life and in his family life.[29] —*Mbayo Mujinga (ordained elder and conference evangelist)*

29. Mbayo Mujinga, interview with the author, July 16, 2015. Original: "Si aujourd'hui l'église s'est propagée, a une époque nous avons connu une implantation de l'église, à l'époque ou Monsieur John Enright travaillait dans l'évangélisation avec le pasteur Mayombo et le pasteur Kabila. A ce moment l'église a connu une grande extension au Nord Katanga grâce à leurs implications, parce qu'il apporter de leur expertisation, c.-à-d. ils donnaient leurs l'argent, ils ouvraient des comptes, ils poussaient un peu que l'église soit implantée çà et là. Vous parlez avec des évangélistes, Nous sommes limites, nous n'avons pas un soutien, parce que imaginez-vous Madame si vous aviez un véhicule, ferions

Since the departure of fulltime American missionaries in North Katanga in the late 1990s, the vast majority of American UMs have come to North Katanga only for short (that is, less than two weeks and often less than one week) visits. In contrast to other regions of the world, North Katanga has not received mission teams coming to do manual labor, such as building or painting structures. This is in part due to the expense and logistical difficulty of sending work teams[30] and that there was neither the established expectation nor desire to ask potential patrons to do physical labor that North Katangans could do themselves. Instead, foreign visitors are usually invited to serve as guest preachers, and, if staying for sufficient time, to teach a seminar on a topic of their expertise. While the Americans interviewed who have led training events in North Katanga generally have a positive assessment of their contribution as educators during their visits, my interviews of North Katangans suggest that many times these workshops have been exercises in flattering the patron rather than fruitful educational endeavors. It may even be appropriate to suggest that we have reached the level of workshop fatigue—at least on certain topics. Two of the main critiques of these workshops is that they are given without the instructor having an adequate understanding of the context and that, since

---

tel espèce de travail, nous n'avons pas de fonds, nous n'avons de véhicule, nous devons nous débrouiller, courir derrière certaines personnes pour leurs dire aidez-nous, donnez autant de dollars pour aller évangéliser mais nous avions nos propres moyens comme à l'époque de Monsieur John Enright, on a implanter l'église a Mitwaba—un peu partout parce qu'il y avait la disponibilité de moyens c'est la vision, c'est la vision des missionnaires qui voulaient que le l'Église soit répandu, comme il est répondu à la mission de jésus, dans Mathieu chapitre 28, verset 19: Allez partout . . . Donc cette mission était d'aller partout, allez annoncer la bonne nouvelle, c'est ce qu'il visait et puis c'était une vision positive, parce qu'il fallait annoncer la bonne nouvelle ensuite, les missionnaires, l'Église ont voulu l'épanouissement, l'expansion de l'homme africain, son épanouissement spirituelle, moi j'ai vu Monsieur Everett Woodcock , quand nous étions encore enfant dans le groupe de GPC, Monsieur Everett Woodcock, organisait des compagnes on les appelaient les camp meeting, on allait en brousse a quelques 80km de Kamina, beaucoup de gens étaient dans les véhicules, un grand véhicule organisé par Woodcock, pour aller prier en brousse et là les gens étaient dans la retraite. Ils n'y avaient pas que les missionnaires, il y avait les américains, les missionnaires suisses entre autres Monsieur Verner Eschler, il a travaillé parmi les jeunes, il a réalisé une grande œuvre, il a poussé les jeunes à la vie spirituelle, des nuits de prières, des veillées de prières, de compagnes d'évangélisation avec Monsieur Verner Eschler. Le souci de l'Église américaine était de voir l'Église s'épanouir et aussi l'épanouissement spirituel, physique et spirituel et intellectuel, pourquoi?, l'épanouissement se trouve dans la Bible, jésus grandissait spirituellement, moralement et même dans la stature. C'est ça ce que l'Église américaine visai. L'épanouissement de l'homme noir, intellectuellement en lui offrant des écoles et aussi moralement et dans sa vie pratique et dans sa vie familiale."

30. Until recently, the only transportation option for reaching North Katanga deemed safe enough for Americans was a six to eight-seater aircraft that ran on Avgas, a fuel that is hard to acquire locally. A Cessna Caravan was purchased in 2013 with funds given by American partner conferences.

attending all these training events does not result in one earning a degree, they do not address the problem of North Katangan leaders who lack official professional qualifications from accredited schools.

> When the American missionaries come they don't really understand all the local thinking. So this is the mistake I see. The American missionaries first come and give this leadership [training] but without understanding the real problem. On the other hand, there is a problem of truth—something I want to really emphasize. There is a problem of truth in our mind; sometimes we do not reveal to the people that want to help us the truth of our communities, and this is a very bad virus. If they come but don't understand what is happening, there is no way that this management, this leadership [training], can go very far. What I see as the mistake in my community is that we should normally exhume all the local reality. Because it is like a very simple example; it is like a patient who wants to get healed but does not then tell all the symptoms to the physician. And on the other way, if the physician would provide the medicine without knowing the real problem, this will not solve anything, so I think this is the very big mistake because we should normally present to you the whole reality . . . : What kind of society are you meeting? What are the values of this society, and what is the negative of this society? [With this knowledge] then, that management [training] could really adapt to the local reality.[31] —*Shabana Banza*
>
> I'm not sure about workshop, workshop. Me, I want to push them [women] in the area of education. Because workshops, they are there. Workshops for women, for HIV and about that. . . . That money for doing workshops, you can just use this money [and instead] let us support [with a university scholarship] even one woman from, for example, one district this year, another year, like that, we can do that than just coming with many women, giving them workshops. The workshops are not bad, but what is coming from the workshop? People they just come together, after that they can go—Are they going to apply those teachings in their churches? We don't know. But if someone just learned and got a diploma from the university, [s]he can help the church and society.[32] —*Kisimba Suzanne (wife of pastor and Africa University graduate)*

---

31. Horace Shabana Banza, interview with the author, July 11, 2015.
32. Suzanne Kisimba, interview with the author, June 14, 2015.

In the interviews, North Katangans frequently noted university scholarships and the resulting increased number of North Katangans with advanced degrees as one of the most appreciated contributions of American partners in recent years. In the same breath, there was also a call for more emphasis on scholarship funds, fair and transparent selection processes for the distribution of scholarships, and a diversification of scholarships such that church leaders interested in topics other than theology could receive financial assistance.

> Why do Americans only want to train people to be a pastor? In any case, even pastors can be trained in other fields! When I was in the United States I found those who were a doctor of one field and also a doctor of theology. We too can take some pastors and train them [in other domains]. For example: a pastor who studies medicine, a pastor who is trained as an economist, a pastor who can be trained as an agronomist, a pastor who can be trained in international relations. So, that's what I request. The bursaries we give [right now] are [too] limited.[33] —*John Maloba*

In 2017, the newly elected Bishop Mande decided to strategically leverage the knowledge of American partners by instituting an annual pastors' school, which is a five-day series of free seminars and workshops occurring directly after the annual assembly of the North Katanga Conference that clergy, clergy spouses, and select lay leaders are encouraged to attend. A committee of North Katangan leaders decide the topics for each year, and the classes are taught by a mixture of North Katangan and Americans coming from the partner conference which financially sponsored the event. Each presenter holds professional expertise in the topic they teach. Time is budgeted into each talk for attendees to pose questions and engage in dialogue with the presenters. The impact of this new program awaits to be seen, but thus far there seems to be a general appreciation of it.

---

33. Mulume wa Umba John Maloba, interview with the author, July 12, 2015. Original: "Pourquoi les américains veulent seulement former les gens a être toujours pasteur? Au lieu, quelqu'un qui est pasteur, un peut le former aussi dans d'autre demains! Puis que j'étais aux États-Unis on peut trouver qu'il est docteur, a tel demain, il est docteur aussi à théologie. Alors, que'est-ce que prennent que, on ne peut pas aussi prennent quelques pasteurs, les forme pour exemple. Par exemple, un pasteur qui est former comme médicine. Un pasteur qui est former aussi comme un économiste. Un pasteur qui peut être former comme un agronome. Un pasteur qui peut être former en relations internationaux. Alors, c'est ce qui me demande. Les bourses qu'on donne sont limiter."

6.2 POWER, RESPECT, AND MONEY

In the early part of the formal interviews, respondents were asked to discuss the recent history of American–North Katanga mission collaborations. This was followed with a question about who had control over resources and decision-making authority in these activities. The majority consensus of those with knowledge of the relationship's history was that despite an official policy of mission priorities being established democratically via bishops, cabinets, and annual conference votes, there has been a direct correlation between who has the ability to raise funds and who ultimately has had decision-making authority. In the follow-up questions about critiques of those involved in these partnerships, the tensions in the interplay of authority, respect, and use of money were raised—especially by North Katangans. Issues concerning who is not treated with respect frequently came up in the responses:

> Congolese church leadership needed to be respected, and I didn't feel it was being respected. It was kind of like that "Oh when they are ready, we'll turn it over" and it was not happening fast enough in my opinion, although when I would ask about it, it did seem that the missionaries present thought that that transition had already happened. I could watch in things like the seating order in the airplane—who got seats, and who got the good seats and who were left behind. In practical applications, the missionaries still were the priority, and the church leaders came second. There was a ham radio network—there were, in fact, two ham radio networks. There was a network that was missionary only, and there was a network that was church leader network, and the church leaders were not allowed to operate on the missionary network.[34] —*Bob Walters*

North Katangans themselves also expressed frustrations over condescending comments and behaviors of American missionaries and pointed out that missionaries were being sent to Belgium—the very country that had colonized and was oppressing Congo—to receive their language and cultural orientation before arriving in Katanga:

> [In the post-war period] relationships [with missionaries] were bad; they never came back when the war was over, and there was a lot of criticism in North Katanga. . . . Not all the missionaries,

---

34. Bob Walters, interview with the author, January 11, 2016.

> I apologize, but some have a bad view of the Congolese, they say any [insult about] Congolese. Those who do not think that Congolese are men too, and that they must be respected.
>
> It was a minority [of the missionaries], and maybe it was really the one person [in particular]. Not only Methodist missionaries [had negative attitudes] but also others. According to my analysis, some have the spirit of colonialism—the Black or the Congolese are not on their level, cannot do good; they are always below. What expresses the superiority of one over the other; this Black cannot do anything without me. Some were there at the time of colonization, and then they came back, but they still had that mentality, that education they received. In the past, any missionaries coming to the Congo had to first go to Belgium to receive their orientation training.[35] —*Joseph Mulongo (ordained elder, District Superintendent, and Friendly Planet Missiology country director)*

Such tensions—dealing with the interplay of power, respect and money—are the focus of this section.

6.2.1 Power of Communication: Relationship Bridges and/or Gatekeepers

When raising the question of relationship dynamics, the point was made a number of times by respondents that, on the North Katanga side, the identity of who specifically is in the relationship has changed. Initially, North Katangan church leaders (and even then, not all) only had access to relationships with American missionaries serving in Katanga itself. The missionaries then communicated with Americans back in the USA for program support. While using American and European missionaries as conduits for communication and financial flows helped assure trust levels

---

35. Joseph Mulongo, interview with the author, July 18, 2015. Original: "Les relations étaient mauvaises, ils ne sont jamais rentrés, quand la guerre est terminée et y a eu beaucoup de critique au Nord Katanga . . . mais ce n'est pas tous les missionnaires, je m'excuse, mais certain ont un mauvais visage du congolais, ils disent n'importe quoi des congolais, et qui ne pensent pas que les congolais sont aussi des hommes et qu'ils faut respecter. C'est une minorité et peut être c'est l'ais d'une seule personne pas seulement des missionnaires méthodistes mais aussi d'autres, selon mon analyse, certains ont l'esprit du colonialisme, le noir ou le congolais n'a pas le niveau, ne peut pas faire de bon, il est toujours en dessous. Ce qui exprime la supériorité de l'un par rapport à l'autre, ce noir ne sait rien faire sans moi. Certain étaient là au temps de la colonisation et puis ils sont revenus mais ils avaient toujours cette mentalité, cette éducation qu'ils recevaient. Avant tout missionnaires avant de venir au Congo; devait passer en Belgique pour leurs fournir des renseignements."

amongst foreign donors and a steady stream of donations, North Katangan church leaders often felt frustrated with the lack of authority/control this gave them when it came to shaping the narratives, emphasizing fundraising priorities, and managing the resources received. As will be revisited in the next subsection, anecdotal stories of misbehaving missionaries (drunkenness, for example) along with the perception of lack of transparency in terms of funding streams and use of funds created an atmosphere of suspicion and resentment among some North Katangan church leaders towards certain missionary gatekeepers.

This was the situation all the way into the early 1990s when even Bishop Wakadilo himself had neither the English language skills nor access to technologies to facilitate communicating directly with the USA. This began to change when his clergy assistant, Ntambo Nkulu (later became Bishop Ntambo), who had served in anglophone parts of East Africa, began to travel to the USA and build friendships and donor relationships. After the evacuation of the missionaries in the late 1990s, Bishop Ntambo (and his missionary pilot son, Gaston Ntambo) became the primary communication bridges between North Katanga and the USA. As noted by a United Methodist leader,[36] the fact that Bishop Ntambo's son provided the only safe way in and out of North Katanga meant that, unlike nearly all other countries where American UMs go for mission collaborations, any foreigner who wanted to visit North Katanga had to request and acquire the bishop's permission.

The following is Bishop Ntambo's account of the transition from missionary-controlled to bishop-controlled partnerships:

> But that connection with *Wazungu*, through America, it was limited just to missionaries who were White. Missionaries as White people. Because the financial assistance to local churches here was a connection between individuals in America with the church here. Which means each missionary was supposed to raise funds to develop his own area or his own people. As a result, the development of the church in North Katanga was under missionaries. No Africans were able to go to raise funds because they had no connection. And it was there, strongly, and they did good work. The churches were built, they supported schools, they bought airplanes. The program of health, education, church growth—it was going so well.
>
> And here comes the time when the war came and all the missionaries had to flee because of the war. At the time they left, the African church, which had no White people, just collapsed. How will we build materially North Katanga? And

---

36. This interviewee requested her/his observation to be anonymous.

> Bishop Ngoy [Wakadilo] died. Now comes my own time. I got to be elected as a bishop and started on how we could build North Katanga. That connection started with your family—your father, and then yourself.[37] —*Nkulu Ntanda Ntambo*

Another account was given by George Howard, an American who has visited North Katanga many times and has firsthand knowledge of this transition:

> Bishop Wakadilo was the bishop in 1990, and his English capacity was—I don't know if it was non-existent, but I could only talk to him through a translator. So he did not build relationships with leaders in the USA. One of his assistants was Ntambo Nkulu Ntanda, and Ntambo was proficient in English and would come to the USA to develop relationships with churches and leaders. Particularly he was seeking support for a program of bicycles, Bibles and hoes to help village leaders to get transportation—that each one would have a Bible and a hoe so they could have their own garden and move towards self-sufficiency.
>
> There were also some American missionaries serving in North Katanga, and they would not only serve there as pilots—primarily—they would also come back to USA to raise funds and occasionally convince someone to come to North Katanga, but it was difficult and did not happen very often. It was difficult to get into North Katanga because of the size of the airplane—it would only hold 4/5 max.
>
> From the beginning at that point, North Katanga began sending key leaders to Africa University for training in health education and theology. They developed English language skills so they could study. They became ambassadors for North Katanga as they worked closely with UMs across the US. In 1990, at the request of Bishop Wakadilo, I developed a relationship with Gaston Ntambo—brought him to the United States, helped him get a degree in accounting and then in aviation, so he became the first Congolese pilot serving in North Katanga. He went on to get training in mechanics as well. So, it was the developing of indigenous leadership that spoke English that was able to build stronger relationships with churches in the US. Ntambo became bishop in the 1990s and then his work in

---

37. Nkulu Ntanda Ntambo, interview with the author, July 20, 2015.

> building relationships intensified.³⁸ —*George Howard (laity on staff at Global Ministries)*

Another interviewee selected for her/his position in the denomination and multi-cultural vantage point offered the following comments based on observations over the past fifteen-plus years:

> The problem is that the relationship as far as I know has always been through the bishop. The bishop is the key connector—the key entry point. He owns the relationship. He coordinates the relationship. There is no way in or out by bypassing the bishop. . . . All these years he has been bishop is a good example of that kind of relationship. Our structure within The UMC allows for this extremely independent role of the bishop in the African context. And North Katanga has been a good example of this—for the good and the bad because it does not allow other relationships to really grow and to let others have access to relationships in a more democratized way which would also bring critical voices to the table. The other reality for North Katanga is that it is so far—you cannot easily fly there if you do not have the son flying you. You can control anybody because how would people go there. So that is what I see as the characteristic of North Katanga and the USA.
>
> And then you have bishops here like Bishop Ough [of the West Ohio Conference]. West Ohio has been a key partner for many years because it can use Bishop Ntambo almost anywhere to be an amazing speaker. So it an easy relationship because you do not control and coordinate too many side conversations because you have a bishop who is kind of a speaker . . . and everything else is control by his office. It is very different from when you go to Guatemala or Honduras or Haiti where everybody travels all the time. Nobody controls anything.³⁹ —*Anonymous*

Control over communications did not begin to change until the advent of affordable cell phones, internet connections, and the first graduating classes of North Katangan clergy from Africa University in Zimbabwe (all happened around 2005). The dramatic increase in the number of North Katangans who have studied English and have been to the USA as General Conference delegates, the spread of smartphones and social media

38. George Howard, interview with the author, January 8, 2016.
39. This interviewee requested her/his observation to be anonymous.

accounts as well as the decision at the 2004 General Conference to encourage denominational agencies beyond GBGM to collaborate with Central Conferences have been a game changer in terms of who from North Katanga and the USA can build relationships. Today, all a North Katangan needs is access to a smartphone (which are now readily available for sale in towns) and a cell tower signal to be able to speak or write directly with countless potential friends or mission partners domestically or in other countries. As of my last count,[40] I have just under one hundred and fifty friends from North Katanga as my friends on Facebook in addition to the significant number of close North Katanga friends who call and message me regularly via Whatsapp. Compare this to the 1990s and early 2000s when North Katangans would have to rely on foreign missionaries and visiting Americans to carry, stamp, and mail hand-written letters to overseas contacts. The arrival of affordable smartphones has destabilized all partnership models involving communication gatekeepers.

> Before . . . there was interaction between America and North Katanga, but it was limited. It was as if only bishops and their office could create that partnership with the USA. So, when I went to Africa University, that's when I now noticed it is possible to get in touch with America through the internet, through all those agencies. That's when I noticed that even a local church can get in partnership with America. Even an Annual Conference, a district. Some individuals can get in touch with America—but not only America. . . .
>
> We interacted more with Switzerland because we had a missionary who was from Switzerland. We worked in the 1990s with that missionary for a long time until he went back. And then, we remained in touch with Europe through that missionary. (I was the youth leader and he was the missionary for youth.) Then, when he left, he essentially left me running what he was doing. So this one maintained our relationship with Europe through Switzerland. But during the time that I ran the youth movement, (we also started around 1995 or so) we started receiving some grants that were sent to youth all over the world. We received some grants from the USA, the global church, and we started being connected to America even before 2000—we started through the fact that I was a youth leader at the Annual Conference level. I was using the grant to lead the youth.[41] —*Nday Bondo*

40. July 25, 2018.
41. Nday Bondo, interview with the author, July 14, 2015.

This emerging democratization of relationships has its advantages and disadvantages. More direct relationships can at times mean less pressure on the bishop to single-handedly manage and tend to every single American donor/fundraiser. For better and for worse, it also means it is no longer possible for the bishop or bishop's assistant to control what messages are being sent to Americans and vice-versa, opening the door for sabotage efforts by rivals via "poison pens" as well as access to information about opportunities that previously would have been distributed to handpicked individuals. Only time will reveal the full ripple effects of this revolution in communications technology.

6.2.2 *Money and Agency: Who Controls and Who Decides*

Over the years, the answers to the questions of who controls communication flows and who has decision-making authority over spending on initiatives in North Katanga have been highly correlated. Bluntly speaking, the dynamics have followed the old cynics' golden rule: the one who has the gold makes the rules. While officially the transfer of decision-making authority (related to the selection of funding priorities and management of programs) from foreign missionary to local church structures occurred long before the missionary exodus of the 1990s, the reality as it has been reported to me was complicated and often conflict-generating—especially due to differing financial priorities and suspicions on both sides of potential misappropriation of funds. What follows in this subsection are excerpts of interview reflections on the dynamics of money and power when it came to North Katangan and American collaborations:

> In North Katanga there were projects that belonged to missionaries; they were doing various projects in different locations. But there were also projects that concerned pastors and lay people in their work of evangelization, and I benefited in those years from them. . . . On his arrival the bishop [Ntambo] urged people to farm and have farms. . . . A big project of North Katanga was bicycle distribution. I was in the Tanganyika Conference where I met for the first time Pastor Bob [Walters] in Manono; he distributed bicycles throughout the whole conference and all the region of North Katanga, and this project was very beneficial for pastors for the whole community. There was the distribution of Bibles, and materials for agriculture. It had affected all of northern Katanga, all pastors and lay people.
>
> Currently what we are seeing is different from the projects of the missionaries. The missionary with his project, he did it

> and everyone observed it in his work. Those projects did not require the consent of the people. It was only the missionary's choice, but people did not always think the project was useful. They [the missionaries] were themselves responsible and set up and managed their own projects. It was not the projects of the population, but that of the missionaries. When the missionary left, everything stopped. And each project was named after the missionary who was in charge of it. Since they left, their projects were left behind.[42] —*Joseph Mulongo*

John Enright echoed the tension Rev. Mulongo pointed to, but from the missionary point of view.

> The power structure was always ambivalent because the missionary would have their Advance Special, their project. That project would then get funded, then the missionaries would have around them a bevy of supporters—African colleagues and so on—who got their income from that project. And the project generally did well until the missionary left and the funding stopped and it went away.
>
> On the other hand, all power resided with the bishop. The Methodist structure presupposes a Western-democratic approach to life. So, when you impose the Western structure on the

---

42. Joseph Mulongo, interview with the author, July 18, 2015. Original: "D'abord au Nord Katanga y avait des projets de missionnaires ; qui faisaient différents projets dans différents milieux. Mais il y a un projet qui concernait les pasteurs et les laïcs dans leurs travail d'évangélisation et moi j'en ai bénéficié dans ces années-là. Les pasteurs faisaient de longues distances à vélos. A certain moment notre pays était en crise économique. A son arrivée l'évêque a exhorté les gens à cultiver et avoir des fermes, ce qui n'était pas facile d'avoir de l'eau ou roue et une machette. Un grand projet au nord Katanga était la distribution de vélo.

J'étais dans la conférence de Tanganyika ou j'ai rencontré pour la première fois le pasteur Bob à Manono, il avait distribué des vélos à travers toute la conférence et toute la région du nord Katanga et ce projet était très bénéfique pour les pasteurs pour toute la communauté. Il y avait la distribution des Bibles, et matériels pour l'agriculture. Cela avait touché tout le Nord Katanga, tous les pasteurs et les laïcs. Actuellement ce que nous sommes entrain de voir ; c'était différent avec les projets des missionnaires. Le missionnaire avec son projet, il le réalise et tout le monde l'observe dans son travail. Le projet peut être agrée avec le consentement des gens ou soit. C'est seulement dans le consentement mais les gens ne savent pas toujours de son utilité ou pas. Ils étaient eux même les responsables et montaient et gérer eux même leurs projets. C'était les projets de la population mais celle des missionnaires. Quand il part, tout s'arrête. Et chaque projet est nommé suivant le missionnaire qui était en charge. Depuis qu'il est parti son projet est resté."

> chieftainship/king system, the democracy side doesn't play very well, so the bishop was all powerful and remains all powerful. However, the missionaries were significantly powerful because of their role as the court mercenaries, the sort of foreign injection... gave them a special status. Plus, they had money. Now, it wasn't a lot of money in absolute terms, but in the context of North Katanga where people were earning a few dollars a month, a missionary salary—my wife and I would have earned about four thousand US dollars per month, which was princely. Our entire workforce of fifty/sixty people I paid entirely out of my own salary. So, we had this very high income. And, then we raised a substantial amount of money. I was involved in the aviation program, the construction program, the river boats, the building of Nyembo conference center, and all of these brought in significant amounts of money. The agricultural missionaries had their ag budgets. Tom Crowe had his clinic and ag budget. There was always tension around that because designation of Advance Special meant the church could not touch the money, but the church is sitting saying, gee, we feel the church would be better served doing this; the missionary is saying "don't touch my project money; I raised it; this is what it is supposed to be used for. You told me to do this project; that's what I'm doing" So, there was always tension there.
>
> 1994, Bishop Wakadilo attempted to take 10 percent of all Advance specials for the function of the bishop as an administrative fee, and the New York board forbade that. New York wanted the aviation programs to be united; the bishops did not want that. They wanted each conference to have their own aviation program, and each program would be directly under the bishop and answerable to the bishop.
>
> So these are the tensions, but by the mid 1990s, the role of the missionaries was diminishing. By the late 1990s, they were gone, and the only North Katanga missionary that went back was Tom and Sharon Crowe. They went back for a couple of years and then they retired.[43] —*John Enright*

Bob Walters, who first began traveling to North Katanga in the early 1990s and briefly lived there as an official GBGM missionary from 1997 to 1998, synthesized the power dynamic this way:

> Well the Americans had all the agency because they had access to the resources. The missionaries struggled to raise money for their projects but they did have access to local congregations

---

43. John Enright, interview with the author, January 6, 2016.

> back in the US that supported their projects and supported their salaries. Missionaries certainly were an economic engine wherever they were planted. The poverty was so desperate—is so desperate—that anyone bringing in that kind of money for jobs and projects—my observations was that, from the Congolese side, every project was seen as a salary mill—some place where you could get an income—and the missionary was going to be the source of the salary. The bishop was the only person in the conference who was paid a salary from an outside source. So, pretty much, any of the Congolese church leaders would look to the missionaries for a salary. Now that began to change in the 1990s with some programs initiated by the general church through GBGM and the Council of Bishops, so there did become a few salaries that were supported either through GBGM or another program. . . . There were some jobs that had a salary. It was a small salary compared to an American salary, but it was a large salary compared to the nothing that others were getting. But, early on, the missionary was the source of any financial support and that certainly defined the relationship. So even if on the organizational chart the missionary worked for a particular person, they were still the source of the income.[44] —Bob Walters

The fact that foreign missionaries were often seen as the only possible source of program funding or a decent salaried job meant, as previously discussed in the section on the meaning of *Mzungu* in chapter 5, that there was (and, I believe, still is) fierce competition to gain and retain favored status with an American or European missionary/partner. After listing the many things he appreciates about what American partners have done to help North Katanga, conference evangelist Mbayo Mujinga offers the following critique about the tendency for favoritism over the conference leadership priorities when it came to project funding, as well as a history of suspicions of financial misconduct:

> Some churches were built where there were the friends of the missionaries . . . [in places where] we do not really need a beautiful church.
>
> And then there are critiques of the Congolese church concerning the budget and the accounts—some missionaries received them; some used them really with the spirit of God. But the others, when we were children, we heard that when a missionary receives an account, he uses it a little and [keeps the

---

44. Bob Walters, interview with the author, January 11, 2016.

> rest for himself]; that's what I heard. So, some pastors, when the missionaries would give them money, a lot of them did not use it as instructed.⁴⁵ —*Mbayo Mujinga*

As the control of funding relationships shifted from missionary to bishop, so did control over fundraising priorities and use of money raised:

> Twenty-five years ago, the missionaries held the power, and the missionaries decided what the priorities were. As the Congolese leadership developed and developed their English capacity, the shift began to happen. They used to ask me when I would come over back in the 1990s, "What do you want to fund?" I would say, "That's not the right question; the question is, what are you doing that we can accompany you with?" And it took time. Eventually they started saying, "These are the projects we are working on, in what ways can you work with us?" And so, the ownership of the projects became more local vs. US-driven. Instead of the money driving it, it was the local priority driving it. And with that came the power to decide what was important. I never would have raised money for an airplane, but because that became their priority—in 2010ish—I shifted my priorities to match theirs and we raised 2.2 million US dollars for a refurbished Cessna Caravan. And that is an example of their taking control of the agenda. They decided they needed a university in Kabongo. Again, that would not have been my priority, but it was theirs, so we worked together on it. So, they are naming the projects, they are controlling the power.⁴⁶ —*George Howard*

Mpiana Disudiampasu (one of the oldest living pastors of North Katanga) was appointed as conference treasurer from 1954 to 1976 and 1981 to 1989. After returning from a management studies program in the UK, he was hired by GBGM to serve in the general treasurer's office⁴⁷ of the re-

---

45. Mbayo Mujinga, interview with the author, July 16, 2015. Original: "Certaines églises étaient construites là où il y avait les amis des missionnaires. . . . On n'a pas besoin de voir tellement une belle église à tel endroit. . . . Il y a eu des critiques: l'église du Congo, concernant le budget et les comptes, certains missionnaires les recevaient, certains d'autres les utilisaient vraiment avec l'esprit de Dieu là où il fallait le faire. Mais les autres, quand nous étions enfants, nous avons entendus ça quand un missionnaire reçoit un compte, il l'utilise peu et d'autres il les rentre avec ça, c'est ce que j'avais entendu. Aussi certains pasteurs, quand les missionnaires lui donnent l'argent, beaucoup d'entre eux ne faisaient pas ce qu'on leur recommender."

46. George Howard, interview with the author, January 8, 2016.

47. Until the mid-2000s, GBGM maintained a foreign missionary in the general treasurer's office who worked with locally hired treasurers to, in theory, create a checks

gion from 1993 until his retirement in 2006. His job included, among other things, supervising construction projects in Kamina and managing payroll distributions. When asked about the dynamics of money and decision-making authority, he offered the following account:

> In principle, the decision to start a project was the responsibility of the [conference's] executive committee, which is generally headed by the bishop. Together they decide the wheres and whens of a project and estimate of the costs and funds necessary for it. Then [the proposal] is sent to the USA [via] GBGM, and those who accept it send money, which goes directly to the general treasury. The treasurer of the conference comes and gets this money.... At that time, it was Mr. John [Enright] who was in charge of the construction of the churches in most of the parishes in the districts. As for the parsonages in Kamina, I was director of construction and construction supervisors, but in the inner districts, it was John.... When we came to the executive committee meeting, we had a right to review the funds in the general treasury, and Mr. John was responsible for the funds earmarked for parish buildings....
>
> When the war came, most missionaries left for Zambia and others for the USA. I was already here at the general treasury with Mr. Tom Rider. When Bishop Ngoy [Wakadilo] died [in 1995], the United States no longer sent a lot of funds....
>
> When the war [that is, that early 1990s wave of violence] ended, Bishop Ntambo was elected in 1996. He saw the lack of funds and went to the USA. There he received a lot of assistance, so we could build primary and secondary schools. Before him the pastors did not have good parsonages.... At that time there were many construction projects.[48] —*Mpiana Disudiampasu*

and balances system.

48. Mpiana Disudiampasu, interview with the author, July 2015. Original: "En principes les décisions prises pour démarrer un projet, était la responsabilité du comité exécutif qui est souvent dirigé par l'évêque, ensemble et de suite décide du lieu et du moment de sa réalisation ainsi de l'estimation des couts et fonds nécessaires pour la concrétisation du projet, envoyé au usa—34:10—le GBGM, et ceux qui sont accepter, envoie l'argent qui est verser directement a la trésorerie générale et c'est au trésorier de la conférence de venir chercher cet argent pour financer ses projets aux endroits déterminer... en ce moment là, c'était Mr John qui était chargé de la construction de l'église, la plupart des paroisses dans les districts. Quand aux projets des maisons pour les pasteurs a Kamina, j'étais directeur de construction et superviseurs des constructions notamment a Kamina mais dans les districts intérieurs, c'était John... Quand on arrive au comité exécutif, on a un droit de regard sur les fonds dans la trésorerie générale, et Mr John était responsable des fonds réservés aux constructions de paroisses... Quand la guerre est arrivée, la pluspart des missionnaires sont parties en Zambie et d'autres vers les USA. Moi j'étais déjà ici à la trésorerie générale, avec Mr Tom Rider. Quand

One of the biggest shifts that has occurred in terms of agency over the past twenty-five years is, according to Bishop Ntambo and Americans such as Bob Walters and Pam Couture (who have both written books addressing this period), that when the missionaries fled, Congolese leaders were promoted to replace them.

> I think the most radical change is that with the war coming and the White missionaries having to leave not only for their own safety but for the safety of the Congolese (because they could not keep the White people safe—they created suspicion and such), the bishop systematically replaced those people with Congolese—so it is Congolese doctors, nurses, administrators, appointed as mission people. I found it one of the most fascinating transitions that was facilitated by the war. . . . Instead of bringing them [the missionaries] back into North Katanga, the bishop has largely brought local people into those positions and they've gotten salaries and education and the support of Global Ministries.[49] —*Pamela Couture*

It is in this sense that one can assert that the war which began in eastern Congo in the late 1990s served as the impetus for a kind of structural decolonization [in terms of who holds power within the conference] of the North Katanga Conference. This change, alongside Bishop Ntambo's series of speeches at North Katanga Conference gatherings over the years about the ability of Congolese to build, work, and lead together (including admonitions against simply "squatting" in the properties left by Belgians and former missionaries) has assisted the decolonization of North Katangan minds that was discussed in section 5.3.1.5.

6.2.3 Where Did the Money Go? Causal Factors and the Elephant in the Room

Another theme that came out of the interviews with North Katangans was a frustration that American financial support for programs is not at the levels it once was. The general perception was that the funding has dried up. When asked why this is so, initial responses by North Katangans tended to

l'Évêque Ngoy, était mort, les états unis n'envoie plus beaucoup de funds . . . Quand la guerre est terminée, l'Évêque Ntambo est élu en 1996, avait remarqué le manque de fonds, allant aux usa, a reçu beaucoup d'assistance, on a pu ainsi construire des écoles primaire, secondaire, avant lui les pasteurs n'avait pas de maison alors sans pasteur pas de paroisse. A cette époque il ya eu beaucoup de constructions."

49. Pamela Couture, interview with the author, January 8, 2016.

place the blame on outside forces, such as the death of Bishop Wakadilo, followed by the departure of missionaries during the war, and the crash of the economy in the USA in the 2000s. When pushed further, some posited that reporting/communication issues could have been a contributing factor.

> From 1990 to 1996, especially after the bishop [Wakadilo] died, [finances] were not good. . . . So when Bishop Ntambo [was elected], he went to speak with the North Katanga partners. We started to receive funds . . . that helped build sanctuaries, pastoral homes, and even some other buildings for the church. Even [money] to build schools. Then in 2001 the problem in the United States. . . . September 11. . . . So [after that] the funding dropped down to the present day. Even when we receive funds, it is not like during the period from 1996 to 2000, where we received a lot. Also, during this period from 1996 to 2000, there was the war in Congo. There are things that were bought by the church that the rebels stole. They looted everything. So, since then, the funding is not that good. . . . The funding relationship really is diminishing . . .
>
> Other reasons? Yes. Other reasons for one, you know when you give money, you need to give a report. . . . There was also the problem of giving the report in time. From time to time, the reports were delayed. And, the people who send the money are unhappy, say no, you gave us this period to give the report but you do not give. So we cannot continue to fund you . . .
>
> I do not know if it is that we manage very badly that we are not given the money. But in other conferences, there are projects that receive . . . even one million dollars. . . . But, I did not see a project here that has received money like that. I am at Africa University in Zimbabwe. There is a conference which gave one million to build their university chapel. . . . Why have we never received a budget . . . [like that]? But for a single project, a million. I'm asking, is this injustice? It's justice?[50] —*John Maloba*

50. Mulume wa Umba John Maloba, interview with the author, July 12, 2015. Original: "De 1990 à 1996, vraiment, comme l'évêque était décidé, les histoires n'était pas bon . . . Alors, quand l'Évêque Ntambo est entre comme évêque, il est parti parler avec les partenaires de Nord Katanga. On a commencé à financer . . . D'ailleurs, c'est projet qui a les aides à construire les églises, les maisons de pasteurs, avoir même quelques bâtiments pour les église Méthodistes. A construire même des écoles. Arrivé à 2000 . . . c'est 2001 o ou ai le problème de la maison blanche aux États-Unis . . . C'est le 11 ? Septembre ! . . . Alors, le financement a diminué jusqu'à nos jours. Même si on finance, on ne finance pas comme on a financé pendant cette période de 1996 à 2000, là où on a donné beaucoup. Et en plus et encore, c'est arrivé que pendant cette période de 1996–2000, il y avait la guerre au Congo. Il y a même les histoires qui était acheté par l'église que les rebelles ont volée. Ils ont pillé tout. Alors, jusqu'à la, les financements

Americans interviewed tended to be reluctant to speak candidly on a recording device about their theories on why the funding levels have collapsed—especially since the early 2000s. Those who did comment gravitated to observations such as lack of effective communication and reporting as well as donor fatigue.

> There are several things [causing the overall funding drop]. One is donor fatigue: people get tired of funding the same thing over and over again. The second thing is that Americans have a short attention span. They do something and they think, therefore, it is done; they don't have a long-term commitment to it. So, funds that they've been pouring into a clinic or hospital or scholarship program over the last five or ten years or so—now they want to do something different [with their money].
>
> The flip side of that is what has been created in Africa and other places is a dependency mindset—a dependency trap—and we have not found ways to develop self-sufficiency to the extent that we need to. Salaries and things are still being relied upon outside of the community. So, until churches and communities in the conference figure out how to become more self-sufficient for the day to day, the struggle will continue. I believe that the role of the partners is not the day to day kind of expenses, but is the add-ons. It is when the roof needs to be purchased after they've made the bricks and collected the stones. It is some of the extraordinary that we need to step in. Where a hydra-form brick piece of equipment needs to be bought. Not in the daily use of it or maintenance or salaries. So, the reduction in finances is tied to not building the capacity locally quickly or even seeing that is a priority, donor fatigue and the shrinking numbers of people who provide many of those dollars in the United States

---

ne sont pas que même bons . . . Puis que, jusqu'à là je ne crois pas que il y a même des projets qui peuvent aller au de la-de 100 mil, no. Les projets, vos est ici, la relation de financement vraiment on diminue . . . D'autres raisons? Oui. D'autres raisons par fois, vous savez quand on donne l'argent, il faut de la report. De fois, si vous ne donner pas le report a temps, il y avait aussi le problem de donner le report a temps. De fois, on a donné le report avec retard. Et, le gents qui envoie l'argent sont mecontent, dissent que no, vous a nous donné cette period pour donner le report mais vous ne donner pas. Alors, on ne peut pas continuer à financer pour vous . . . Je ne sais pas si c'est parce que nous gérons très mal que nous ne donne pas l'argent. Mais, dans autres conférences, il y a des projets a 2 mil, 10 mil, même 1 millions de dollars que on donne . . . Mais, je n'ai pas vu un projet ici qu'on donne comme ça. Sur tout à Nord Katanga. J'ai un exemple. Je suis à Africa University a Zimbabwe. Il y a une conférence qui a donné 1 million pour construire la chapel de l'université. Alors, je suis entrain de me demande. On n'a jamais été un budget de 2 millions pour tous que nous donne. Mais, pour un seul projet, un million. Je suis entrain de demander, c'est l'injustice? C'est la justice?"

> and Europe.⁵¹ —*George Howard (GBGM executive; former chair of West Ohio Conference's Mission Committee)*

What I found most fascinating was that none of the interviewees explicitly asserted what I believe to be the primary reason funding from American church and conference partners dropped considerably—especially after the departure of the of last foreign missionary general treasurer in the mid-2000s—and that is the loss of trust among Americans that funds were being used as designated. This loss of trust in financial management has been raised in numerous off-the-record conversations over the years (both with Americans and Congolese); I believe that the fact that it did not arise in the recorded interviews is more a reflection on the taboo surrounding public criticism of financial management in the partnership than an absence of awareness of the issue—at least among Americans. I have no way of measuring how many interviewees secretly shared my belief, although some danced around it, even hesitantly mentioning it as a blink-you-missed-it quandary. I see it as the proverbial elephant in the room—no one wants to mention it out loud for fear of being branded a racist or a traitor—but over the years, I have heard many a former donor express exasperation that no proof had been sent that the project they had funded had been built. In 2006, there was a family in Indiana threatening to take legal action because they believed they had waited an excessive amount of time for a photo of the church that was to be built in their family member's memory. A North Katangan who immigrated to the USA reported to me that he received a vitriol-filled rebuke and warning from members of a certain United Methodist congregation when he attempted (within the past ten years) to raise funds for North Katanga initiatives; the congregation (and many others) had been told via former American missionaries to North Katanga that Bishop Ntambo could not be trusted. I have also had numerous Katangan colleagues lament to me over the years that they were being pressured to give inaccurate reports about amounts they had received for partnership projects they managed and what had been built. Even I faced extreme pressure⁵² in 2015 to remain silent when a team from a wealthy American congregation was shown construction projects my NGO had supported (they were led to believe that these projects were accomplished with funds they had sent).

---

51. George Howard, interview with the author, January 8, 2016.

52. For me as an American to travel to Kamina, I need a notarized invitation letter for a visa and a seat on the church plane. If I were branded as disloyal, I would have been blocked from returning, as I was in 2006.

Even as I monitor my word choice because I know that some matters I should not print in this thesis, I find myself pondering *why* certain things are taboo to say plainly—why they must only be transmitted in whispers, becoming the thing everyone knows but no one will say aloud—and what such taboos say about the nature of postcolonial partnerships, especially as North Katangans are whispering these secrets to their American friends, such that now it becomes a collusion between North Katangan leaders and their primary American partners to together present an idealized narrative to potential new donors. This is a question I am certain I will continue to wrestle with in future research.

I suspect that it has something to do with the social dynamics of secrets and shame and airing dirty laundry in public. (Even in Kiluba there is a proverb about dirty laundry which admonishes the sharing of shameful family matters with outsiders.) It might be enlightening to juxtapose this elephant to the research on children raised by abusive or addicted parents and the pressure they are under to not reveal the family secret. I also think scholarship on the White privilege of being seen as an individual actor could also inform such an exploration. While the pressure to cover up potential scandals exists in all organizations in the world, I suspect that such pressure is more intense in certain demographics. As has been pointed out numerous times, especially in the context of how mainstream media in the USA speaks about mass shooters,[53] when a White person commits a scandalous act, s/he is portrayed as a lone wolf—an individual whose actions are not seen as an indictment of all White people. Yet when a person of color commits the same or similar act, the reputations of everyone who society has placed in her/his ethnic demographic are further tainted in the process. Perhaps this is another reason why I have observed North Katangan leaders being under immense pressure to not publicly call out the misconduct of colleagues while Americans are in the room, yet at the same time they are quick to vent their indignation about such acts to American friends whom they trust not to hold the misconduct of a colleague against them personally.

This topic is explored more in the following section on governance and administration. While American UMs in leadership positions in the denomination tend to speak euphemistically about accountability and transparency when referring to issues of lack of trust in financial management, I found it interesting that some North Katangan interviewees chose to critique their colleagues (while still never naming names) by speaking against impunity when it comes to such matters, asserting that this impunity has undermined

---

53. E.g., Metzl, "When the Shooter Is White."

initiatives of the church, although they did not go so far as to suggest aloud that this impunity has impacted foreign partnerships.

6.2.4 Power Shift

Curiously, the topic of how the meteoric growth of North Katanga's official membership statistics over the past twenty-five years has impacted power dynamics in the partnership was rarely even hinted at in the interviews. During the time period of Bishop Ntambo, North Katanga officially became the largest conference in The UMC. This meant that it also received the largest number of delegates to General Conference (the quadrennial legislative gathering of the denomination). As noted in the introductory chapter (see 1.6), this resulted in caucuses on all sides of hotly debated proposals seeking to gain influence over the votes of North Katangans. I personally witnessed—and was involved in coaching—many North Katangan delegates shift from seeing themselves as outside observers and/or beggars at General Conference to claiming their seats at the table, recognizing the power their voting block wielded, and leveraging this power to push forward their agendas and get North Katangans chosen as members of denominational-level boards and committees. However, since this was not a topic explicitly raised in the interviews, I note my observations of this dynamic here simply to provide additional context on the shifting power dynamics. While there are legitimate critiques that could be made of it, overall, I see this shift as a positive step in the decolonization process in that it has provided North Katangans the ability to stand tall and speak boldly when engaged in conversations on the denominational-level.

6.3 GOVERNANCE AND ADMINISTRATION

Interview participants often touched upon issues pertaining to governance and administration of church programs. This included discussions about the shift from American to North Katangan program administration, the impact of American missionaries and the North Katangan church operating in parallel isolated systems, the differences between church governance models in America versus North Katanga (and American lack of understanding of these differences), the conflicts over funding priorities and the use/distribution of resources, the tensions created by reporting requirements, and the impact of impunity when it came to mismanagement of programs.

While American respondents tended to shy away from open criticism of North Katangans,[54] many North Katangan respondents were quick to

---

54. I suspect but cannot not prove that this particular reluctance to openly

express their frustrations with administration and governance issues within their conference (while passionate in their critiques, the names of those being critiqued were always left to be inferred). The issues that kept resurfacing were nepotism (although never named as such) and impunity—the sense that those who fail to perform their appointed task effectively, either due to incompetence or deliberate disregard of expectations (e.g., redirecting designated funds, not working on task, etc.), faced no negative consequences.

> For my critiques, I begin with us the Congolese. We did not arrive at good management, administration, leadership, and good governance. We really have not tried to put it in practice yet. Sometimes, we manage very badly. One can give you a project, you finish it well or not; one does not send reports. You can have a project and say it's for auto-financing, but you do not produce any money. But you have even said to partners, "Give us the money, and we will produce ourselves." But, you do not produce. These are the bad issues for us Africans.
>
> And then, to leadership, it must be what is called distributive justice. That is to say that everyone is represented instead of selecting only ones who come from my family or territory. No, this [practice] weakens the people who are at risk of being forgotten, the minority. So, you need everyone. Even with the selection of those who are going to study, or those going to General Conference, one must always include everyone so that everyone feels that this is our church. Here, it is our church. But sometimes we forget because we have not studied much. So, this is what is not good.[55] —*John Maloba*

criticizing North Katangan leaders comes from the very realistic fears of being accused of racism/(neo)colonialism and to be labeled *persona non grata* by both the bishop and denominational agencies in the USA.

55. Mulume wa Umba John Maloba, interview with the author, July 12, 2015. Original: "C'est que j'ai comme critique je commence avec nous les congolais. Nous ne sommes pas arrivés à la bonne gestion. L'administration, le leadership, et la bonne gouvernance. Ça vraiment nous n'avons pas encore essayer au mètre en pratique. De fois, nous gérons très mal. On peut vous donner un projet, vous les terminer bien or pas, on ne donne pas les reports. Vous pouvez donner le projet pour dire que c'est projet et pour l'autofinancement, mais, vous ne produisez pas l'argent. Même vous avez dit aux partenaires, donnez-nous l'argent et nous allons produire nous-même. Mais, vous ne produisez pas. C'est les mauvaises cotes pour nous les africains. Et puis, au leadership, il faut qu'il soit ce que on appelle la justice distributive. De dire que, que tout le monde soit représenté au lieu de prendre seulement at dire l'autre il vienne de ma famille, il vienne de mon territoire. No, puis que ça faiblit. Les gens qu'ils sont beaucoup il risque d'être oublié, la minorité. Alors, il faut tout le monde. Même avec la sélection, pour eux qui vont aller étudie, qui soit pour le conférence général, il faut toujours inclure tour le

This section seeks to explore the realities, misunderstandings, and critiques of church governance and administration (especially in terms of programs funded by Americans) in North Katanga as well as comment on how Americans have tended to respond.

6.3.1 Bishop as Paramount Chief and Spiritual Leader

One point of tension and misunderstanding between American and North Katangans identified in the interviews is the differences in the role and authority of the bishop in their home conferences. John Enright asserted in his interview with me that United Methodism in Katanga is a baptized version of the traditional Luba and Lunda political structures, and that in it the bishop plays the role of Paramount Chief. This subsection explores Enright's assertion, comparing the model of church governance that is the norm among American United Methodist bishops to what I and others have observed about the realities of being the bishop of North Katanga. It is intended as a continuation to the conversation in chapter 3 on the dynamics of the Luba chieftaincy system (see esp. 3.1.3).

> In the ancient tradition you have the tribal structure which has the paramount chief, the land chief, which the Belgians gave government status to. Below that you have . . . the chief that is the owner of the land for hunting and below that you have the village chief, and then the section of the village—all the way down—everyone has their place in the structure, and, within the structure, what United Methodism did was to basically take the African traditional structure and baptize it. The bishop became the paramount chief, the district superintendent became the land chief, the parish pastor became the area chief and all the way down. And these structures very much remained the same, intact and operational.
>
> For example, in North Katanga when the bishop comes to the village the people sing words that mean "Rejoice upon seeing the chief. Let us all sing with a big voice, Alleluia! Rejoice upon seeing the chief." Now, the song is about Jesus, but kind of strange that the song is sung only when the bishop arrives and the word used for the bishop is the same word used for the paramount chief. It just ties back into the whole tribal structure. This is the real world.[56] —*John Enright*

---

monde. Pour que tout le monde sent que c'est notre église. Ici c'est notre église. Mais, par fois on oublie parce que on n'a pas étudié beaucoup. Alors, c'est qu'il n'y a bon."

56. John Enright, interview with the author, January 6, 2016.

Enright's assertion that in The UMC in North Katanga the bishop steps into a role similar to that of a paramount chief (with its benefits and burdens) is consistent with my observations over the years. Luba chieftainship traditions, Methodist traditions, and modernity co-exist, as could be seen via numerous photos and videos posted on Facebook[57] by Congolese United Methodists over the last weekend of May 2017, when Bishop Mande Muyombo's installation was celebrated in Kamina. In addition to the formal vestments, processions, and regalia one would expect to see in an ordination service in a UM conference in the United States, there were photos documenting all the people and groups who presented gifts to the new bishop as well as choirs accompanied by traditional Luba instruments. Bishop Mande's speech at his installation (which was printed and distributed) begins with two pages of acknowledgements (lengthy lists of public acknowledgements is the norm in speeches in North Katanga) and followed with his priorities going forward.[58] Noted priorities included the clergy pension initiative, auto-finance via income-generating programs, the increased use of the leadership skills of laity, and increased collaboration with the other UM bishops in DR Congo. The theme of the spiritual retreat[59] he offered the next day to the gathered crowd was "when you are in Christ, you become a new creature."[60] In this way, it was evident that Bishop Mande attempted to set the tone of this new episcopacy by affirming traditional and modern practices while simultaneously promoting independence and mutuality.

In United Methodism in the USA, the role of a bishop is more limited than what is expected of a UM bishop in Congo. Officially, a bishop is to chair annual conferences[61] (that is, the annual meeting) and to make appointment decisions within those conferences in consultation with the appointed district superintendents. The bishop is also expected to spend a significant amount of his/her time making public appearances at church events as well as preach at them, serving as a spiritual guide. A bishop's vision for a conference's mission agenda is influential, but that theoretically comes from his/her power of persuasion—not legal authority.

As touched upon in the section on tributes, in North Katanga the status and role of bishop is larger than this. I have witnessed on numerous occasions over the years the arrival of Bishop Ntambo into a community

57. I observed this trend on my own personal Facebook newsfeed.
58. Muyombo, "Episcopal Installation."
59. That is, a retreat for learning and discussions.
60. Kazadi, "When You Are in Christ."
61. The term "annual conference" can be confusing; in United Methodism, it refers both to the congregations in a delineated region as well as their annual gathering, which is attended by clergy and lay delegates from each congregation.

being met with great fanfare. In some instances, the cloth traditionally used as wrap-around skirts is placed on the ground for the bishop to walk upon. Choirs sing and large crowds gather to witness the event. When traveling in more remote[62] regions, Bishop Ntambo frequently had a protection detail, consisting both of uniformed scouts and armed police (the police were there because of his status as an elected senator).

Early each morning, a long line formed at the gate of his residence. The bishop met with each visitor in a semi-private outdoor space. When at his homes in Kamina and Lubumbashi, he would meet with visitors in the paillote (a gazebo-like structure in the front lawn with many chairs inside, including a grand chair designated for him). Bishop Ntambo once told me that this process of meeting with individuals tends to begin around five o'clock in the morning and continues until he must leave for other business. The topics of these conversations typically ranged from requests for intervention in a personal problem (money for school, medicine, etc.) to reports from appointed program heads with requests for authorization on next steps. When I asked the bishop why he did not require these visitors to schedule an appointment with his official secretary or delegate these sort of issues/decisions to someone else, he replied that such an approach would not work in this context. He alluded to issues of trust (that is, people wanting to speak to the bishop directly instead of trusting that someone would effectively pass their message along and accurately report back the bishop's reply), but it appeared that the trust issues went in both directions; program managers all spoke directly to the bishop instead of a mid-level supervisor when it came both to reporting and obtaining approval for actions.

Contrast this to the role of a United Methodist bishop in the USA. While the official visit of an American bishop to a congregation within her/his annual conference is also generally met with an effort to show hospitality, a larger-than-average attendance at the service/event, and an above-average performance by the music ministry team, there is a substantial difference between this and what is practiced in North Katanga. In America, the expectation is that the bishop will preach a good sermon and offer words of praise and/or encouragement to the congregation for its ministry efforts, but little is expected to come from the bishop's visit beyond this. Whenever Bishop Ntambo visited a community in one of his conferences, the expectation was that this would result in him bringing solutions to many of their problems (both on the individual and group level). The former is welcomed as a distinguished guest; the latter is greeted like a king and savior.

62. For lack of a better term, I use "remote" to express that the location is difficult to reach (lack of train, broken roads, no commercial flights, etc.) and rarely receives friendly visitors.

During the time that I lived in Kamina as the appointed director of Community Development (2005), I noticed that church departments sprang into action when the bishop was in town but halted the moment he left and a decision needed to be made. This is quite different to the way church leaders operate in relationship to United Methodist bishops serving in the USA. In the USA, it is an unwritten social taboo to go to the house of a bishop (or boss or any high-ranking person) without an invitation,[63] and to meet with the bishop, one should request an appointment, which is often done through a bishop's office assistant. It is also implicitly understood that to approach one's bishop with a request for money for a personal matter is both inappropriate and ineffective; such issues are to be handled on a family/congregational/community level or, in these days of social media, through friendship networks. Likewise, fundraising for church ministries are handled at lower levels (with the occasional exception of a bishop deciding to be a spokesperson for a campaign), and management of such projects is outside of the scope of the bishop's concerns unless there is an accusation of mismanagement by an appointed clergy member. It will be interesting to watch how the newly-elected Bishop Mande, who is well-acquainted with the leadership models of both American and Congolese bishops, will choose to navigate these differing models and expectations.[64]

Another important distinction between American and North Katangan UM bishops relates to their salaries and the pressures put upon them to share their salaries. The UMC does not take the additional roles of a Congolese bishop into account when calculating the salaries of bishops. In 2016, all UM bishops in the USA had the set salary of one hundred fifty thousand US dollars plus housing,[65] but UM bishops in Africa received considerably less. By agreeing to leave his job at GBGM to become the bishop of North Katanga, Bishop Mande took a large reduction in his monthly income. The assumption has been that a bishop's salary should "reflect local economic conditions

---

63. In these days of cell phones and email in the USA, it has started to become taboo to knock on the door (with the purpose of visiting/conversing) of anyone but a close friend without having contacted them in advance and received their invitation. This is not (yet?) the case in North Katanga. When I was living in Kamina in 2005, it was common for me to be woken early in the morning with a knock on my bedroom door with the message that someone (occasionally a stranger) was already in the living room waiting to speak with me. It will be interesting to see if the growing ubiquity of cell phones and the dropping of usage fees in North Katanga will change this practice in the coming years.

64. When I requested a comment from Bishop Mande after his election on what—if any—changes he planned to make concerning these sorts of issues, he declined to say anything on the record, citing the sensitive nature of the topic.

65. "Frequently Asked Questions."

and cost of living," but the fact that in North Katanga (and other places) the bishop is expected by the members of his[66] conferences to use his personal financial resources for addressing needs of the members has not been properly addressed and acknowledged. It would be enlightening to know exactly how much of Bishop Ntambo's personal money was given to other family members or individuals over the year he was bishop, but an investigation into that touches too much onto sensitive topics and would be impossible to calculate due to lack of record keeping. In his autobiography, Bishop Ralph Dodge, the last American UM bishop of the region,[67] spoke about this pay gap and the financial sacrifices he and his family made in accepting to serve as bishop in Africa (1956–1968), making considerably less than his colleagues in the USA.[68] He also remarked that he never felt like "one of the group" when meeting with his episcopal colleagues in the USA; this was in part because American UM bishops met semiannually, while during those years "it was considered an extravagance for us 'overseas' administrators to make the costly trip so often."[69] Such differences in personal economic realities between UM bishops in the USA and Africa are, I believe, a factor to be considered in any holistic conversation about decolonizing relationship dynamics between American and African UM conferences and their bishops.

6.3.2 Critiques and Conflicts: Decisions, Suspicions and Misunderstandings

As previously stated, this thesis deliberately avoids investigating or rehashing specific allegations of misconduct, scandals, or conflicts between individuals. Interviewees themselves—especially North Katangans (there were some exceptions among Americans interviewed)—refrained from raising complaints about the actions of any specific individual. When the interview reached the question encouraging reflection on mistakes, misunderstandings, or critiques relative to the history of American-North Katangan collaborations, criticisms by North Katangans about Americans on the recorded interviews were always prefaced with words of appreciation for the assistance received from Americans over the years. Since at least two of the North Katangan interviewees were significantly less candid with me on their

---

66. Thus far, there have been no female United Methodist bishops elected in DR Congo.

67. As United Methodist membership increased in central Africa, additional episcopal areas were created. In Bishop Dodge's time, he oversaw an area that includes what is now Zimbabwe, Zambia, Angola, and DR Congo.

68. Dodge, *Revolutionary Bishop*, 111.

69. Dodge, *Revolutionary Bishop*, 131.

recorded interview about frustrations/critiques of the relationship dynamics than they had been with me in confidential conversations over recent years, I suspect other respondents may have also muted their responses, but I am unsure to what degree. As one American respondent noted, the desire to not upset or offend American partners for fear of damaging the relationship (and thus the assistance that comes from it) results in a lack of candidness by North Katangans with all but those who they trust to be discreet. The same, of course, can be said of nearly all human interactions where there is a strong motivation to gain/retain the support of another.

> Missionaries are held in esteem in many respects. I think the Congolese have a balanced perspective in that they know the contribution that missionaries made to building durable institutions. . . . And they seek the sort of support that they can get through mission connections . . . and so they are very reluctant—until you build enough trust—to "bite the hand that feeds them" so to speak.[70] —*Anonymous*

That said, important themes could be found in the interview responses to questions about criticisms or misunderstandings regarding the relationship. While certain issues were danced around, some, including ones pertaining to money and use of power by administrators, were said bluntly.

6.3.2.1 Segregation, Superiority Complexes, and Decolonizing Taboos

As was touched upon in chapter 4 as well as interview excerpts included earlier in this chapter, despite numerous affirmations by North Katangans that most American UM missionaries in living memory were appreciated for their attempts to live among the people they had been sent to serve and promote Congolese leadership, in very real ways the missionaries lived and socialized apart from North Katangans. I see there being both healthy (e.g., the desire to spend time with people who share one's mother tongue and experiences) and toxic (e.g., segregation based on ethnicity as a way to establish boundaries in a blanket response to objections to the behaviors of specific church leaders) reasons why such segregation occurred. As Bob Walters recounted to me, in the late 1990s, the communication breakdown between missionaries and local church leaders was such that he found in the same region a district superintendent trying to sell seed corn and an American missionary trying in vain to find such seeds for sale—neither

---

70. This interviewee requested her/his observation to be anonymous.

were aware of the other's situation. When GBGM was evacuating missionaries in 1998, their New York office called my mother in Indiana to say that my father was missing and asked if she had any clue where he had gone. My father would frequently cite the incident as proof that the missionary network functioned inside of its own bubble. Many North Katangan leaders knew exactly where he was—attending a major gathering organized by district church leaders—and this information could have been ascertained quickly by switching ham radio frequencies and asking operators on the church's network. While Walters did not hesitate to speak openly about these frustrations (and was socially ostracized in certain circles in the USA for it), other Americans spoke candidly with me—on the condition of anonymity—about their observations of (neo)colonial/racist attitudes among American UMs.

> The impression I got from [a former head of GBGM] was that Wings of the Morning [the aviation ministry in North Katanga] was disorganized, that Congolese didn't know how to plan. . . . It contributed to this kind of generalization that was coming from the missionaries in Congo that the Congolese were inherently violent and inherently corrupt, lazy, and disorganized. . . .
>
> You go to things like the obstacles of building a church when you haven't got a working truck. And the effort—it totally undoes those generalizations—the effort that goes into relief distribution. . . . They are all up against the same things. . . . I think I quickly formed impressions of the kinds of things that were being said about the Congolese, and that got repeated in a couple of different places.[71] —*Anonymous*

As a number of North Katangans interviewed noted, this lack of trust and *de facto* segregation also negatively impacted the transfer of responsibilities when the missionaries left; there was a dearth of local leaders who had the experience and knowledge of exactly how the missionaries had been managing certain programs. Below is a sampling of critiques about segregation and the lack of integration of Congolese into leadership roles found in the interviews.

> What I am seeing as error, at the beginning we did very good evangelization [efforts], and we are very grateful [to missionaries], but there are some errors that spoiled the Methodists

---

71. This interviewee requested her/his observation to be anonymous.

> [here]. . . . What I personally find wrong is not to get people to participate in the projects that the missionaries were doing. For our own health center, the missionaries had to buy everything, do everything for us . . . [things] that we can do ourselves: the stones that we gather and then transport somewhere, the bricks that we can make ourselves. But the missionaries came and bought everything and it was a church of money, and we created lazy people who wait for everything from the missionary.[72]
> —Joseph Mulongo

Most of the past quarter-century has been during the post-missionary period—the time of long-distance direct partnerships and hosting of short-term visitors. Thus, we must also question to what degree superiority/inferiority complexes and social segregation have impacted relationships since 1998. I offer a few thoughts on this below and return to the question in other subsections, including the section on the psychology of reporting (see 6.3.3).

> I think that before, the missionaries who lived with us were a bit isolated to themselves. They were not completely in direct contact with the Christians. Now, I think that there are no longer boundaries. The missionaries [that is, American partners] are surrounded (entouraged) by Congolese Christians. They launch projects with Congolese Christians, they work with Congolese Christians. This is something to emphasize.[73] —Daniel Mumba (ordained elder and District Superintendent)

---

72. Joseph Mulongo, interview with the author, July 18, 2015. Original: "Ça c'est vrai, ce que je suis entrain de voir comme erreur, au départ on a fait une très bonne évangélisation, nous sommes très reconnaissants et on a gâté, les chrétiens, les fidèles méthodistes. On devait faire tout sans leur participation, même les missionnaires ont fait une bonne chose. Mais ce que moi personnellement je trouve comme erreur c'est de ne pas amener les gens à participer au projet que les missionnaires faisaient. Parce que pour notre propre centre de santé, les missionnaires devaient tout acheter, tout faire pour nous, même les fables—18:07 que nous pouvons creuser nous même, les pierres que nous caser et puis amener quelque part, voir les briques que nous pouvons faire nous-même. Mais les missionnaires venaient et acheter tout et c'étaient une église d'argent et on a créé des paresseux qui attendent tout du missionnaire."

73. Daniel Mumba, interview with the author, Kamina, July 13, 2015. Original: "Je pense que, auparavant, les missionnaires qui habitaient avec nous étaient comme des missionnaires isolés par lui-même. Parce qu'ils n'étaient totalement en contact avec les chrétiens. Mais actuellement, il n'y a pas des limites. Les missionnaires étaient entourés des chrétiens congolais. Les missionnaires montent ces projets au chrétiens congolaises. Les missionnaires travaillent avec les chrétiens congolais. Et, c'est quelque chose qu'il faut encourager et quelque chose qu'il faut pousser."

The expressed perceptions were that the segregation of the past has ended, and to an extent I agree. My late father is an example of an American who was acutely aware of the (recent) history of missionaries opening their homes to other missionaries but not to their Congolese colleagues, and so he consciously chose to eat and sleep in the homes of North Katangans during his visits. That said, we are comparing the behaviors of Americans who were living in North Katanga full-time for several months, years, or even decades to Americans since the late evacuation who, with very few exceptions, only visit for a couple weeks at a time and are explicitly there as invited guests of the bishop. I would push back on any assertions that the (neo)colonial period of segregation is fully behind us. Over the past thirteen years of my regular travels to North Katanga, I have observed the behaviors of numerous American visitors from a number of conferences and agencies. With rare exception, the Americans spend nearly all of their non-scheduled time decompressing at the guarded guest house and/or socializing with other Americans or a few of their official North Katangan handlers. Regular North Katangan pastors and lay leaders get little more than a handshake, if that. Even the youth living at the UM orphanage in Kamina have told me that despite the many years of American partners being flown into Kamina and the countless obligatory orphanage photo-ops—including with those from the conference which is the primary financial sponsor—I (and the few persons I have deliberately brought over with me) am the only American who has made an effort to truly get to know them as individuals and maintain a relationship. Thus, while I agree that much has improved in this regard the past quarter-century, American UMs in general still have soul-searching to do on the degree to which they are confusing the radical hospitality they receive when they arrive with them being actual VIPs who need not socialize with regular people.

Among the Americans interviewed, I sensed conflicted emotions even among those who kept the general tone of their comments positive/optimistic when asked to identify current or past mistakes made in the partnership. Whenever participants moved past stating politically correct rhetoric and pointing to things that could be celebrated, I found expressions of skepticism, cynicism, and deep ambivalence about the partnership, yet for most there appeared to be a reluctance to critique North Katangans.[74] I believe I know what was going on beneath the surface of many of these conversations because I recognized it in myself: cognitive dissonance and fear of the social consequences of reporting what I see. I firmly believe that, in

---

74. See esp. transcript excerpts in section 7.1.1.2.

general, the White Americans I interviewed[75] fell into the category of persons who believe intellectually that racism is wrong, and they consciously avoid making criticisms that could be judged racist.[76] Thus, when they observe something that could potentially support a view that North Katanga's leaders are morally or intellectually inferior (e.g., issues of sexual abuse and domestic violence, theft or reallocation of funds, reports of sabotage—even through witchcraft, etc.), they try to avoid talking about it. Such is the sense of taboo[77] and shame associated with being seen as racist that, when participants would make comments about racism (especially when identifying racist statements or actions they had observed from American colleagues in regards to North Katanga), they would almost always afterwards request for their statement to be removed from the transcript.

What results from this fear of naming and exploring criticisms—of appearing to be racist or risking the fallout of suggesting another is racist—is internal confusion and unhelpful broad and euphemistic language. For example, instead of speaking about having reasons to believe that a specific misconduct has been committed by specific person(s), frustrated American partners and agency heads tend to talk about the needs for more "transparency" and "accountability." This sort of language is not helpful. It neither gives leverage for change to those negatively impacted by wrongdoings nor does it assist in the decolonizing of relationship dynamics. It also relativizes moral decisions in such a way that assumes that respectful cross-cultural understanding cannot be reached. For example, instead of conversing about complex decisions (e.g., designated partnership funds were redirected, lies were told, persons found guilty of theft or rape were appointed to manage a project receiving partnership funds), both Americans and North Katangans speak to each other about such things only in whispers. While both in the USA and Katanga UM clergy misconduct trials and sentencings happen behind closed doors, when accusations are widely known and it appears that the person(s) were not held accountable, mistrust festers.

---

75. All of my participants who had been American citizens since birth were White due to my difficulty in locating American POCs with a significant history of partnering in North Katanga. In future research, I would like to explore the recent emergence of North Katanga partnerships with Black Americans as well as North Katangans who have permanently immigrated to the USA.

76. This conclusion is based both on the nuances in how they responded my questions and that, for all my American interviewees, I had interacted with them in the past or at least knew about them through things they had said and done in the capacity of their work in The UMC.

77. Refer back to the discussion on the relationship between shame and silence in chapter 5.

In later subsections in this chapter, the topics of impunity and redirection of funds return. What I wish to highlight here, though, is how this relates to conversations in chapter 5. I assert that the fear/shame of being accused of racist/(neo)colonial behavior (i.e., White Fragility) is a hindrance to true decolonization of the relationship. Brown's distinctions between shame and guilt (see 5.4) are useful in addressing this issue. Internalized racism and fear of being called racist are both about shame; the assumption made in shame responses is that any ignorant or immoral action made is a reflection on the underlying essence of that person. A guilt response, in contrast, focuses on the specific action, with the understanding that it is possible to criticize the action itself without making a judgement on the moral and intellectual character of an individual, let alone an entire community.

What would be possible if both Americans and Katangans felt free to openly discuss criticisms with each other? What if we were able to say "I name these problems; I seek to understand their causes, and I reject any answer built upon (neo)colonial assumptions"? To decolonize a partnership—to remove the element of shame and build mutual trust and respect—we need a safe space to explore frustrations and questions. For example: "Is it neocolonial to insist on detailed reports and independent auditors?" I believe that the answer depends on the motivation. If a system of reporting is built on a desire to facilitate communication and to protect partners from false accusations, then yes, they can exist in a decolonized partnership. If the system is about controlling the actions of someone one does not fully trust, then it is neocolonial in nature. This raises for me a question I struggle to answer: If one seeks a decolonialized partnership, but one does not trust leaders in the partnership, what is the healthy way forward?

6.3.2.2 Designated Funds and Conflicting Priorities

Another point of tension over the years has been that of what needs getting funded and when exceptions should be made to policies concerning designated funds and resources. This issue has manifested in different ways. The Advance system, which is managed by GBGM, allows donors to earmark their contributions to specific projects. Church leaders, with the approval of the bishop, can establish an Advance number for their project. The official policy is that funds given for one project must not be used for another. The problem is that the creation of an Advance number does not guarantee funds will be given to it; there must be someone actively fundraising for it. Historically, this meant that Advance projects managed and fundraised for by missionaries tended to receive funds, while projects created by North Katangans could have empty accounts despite sometimes being seen as more urgent needs by local church leaders. Conflicts would frequently occur when the bishop or other church leaders wanted to reallocate or borrow[78] funds to address urgent issues, such as lack of transportation, medical procedures, etc. Such conflicts took on an additional level of tension when the perception was that there was a desire to use church resources to address issues of an individual, not the church as a whole.

> The Americans who used to be here . . . as missionaries. They managed the money that they brought here themselves. . . . Sometimes when the church needed it, they would say, "No, no, the money I brought is for other things." Then the church management is not happy. The church there has no roofing; the rainstorms destroyed it. So the one who has the money says, "No, no, it is for medicines," for example. He does not give the money [to repair the roof]. And one cannot be happy when there is a need like this that is urgent. From time to time, the problem arose that there was no road [to get somewhere], and the missionary pilot refused to fly the bishop when he said, "No, no. You take me, I have a meeting to attend." The bishop has his plan. So, with these things, sometimes an understanding was not there.[79] —*John Maloba*

After the foreign missionaries left, the tug-of-war game over use of designated funds was won by the bishop. Although officially there were still outside audits by GBGM, discretion over how to handle financial shortfalls (such as using funds in the bank to cover an urgent crisis with the intent to use the funds in the next bank wire to replace them) now fell to the bishop.

---

78. The trouble with borrowing funds is that this assumes that there will one day be the ability to repay them. See my later comments on the problems related to "temporarily" re-allocating resources.

79. Mulume wa Umba John Maloba, interview with the author, July 12, 2015. Original: "Les Américains qui ont été ici auparavant, de fois ils ont travaillé, ils étaient ici comme missionnaires, l'argent qui ils ont amené c'est eux même qui géré. Alors avec un objectif quelconque. De fois quand l'église dissent qu'ils ont besoin de ça, ils dissent que, no, no, moi l'argent que j'ai amené c'est pour autre choses. Alors, à ce moment-là, de fois, le dirigent n'étaient pas contents. Puis que, j'en voulais que, on n'est allé pas, l'église là-bas, il n'y a pas de toit. Le puit a-t-élevé tour les toits. Alors, que lui qui a l'argent il dit que no, no, ça, c'était pour les médicaments, pour exemple. Il ne donne pas. Et, on ne peut pas être content puis qu'il y a eu cas qui est urgent. De fois, le problème qui est là, il arrivé que, comme il n'y avait assez de route, il y avait le missionnaire comme pilot, il ne voulait pas accepter que l'évêque dît que No, no. Vous m'amenez, j'ai une réunion ici. No, pour lui l'évêque a ses histoires soit planifier. Alors, avec ses choses, de fois l'entendre n'était pas là."

Even the aviation ministry was now in the hands of the bishop's son, who became both the sole pilot and manager for the program; any disagreement between the bishop and pilot over the use of the plane and fuel funds had the added dimension of being a son saying "No" to his father and boss.

While the departure of the last of the foreign missionaries gave full control of the treasurer's office to the bishop and his staff, tensions still remained in that many foreign partners continued to earmark their financial contributions for specific projects, which were not always determined by the bishop to be most urgent needs.

6.3.2.3 Short Term Mission Teams: True Partners or Fair-weather Friends?

As has been previously touched upon, Americans coming to serve in North Katanga tend to be unaware of the dynamics at play in their interactions with North Katangan church leaders. This applies both to the long-term missionaries of the past and the short-term mission teams that have been coming since the final evacuation. While these groups of visitors are welcomed in North Katanga and viewed as current/potential allies/financiers, there is a reluctance to be candid with them in terms of whether the words and actions they offer during their visit have been helpful or even make sense in the North Katangan context. This reluctance is both out of desire to not shame well-intended guests and to not damage the relationship. It is also, I believe, due to the sense that these relationships are fragile, that the Americans are fair-weather friends, and therefore their egos must be stroked. Thus, all guest preachers and lecturers are praised regardless of whether their teachings were contextually appropriate/useful. Gratitude is expressed for all gifts even if they create more headaches than they solve.

> I asked Dr. Mireille about her perspectives on the medical missions that came in. She said it was a great learning experience for the physicians that came in. . . . But that the medical mission teams didn't realize that they would come in a treat ten thousand people or whatever number it was—and then wouldn't recognize that Congolese physicians had to do the follow-up, and that there were physicians left without travel money—had to get back to Kabongo, for example, or expenses to stay in Kamina to do the follow-up. It is the same phenomenon of building the school and not providing for maintenance and teachers and what it takes to run the school. You think you've done a great job in building the school, but then there is the execution of education that has to be provided.[80] —*Anonymous*

---

80. This interviewee requested her/his observation to be anonymous.

> When two Christians sit together in holy conferencing, it requires not only listening to one another but listening to where God is in the conversation. One of the things that troubles me is folks that I see from particular theological or political perspectives going to North Katanga or other parts to convince them about a particular strategy or theology that does not take into account the experiences and insights of the African context.[81]
> —Anonymous

From what I've heard and observed, this reluctance to be candid with critiques is not simply about hospitality norms. It is evidence of a relationship that is not fully decolonized—of partnerships that merely exist on paper. When partners in mission fear offering each other critiques, this is evidence of power imbalances and lack of trust that the relationship can withstand constructive criticism. Healthy missional partnerships involve a level of mutual trust and respect that is strengthened—not weakened—by honesty. Also, by treating American visitors like one would treat a financier one is trying to court instead of a co-collaborator, one is placing them outside the system of governance and administration of missional programs. This is not a healthy mission partnership; it is a donor-client relationship, and an unhealthy one at that.

Under Bishop Mande's leadership, there are signs of the existence of candidness and friendships without power imbalances between Bishop Mande and certain American allies, including some American bishops and friends he made during his years living and working in the USA. This indicates that relational dynamics are changing along a healthy trajectory. A question that could be explored in future research would be whether healthy decolonized mission partnerships can involve both true international partners *and* fair-weather financiers.

6.3.2.4 Impunity and Nepotism

As previously mentioned, one of the topics that was frequently raised by North Katangans when asked to critique the North Katangan side of the partnership was that conference leadership did not penalize those who failed to do their jobs. While I have framed the issue as "showing an abundance of grace and mercy"[82] when required to speak of it diplomatically in certain set-

---

81. This interviewee requested her/his observation to be anonymous.

82. On more than one occasion over the years, Bishop Ntambo has expressed to me his reluctance to fire, suspend, or press legal charges against a person who abused their position in the church because, by doing so, he would also be punishing all the people who depend upon that person's salary to survive—with potentially deadly consequences.

tings, the North Katangan respondents did not frame it that way. For them, the problems were stated as promotion decisions being heavily biased by family/friends connections, the failure of church authorities to punish bad managers, especially those who were relatives, and those appointed to managerial positions using their authority for personal gain instead of community development. The resounding complaint was that instead of taking punitive or corrective actions against those who mishandled church resources, those in authority had set a precedent of impunity in the church.

> The problem [on the North Katanga side] . . . is poor leadership. Why do I say poor leadership? When a leader appointed someone to a project, he [sic] needs to see if that person is able to accomplish that task on time. But if that person is not working well, you need to remove and chose another person. . . . But most of the time, those people who want to work well, they are not chosen to do that work. That is the major issue we have as Congolese. We are not seeing ahead, which [project] is properly working. Then maybe we have the sentiment to think that . . . "Kora is my friend." [i.e., nepotism] If I put Kora there, . . . then I am not putting in place the person who is capable to work on that issue. That is my own point of view what I'm seeing as Congolese. And then, also most of the time we do not want to work for people. We are working for our own [personal benefit]: If they have money, I need to spend maybe 20 percent for the church and 80 percent for myself. But this is dangerous. We need to flip that rate—maybe to work for people 80 percent and then maybe for us maybe we can get 10 percent as human being that would be helpful for our society to change and to make a good job.[83] —*Floribert Mwamba Kora*

Kabila, the oldest living (retired) pastor in the North Katanga Conference spoke passionately about what he saw as a destructive trend in administration practices. He compares the early days of his ministry (he was ordained in 1966, becoming an elder in 1968) to what he has observed in recent years. Kabila states that "impunity" is the reason for the high failure rate of church projects today. In the past, pastors were suspended for mismanagement and required to repay any funds or materials taken for personal use. In recent years, he argues, bad managers are, at most, reappointed, but not forced to

---

83. Floribert Mwamba Kora, interview with the author, July 14, 2015. (Kora's responses were in English, but some edits were made for better understanding by anglophones.)

make amends. When asked when these changes occurred, he says he cannot (or will not?) say except that the shift occurred gradually.

> If projects do not succeed, it is [because of] impunity; those responsible do not punish those who bring down projects. I still remember when we were young pastors: once we give you a project we do not insist directly; we put you on suspension.
> Do today . . . we have that? When there is someone who lets a project fall down, fine, it is finished. Sometimes we only dismiss it, and give him another job. In the past years . . . if you have lost money, you are required before you are re-established [while on suspension] to at least repay the money there. . . . I have no precision [on when this change happened]. These are things that came with time and eventually it got worse, but I cannot tell you and specify.[84] —*Kabila wa Kubangimayo*

While an expectation of impunity has allegedly led to rampant mismanagement in the conference, this is not to say that all church leaders have chosen to personally profit from it. Kabila is quick to note that one should not assume that just because one pastor took church resources that another pastor cannot be trusted.

> Yes, there have been some changes [in behaviors] but you cannot generalize. For example, you can give me money to manage today—me, as an individual, Pastor Kabila. If I abuse and divert this money, it should not be considered that Maloba did it. No, the distinction must be made. If Kabila has bad management, do not generalize that all the pastors, that all the laity [are bad managers]. . . . In the past years, when I was still young, the church in America donated the construction money, gave the sawmill money and supplies. . . . That is to say, we gave machines,

---

84. Kabila wa Kubangimayo, interview with the author, July 22, 2015. Original: "Si les projets ne réussissent pas, c'est l'impunité. Les responsables ne punissent pas ceux qui font tomber les projets. Je me rappelle encore quand nous étions pasteurs jeunes. Une fois on vous donne un projet on n'insiste pas directement. On te met en suspension. Est-ce qu'aujourd'hui et aussi d'autres années passées, nous avions ça? C'était quelqu'un qui faisait tomber les projets mais bon c'était fini. Parfois on l'écarte seulement. On lui donnait un autre travail. Dans les années passées, on n'assiste pas directement et si tu as perdu l'argent, on t'oblige avant que tu sois rétabli du moins que tu donnes que tu rembourse cet argent là. C'est la seule différence avec la question que vous avez posée avant . . . Là, je n'ai pas de précision, ce sont des choses qui venaient avec le temps et finalement cela s'empirer mais je ne peux pas vous dire et préciser."

bicycles, or other things like that. You will find at a pastor's house, when he leaves this church, he leaves all the equipment with the church, but another he takes everything when he goes away. That's why I said that we should not generalize things.

Whoever left with the [church property], this one was bad. It happens even today, we can give money for something, but sometimes the individual can appropriate, and it's bad; I consider it a sin. . . . The one who diverts money, the one who diverts the goods, and the one who does not handle the sheep of Jesus well, are bad. That's what I understand in my conception of theology. It's like that. But you have to be fair and manage the property of the church properly, manage the sheep of the church properly, you cannot take Christians as your personal workers. No, they are Christians, they are in the church, your duty, is to keep them, to protect them, to pray with them, to evangelize them, or to preach to them. So if you start taking Christians as your subjects or as your slaves, it's a sin; you must not do it. When you are given the money to build, and you divert that money to something else—the funds that were given to the construction, it is a sin too. It is [like] he who commits adultery. This is my understanding of the faith.[85] —*Kabila wa Kubangimayo*

---

85. Kabila wa Kubangimayo, interview with the author, July 22, 2015. Original: "Oui il peut y avoir des changements mais qu'on ne peut pas généraliser, par exemple, vous pouvez me donner l'argent à gérer aujourd'hui, moi, autant qu'individu, pasteur Kabila; alors si j'abuse, je détourne cet argent, il ne faut pas considérer que Maloba a fait, non, il faut un peu de distinguer les choses, si Kabila a mal gérer, il ne faut pas généraliser que tous les pasteurs, que tous les laïques, c'est un bon système, c'est ce que moi je comprends. Dans les années passées, quand j'étais encore jeune, l'église d'Amérique donnait l'argent de construction, donnait des budgets à la scierie et des fournitures en caches, c'est à dire ; on donnait des machines, des vélos, ou d'autres choses comme ça. Vous trouverez chez un pasteur, quand il quitte, cette église, il laisse tous à l'église mais un autre il prend tout il s'en va. C'est pour cela, Jai dit qu'il ne faut pas généraliser les choses. Celui qui est partis avec les choses, celui-là était mauvais. Cela arrive même aujourd'hui, on peut donner l'argent pour telle chose, mais parfois l'individu peut s'approprier et c'est mauvais, moi je considère cela comme un péché. Nous ne pouvons pas peut être pas considérer le pêché dans certaines choses et dans d'autres non, ah non, ça c'est mauvais. Celui qui détourne l'argent, celui qui détourne le bien et celui qui ne gère pas bien les brebis de jésus, tous sont mauvais. C'est ce que je comprends dans ma conception de la théologie. C'est comme ça. Mais il faut être juste et gérer bien les biens de l'église, comme il faut, gérer les brebis de l'église comme il faut, vous ne pouvez prendre les chrétiens comme votre personnel, comme vos travailleurs, non, ils sont chrétiens, ils sont dans l'église, votre devoir, 'est les garder, les protéger, prier avec eux, les évangéliser, ou bien les prêcher. Alors si vous commencer à prendre les chrétiens comme vos sujets ou comme vos esclaves, c'est un pêché, il ne faut pas le faire. Quand on vous donne l'argent pour construire et que vous détourner cet argent a autres chose, les fonds qui étaient donnés à la construction, c'est un pêché aussi, c'est lui

One thing I found noteworthy is that while over the years I have heard American partners openly and frequently speak about the need for accountability and transparency in how funds are used in North Katanga, there is a general taboo to actually suggest that any resources have been mismanaged—it is only socially acceptable to say that the management has been poorly documented. Many North Katangans themselves, however, do not hesitate to assert that they have seen church resources embezzled, misdeeds unpunished and honest workers passed over for promotions. In fact, in the interviews in 2015 there were a number of North Katangans whose responses indicated that the problems of impunity and embezzlement were getting worse.

> On the Black [Congolese] side, we also noticed, without control, there was abuse in management. . . . It was much later when people began to understand, that is to say after the failures, after several times, we realized that the issue is our church; we must take our responsibilities. We must not divert what we are given by our members or the American church. We have to manage it carefully to achieve the same goals [as] when the missionaries are there.
>
> This change began with the departure of the missionaries. When the missionaries were there, it was they who were the bosses, they were the ones who managed. . . . It's true, even the time when the missionaries were there, there were pastors, even superintendents who lost [that is, took] church property. Sometimes we could punish them harshly; sometimes the missionaries intervened [saying] "No, let it go; we'll give others." All this was a situation that did not leave good lessons when the missionaries left. . . . There are who continue until today to lose the goods of the church. . . . There was the cement taken and we let them go; they leave with the cement. He [the bishop] is supposed to manage, to take care until the end, that's what he said tonight. It reminds you of the reality we just talked about. It was a pressure, you must be there, and finish what you started before you leave, it's safer.[86] —*Guy Nyembo Kinkundulu (ordained elder and conference evangelist)*

---

qui fait l'adultère, c'est ma compréhension de la foi."

86. Guy Nyembo Kinkundulu, interview with the author, July 15, 2015. Original: "Cote noir, nous avons remarque aussi, sans contrôle, il y avait l'abus dans la gestion, quand il ya conflits entre nous, et le blanc n'etait pas la, chose ne marchait pas, c'est plus tard après que les gens commençaient à prendre conscience, c'est a dire après les échecs, après plusieurs temps, on s'est rendu compte qu'il s'agit de notre église, nous devons prendre nos responsabilités, il ne faut détourner ce qu'on nous donne, soit des membres, soit de l'église américaine, on doit gérer ça, soigneusement pour aboutir au même objectifs et quand les missionnaires est la . . . Ce changement a commencé avec

Bishop Mande is aware of these accusations and sentiments within the conference and has openly said/warned that under his episcopacy abuses of power and misappropriation of church resources will not be tolerated. A considerable number of reappointments were made in his first full year as bishop, including removing from powerful appointments those known to have abused those positions. Addressing such abuses is not simply a pragmatic matter; it is a theological one. As J. N. J. Kritzinger notes, a theology of stewardship, based on the creation narratives and the image of God, strengthens a sense of accountability to God our Creator, "which sets us free from all human domination and colonial manipulation."[87] This I view as a significant step in the decolonizing process—to refuse to have a lower standard for Congolese leaders than for foreign missionaries in terms of stewardship, and thereby reject the internalized (neo)colonial assumption that Congolese leaders are inherently less trustworthy in their management of resources (and thus the only way to control them is to demand more accountability and transparency in their reports).

What remains now is to deal with the second half of the (neo)colonial assumption: that Congolese are inherently less intelligent/competent, so it is to be expected that they do not meet international standards in their job performance. One factor that has reinforced this belief is the gap in training for their job that North Katangans have received compared to their American counterparts. With the appointment system, oftentimes one's perceived trustworthiness or loyalty results in one being appointed to manage a program outside one's area of knowledge. This problem is exacerbated by the previously mentioned dearth of scholarships available for church leaders outside of theology majors.

---

le départ des missionnaires, quand les missionnaires étaient là, c'est eux qui étaient les patrons, c'est eux qui géraient, y a pas moyen de montrer leur incapacités, c'est vraie, même a l'époque quand les missionnaires étaient là, y avait des pasteurs, même des surintendants qui perdaient, l'histoire de l'église, les biens de l'église parfois on peut frapper fort, parfois les missionnaires interviennent : non, laisser, on va donner d'autres. tout cela c'était une situation qui n'est pas donner, lier a de bonnes leçons quand les missionnaires sont parties, les gens ont commencés à réaliser, et y'en a qui continue jusqu'à aujourd'hui à perdre les biens de l'église, il y avait des choses de l'église de l'évêque, la bas, il a dit bon, nous ne pouvons faire beaucoup de changements . . . Il y a avait le ciment déposé la bas et nous les laissons partir, ils partiront avec le ciment, il doit gérer, s'assumer jusqu'au bout, c'est ce qu'il a dit ce soir. Ca vous rappelle cette réalité dont on vient de parler; c.-à-d., c'était une pression, vous devez être là, et terminer ce qu'on a commencé avant de partir, là c'est plus sûr."

87. J. N. J. Kritzinger, email with the author.

> [One reason] that the church here does not know how to manage well is that sometimes the church is appointed somebody to do a job [s/he] has not studied because [s/he] is a pastor. "No, you will be an agronomist." He has never been agronomist. How can he lead this project? So, here is at least what I find with the Americans: [they should support] ways to train the people in finance and different [subjects other than just theology].[88] —*John Maloba*

This issue is trickier because, while the response to deliberate abuse of power can be sanctions and required restitutions, the response to poor management due to incompetence—potentially due to nepotistic hiring practices—could either be demotion (which can shame/punish a person for the inability to succeed in an appointed job) or training (while temporarily accepting a subpar performance). Mande appears to be doing a mixture of the two responses in attempts to dramatically improve performance levels. He is organizing training programs as well as seeking graceful ways to reappoint persons to jobs that better fit their skill sets. It is too early to measure the impact of these recent changes or to what degree political pressures (threats/intimidation) or contextual challenges (e.g., power outages, insufficient wages requiring moonlighting, chronic illnesses, etc.) will undermine the process.

Accusations of playing favorites and protecting those accused of serious crimes were not limited to Congolese in positions of authority. American missionaries were also observed doing this. The interview with conference evangelist Guy Nyembo Kinkundulu expressed this critique best:

> Also we noticed, on the American side, when one is a friend of a missionary, one can become untouchable—someone who must be obeyed. If he raped [someone], the missionary says "No he must be left [that is, not punished]." . . . Someone can be caught in adultery with the wife of others; when you go [to report it] to the church, the missionaries get angry, "He must not be touched." He is his employee. This was a contradiction to our teaching to and how to handle these it who are in close collaboration with the missionaries.
>
> Even the drivers. A driver who is goes to look for pastors who are walking on foot to the conference, if he does not have

---

88. Mulume wa Umba John Maloba, interview with the author, July 12, 2015. Original: "Et alors, que l'église ici ne sais pas bien gérer c'est puis que par fois l'église on donne quelqu'un le travail ou il n'y a pas étudié parce il est pasteur. Non, vous aller être agronome. Lui, il n'a jamais être agronome. Comment il peut diriger ce projet? Alors, voilà au moins ce que je trouve avec les américains : la façons de former les gens y de financer et différent."

> the blessing of the missionary, he does not take them [that is, give them a ride]. And if he takes them, the missionary is not happy. However, if the diocese finds them we pick them up with the help of the trucks. We think that the missionary works for the church.... It was very difficult. It's sad ...
>
> People who worked close to the missionaries, they received a lot of advantages. When a missionary is in good relationship with a pastor, the pastor is saved. The others who are in the same environment, they do not have the chance. Really, there was no justice. It looks like he [the missionary] came for some individual and not for everyone. This is what was observed. It was discouraging for some pastors; the doors are locked. This side of the missionaries was difficult.
>
> And on the side of the Congolese, there are people who wanted to appropriate the missionaries, the missionary became private property. When another person comes, he invents all the reasons sometimes to lie to the missionary to keep the person away, so that [the missionary] remains his property. Sometimes the missionary does not discover this; he does not know that this person is manipulating him so that the benefits are granted to him alone.
>
> But for the distribution of goods, there were at Christmas clothes, and those who profit from this are people close to the missionaries. And we, the other pastors, the other laity, we are a little distant. Honestly, we saw the missionaries let [undistributed] clothing rot in depots, and then they were taken out and burned. We truly saw this in some places. We felt the difference of cultures, a little exaggerated selfishness. It felt like that, because it's better to give someone something than to burn it. A lot of old things—not just medicines.[89] —*Guy Nyembo Kinkundulu*

89. Guy Nyembo Kinkundulu, interview with the author, July 15, 2015. Original: "Aussi on a remarqué, du cote américain, quand on est ami d'un missionnaire, y en a qui étaient intouchables, on doit obéir aux services, s'il a violé, le missionnaire dit non il faut le laisser ... quelqu'un peut être attrapé par un adultère avec la femme d'autrui, quand vous allez a l'église, les missionnaires s'énervent, il faut pas les toucher, c'est son personnel, ça était une contradiction par rapport à notre enseignement aux et comment gérer ces cadres la qui sont en étroite collaboration avec les missionnaires, même les chauffeurs, un chauffeur qui va chercher des pasteurs qui marchent a pieds qui vont a la conférence, s'il n'a pas l'avis du missionnaire il ne les prend, et s'il les prends le missionnaire n'est pas content, cependant si les diocèse trouve on les ramasse à l'aide des camions, nous pensons, le missionnaire travaille pour l'église, si nous devons l'aider on l'aide, ça c'était beaucoup difficile, c'est triste, nous avons connu aussi des faveurs, des gens qui ont travaillés tout près des missionnaires, ils ont eu beaucoup d'avantages et quand un missionnaire est en bonne relation un pasteur, tel, lui est sauvé, les autres qui sont dans

The issue of giving preferential treatment in the form of gifts, employment, or mercy in the case of crimes is a complicated one that is deeply entwined in and goes beyond the legacy of colonialism and efforts to decolonize relationships. For Congolese church leaders in positions of authority, the sense of moral obligation to support and protect one's family and close friends is at odds with the calls to provide every member of the conference equal opportunities for advancement and access to resources. Foreign missionaries must wrestle with the conflicting desires to promote a meritocracy—instead of nepotism—in church leadership while at the same time building genuine friendships with North Katangans (with all the moral obligations this entails)—instead of socially segregating themselves like in colonial days. The ability to be completely impartial yet fully with a community, is, I have concluded, a myth.

As J. N. J. Kritzinger has noted, the values at odds with one another in such a situation can be described in terms of ecclesial imaginations.[90] For example, when we think in terms of church as a family with a benevolent patriarch, the values of protecting and providing for family members (Grace) outweighs the question of whether they merit such assistance (Works). In contrast, when we think purely in terms of the Church as the Body of Christ, we are more likely to think terms of which person is best suited for which function of the Body.

6.3.2.5 Double Standards: Good Enough for Congo

Another critique, while not a common theme raised, is an important one: missionaries of the past modeled a good-enough approach to construction projects in North Katanga. Conference evangelists Mbayo Mujinga

---

le même milieu, ils n'ont pas la chance, vraiment, il n'y avait pas de justice, on dirait qu'il est venu pour quelques individu et non pas pour tout le monde, cela on a observé, c'était décourageant pour certains pasteurs les portes c'est verrouillés, c'était difficile de ce cote des missionnaires. Et du coté des congolais, on trouve des gens qui voulaient s'approprier les missionnaires, le missionnaire devenait propriété privée. Quand l'autre il vient, il invente toutes les raisons parfois jusqu'à mentir au missionnaire pour éloigner la personne, et comme ça cela reste ca propriété, parfois le missionnaire découvre pas, il ne sait ce que cette personne est entrain de manipuler pour que les avantages soient seulement accorder à lui, a lui seul, c'est un constat aussi. Mais pour la distribution de bien, y avait à Noël, des habits et ceux qui profitent de cela, se sont des gens proches des missionnaires et nous, les autres pasteurs, les autres laïcs, nous sommes un peu éloignés, c'est vraie, on a vu les missionnaires faire pourrir les habits dans les dépôts, et puis on les sortaient pour les faire brûler, ça on a vu, vraiment, quelques part, on sentait la différence des cultures, un peu d'égoïsme exagéré. Ça on sentait ça, parce que mieux vaut on donner à quelqu'un que de brûler, beaucoup de choses périmés, non seulement les médicaments."

90. J. N. J. Kritzinger, email with the author.

Maxine and Guy Nyembo Kinkundulu saw this as a glaring double standard. While church construction standards in America during that time generally included smooth painted interior walls and a ceiling that hid the roofline, missionary-managed construction projects in North Katanga tended to build up to the point of addressing pragmatic concerns (e.g., Does it provide shade and keep out the rain? Is it likely to fall down soon?) and not worry much about aesthetics.[91]

> At a certain moment in the church of Congo, even the buildings that were built, many were hangars; we did not think about quality. For example, in the North Katanga, we should have a big and beautiful church, where all the pastors can gather for the big ceremonies. I can give the example of the church of South Congo: they have all their big gatherings in the church of Jerusalem.[92] But we in North Katanga do not have a big sanctuary. Also the churches [in North Katanga] are not beautiful, not fixed up. When Katanga started having a conference and a diocese, one only considered the number [of buildings] and not the quality.[93] —*Mbayo Mujinga*
>
> I can add to what he [Rev. Mujinga] said about this construction situation. Most of the buildings of missionaries in North Katanga were not finished. There aren't [glass] windows or ceilings in our churches which have been used for fifty years in this state. These missionaries are gone, and afterwards we have copied these models which we think are correct—with ceilings not finished. Now we must finish the ceilings.[94] —*Guy Nyembo Kinkundulu*

91. An exception to this double standard in the region is the chapel at Mulungwishi seminary in South Congo, which features stained glass windows and carved wooden doors all done by Congolese artisans.

92. This is a reference to the large church in Lubumbashi, which was built during the colonial period.

93. Mbayo Mujinga, interview with the author, July 16, 2015. Original: "A un certain moment l'église du Congo, même les bâtiments qui ont été construit, nombreux étaient des hangars. On a pas penser à la qualité, par exemple au Nord Katanga, Il fallait avoir une grande et belle église, là où tous les pasteurs peuvent se rassembler pour les grandes cérémonies, je peux donner l'exemple de l'église du sud Congo, on a, toutes les grandes manifestations se passent dans l'église de Jérusalem, dans les limites sud, mais on au Nord Katanga, on a pas de grande paroisse et aussi les églises ne sont pas belles, pas améliorer. Quand Katanga a commencer à avoir une conférence et un diocèse, on comptait seulement sur le nombre et pas sur la qualité."

94. Guy Nyembo Kinkundulu, interview with the author, July 15, 2015. Original: "Je peux ajouter à ce qu'il a dit, après cette situation de construction, la plus part des

While one could argue that a quantity over quality approach made strategic sense when trying to address with limited financial means the problem of numerous sanctuary walls collapsing every rainy season and grass roofs needing constant maintenance, the standard of what made a sanctuary, parsonage, or other project building good enough to be declared completed was not the same as the standard applied to the construction of missionary homes; this discrepancy was not lost on the evangelists, nor have I failed to notice that every Jehovah's Witnesses' kingdom hall I have seen throughout the region is well-built and painted.

While architectural styles have changed over the years in the USA, with "open concept," "exposed pipes and beams," "distressed walls," and even concrete slab flooring now being viewed as an legitimate aesthetic choice found in fashion magazines, I have found that suggesting to North Katanga church leaders today that the dropped ceilings which they want to install are both impractical (quickly stained) and out of fashion is a tone-deaf remark. It is one thing for people to choose an "industrial look" for their home, office, or sanctuary. It is another if that is all they have ever been able to afford and experience, and they desire an aesthetic that has until now been out of their financial reach. I also recognize within myself a dual-standard (that is, neocolonial attitude) at play. It would not occur to me to judge a congregation in the USA for deciding to install wall-to-wall carpeting (which is also quickly stained and out of fashion) in the sanctuary, build a ceiling that hides the wires, or to put plaster or drywall over old walls. Such things convey to the congregation and community that this is a vital congregation—not a tired one that can't even manage to maintain its own building. Yet, my knee-jerk reaction has been to judge congregations in North Katanga for wasting money on similar efforts of vanity when those funds could have been spent on more pressing needs. This is similar to the dual-standard I once had about church choir uniforms: In the USA, they seem like a reasonable choice that can build a sense of belonging to a team and provide a solution to members who can't afford a wardrobe as nice as wealthier members,[95] but in Congo I initially thought it ridiculous to be asked to contribute hundreds of dollars for choir uniforms when the majority of the congregation was facing basic

---

bâtiments au Nord Katanga des missionnaires étaient inachevés. Il n'ya des vitres ni de plafonds dans nos églises et on les a utilisés pendant 50 ans dans cet état. Et ces missionnaires sont partis, et nous par la suite nous avons copie ces modèles que nous pensons correctes avec des plafonds non terminer. Maintenant il faut terminer les plafonds."

95. My mother pointed out this benefit to me years ago. After noticing that a fellow choir member was distraught at the talk of the choir abandoning its use of robes, she then found out that the member had joined the choir in order to have something suitable to wear to church.

survival issues, such as feeding their family each day. It took me time to start to understand the numerous reasons why a congregation would prioritize choir uniforms over, for example, nutrition programs.

These double standards could be analyzed through the lens of neocolonial critiques (i.e., racially-based assumptions of superiority), but conversations about classism, such as the harsh judgements frequently made in America about Americans receiving charity or government assistance, are also applicable. The societal expectation in the USA is that in order to be worthy of receiving financial help, a person must not own or purchase anything that is associated with comfortable living, such as nice clothes, electronics, or an attractive home or vehicle.[96] Even eating food not associated with poverty is judged.[97] Likewise, divergences from these sorts of expectations in North Katanga can be seen as comical to American visitors (e.g., a mud and grass hut with a satellite dish on the roof) since the belief is that there is a set order to what items one should acquire first. For example, purchasing a fashionable outfit or a television when one is malnourished is viewed negatively. Yet, from the perspective of the one making the purchase, it is a smart strategic decision; using that money on food won't solve the long-term battle with hunger, but being able to look nice in public or have access to information and mental escape via electronic devices provides a number of long-term benefits, including increased social status. A perfect example of this decision-making logic can be found in the *Sapeurs* of Kinshasa, DR Congo. This internationally famous society is composed of Congolese men who spend large percentages on their incomes on high-fashion suits despite most of them living in what Americans would consider impoverished neighborhoods.[98]

Circling back to the topic of standards of church construction, one could argue that quality should not be treated as a luxury but as a core value.[99] Instead of modeling the value of quality by building each sanctuary as if one would if it were for an expat congregation, a "good enough for Congo" precedent was set. While North Katanga leaders are beginning to challenge what defines good construction by building at standards that far surpass those of the past,[100] the damage done by (neo)colonial double-standards

96. E.g., Cunha, "This is What Happened."
97. E.g., Holley, "Republican Lawmaker Wants to Ban Welfare Recipients."
98. Barnett, "Fashion Cult."
99. I credit my father's love of talking about the points raised in Robert Pirsig's manifesto *Zen and the Art of Motorcycle Maintenance* for first challenging me to ponder the importance of quality as a core value.
100. For example, The UMC conference center in Kamina now has a dropped ceiling, and plans for the building of a modern cathedral have been launched.

when it comes to not raising the expectation of craftsmanship and the value of quality work in all efforts still remains.

6.3.3 Reports: Pragmatic and Psychological Divides

One of recurring themes I noticed in the interviews with North Katangans was a frustration over donor demands for official reports, which were often seen as unreasonable considering the logistical and political challenges involved in meeting report requirements and deadlines. Underneath the tensions over reports was the sense of being accused of wrongdoing. As has been explained to me over the years by Bishop Ntambo and other North Katangans, the formal written reporting process that is considered normal bureaucratic procedures in the USA and many other countries was initially foreign to Bishop Ntambo and his generation of church leaders. Demanding a project leader to submit a financial account of intake and spending along with a list (and photos) of accomplishments and property belonging to the project itself was heard as an accusation of wrongdoing—a challenge to prove one's innocence.

I witnessed this firsthand during my brief stint in 2005 as the interim director of the conference's development department. Dumbfounded by the difficulty I was having persuading project directors to submit basic written reports at our monthly meetings (I naively thought I could solve the problem of each director vying for an audience with the bishop by creating consolidated briefing papers for him to review, which listed the major accomplishments as well as any issues requiring assistance/intervention), I began to ask Congolese friends why this was happening and why, despite regular face to face meetings, directors refrained from mentioning even urgent crises (such as, "All the conference's cattle are starving due to the pasture being burned by vandals"). It was then I was told that requesting reports was heard as questioning one's integrity and competency. When I asked questions such as "How many pigs do we have at the farm?" what was heard was "I accuse you of stealing pigs." The most explosive example of this was when, at a day when malnourished children were being fed during a visit of Americans, I noticed that the amount of food in the pots did not look like it could feed all the children in the program, many of which had been standing in line a long time and were crying. I asked the bishop's wife whether there would be enough food for them. As I soon learned, this was heard as me publicly accusing her of stealing funds from the program, and she became furious at me.

All that said, I have seen plenty of counterexamples to these anecdotal stories that makes me question whether I really was committing a cultural *faux pas* by asking such questions. At each annual conference, each department and district is expected to submit an oral and written report, and after each report people come forward (usually more than the allotted time allows) to question elements of the report. There is rarely reluctance to point out inconsistencies or question the validity of statements made, although even then praise tends to come in the form of statements and questions are usually in actuality critiques. I have also observed that those in North Katanga who are doing highly effective work tend to be eager to present detailed reports that show what they have accomplished. This makes me wonder if the underlying issue has more to do with a reluctance to submit reports or answer questions that could bring shame upon the individual, expose misconduct of an authority figure, and/or potentially shut down a funding stream.

Below, Bishop Ntambo expresses his analysis and frustration when it comes to American donors asking for reports.

> For us, first, the great critique [we face] is [lack of] credibility, accountability. We grew up far away from dollars. But, when you receive . . . money, one part is that Americans want to know each penny—how it has been used. Another side is Congolese. The part Congolese is how things are to accomplish the need of that money given. The Americans have time limit. "We gave you for the church building. We want, after three months, for you to come and ask—I mean, with auditor." They forget that we have problems with roads; we have problems with communications. We have problems with security matters. We have problems with the system—how it's used in Congo. Which means, you gave me ten dollars. The government agency of Congo wants also to tax and for you to finish to move quickly, you need out of the ten dollars you give one dollar so someone can help you and make things go. For Americans, they don't understand. If we don't use it, things cannot move. Well, for some that is corruption, but it is the system. If you don't do it, you can't move. I think you went through different ways in that area. It is not the fault of the church, but it is a system. And that is one side for the misunderstanding that is in between.
>
> You say "stealing," but why to steal? Africans, they give a lot. I mean, when you bring building, we have land to offer ourselves, we have concrete to offer ourselves, we have sand, bricks offered by ourselves. Sometimes we bring wood [beams]. And the assistance we receive is basically cement and roofing. Well, when you

> look, 80 percent is given by local people. Twenty percent is given by assistance. And that assistance, when we say "This church has been built by the church in America," it is a connection. We are proud of that connection, but it is not that 100 percent was given by the church in America. No, 80 percent was done by ourselves, but we want to honor the one who has given money. And this is why—even the ones you saw who came—it is not the whole thing that was done with their money. But we are proud to share that "Florida has come to contribute with this and this to us" and we enjoy to keep that relationship because we know that if that relationship will continue, with the willing of the people to have churches in their communities, they will continue to make bricks and that offer of buying cement will continue, so we can build our country.[101] —*Nkulu Ntanda Ntambo*

While expressing frustration about the reporting system, some North Katangans also expressed a criticism that American donors did not do enough to verify and insist that funds sent for specific projects reached their intended destination. A few offered comparisons to how the "Swiss Board" (that is, Connexio, the mission agency of The UMC's France-Switzerland-North Africa Conference) interacted with North Katanga. While Connexio sent significantly less financial assistance to North Katanga compared to the USA, it was repeatedly noticed that the amount of funds they sent were predictable so long as follow-up reports were submitted.

> The relationship with Switzerland/Europe was very demanding. They were doing follow-up on what they sent. That was not the case in what [funds] we were receiving from America. The follow-up was not really there.... But for the relationship with Europe—with Switzerland, they were making follow-up—they need to receive your report. They also come and make a follow-up of what they have sent, and they want to see if things are ok. If they are not ok, they stop giving you their assistance. I remember that when I left to pursue my studies at Africa University, those who remained and were the new leaders of the youth did not send reports, and it led Switzerland to stop their assistance. So, they were so demanding. They wanted to make sure that what they are assisting the church with is fruitful. If the fruit is not there, they stop. This was not

---

101. Nkulu Ntanda Ntambo, interview with the author, July 20, 2015.

> the case with the Americans. The receiving was just there and sometimes no follow-up . . .
>
> I did not see [a relationship between American funding and whether reports were sent]. It was something that was conceived and decided. And, if it released, it is released. How are you going to use it? You don't know; they don't know. They may not need—until the next assistance, if there is a new grant, it was sent. But that was not the case with Switzerland board because they were making a follow-up. What they were sending was not as big as America, but at least with their smaller amount they were making a follow-up because they wanted to see what they were sending was being used in the correct way.[102] —*Nday Bondo*

During the time before the ordered evacuation, missionaries were heavily involved in the oversight and reporting process of projects in North Katanga. When they left, church leaders faced the unplanned handover of these duties while at the same time responding to a humanitarian disaster which engulfed much of the region. The task of collecting receipts, uploading photos, scanning documents, tracking spending, creating itemized reports, and meeting submission deadlines when working in locations lacking computers, access to internet, or even stable electricity—where the idea of getting store receipts or multiple bids was laughable—was such that oftentimes reports were not submitted correctly or at all. Those tasked with submitting reports on behalf of the conference were located a several day's journey from those working on the ground; hence, breakdowns of communication happened on multiple levels. Even the logistics of transporting materials and money meant that slippage and theft frequently happened. No one wanted to report back to America that their contributions had been lost en route or that someone in the chain of command had re-allocated the resources for another purpose. Oftentimes, Americans seeking follow-up information found that their calls and emails were left unanswered. For North Katangans working on the ground who felt undermined by financial re-allocation decisions, it felt as though Americans were enabling these decisions by not insisting on proof of the accuracy of reports and not holding accountable those who did not send it.[103]

---

102. Nday Bondo, interview with the author, July 14, 2015.

103. I am writing here not just about what was said in the interviews but also about numerous conversations I have had since 2005 with both Americans and North Katangans who shared their frustrations about reports and the lack thereof.

> Before the war, nearly all of the projects were financed and directed by the missionaries. It was the missionaries who brought the needed things; it was the missionaries who paid people, it was the missionaries who did almost everything. The Christians were there like workers. But, with the evolution that we've had—after the war—with the philosophy that we appreciated from the American missionaries who now give the responsibility to the Congolese people. The missionaries sent funds and it is now the Congolese Christians who operate the work. There is a large evolution—because now the Congolese Christians have recognized their responsibilities—that he receives a fund, and he does everything he can to make sure that these funds do good things....
>
> The mistakes are shared. First, I'd like to share something I see that is wrong on the side of the missionaries. When they give funds, I think they should follow what happens with those funds. Money is given for a certain task. Sometimes he gives money, and he abstains [from follow-up]. I think that when they are collecting funds for a project, the construction of a clinic somewhere, or a church, they should follow things until the point that the church is completed. Sometimes missionaries give, and then leave it.
>
> And us, the Congolese, sometimes we receive money. The money is given for the functioning of a specific program. Sometimes, I don't know, we search for the money, for example, for a church—the foundation up to the roof. But it isn't the fund for the repairs of another church. Sometimes we do what is called the *virement de compte* (transfer of account)—that is what is bad. Sometimes there are projects that are unfinished because the money that was given for one project was used for another. When there is supervision, the mismanagement of funds will be diminished.[104] —*Daniel Mumba*

---

104. Daniel Mumba, interview with the author, July 13, 2015. Original: "Avant la guerre, presque le grand parti des projets était supporté et dirigé par les missionnaires. Ce sont les missionnaires qui amènent les nécessaires. Ce sont les missionnaires qui payent les gens. Ce sont les missionnaires qui faisaient presque tout. Les chrétiens étaient là comme des travailleurs. Mais, avec l'évolution actuel qui nous avons après la guerre, avec la philosophie que nous apprécions dès les missionnaires américaines, qui donnent maintenant la responsabilité au peuple congolais—le missionnaires envolent des fonds et ce sont maintenant les chrétiens congolais qui font fonctionner ces travaux. Il y a une grande révolution. Parce que on amène les chrétiens congolais à reconnaitre leurs responsabilités qu'il reçoive un fond et il doive tout faire pour que ce fonds puis donner de bons... Les erreurs sont presque partagées. D'abord, je vais dire quelque chose que je

Another issue raised in the interviews was that the ones tasked with reporting have often not been the ones managing the program itself. Thus, those receiving the benefits from the work can be penalized for the (in)actions of those appointed to submit reports on behalf of the conference.

American partners were faulted for taking the official requests and reports they received at face value, instead of traveling to North Katanga to see for themselves. Such a critique highlights to me the use of Americans as pawns in conflicts between North Katangans themselves. By playing the role of distant donor instead of investing the time and expense required to personally know the strengths and weaknesses of individual leaders and the relational dynamics between leaders, Americans can inadvertently enable unhealthy actions. This *doing for* versus *being with* response may seem the most efficient and fiscally responsible course of action, but, as will be discussed in chapter 7, both theologian Samuel Wells and economist Dambisa Moyo agree that sending aid in this way is a recipe for increasing—not solving—problems.

> The mistakes . . . maybe [are] in the way they [Americans] are asking; they are asking and then they are making conditions: "If you don't give feedback; we stop sending help and gifts." Maybe people are working. People are receiving. People are forgetting maybe to send a report to that side. When those people stop [sending funds], no leader will suffer, but the one who is getting that help will suffer more. If those people who are getting that support could send the report themselves, that would be fine. . . . Another part which is not well done is to send the report on time, and then people are suffering more. And then maybe [another mistake is to not] ask to [physically] come and to follow-up on that. Because if you send something, you need

---

vois de mal de nos missionnaires. Lorsqu'ils dont un fonds: moi je pense ils doivent avoir un grand suivi pour ces fonds. L'argent est allé pour telle travaille. Par fois il dont ces fonds et il s'abstient. Ça ce ne pas bien. Moi je pense que lorsqu'il est un train de collecter un fonds pour, par exemple la construction d'un clinque quelque part—dans un village quel conque ou la construction d'un église—ils doive nécessairement poursuivre jusque que cette église est terminée. Par fois nos missionnaires donnent et ils laissent. Et nous, les congolaise. Parfois nous recevons de l'argent—argent désigné pour le fonctionnent de tel problème. Il y a de fois—je ne sais pas—nous cherchons a—c'était l'argent pour un église—c'est-à-dire une église de la fondation jusqu'à la toiture. Mais ce ne pas la fond pour la réparation d'une autre église. De fois nous faisons ce que on appelle le virement de conte. C'est ce qu'est mauvais. A ce moment vous voyez qu'il y a les projets qui sont inachevé parce que l'argent qui était loué pour telle mission a travaillé aussi pour une autre mission. C'est qui est bonne : Quand il y a la suivi, je pense que le détournement des fond va diminuer."

> to come and ask ... where people are living. If you ... stay in the US sending only money, only money without coming and see what the money is doing. ... Those are the mistakes people are making. ... Because if you send the money, maybe to pay school expenses, maybe for orphanage children, you need to come and to see if those children are getting those funds. If people are suffering here, and then they get the report that we paid school expenses for children, and the children do not get that money, the children are suffering about that money which is not reaching them. That is the mistake: to not follow where the money is going. And then, the second thing is to be aware of which projects you need to support and which projects are not good to support. That is maybe not being on the ground to know what is going on.
>
> Maybe if you get something which is like a project, you must know, this project will be helpful on the ground or not? If you didn't know, maybe you will spend money which will not respond to the issue which is on the ground. That is, maybe when people are getting some projects, they need also to send someone to come on the ground to see if this project will be helpful. Then, even if they send money, they need also to follow and then to see if that project was well done. Maybe that will be fine[105] —*Floribert Mwamba Kora*

Since his election as bishop in 2017, Mande Muyombo has tried to rectify the problem of reports being overdue or missing by stressing to program and department heads the importance of professional reporting. One year into his episcopacy, the results of this effort remain mixed. At the North Katanga Conference's annual meeting in June 2018, the bishop tasked me with presenting a talk to all the clergy and laity gathered for the conference on the topic of decolonizing relationships and the importance of submitting reports. The talk began by naming psychological contaminations of colonialism—(a) the belief that *Bazungu* are smarter than Congolese; (b) the belief that *Bazungu* are more trustworthy; (c) the belief that *Bazungu* are more competent project leaders—emphasizing that both Americans and Congolese have been contaminated by these ideas, and how this has negatively impacted partnerships until today. It identified frequent complaints made by those in the partnership (e.g., lack of understanding, lack of reports) and then contrasted this with the marks of healthy friendships between peers (a) trust; (b) respect; and (c) communication. The talk received

---

105. Floribert Mwamba Kora, interview with the author, July 14, 2015.

much praise from North Katangans and had a high-level of congregational engagement (finishing my sentences aloud, nods, and audible sounds of agreement). It appeared clear to me (as well as visiting Americans present) that I had touched upon what Paulo Freire called a generative theme of the community.[106]

All that said, there continue to be some program heads who submit professional reports in a timely manner, and an alarming (by American expectations) number who do not. I do not know the reasons each person has for failure to submit; I suspect that in many cases it is more complicated than incompetence or insubordination. It waits to be seen what actions and/or consequences Bishop Mande will implement in response, but freezing salaries of those who neither meet deadlines nor request extensions is being considered as an option.

6.4 RETURN OF FULLTIME AMERICAN MISSIONARIES?

As previously discussed, the waves of violence in Katanga throughout the 1990s led to multiple missionary evacuations, resulting finally in a *de facto* foreign missionary moratorium[107] by the end of the decade which has, with a couple debatable exceptions, continued for two decades in the North Katanga Conference. Is it time for the moratorium to be lifted? What did interview participants think of this, and did they believe it would be good for there to be American missionaries living in North Katanga again? When asked directly,[108] all except one North Katangan participant (who declined being recorded or referred to by name) expressed a positive view of the idea of American United Methodists coming now to live in North Katanga. The Americans and Europeans I spoke with formally and informally had mixed opinions, however, with a number expressing ambivalence about whether the era of American missionaries living in North Katanga is and/or should be over.

Daniel Mumba, a district superintendent, expressed what appears to be the majority view among North Katangan United Methodist leaders based on the interviews conducted and conversations I have heard and engaged in over the years:

---

106. That is, an issue that generates high levels of emotion when raised and thus can be used to leverage community action. One could also call this a "hot topic."

107. Referring to missionaries who move to North Katanga to live, not those who come for visits.

108. Since the interview with Bishop Ntambo had to be cut short due to an urgent matter, he was not asked directly.

> We are called to work together. There is experience that we receive from foreigners, and there is our experience that we put together with the foreigners to make programs move forward . . .
>
> When one wants to work together with a *Mzungu*, one sees that one is ready to receive the gifts one needs. . . . Where there is a *Mzungu*, there is someone who wants order, someone who wants transparence, someone who wants a job done well. If someone is working with a *Mzungu*, he will do a good job well supervised. . . .
>
> The presence of a *Mzungu* pushes people to work. The Congolese people work when they see the presence of a *Mzungu*. This partnership with missionaries and the Congolese can succeed. We want to work with their support and assistance.[109]
> —Daniel Mumba

John Maloba's interview presents a more nuanced reflection of the potential benefits of foreign missionaries returning and whether their presence is essential to project success.[110] He also criticizes missionaries of the past for not adequately preparing local leaders to take over their roles.

> The thing that made the American missionaries leave was the war. There was no peace in the country. The Americans who were in Luana during Mobutu's time, they experienced looting. All their belongings were stolen. Thus, they were ill at ease. That's why they left. . . . There are those who were in Nyembo; also with the war they fled to Zambia. . . .

109. Daniel Mumba, interview with the author, July 13, 2015. Original: "Nous savons que nous sommes appelés à travailler ensemble. Il y a des expériences que nous recevons de bazungu—les étrangers—et il y a notre expérience que nous mettons ensemble avec les étrangers pour faire évoluer les projets au Nord Katanga . . . Alors, quand on veut travailler ensemble avec un Mzungu, on se voit que on est prêt à recevoir ces dons on a besoin. Ça c'est l'impact. Alors, l'impact est là que même là où il y a un Mzungu c'est quelqu'un qui veut d'ordre, c'est quelqu'un qui veut la transparence, c'est quelqu'un qui veut un travaille bien soigner. Vous verrez que même c'est lui qui voulait fainéante parce qu'il y a le présence d'un Mzungu a cote de lui, il va faire un bon travail—un travail bien soigner . . . La présence d'un Mzungu pousse les gens à travailler. Le gens congolais—les fainéante congolais qui ne veulent pas travailler mais quand ils voient la présence d'un Mzungu, ils travaillent. C'est pourquoi j'aimerais que ce partenariat entre les missionnaires et les congolais puis aller parce que nous voulons aller l'avant et nous voulons construire beaucoup avec leur appuis et assistance."

110. As documented in section 5.3.1.5, a number of North Katangan leaders interviewed expressed changing beliefs when it comes to making the distinction between foreign missionaries being beneficial vs. essential to success.

Since the time of Bishop Ntambo, I have not seen a missionary living here in North Katanga. There are only the partners, the friends of North Katanga who come to help North Katanga if they have some funds. One gives to someone's project and returns home. . . .

What I think is that [the absence of missionaries] is good, yes, but it is also not good. The problem that exists it that missionaries who came should have taken time to teach the people how to raise money, how to manage things, and prepared our leadership on everything about administration and management of property. Then, if they did not teach [these things], really, it was not good. I think they should have been there to teach us and then, after having taught us, they come back and verify if what we have been taught is really what we now practice. . . .

Yes, we have missionaries here [that is, North Katangans paid by GBGM], but these missionaries that we have, they are not like the American missionaries. The Black missionaries who travel to do fundraising do not find funds like the White missionaries, the Americans. So, that's the problem we have. [The reasons for this are] (1) One cannot give to someone one doesn't know. (2) In order to give money, you have to trust the person [who is collecting funds]. So here it is, what happens. But, when it is a White person, people know that this person is from a certain conference; they can even know their life story. So, they are right sometimes to doubt giving to someone else whom they do not know. Will they do good work? Will they give you a report? Will they bring the materials to the intended recipients? That's it.

There is change in the mentality of people in North Katanga. At the beginning it was only White missionaries who went to the United States and brought the project and construction money. And now, Blacks go there in the name of the church. They also bring back money for the construction and other projects of the church. It is the example of the other period of Bishop Ntambo: When he started going to the USA himself to search for funds from our partners. And he brought back money so we could construct churches, schools, and even parsonages and launch other projects. At first it wasn't that way—it was only the missionaries who went. Then the Black men said the Americans don't just help their friends, but they will help everyone for the development to help everyone. There is also a change in the mind of people—development doesn't always require a White person. A Black can manage things well, and can receive help from a White person.[111] —*John Maloba*

---

111. Mulume wa Umba John Maloba, interview with the author, July 12, 2015.

Susanne Kisimba Bisibo, Africa University graduate and wife of a pastor and Africa University lecturer from North Katanga, compared the relationship between North Katangan and American UMs to a marriage, arguing that by living together again, we can grow closer and understand each other better.

> I want also to compare in a marriage: two people they will be together. They are one, but they are two different people. . . . To understand is difficult. In a relationship, as a partnership,

---

Original: "C'est qui a fait que les missionnaires auparavant quittent les américains, c'était la guerre. Il n'y avait pas de paix à la paie. Telle que les américains qui ont été à Luana, au temps de Mobutu, ils ont connu de pillages. On a volé tout. On a pris leurs biens. Alors la raison ils étaient malcontent. C'est pourquoi ils partirent, les américains. Il y a ces qui étaient à Nyembo, aussi avec la guerre ils ont fui pour aller en Zambie. . . . Au période de l'Évêque Ntambo, je ne vois pas un missionnaire vivre ici au Nord Katanga. Il y a que les missionnaires, les partenaires, les amis de Nord Katanga qui viennent aider le Nord Katanga s'ils ont quelques fonds, on donne pour un projet quelconque et ils rentrèrent. . . . C'est que je pense, c'est bien, oui, mais c'est aussi ce n'est pas bien. Puis que, le problème qui est là, je pense que c'est lui les missionnaires qui étaient venus du d'avoir le temps pour encenser les gens comment il faut trouver l'argent, comment il faut se prendre en charge, et faire assoir [?] notre leadership sur tout dans l'administration et la gestion des biens. Puis que, s'ils n'ont pas encensé, vraiment, ça n'était pas bien. Moi je pense ils devraient être là pour nos enseigner et puis, après avoir nos enseigner, ils rentrent et nous vérifions maintenant si c'est qu'on a étudié, c'est qu'on a appris de, vraiment, c'est que on pratique ça. On est en train de mettre ça en pratique. C'est oui, nous avons de missionnaires ici, mais ces missionnaires que nous avons, ils ne sont pas comme les missionnaires américains. Puis que, les missionnaires noirs que partent de vont faire le "fundraising" ne trouvent pas de fonds comme les missionnaires blancs, les américains. Alors, voilà le problème que nous avons. Les raisons, oui. (1) On ne peut pas donner à quelque qui on ne connait pas. (2) Il faut, pour donner l'argent, il faut avoir la confiance a cet homme que vous donnez là-bas. Alors, voilà, ce qui arrive. Mais, si c'est pour un blanc, on connait celui ici est de telle conférence, il est ici, il est ici, on peut même connaitre son histoire, on peut connaitre sa vie. Alors, ils ont raison par fois de douter quelqu'un de donner à un autre quelqu'un qu'il ne connait pas. Est-ce qu'il va vous rendre un bon service? Est-ce qu'il va vous donner le report? Est-ce qu'il va amener ses histoires au gents destiné? C'est ça. Il y a de changement dans la mentalité de gens aux North Katanga. Puis que, au début c'était seulement les missionnaires blancs qui partit aux États-Unis et emmené l'argent de projet et construction. Alors, maintenant il y a aussi les noires qui vont là-bas en nom d'église ils amènent aussi l'argent pour la construction, pour des autres projets dans l'église. C'est l'exemple de la période de l'Évêque Ntambo. Quand lui a commencé, lui-même allait aux États-Unis, pour chercher l'argent chez les partenaires de notre église. Et il a amené l'argent, en effet que nous puisent construire des églises, des écoles, même les maisons de pasteur et fait aussi de autres projets. Alors, au début ce n'était pas le cas ; c'était seulement les missionnaires qui partent. Alors, avec ça, l'homme noir dit que non! L'homme blanc n'aide pas seulement son frère mais il aide tout le monde pour le développent, il est là pour tout le monde. Alors, voilà. C'est qui fait que, il y a aussi un changement dans la tête de gens du Nord. Le développent ne peut pas se faire toujours avec un blanc. Même un noir qui dirige bien il peut être assister par un blanc."

> we need also to move as a couple; we can also move. If we say, "Let us accept the weakness of that side, and other to accept the weakness of that side," we can move together and also accept the force this side and the other side. We can build together. Even in the couple, when you are not in the same language, we cannot move. This is the reason why we can find many divorces among the couples because they are not moving together. Me, I was thinking about the partnership; we need to move and to live as a couple to understand each other. To be one, it is not easy, but with the help of the Spirit—like as we say—the Spirit is moving—with the help of the spirit we can move as a couple. Otherwise, it is hard because we are coming from different backgrounds. American/*Mzungu* have got their own background as African/North Katangan we've got also another background. It is difficult.... Now, that is a problem faced.
>
> To live again together, we start to understand each other. It is not easy, but with the help of the Holy Spirit we can move together. [This is the] reason why you can see there are also couples living together with children. In that partnership we need also to understand each other and accept each other and to accept first the background of each other and to start moving together. I think we can make something.[112] —*Suzanne Kisimba*

Shabana Banza, a lay member who I believe to be the youngest person I interviewed, responded to the question about the merits of a foreign missionary moratorium with both a theological and pragmatic answer about the importance of collaborating with others:

> God wants us to share. What is wrong if what I know as experience I share with my neighbor? This is what God is pleased with, sharing what we know, what we have with our neighbors. Because, you know it is in [the Bible], "My people perish because they don't have knowledge." I have seen changes happening with the missionaries. There is so much I have seen with these partnerships. People have been blessed, and even the local communities. Places where we couldn't find even a clinic, today are hospitals. People are getting medicines, mosquito nets, to prevent against malaria. And in all these we have seen the wells being built. I remember . . . where my father [a pastor] was living, it was hard—very hard—to get water. I visited the place where my mother used to go to fetch water. It was terrible, terrible. A

---

112. Suzanne Kisimba, interview with the author, June 14, 2015.

> mountain very difficult to climb, but they used to do that. With things of water on their head, helping each other, it wasn't really beautiful to see. But, in this partnership, there is a well today. Not only the pastors, the members, the whole community are drinking water from that well. So, I don't think that solving this problem will be by asking some other people not to participate. Even if we will be able to do by ourselves, but why we should ask some other people to leave?
>
> With my experience, I know that people who build the community are those who come from other areas. You could see Kamina before the war, but after the war Kamina is developed. New buildings and so on because it has received different people from here and there with their experiences, with their expertise, they have built the country. This is the same with Lubumbashi. Lubumbashi hosts everyone, and now it's a big city. And the people who are building, most who you see, they come from different places. I think even in some other countries, we cannot say that just the Americans built America. People came from there and there, so they then built the country. I don't think we can solve the problem by saying, "Okay, we are now able, so we think you are a problem."
>
> You are not a problem. The problem is there; the problem is known; everybody knows the problem, but everybody is not talking about the problem; everybody is not thinking about the problem. They know the problem; we know the problem; maybe you don't know the problem, but we know the problem. Yes, there are some other problems we can fix by ourselves, but to develop the problem, including development, I think it is global. It implies everyone to participate. I think it is boundless, it is open to everyone. And it is now my opinion. We now have doctors in theology and in different domains thanks to this partnership. We now have Africa University, so there are now many projects. In North Katanga we now have a beautiful gem, the plane. Thanks to such a partnership. So, we have people going to America everyday. We have General Conference. I've never had the chance to be there, but the people who go there, when they come back they testify. And where we don't pay the bills, but we have all this help . . . So you can see right now North Katanga is growing and growing because of such partnerships.[113] —*Shabana Banza*

Bob Walters, in contrast, began his official time as GBGM missionary in North Katanga with a strong belief that the foreign missionaries were doing

113. Horace Shabana Banza, interview with the author, July 11, 2015.

more harm than good and were an impediment to the development of healthy local leadership.[114] He initially saw his calling to be to push the all foreign missionaries out (himself included) and lock the door behind him.

> I came out of that [missionary moratorium] movement. That's who I was about, which puts me in a conflict with myself....
> I was a part of that and believed that strongly. And still do. Clearly I think there are allowances for exceptions, and I'm there myself—but off and on—and I have left the Congo three times now intentionally with the words that I would never return. And it may very well be that, although I haven't said it, I may have made my very last tour there. So, I keep looking at my own presence there as much a problem as it is a help. I think that in this period, from the 1990s to the present, any exceptions to that are rare and when those exceptions are made for a particular skill set, I just can't imagine anything that in terms of resources or training or skill set that the church needs that can't be found within North Katanga itself and if not within North Katanga certainly within the African continent. So, whether you are talking about machinery, or technology or personnel, first look is local and then only if it is absolutely pushed to go outside of that. If you can't find it local, maybe you ought to live without it.[115] —*Bob Walters*

In his interview, John Enright repeatedly expresses great cynicism about the relational dynamics and the effectiveness of missionaries of the past, and I have been told by a number of North Katangans that they believe Enright has sabotaged efforts since the late 1990s to build partnerships by advising Americans against sending money to church leaders there.[116] And yet, even in 2016 he still dreamed of returning to the communities where he once lived in North Katanga—not to live there but to set up businesses in order to bring revenue streams to the most vulnerable people.

---

114. It is worth noting that Shabana Banza's primary interactions with American United Methodists have been through acting as a translator for me and Bob Walters on our journeys. This makes the contrasts in their responses to the moratorium question even more interesting to me.

115. Bob Walters, interview with the author, January 11, 2016.

116. The late Kasongo Munza (North Katangan pastor who became Enright's neighbor and ministry collaborator in Zambia) said to me in 2005 that asking John Enright about North Katanga is like asking a man to tell you about his ex-wife after an ugly divorce. That is, the passion was still there, but the pain and anger masked the love that remained.

> In the culture, the court mercenary is an ancient, important game changer. Why on earth would you not want to have this person? . . . If I go to Nyembo, I will be carried through the streets. I am the Messiah. Even when I lived there, I was a demigod. My . . . [local name] meant John of the Fox, which is one of names of God. . . . The missionaries went home because the time of the court mercenary was over. There was no further role they could play because they were now leading the rebellion against the king [that is, bishop]. Or, put another way, the king perceived them as leading the rebellion. . . .
>
> But I will go back to North Katanga, not physically. And we will put up a couple million beehives. I'm one of those people who states it out there and believes it. We will generate about two hundred million US dollars per year. All of it will be focused on women and children and development and creating wealth within the country to lift people up. I think we have the tools to do it now. It is working pretty well [in Zambia].[117] —*John Enright*

Ken Vance also served many years in North Katanga before relocating to northern Zambia and has a mix of emotions and thoughts about the past and the possibility of Americans returning.

> One thing I saw in some missionaries was that they were the *Mzungu*, the big chief. There was an arrogant attitude, "We are superior to you," and it was very blatant, clear and evident even to children. I think that mindset "We are here to save these poor people" led to some of the bitterness and resentment from some of the indigenous people. . . .
>
> From Mobutu to the colonialists—everything for motivation was fear—so bringing transformation through love can empower people to take charge of their own lives. And it goes beyond salvation. What is salvation? Well, there's medical, education, . . . jobs. And, I think at some point the way of going about it had been wrong. I guess I didn't deal with it directly in Congo; I was never told "You need to go home," but we did see a bit of it. There were a couple missionaries asked to leave by the African church during my time, and I think at this point the African church can justify some of their decisions. . . .

117. John Enright, interview with the author, January 6, 2016.

> It is a bittersweet relationship. I've been back to Congo several times since 1998. . . . I think what I've sensed and seen is that the church is maturing and growing and taking on greater responsibility. I know North Katanga still gets a lot of financial support from America. One of our goals was to create self-sustaining projects; it is working in Zambia. In Congo the problem was every three or four years there would be another war that would destroy everything; it was always starting over, trying to build up from the ashes. In Zambia we are seeing what [can be built without the interruption of war]. . . . I'm following [North Katanga] but I'm removed. As you know, you can be in Zambia and it is like being in the US in terms of communication. . . . I'm in contact with Kafakumba pastors . . . we do manage to keep up with what's going on.[118] —Ken Vance

Vance emphasized that living for long periods as a missionary in North Katanga is harder than in Lubumbashi or Zambia, and he is skeptical about what short-term mission volunteers could accomplish with so little time to learn about the context.

> Living in the interior, you are in a sense landlocked. And it is much more difficult. It is a long term—We were there for the long haul. Each of these wars wears on you. When we first went, I was in my thirties. I'm in my sixties now. It gets old and you get tired. I think for today I'm not sure that someone going for a longer term is even practical or feasible. I may be wrong there, but I see the short-term things—I don't know how effective—it depends who and what is being done.
>
> When we went, Bishop Wakadilo said, "If you do nothing your first term but learn the language and study the culture, your term will be successful. I don't care if you fly, preach, I don't care if you do anything else, but I want you to learn the language and understand our culture, because without that you can't be effective." So, the question is, well, if we come in for a short term, we don't have the language skills or the cultural understanding: can we be useful or will we be detrimental? I don't know. But it's changing. The church is changing. North Katanga is changing. The world is changing, and so what was traditional is no longer applicable. It is a different day in mission than what it was when

---

118. Ken Vance, interview with the author, January 11, 2016.

> I went thirty years ago. As Bob Walters would say, we may have seen the last missionary....
>
> Again, there has to be a transition—a change within the church—both the African and the American church on how we do mission. We're kind of grasping at straws and it hasn't really come together ... North Katanga is such a unique place in that what works in Zambia just across the border won't work up in North Katanga. So, we have to come up with different paradigms of mission and how to deal with this—whether it is short term and what we're going to do.[119] —*Ken Vance*

Vance also touched upon the issue discussed previously in this section by John Maloba (see also 6.2.3)—the correlation between having a foreign missionary and having project funding. The belief that funding levels would return to their past heights if Americans came back fulltime is evident in many of the interviews with North Katangans.

> I think the American church did a bad, bad thing there. That is one of the shortcomings we have. When a person is tied to a project financially and the person retires, the people who are underwriting say, "Oh, they are retired. We don't need to support them anymore or what they were doing." And so the project dies. And then again that is where we were trying to establish in the 1980s some infrastructure—even with Wings of the Morning—to generate funds within North Katanga, and that never happened. So there is that liability that with a certain missionary and a certain project that because of the churches—the old school way of raising money in Africa.... And also, we did not prepare for the transition that when someone retired that someone took it over or handed it over to the African church. We did not do a good job transitioning there. So, again the funds were tied to a missionary/the American church. Now that we have more Africans coming to America to visit, there is less of a dependence on the American missionary. However, in reality not that many can come, and the ones that definitely need the funds can't afford to come.[120] —*Ken Vance*

This issue of American donors preferring to tie their financial support to the work of American missionaries adds to the complexity of the

---

119. Ken Vance, interview with the author, January 11, 2016.
120. Ken Vance, interview with the author, January 11, 2016.

conversation of decolonizing missional initiatives while remaining in partnership, especially when we talk about the pros and cons of American missionaries living in North Katanga. What some call a preference for giving to those you feel you know, others call blatant racism. This issue also undermines efforts by GBGM to decolonize the way it selects and sends missionaries. The relatively new From Everywhere to Everywhere motto has involved efforts to hire missionaries from countries such as DR Congo and send them to serve in other countries. A number of these missionaries, however, have reported facing rejection both by the places they are sent and by donors due to not being American. One interview participant shared the following:

> I know that we still struggle with the White man's image. I cannot give you an example from North Katanga, but from another one of our mission initiatives where we changed from a mission superintendent who was American to a mission superintendent who was [African]. And that moment we not only had 90 percent of covenant churches asking for another missionary to support saying with the argument that it was French speaking and they didn't have anybody [to translate]. Whether there was more to it I don't want to question, but we also had the fact that members of the church in that African country left the church with the argument, "If [we don't] have a White man leading the church, what was the point of being United Methodist? We can then go back to our old church or another church because as long as there is a White man we have some relationship with the USA, we have some opportunities which a Black man cannot offer to us." And this was shared with me by the mission superintendent, so I think it is true.[121] —*Anonymous*

In exploring this question, I also sought the opinions of leaders in the denomination's general agencies, especially those with considerable power to influence popular opinion or agency policies. Tim Tanton, director of United Methodist News Service, had the following to say about the idea of a missionary moratorium in North Katanga:

> This is outside my realm of expertise, but I can offer a couple general observations. A moratorium is an absolute thing and I think sometimes absolutes aren't the best way to address a need or a situation. It is helpful to hear Tafadzwa [Mudambanuki]

---

121. This interviewee requested her/his observation to be anonymous.

> talk about his experiences and observations with the missionaries and so on. The point that I make is that being part of a connectional church forces us to ask "What does it mean to be connectional in this context?" If we are talking about North Katanga, for example, "What does it mean to be connectional there?" Does it mean that we have church partnerships that cross national boundaries where people partner together to accomplish ministry—to lift up lives? The Imagine No Malaria campaign is a wonderful example of that. . . .
>
> We also have to go back to the importance of listening and the importance of making sure the ownership of those relationships is properly distributed, so you don't have a patriarchal system where people are coming in from the outside and imposing their wishes. That is not a good thing. I think being a connectional church in The UMC is a special thing. It is very unique and puts us in the special position to think about ministry in a different way that can be very positive and empowering.[122] —*Tim Tanton*

Thomas Kemper, head of GBGM, thanked me for pointing out to him that North Katanga, while having a number of local missionaries on GBGM payroll, had not had an American GBGM missionary living in the conference for two decades.

> We are very proud that our missionaries are from everywhere and going everywhere, but if we are not careful . . . it could create this kind of [missionary] moratorium. Missionaries from everywhere does not mean that we are not sending American missionaries anymore. So if this kind of hides that certain parts of the world where life is difficult we do not have American missionaries anymore; we have got something wrong. . . . I look at the big picture and have seen the number and diversity of missionaries increasing . . . [but] what does it mean in a concrete place? . . . It is the diversity of missionaries that is the message. So it includes American missionaries and it includes American missionaries together with other missionaries. But if we come to a point where only African missionaries are willing to go to difficult places in Africa, then we have made a mistake in this process of diversifying our missionary community.[123] —*Thomas Kemper*

---

122. Tim Tanton, interview with the author, January 7, 2016.
123. Thomas Kemper, interview with the author, May 11, 2017.

While still a director at GBGM, Mande Muyombo shared with me that he believed that idea of a missionary moratorium was too extreme and that North Katanga should once again receive foreign missionaries, provided that they took an incarnational approach. His response focused on what a healthy mission relationship would look like.

> To me that is an extreme position. As I said to you, if you look at the missionary movement as a whole, and you look at the context, the timing, you have to give them credit for what they did. In most areas in the DRC we have celebrated over 100 years of United Methodism, and this is partially because of the work of the missionaries who brought the doctrine of the Wesleyan movement. Now in the process, there have been conflicts and to me the theological argument is, when time evolves—you look at the colonial era—the postcolonial era—there was a need to develop a new theology of mission. As long as that theology of mission was not yet available, I think we went through a period of crisis where there were some extreme positions or arguments that arose.
>
> I believe that we do need missionaries, and when I say we do need missionaries, I will tell them that North Katanga needs missionaries. The American United Methodist Church needs missionaries. But the way we do mission needs to look at God's mission—*Missio Dei*. Second is to understand that that mission work is now happening in mutuality and respecting the priorities of the local people, giving the opportunity so that both have ownership of the project.
>
> We have a concept that we call "mission roundtable" today. The key principle of the roundtable is to let partners listen to the local priorities of the local people. For instance, you cannot go to Kamina and say, "I want to build a church of 10,000 members," and you develop a plan on computer from the USA, and you want people to own it. It will not work. You need to let the people decide on what kind of building they want to build. How we help a missionary—whether African or American—to serve in a place where you would expect for the local people to take ownership. This is what we call today "incarnational model of mission."
>
> We want the missionary to incarnate—feel with the people, to be with the people and realize that he or she is equal to the people. Not a missionary who is perceived as somebody who has privileges because of the salary and the money that he or she gets. So, I would say those [mission moratorium proposals]

> were extreme positions. I think what is key is how do we look at ourselves, and let's look at mission as God's mission. Second, let's look at each other as equal partners who want to serve in partnership and mutuality. And then, how do we help a missionary to be incarnate? ... And I have to say, it has been hard. Some missionaries have left because of that. But I think that's what we have right now. I think that saying that we don't need missionaries is extreme. ... We need each other.[124] —*Mande Muyombo*

A few months after his election as bishop of North Katanga, Mande Muyombo made a formal request to GBGM[125] for the creation of two new missionary placements—one in North Katanga Conference and one in Tanganyika Conference. Both placements were for tasks identified as priority ministries where persons within the area with the required qualifications could not be found, but at least one qualified American had been identified and was willing to be appointed providing a living wage could be provided. With the exception of a Zimbabwean agronomist who began working in North Katanga this year, neither conference had received a foreign missionary via GBGM since the mass evacuations in the 1990s. To the bishop's surprise, both requests were declined in June 2018. The bishop publicly announced his displeasure with the decision during North Katanga's Annual Conference in July 2018 and pledged to appeal. The results are yet to be known.

What role can or should full-time foreign missionaries play in the decolonizing of mission partnerships? Is there even a place for them in such a relationship? My conclusion is that not only is there is a place for American missionaries in a decolonized relationship, *being with* one another is at the heart of a healthy relationship. This new relationship, however, must emerge from a transformed relational dynamic—one of mutual respect and affirmation of one another's gifts. Such a relationship must be a "two-way street" to move beyond the power imbalances of the past. Hence, I argue that for true balance, it must also include North Katangans serving in America.

6.5 NORTH KATANGANS AS MISSIONARIES IN AMERICA

One topic which was frequently mentioned in the interviews about changes that have occurred in recent years is the presence of North Katangan United Methodists in the USA. While historically only a small number of North

---

124. Mande Muyombo, interview with the author, January 2016.

125. I was informed in June 2018 that GBGM's restructuring/rebranding process has included an acronym change. It now goes by Global Ministries. For simplicity sake, however, I am staying with the better-known name.

Katangans had had opportunities to come to the USA to visit or attend church meetings, these numbers have increased exponentially over the past two decades. I credit this to a confluence of multiple factors: increase in the number of scholarships raised for North Katangan leaders (initially scholarships to Africa University,[126] and later doctorate programs in the USA for clergy), increase in the number of delegate spots allotted to North Katanga for The UMC's General Conference[127] (due to increased membership statistics in the conference), leapfrog advancements in the ease of international travel and communication, and the push by Bishop Ntambo to advocate for conference leaders' opportunities for travel and study abroad.

There are two points I want to highlight about this change: (1) The number of North Katangans who no longer depend on cultural or language translators when in the USA or at international gatherings has increased dramatically. This has changed the interactional power dynamics for denominational/agency-level meetings and well as fundraising efforts. (2) The number of North Katangan clergy with MDivs and doctorates has increased, thereby making them more attractive and capable to serve effectively in congregations in the USA, where by all reports I have received they are growing congregations. We are beginning to even see congregations in the USA led by pastors from North Katanga sending funds for initiatives in North Katanga. This change of status and situation has also led to a considerable number of North Katangans who came to study in the USA officially transferring their membership to conferences in the USA.[128]

Whereas even fifteen years ago I used to say in my advocacy/fundraising talks in the USA that North Katangan leaders have gifts they could offer the church in the USA—especially in the areas of church growth and reconciliation, now I can point to specific examples of flourishing ministries in the USA under North Katangan leadership. These third-culture[129] North Katangan

---

126. A United Methodist university built in Zimbabwe with the goal of creating a world-quality university in Africa where United Methodists (and others) could be sent to study and return home to serve. Groundbreaking was in 1991.

127. Until now, General Conference has always been held in the USA, although there are plans to change this.

128. To my knowledge, Bishop Mande and Gaston Ntambo (pilot paid by GBGM) are the only examples of North Katangan church leaders moving to the USA to study and eventually returning to North Katanga to serve. Despite their initial pledges to return, all others have remained in the USA after graduation.

129. I was tempted to use "bicultural," but I don't think that is accurate. What is emerging is a new "culture" due to increased access to travel and communication technology. What I am referring to is what anthropologist Dr. Ruth Useem was pointing to when she coined the term Third Culture Kid, which was used in the context of children of diplomats and missionaries who grow up around the world and end up with a

church leaders are part of a larger trend in terms of becoming peers at the global table and missionaries to the USA. In the 2013 documentary series *Africa Christianity Rising*,[130] filmmaker James Ault documents not only the growth of Christianity in Africa but also the reversal of missionary flows that has started to occur—with African congregations and pastors investing in evangelism and church planting in North America.

Changes in relational dynamics created by the increased interactions between North Katangans and Americans can be seen in large and small ways. Bishop Ntambo noted:

> I have seen that exchange. For example, the model of hospitality—the way we do it here in North Katanga. Just remember when you are there [in Kamina] all transportation by air, car, lodging, the food you ate, was given free. Was given free. In America they could give you a bill, and here it is free. And once we are also in America, they take care of us. They provide lodging, feeding. So it is learning both sides. It is joy. And the way we organize this time. We have 143 [newly ordained] pastors—it is a lesson to Americans. The [American] lady said, "What?! We had only 14, but here you have 143." It is a lesson. And for us, this spirit of sacrifice. Because when you look here in North Katanga, that's really bush. And you planned to come spend a month with us. That's love. We need our young people to learn from that—so that one day they can do that in Africa or outside of Africa. So, I may say, both sides are learning from one another.[131] —*Nkulu Ntanda Ntambo*

Bishop Mande also believed progress has been made in dismantling the (neo)colonial dynamics in the relationship through these increased interactions on more level playing fields, like at organized mission roundtable events.

> I think we have made significant progress. I now see UM bishops and local churches that are listening to the priorities of the people. They are now letting the people take ownership. They are now looking at mission and partnership with humility. I think that there has been significant progress. And this is where I'm blessed to be in the position I am right now because, as you said, I'm in a better position to understand both contexts, but

worldview that is beyond any specific culture, larger than the sum of the parts.

130. Ault, *Africa Christianity Rising*.
131. Nkulu Ntanda Ntambo, interview with the author, July 20, 2015.

> I also recognize that on the side of North Katanga and other episcopal areas, I think that they also have to look at Americans as partners not necessarily as people who are cash cows. I think they also have to value the relationship first than to value the money. I think that money comes next. I have to say that there has been significant progress in that regard, and I do give credit to local churches who now understand there is a new concept of mission, there is a new concept called roundtable—a new understanding of partnership and mutuality. Even the new missionaries that we've commissioned [at GBGM], we have a new brand of missionaries. We don't have the old day of missionaries who were looked at like people with privileges. I have to say there has been significant progress, and we have to work to allow folks on the ground to have ownership.[132] —Mande Muyombo

The long-term impact of North Katangans demonstrating both to Americans and other North Katangans that they are capable of holding their own in intellectual discussions at meetings as well as serving fruitfully in ministries in the USA cannot yet be measured, but I am convinced it will be game changing. Assumptions (conscious and unconscious) of moral and intellectual superiority are hard to hold onto when repeatedly staring directly at contradicting evidence. Thus, while on one hand I lament the brain-drain of some of North Katanga's brightest scholars immigrating to the USA, I also celebrate that this reverse flow can contribute to the decolonization of the relational dynamics in the partnership. While my research did not include an in-depth examination of the impact the North Katanga diaspora is having on the perceptions and interactions between Americans and North Katanga, this topic merits further exploration.[133]

With the arrival of social media, smartphones, and 3G networks in Katanga, North Katangans no longer even have to leave Katanga to participate in conversations that are taking place between United Methodists in the USA. This, too, is a tool that can be used for decolonization of relationships, and in the coming years it would make a good topic for focused research.

6.6 ANXIETY ABOUT THE FUTURE

While some interview participants expressed optimism about the future of the partnership, many expressed anxieties about the future of The UMC in

---

132. Mande Muyombo, interview with the author, January 2016.

133. This was initially a topic I considered for the focus of my thesis, but I concluded that other topics needed to be explored first and this could be revisited in later research.

North Katanga. Reasons for this included both local and denominational-level issues in the church.

6.6.1 Neo-Colonialism in Church Politics: Homosexuality and Schism

One of the proverbial elephants in the room when talking about the future of The UMC and the current power dynamics between American and African United Methodists is the ugly battle that has been playing out for years between the "traditionalists" and "progressives"[134] in the denomination over the topic of blessing/officiating gay marriages and the ordination of "self-avowed practicing homo-sexuals."[135] Within The UMC in the USA, opinion is fiercely split, resulting in both conservatives and progressives leaving the denomination. In recent years, the delegates to General Conference (the official legislative assembly of The UMC) from Africa have cast the deciding votes. This has created considerable tensions and accusations on both sides of American caucuses attempting to use African delegations as pawns in their political agendas. I myself have been one of the voices calling attention to the racist comments and strategies I have observed in this conflict. In a piece I wrote in September 2013 that went viral on multiple social media platforms,[136] I called out both progressives and conservatives for patronizing African delegates, and I criticized Bishop Minerva Carcaño (a social progressive) for making the following public statement: "Delegates from Africa once again proclaimed that their anti-homosexual stand was what US missionaries taught them. I sat there wondering when our African delegates will grow up. It has been two hundred years since US Methodist missionaries began their work of evangelization on the continent of Africa; long enough for African Methodists to do their own thinking about this concern and others."[137]

Kabala Chali, a United Methodist pastor who immigrated from Congo to the USA, has also written about what he sees as neo-colonialism wrapped in religion. His most recent article on the topic caused considerable anger in certain circles because he focused his criticism on the largest conservative caucus, Good News. Chali writes:

> Each time before Annual Conference session in several African Annual Conferences, Good News would send someone

---

134. I put these words in quotes because I believe they are poor labels for the division, but they are the ones most often used.
135. "Homosexuality: Full Book of Discipline statements."
136. Denyer, "Africa, Reconciling Ministries."
137. Carcaño, "Bishop Carcaño on the Good and Bad."

to speak and tell people how they should vote. These things happen without any discussion on the things brought forward. In addition, this week, leaders from various African countries were invited to attend an event in Nairobi, Kenya. This event was called Africa Initiative UMC: Prayer and Leadership Summit. While the title suggests something initiated by Africans, it is something organized and sponsored by a US-based caucus group. The intent: let's tell them how to vote during the special General Conference 2019.

One then asks, while US groups come to tell some African delegates and leaders what they need to support, when do our leaders ask US groups to make priority the issues African church contexts are facing? When would Good News come to listen to the challenges facing Zimbabwe with oppressions or the DRC with political instability and how the church can be an agent of peace and stability? Or why isn't African migration, both internal within the continent and beyond, not included in an African summit? Or how about climate change, the consequences of which affect much of the African population? Good News is a US group using African UMC leaders to manipulate many of our laity and clergy, because they fear if they question things our leaders allow, they may get in trouble.[138]

This concern about Americans trying to control the political and theological conversations was voiced by a few American interview participants, yet with fear that making such comments publicly would create problems for them. Below is such a response, which was immediately followed by a request to cite her/him anonymously.

> When two Christians sit together in holy conferencing, it requires not only listening to one another but listening to where God is in the conversation. One of the things that troubles me is folks that I see from particular theological or political perspectives going to North Katanga or other parts to convince them about a particular strategy or theology that does not take into account the experiences and insights of the African context.[139] —*Anonymous*

With debates about homosexuality and talk of denominational schism (which is a very real possibility for 2019) dominating General Conference sessions the past two decades as well as the efforts various caucus groups

---

138. Chali, "UMC Nairobi Meeting."
139. This interviewee requested her/his observation to be anonymous.

have made to speak to African delegates about these issues, it came as no surprise that, although my interview questions did not touch upon homosexuality, many interview participants raised it when I asked about their thoughts on the future of partnerships with American United Methodists. Fears include both the potential impact of a church schism as well as the response of Congolese in general if The UMC as a denomination voted to accept homosexuality. Bishop Ntambo asserted the following:

> The danger we have—I want to be honest with you—is this matter of homosexuality. It will affect both sides because the misunderstanding is great. We have our culture—I mean in Africa—which we never see such kind of things. We see the other side is like America-promoting this, supporting this, I mean some people there—it is a clash. Africans are saying "No. We can't." Some Americans are saying "No. It's freedom." So that misunderstanding between them can put the church in a very difficult union. . . . I don't understand better what Americans are thinking. I understand better Africans. You were in Kamina. You were in Mulongo. Have you seen even one woman—one couple—claiming "We want to be lesbian"? [Interviewer responded "Yes."] . . . Only in Kinshasa—Kinshasa which is not really—[those are] ideas brought in by outside. Not Kinshasa people. Young people who were in Europe who bring ideas to have money—to have money. Such kinds of things is a shock, and that shock is deep. My hope is that the church will continue to be united and my hope is that in General Conference people will continue—not to support African side—but that The UMC would remain without accepting such things in the church.[140] —*Ntambo Nkulu Ntanda*

Part of the anxiety expressed was the scandal in DR Congo of being potentially part of a denomination that accepts homosexuality. The other part is the financial impact of what may become an expensive divorce process and the question of whether certain groups and congregations will continue to send funding once North Katanga is no longer seen as a necessary political ally.

> Yeah, it [the predicted schism] is going to affect us all. A part is the resigned, "Well, we'll still be the African church and we will continue on." But, there is that thinking, "How will we survive?"; "Where will our money come from?"; "Which churches

---

140. Nkulu Ntanda Ntambo, interview with the author, July 20, 2015.

> will support us?" Financially, it could be a big disaster and the African church would feel the fallout from that. So, yes, there is fear about that.[141] —*Ken Vance*

While my research deliberately treaded lightly on this hot topic, it is clear that neocolonial attitudes about Africans have been on display by American church leaders (regardless of their beliefs about human sexuality) throughout the political process. It is also clear that what happens in the near future regarding this conflict will impact partnerships between American and North Katangan congregations and conferences. It is too soon to know for certain what this impact will be.

6.6.2 Clergy Giving Up

Another issue that was raised in the interviews has mostly remained a secret kept from American partners: the growing levels of burnout among church leaders in North Katanga and the impact this has on the conference as a whole. Bob Walters first alerted me to the problem when he returned from his bicycle tours of the conference. In village after village he found clergy and lay leaders who looked exhausted and malnourished. They spoke to him about feeling abandoned. And, as has been whispered to me by Walters and numerous others, church attendance in many communities isn't what it once was. Adult children of pastors do not want to follow in their parent's vocational footsteps, fearing the financial suffering that would come from it. People are tired and disillusioned—so tired that there is a real risk of mass exodus if change—or at least renewed hope—does not come soon.[142]

> For the future, Pastor Taylor, I'm scared. If the church does not think of producing, there are many people who will leave the church to look for work elsewhere because they are human beings. They eat. They have children. The children must study. . . . I am talking about the case of a pastor: he is in the church, the church does not pay him, these children do not study, he says "No, I quit. I will work in the company to have money for my child to study." So, my plea to the church is this: the church must think how to take care of its personnel who are the pastors.[143] —*John Maloba*

---

141. Ken Vance, interview with the author, January 11, 2016.

142. The same can be said of The UMC in much of the USA.

143. Mulume wa Umba John Maloba, interview with the author, July 12, 2015. Original: "Sur l'avenir, Pasteur Taylor, j'ai peur. Si l'église ne pense pas à produire, beaucoup il y a les gens qui vont abandonner l'église pour chercher le travail ailleurs. Puis que, ce sont des humanes. Ils mangent. Ils ont des enfants. Les enfants doivent

Bishop Mande is acutely aware of this issue and has made addressing the needs of clergy a top priority. His strategy is multipronged, a major part being finding American partners to pledge to subsidize clergy salaries (and thus giving pastors appointed to impoverished congregations the same type of support given to other kinds of missionaries) as well as creating opportunities for advancement through scholarships and sponsoring continuing education programs.

While clergy and laity burnout (either in North Katanga or in the USA) was not a focus of my research, I am convinced it is a factor affecting partnerships and their future. On one hand, burnout results in reduced levels of fruitful activity as well as reduced levels of generosity (causing a downward spiral). On the other, healthy partnerships can serve as the remedy to burnout. As will be discussed in the following chapter on theological reflections, at-one-ment has restorative powers.

6.7 CONCLUSIONS

This chapter has, through documenting the themes and major points found in the interviews, demonstrated that (internalized) colonial assumptions about White American superiority have and continue to impact the dynamics of the partnerships between North Katanga Conference and American individuals and groups. It has also shown that change is happening—old beliefs are being challenged, and new healthier relationships are forming. While there is still far to go before declaring these relationships decolonized, I am optimistic about the trajectory we are on and the leaders who are currently in place.

The last phase of the interviews, a request to reflect theologically upon the relationship, is the focus of the first section of the next chapter.

étudier. S'il est à la maison lui est, par exemple, je parle du cas d'un pasteur, il est dans l'église, l'église ne lui paie pas confortablement, ces enfants n'étudient pas, il dise 'no, je laisse. Je vais travailler dans la société pour avoir de l'argent pour que mon enfant peut étudier. Alors, mon interpolation a l'église: l'église doivent penser comment gérer les personnelle qui sont les pasteurs."

7

Reflecting Theologically on the Relationship

UNTIL NOW THERE HAS been very little theology discussed in this thesis; this was intentional. When moving through the mission praxis matrix, I wanted to first explore the other matrix points before identifying pertinent theological understandings of the participants, Methodist traditions, and the theological concepts I have found to be most useful in interpreting these partnership dynamics and discerning healthy next steps in the relationship. As shown in section 1.8.2, spirituality sits at the intersection point of the mission praxis matrix. Thus, to effectively discuss spirituality in this partnership, I needed to first to have all the previous explorations in this thesis.

There are numerous Scripture passages and theological concepts that can be used to critique the history of North Katangan-American United Methodist interactions and to discern methods and reasons for striving to decolonize mission partnerships. This chapter does not attempt to mention them all. Instead, I have organized it into sections based on three main modes of inquiry: (1) How do the interview participants understand the partnership in relationship to Scripture and theological concepts? (2) What theological resources are there in the Methodist tradition that can be reclaimed/mobilized/activated to foster a decolonising partnership? (3) What can be said in terms of identifying a theology of partnership, especially ways to heal and/or build relationships?

7.1 INTERVIEW RESPONSES

Near the end of each interview, I asked participants to reflect theologically on what they had discussed thus far. In this section I have summarized responses I received. These responses were based on what first came to their minds, having not been given time to ponder the question for an extended period. For this reason, I asked two or three variations of the question, frequently to the same person, in attempts to allow time for responses to become deeper and fuller. These questions included: "How do you see the Spirit of God at work in this relationship?"; "What Bible passages or themes come to mind when you think about this discussion?"; and "If you were to preach on the topic of this partnership, what would be the main points in your sermon?"

The North Katanga responses generally fall into four areas (some touching upon more than one of these): (1) Helping/Love; (2) Courage, Self-Assertion, and Autonomy (not needing outside help, but appreciating it); (3) Numerical Growth/Evangelism; and (4) Advanced Education.

Interestingly, despite all the questions in the interviews being explicitly about the relationship between North Katangans and Americans, when it came to the theological reflections, some North Katangans gave responses that did not explicitly mention foreigners but instead focused on what they saw as scriptural responses to pressing issues within North Katanga. While one might say that they were not answering the question at hand, in an important sense they were. Despite having just had an extended conversation about North Katanga's relationship with Americans, when asked to reflect on what God is doing and/or what message should be preached, many expressed what I see to be decolonized thoughts—that is, while they had already expressed appreciation for the contributions of Americans, their understanding of what God is doing and what North Katangans are called to do existed beyond the conversation about foreign partnerships. This suggests that a number of interviewees hold an identity and relationship with God that is not trapped in a (neo)colonial narrative; in this sense, their minds are already *de*colonized.

7.1.1 *Spirit of God at Work*

The responses I received to the question of where the Spirit is at work were varied, and each of these merits inclusion in the discussion. This section includes excerpts from several responses. I start with those from North Katangans and follow with the American points of view.

7.1.1.1 NORTH KATANGAN RESPONSES

The North Katangan interview participants all affirmed that the Holy Spirit is at work in North Katanga. Both what has been accomplished through the partnership and the changes that are occurring both with and without collaborations are identified as the Spirit of God at work. That is, the evolution of the relationship itself is seen as Spirit-led. An implicit assumption found throughout these responses is that when the Spirit is at work, the church grows. The following transcript excerpts are examples of these responses and are organized to highlight the four areas.

Daniel Mumba focused on of the helping/love aspect. He saw the existence of the partnership itself as an act of God—strangers being moved to send help to strangers:

> When I think about the history of this relationship, God is acting. Imagine you, my sister Taylor. Americans are moved by the spirit of love and fraternity. Someone who helps someone that he doesn't even know—someone who he doesn't even see. You will never even see him, but you hear that there is cholera in someplace, and you release funds for medicines to help these people. Me, I think that this is the love of Christ. Our brother/sister missionaries work with the love of Christ. They want to help us because they love us like they love themselves.[1] —*Daniel Mumba*

Shabana Banza also focused on helping/love while touching upon advanced education and peacebuilding through love. He lifted up the foreign missionaries who came during war time as well as what has been accomplished through those partnerships. He also asserted that for God to work in a community, there must be love.

> What I see is that God is working in creating such partnerships, because Africa is not just Congo. There are so many places in Africa where all this partnership should go. But when I see much interest of the American missionaries in North Katanga, I see that God is working within them—courage and willingness to come and help—because I've seen missionaries coming even in critical times. We have been living with the missionaries even during the war.[2] Even during this time—this difficult time where

---

1. Daniel Mumba, interview with the author, July 13, 2015. Original: "Quand on réfléchit dans cette histoire, on voit que Dieu agie. Parce que, imaginez-vous, ma sœur Taylor, les américaines sont pousser par l'esprit de l'amour de fraternité. Quelqu'un qui aide quelqu'un qui il ne connait pas—quelqu'un qu'il ne voit même pas-ils ne sont pas amis. Vous ne là jamais vu, mais vous entendez qu'il y a de cholera quelque part vous débloquer l'argent pour la charge de médicament assister ces gens. Moi je vois que c'est ça l'amour de Christ. Nos frères missionnaires travaillent avec l'amour de Christ. Ils veulent nous aider parce qu'ils nous sont aiment comme eux."

2. Referring to those who came and stayed for many weeks/month—in particular,

> the country was really unsafe and much conflict—but they used just to come. So, I am trying to understand that really God is working in all these construction projects and all the help and support I've seen happen.
>
> I've seen so many people even getting the scholarships to learn abroad and then coming back with their expertise and trying really to elevate God's work in North Katanga. . . .
>
> There is much to do in the North Katanga. I think God wants the church to play a very important role of not just bringing community development, even of the local communities, but also getting all these people involved in his ministry. The church has much to do, and God what He wants us to do as the church is to unite all these divided tribes, because in North Katanga the other problem is, "I am from this tribe, but he is from the other one." So God wants us to play this role of peace building with all the communities, all the tribes, so we can live as one. I don't think that God works where there is division, because where there is division there is not love; where there is division, there is not justice, and where there is not justice and love, God is not there. So God wants the church to play the role of developing all these communities with love, justice, truth and faith.[3] —*Shabana Banza*

Nday Bondo spoke to the area of helping via partnerships and asserted that the corrective measures that are being taken to improve the partnership—including the inspiration for me to pick decolonizing this partnership as my doctorate research—are led by the Holy Spirit.

> I also see that the Spirit is working. Sometimes we start things from nowhere. We say that it is from nowhere, but by the end of the day we notice that God is in control. Because the intention of the partnership is to help one another.
>
> The move that we took was "I noticed some weaknesses on the Africa partners, so let us go and assist them so that they may grow and they can start moving by themselves." Even though we have said that it has failed because the procedure, that what they started with is not good, but now we have noticed that we are correcting some of the things during the process. . . .
>
> Let us improve that weakness. We are improving arranging that partnership in order for it to become a fruitful and effective

---

myself and Bob Walters, who he accompanied on journeys.

3. Horace Shabana Banza, interview with the author, July 11, 2015.

> partnership. This one is led by the Holy Spirit. Even when you are now thinking of a topic like this one, this is already showing "Where did it come from?" The Spirit should have moved you to think of, when you said this is my topic—this is what I want to research on. Yes, it cannot come just from a human mind. You have been in this partnership, you have been in this church, and you are now seeing that are changing. So let us talk of that change that has occurred and let us see the impact of that change. So, the Spirit is leading us and the Spirit is illuminating our mind in order to see how we can improve it. So, for me, the Spirit is at work.[4] —*Nday Bondo*

While appreciating the contributions foreign partners have made, Gertrude Mukalay Mwadi, a pastor from North Katanga who was at the time a lecturer at Africa University,[5] pointed to the shift to autonomy. She saw the Spirit at work in how North Katangans now see the gifts of Jesus Christ not requiring Americans as intermediaries:

> The example of these American preachers who are preaching Jesus; they are telling people, "It is not us who can give you these things but Jesus Christ." If you just deepen your relationship with Jesus Christ, he is there to respond to your needs.... There are some people who are thinking that, "If a *Mzungu* comes, he is the one who can change my situation, my involvement." But now there are others who saying, "Even you are the one who can receive directly from God." So that aspect of believing in God is very important in our conference. We are challenging our pastors to teach people. It is possible for them to make that relationship.... Like the report I heard yesterday from Kanene. People are poor, but they managed to build—even to cover—their churches and houses and schools by themselves. Now people are starting to understand that when we trust in God, when we pray, He is able to respond to our needs. To give us strength. To make us able to respond to our situation. Even though *Mzungu* is not there, God is able.[6] —*Gertrude Mukalay Mwadi*

John Maloba pointed primarily to the areas of numerical growth and advanced education, while still touching upon the partnership helping. He

4. Nday Bondo, interview with the author, July 14, 2015.
5. She has since immigrated to the USA and serves as a UMC pastor in Michigan.
6. Gertrude Mukalay Mwadi, interview with the author, July 14, 2015.

spoke of the increase in the number of pastors and congregations as well as increased opportunities for advanced theological education:

> Yes, the Spirit of God is doing something. . . . In our past we had few pastors. But since Bishop Ntambo arrived we increased. We created universities where we train pastors. Really, God is at work because the number of churches increase. We have many Christians; we have many pastors. And even our partners help us . . . [There are] scholarships. . . . The spirit of God is working in theological field.[7] —*John Maloba*

Joseph Mulongo pointed also to the courage and self-assertion displayed by pastors during the recent war:

> The Spirit of God is working in North Katanga [in] the courage and the way pastors in North Katanga have worked. Let's take the example of the difficult period of the war: we saw the church being built and growing; health centers were opened. Even in difficulty God is present and doing things. The Spirit of God is working. The great change in North Katanga during the war shows that the Spirit of God works.[8] —*Joseph Mulongo*

Susanne Kisimba Bisibo talked about the problem of lack of spiritual maturity among the people of North Katanga and the need for more evangelism—more preaching, praying, and teaching/training—while acknowledging physical needs as well. She believed that what blocks effectiveness is when there is a difference between the evangelist's or missionary's agenda and the goals of the community (e.g., you go to preach and they want

---

7. Mulume wa Umba John Maloba, interview with the author, July 12, 2015. Original: "Oui, l'esprit de Dieu est entrain de faire quelque chose. Oui, dans le domaine théologique . . . Puis que on a vit on avait peu de pasteurs. Mais pendant que l'évêque Ntambo est arrivé on a augmenté l' [?] Puis que on a créé des universités là où on forme les pasteurs. Vraiment, Dieu est entrain de faire puis que le nombreuse de églises augmentent, on a beaucoup de chrétiens, on a beaucoup de pasteurs. Et même nous partenaires aussi on aide, les américains avoir des pasteurs . . . une bourse . . . L'esprit de Dieu est entrain de travailler dans le domaine théologique."

8. Joseph Mulongo, interview with the author, July 18, 2015. Original: "L'Esprit de Dieu est entrain de travailler au Nord Katanga, le courage et le travail des pasteurs au nord Katanga ont travaillé. Prenons en exemple, la période de la guerre qui était difficile, mais nous avons vu l'église se construire et grandir, des centres de santés s'ouvrirent, même dans la difficulté Dieu est présent et fait des choses, l'Esprit de Dieu est entrain de travailler. Le grand changement qu'a connu le nord Katanga pendant la guerre montre que l'Esprit de Dieu travaille."

physical healing) or when one's agenda is not in line with what the Spirit is directing. This issue is what she identified as why the Spirit does not appear to be working well in some places.

> I think the Spirit of God is moving.... These people, they are not mature in the Word of God. When we go there, with the objective to preach, to pray with them, ... and to teach them the Word of God, the Spirit of God is going to move. If you go there [to preach], [but] their objective is healing ... [or] maybe their problem is education, [but] you go there with the [agenda] of healing—I think it cannot work very well....
>
> When we see those people, we need to train them to leave the world and to work for God.... When they receive it, they will be able also to work for other people and to preach.... But when we do not know ... your agenda, when you are coming as a *Mzungu* ... even you are preaching—you see ... they need this and that. And after that, you are also are going to do this and that.... Maybe it is ... first to preach the Word of God. Maybe it is not just the Word of God they need, for example, clinics. They need education. You know, the Spirit of God is going to direct you as a *Mzungu*.... But when there is no connection, no agenda, sometimes the Spirit of God is not working properly. It is like you are forcing the Spirit of God, and you are seeing other things are not working very well.[9] —Suzanne Kisimba

Mbayo Mujinga addressed the question of the Spirit's movement through a longer lens of the partnership's history and talked about how the public perception of Methodists has changed over the decades. He celebrated the numerous North Katangan church leaders with powerful spiritual gifts, and he interlaced his conversation about the work of the Spirit with his frustrations about not currently receiving the support needed to answer the call to evangelize.

> The Methodist Church has its spiritual history. At first people thought that the Methodist Church was not spiritual—that the Methodist church was not engaged in prayer. It was thought that people drank alcohol, people were doing debauchery, and it was not a spiritual church, but I tell you the language has changed.
>
> We shared with some missionaries the time of prayers. ... We have seen the manifestations of the Holy Spirit; we

---

9. Suzanne Kisimba, interview with the author, June 14, 2015.

have had missionaries who commit themselves to prayer—the missionaries who loved prayer and missionaries who wanted to evangelize from one place to another. . . . The missionaries wanted to see the spiritual pastors, the pastors who were engaged in the Holy Spirit. . . .

The Americans assisted the Congolese. . . . I do not say that you always have to reach out to the missionary. Perhaps you were touched by the LORD, and said, "No, I must also help. We must also help widows, orphans because they do not have enough means."

The missionaries had a complete vision of the fulfillment of man. Spiritually, he knows God; he is a man of prayer; he is filled with the power of God. Today, there are Pentecostal men who lead life like that of John Wesley. There are those who speak in tongues . . . there are pastors who have spiritual gifts, the powerful ones. They are among the pastors, among the laity. We have worked with the young people who have the power; you will hear the prophecy that has just been said, and indeed it is God who speaks. And we are going to prepare pastors who are very strong.

Members of the youth today are very strong pastors. They preach, and they have the Word; they also have prayer, and they live far from sin. And even those churches that once thought we were a drunken church—today they confirm this we are not. For example, I worked for twenty-two years with the Pentecostals. I saw what they were doing there. I preach with them. I prayed with them; they are the fruits of the Methodist Church. In my opinion, the Methodist Church wants the complete expansion of man. I repeat: spiritual, physical, intellectual, and moral.[10] —*Mbayo Mujinga*

---

10. Mbayo Mujinga, interview with the author, July 16, 2015. Original: "L'église Méthodiste a son histoire spirituelle, dans un premier temps, les gens ont pensé que l'église méthodiste n'était pas spirituelle, l'église méthodiste n'était pas engagé dans la prière, on a pensé que les gens s'enivrer, buvaient l'alcool, les gens faisaient la débauches et ce n'était pas une église spirituelle, mais Madame je vous dis le langage a changé. Nous avons partagé avec certains missionnaires le temps des prières, moi personnellement nous avons partagé un temps de prière, nous avons vu les manifestations du Saint Esprit, nous avons les missionnaires qui s'engager à la prière, les missionnaires qui aimait la prière et des missionnaires qui voulaient bien évangéliser d'un lieu à un autre. Donc la mission de l'église a été presque accomplie avec les hommes, les missionnaires ont voulu voir les pasteurs spirituels, les pasteurs qui étaient engagés dans le Saint Esprit, dans la puissance et dans la plénitude du saint esprit. Certains missionnaires ont aimés ce pasteur parce que il était dirigé, utilisé par le Saint Esprit et puis quand on le voyait prêcher, il était beaucoup apprécier et nous aussi il y avait une certaine influence

Thus, for the North Katangans interviewed, the Spirit of God can be seen at work in Katanga through relationships built on love (e.g., foreign partnerships, care for the vulnerable, etc.), shifts of mentality that decolonize the mind (e.g., believing in one's own capabilities, increased spiritual maturity, higher education levels), and numerical growth of the church (increase in pastors and buildings). While there remained in some of the interviews a yearning for foreign partners to help them address their problems, overall the rhetoric was that of North Katangans affirming their own ability to accomplish things through the power of the Holy Spirit as well as recognizing their responsibilities to be in ministry, addressing needs in their own communities. This once again indicates that these North Katangan church leaders are not exhibiting an inferiority complex (i.e., internalized racism) to *Bazungu* when it comes to their capacity to receive the gifts of the Holy Spirit and to engage in evangelization and peacebuilding activities.[11] Overcoming of internalized racism is a key ingredient in decolonizing North Katangan-American mission partnerships. How to facilitate this process is revisited later in this chapter (7.3).

---

de certains missionnaires qui poussaient les pasteurs soient spirituels. Le thème que nous pouvons dire aujourd'hui . . . Les américains ont assisté les congolais . . . Je ne dis pas qu'il faut toujours tendre la main au missionnaire et même qui était touché par le seigneur, et qui disait non, je dois aussi aider, on doit aussi aider les veuves, les orphelins parce qu'ils n'ont pas assez de moyens. Les missionnaires avaient une vision d complète de l'épanouissement de l'homme. Spirituellement, il connait Dieu, il est homme de prière, il est rempli de la puissance de Dieu. Aujourd'hui, il ya des hommes pentecôtistes qui mènent la vie comme celle de John Wesley, il ya ceux qui parlent en langues, vous pouvez refuser, Madame, je vous dis, moi je la parole de Dieu, vais vous convaincre, il ya des pasteurs qui ont des dons spirituels, les puissants. Ils sont parmi les pasteurs, parmi les laïques, Nous avons travaillé avec les jeunes—nous deux—qui ont la puissance, vous entendrez la prophétie qui vient de dire et effectivement c'est dieu qui parle. Et on est entrains de préparer des pasteurs qui sont très forts. Des membres parmi les jeunes, aujourd'hui, sont des pasteurs très forts, ils prêchent et ils ont la parole et ils ont aussi la prière et ils vivent loin du péché. Et même ces églises qui nous considérer au début que nous étions une église des ivrognes. Aujourd'hui ils confirment ce n'est pas ça. Par exemple, moi j'ai travaillé pendant 22 ans chez les pentecôtistes, moi j'ai vu ce qu'ils faisaient là. J'ai prêcher avec eux, j'ai prié avec eux, ce sont toujours les fruits de l'église Méthodiste.

Selon moi l'église Méthodiste veut l'expansion complète de l'homme, je reprends, spirituelle, physique, intellectuelle et morale."

11. At the same time that I state that (neo)colonial inferiority complexes have plagued North Katangan leaderships in terms of beliefs that bazungu are necessary to successfully lead church programs, I also recognize that throughout the history of Methodism in Katanga there have been Congolese evangelists exhibiting confidence and effectiveness in their ability to grow the church and manifest spiritual gifts.

7.1.1.2 AMERICAN RESPONSES

In contrast to the North Katangans, the Americans I interviewed often expressed cynicism mixed with hope—especially among those who have been involved for a number of years—in response to the question of where they believe God is at work in the relationship with North Katanga. Despite the cynicism some felt, there was among the Americans interviewed an underlying sense of a sacred call of the Spirit to be engaged in the relationship.

> My initial reaction is that God is sitting there laughing at us—"Will you ever get it right?" I think behind it all, I see the love of God as the predominant thing that has to bring about transformation. And in Congo we have to break through the whole thing of people living out of fear. To transition into love is a very difficult thing. It is happening. I see God in the midst of all of this, holding people together as best as they can be held together in some of the trying and difficult circumstances.
>
> The Kingdom of God—again we are a global church and this is our community, our brothers and sisters—and some of these are through no fault of their own—they didn't ask to be born into poverty, in the middle of a war, with malaria, typhoid, cholera, AIDs—I see that if we are going to be a community we must somehow empower the African church—our brothers and sisters to rise up—and I think God is there ready to help. This is just a matter of how this is going to come about—to vision, to see how that will be, but there needs to be more unity in the Kingdom of God—with the American church and African church working together rather than different agendas coming to together—building the community, focusing on the least of these, responding in love instead of fear, and doing it in the midst of total chaos, violence, and suffering.
>
> I still see hope for North Katanga. I'm very cynical, yes. I've been there long enough to see it happen over and over, but yet I know people, and you deal one on one with our local church—the village people—it is a whole different reality—they are hurting, they are suffering, they are hungry—through no fault of their own. And we are a local community, a local church that must respond accordingly. How that will be—I don't know—when that will be—I don't know, but we keep trying.
>
> For me, I've seen the transition in Zambia, and I've seen things happen that never happened in Congo in a shorter period of time in Zambia. Then again, there is peace and stability—a different world than North Katanga. For North Katanga, there

> are so many factors working against the local church that it is going to take a lot of coming together, seeking God's direction. I believe it can happen. I am one who everybody laughs at because I think there is hope for Congo despite the wars and rumors of wars—that one day there could be peace there. I may not see it in my lifetime, but we do not want to give up the church. I could say that God has not abandoned the church in North Katanga. God is ready to do whatever needs to be done and we must work together to see that happen.[12] —*Ken Vance*

Bob Walters also expressed hope in the midst of doubt. Yes, the Spirit is at work, but it is also possible that we will screw this up.

> First of all, I'm very reluctant to use God language here because it gets so abused and becomes an explanation of some unhealthy relationships and unhealthy work. . . . On the other hand, there is so much going on that I have no other explanation other than the Spirit of God moving.
>
> Being a good Wesleyan, we can choose to do this well, or we can choose to screw this up real bad. This isn't necessarily something that, in the end, is going to all work out because God is in control. In the end, this could all collapse because we just absolutely refuse to do it well. I'm filled with hope. I see the Spirit of God moving. I also see that choices made by local church leadership, Congolese, choices made by Americans trying to help, choices made by general church agencies, are not always alert to the movement of the Spirit of God.[13] —*Bob Walters*

George Howard expressed a more celebratory sentiment, identifying the shift in power and the emergence of North Katanga church leaders as leaders on the global-level as a change that is Spirit-led.

> North Katanga is the largest (numerically) annual conference in Methodism. There are more people coming from that annual conference and from North Katanga as a whole than anywhere else in the world to General Conference. So they have numerical clout, which also makes them a target for people who want to convince them that they know something that North Katanga

---

12. Ken Vance, interview with the author, January 11, 2016.
13. Bob Walters, interview with the author, January 11, 2016.

> doesn't.... The more I have conversations with people, the more I see leaders thinking for themselves and North America in particular recognizing that they can't do it all on their own without alliances, with partnerships, without relationships with people from North Katanga.
>
> And so it is a shift in power. And North Katanga finally is going to have to claim that shift and claim that power and start talking more about the challenges and breakthrough from their perspective....
>
> At Global Ministries we talk about "missions from everywhere to everywhere" and the map that was designed five years ago had this explosion of missionaries leaving the US and going all over the world and then a few from here and there. We recreated the map this year. We plotted on it where missionaries are coming from. There is still a starburst coming out of North America, but there is another huge starburst coming out of Katanga and the DRC. We are sending missionaries through GBGM from all over the world.
>
> So, when you ask where the Spirit of God is moving, their leadership is stepping up as missionaries, at General Conference—their leadership is stepping up as they are teaching the rest of the world what is happening and the rest of the world is beginning to pay attention—particularly through the partners who have been there long term and have been getting glimpses of what is going on there and what they have to learn from it.[14]
> —George Howard

Tim Tanton of United Methodist Communications also focused on the testimonies he has heard of what has been accomplished.

> When you look at what is being accomplished ... what people are often up against because of some of the conditions they are dealing with, which are very alien to what people in the North [North America] are accustomed to—malaria, [war], clean water ... when you look at what people of faith are accomplishing, ... that is powerful. That is God working through us to fulfill what Christ directed us to do in Matthew 25.[15] —*Tim Tanton*

---

14. George Howard, interview with the author, January 8, 2016.
15. Tim Tanton, interview with the author, January 7, 2016.

Neelley Hicks from United Methodist Communications[16] saw God at work through the learning experiences, and she held this in tension with internal conflicts about how to respond to clashing beliefs about the rights of women.

> It is such an amazing learning experience. There is . . . like the Muslim/Christian relationship there. . . . People [in the USA] don't know. . . . I think we are called to shine a light on where we see God at work.
>
> I think that on honoring women in ministry that is still a challenge. I saw some pretty harsh examples of how women are still marginalized as I was there during my second trip. Not even covertly—in a meeting how women were talked about—it really stunned me—I was faced with "I'm not going to call this person out because I would be the ungracious one in a culture that is really accepting of what he just said about spanking wives or that being ok or women shouldn't have smartphones because they don't have pockets therefore they shouldn't have smartphones." When I tried to offer alternatives and say, "We use purses," it wasn't met very well. So, there is a long way to go.
>
> I think God is asking us to be cognizant of the ways people are diminished—but as outsiders—knowing how we can be gracious in sharing what could be. They have things that they could teach us on in our communities as well.[17] —*Neelley Hicks*

For Pamela Couture, the relationship could be described as a holy mystery—the Spirit is at work in these global friendships, and these formed communities become the body of Christ in the world.

> To me, the Bible came to life [in Congo] because the Congolese society is much closer to [biblical issues]. . . . There are mysterious and remarkable things happening in these relationships that have developed. That the Spirit of God is hard at work when our intimate relationships with people we love and support are strewn across the globe . . . so the relationships are powerful connectors for our life. The way that God's Spirit works internationally to make something new . . . it really is making something new.

---

16. Hicks has recently become highly involved in initiatives in eastern Congo and is now the head of Harper Hill Global.

17. Neelley Hicks, interview with the author, January 11, 2016.

> We can make all our statements about what we want to do, and those statements get exploded into something new. I think that there is a way in which people who engage in these relationships over the long haul . . . that there is a level of irrational commitment, and we not explain that. . . . The assumptions that operate in our society . . . we get committed to these relationships, and that is the vocational aspect. There is something here about ministry and being partners with God at the center—which is strong and makes a claim on us. . . . It becomes all encompassing . . . the way in which we build a community that does become the body of Christ.[18] —*Pamela Couture*

For John Enright, the question of where the Spirit of God is acting in the relationship raised deep questions, and he began his response by reflecting upon the historical pain in Congo as well as what happened when traditional evangelical missionaries arrived. He also expressed what I have noticed to be a point of view many long-term foreign missionaries arrive at: a sense that reality is more complicated than they once thought, and that doctrinal claims that undergird confident claims of who God is and what God is doing are not contextually appropriate.[19]

> Have you read anything by Eckhart [Tolle]? [He wrote] *The Power of Now*. . . . Basically, you have certain understandings, things called ego, pain-body. You have traditions that suffered a great deal and they have a cultural damage and pain that is buried deep within the subconscious of people who went through that. And this is all over the world. There is a great deal of historical pain in Congo, and believe me the White people contributed heartily to it, but not only the White people. The pain is spread around.
>
> Now, where is God in all of this? For me, I think that traditional evangelicalism was the motivating force that brought Christianity to Congo. It isn't that the evangelical tradition won in the sort of liberal/fundamentalist dichotomy of the West. It is that there really is no other tradition in Africa than what Americans would call traditional evangelicalism. Coupled

---

18. Pamela Couture, interview with the author, January 8, 2016.

19. Although many long-term missionaries stand firm in traditional doctrinal beliefs, those who don't seem, based on my anecdotal observations, to go on a spiritual journey that has them questioning everything they were taught, resulting either in disillusionment or comfort with ambiguity (or a bit of both).

with that, traditional evangelicalism is a coat of paint over the ancient traditional religion of Africa, which has a very strong understanding of God. A bit more than the simplistic, for some Americans, grandfather sitting on a cloud in the sky tossing candy to children. The African concept . . . is very deep theological understandings that did not suffer from the simplistic modifications that happened to Christianity to make God palatable and theology accessible to people that really don't know a whole lot about it.

All of that is to say is that I think that the Western understanding of God or the traditional understandings of God simply don't matter here. . . . The sort of theological arguments about prevenient grace and eternal security—my gosh—imagine discussing that in the village of Nyembo when the big issue is the lady eating the spirits of children and flying and the measles epidemic, which is actually witches killing children. It just doesn't pertain.

So where is God in all of this? See, I'm afraid we created God in our image and then took God to Africa. But God was always in Africa, and so we need a really long-term view of this. This is an evolution and a process which Africa is being brought into the community of nations and being subjected to whole worldview changes. It is happening rapidly and the younger people are moving fast. Most of the Lunda young people can't speak Lunda. Most of the Luba young people—in the cities like Lubumbashi—can't speak their own language. . . .

So, things are changing, and I believe that in that change, there is the hand of God. Things that I don't understand are being directed by God. . . .

One other maxim that I think needs to be written in the sky: everything that everyone does they do out of perceived self-interest. No one really does anything apart from self-interest. Altruist acts are in my self-interest. It makes me feel good to help people. Now, when we understand some of these basic psychological principles that are acting out, we realize that God is helping Africa evolve and that our little petty doctrinal issues and little fights and political conniving are just that and really it is all part of the process—some may be a step backwards or forwards—but all is part of a process, and this process is good. This process is how it has to be.

I see no regrets no regrets—nothing that could have been otherwise during that period. It simply was the way it was. The

> statement says there are only three options to health-fully deal with situations: the first is acceptance, the second enjoyment, the third enthusiasm. In what was a very painful period of my life, I have acceptance.... Let's see if we could do better in the future.
>
> I wish I could give you a better answer, but I don't know what God is. I mean, I used to know when I was at Taylor [University], but I don't anymore. I know God. I experience God. I experience God's power tremendously, but I don't have a whole lot of answers about God. I think God can take care of himself—or herself. And is doing a good job as far as I am concerned.[20]
> —John Enright

One of the striking elements of Enright's comments is the element of conversion. Like many long-term missionaries, Enright's experiences in ministry challenged the theology/missiology he was taught in his American seminary, and it resulted in him rethinking what he once thought to be true. While my research did not explore this phenomenon, it is important to recognize that partnerships that cross socio-economic and/or cultural barriers can result in the one self-identifying as "missionary" also having their understanding of God and God's mission profoundly changed in the encounter.

The consensus of North Katanga and American interview participants was that the Spirit of God is at work in the partnership in many ways. Saying this, I emphasize that this is not the same as asserting that everything that has occurred in the evolution of the partnership has been God's will, nor is it the same as saying that the partnership is currently healthy, decolonized, and exactly how God desires it. Instead, it is an affirmation that, despite our follies, there is a holy mystery at work in these relationships, and thus people of faith can cling to the hope that our leaders will grow in their love for one another, and the fruits of the Spirit will continue to be seen.

One lens that can be used to describe Katangan participants' descriptions of the Holy Spirit at work is the Methodist understanding of God's grace (see 7.2.1.). For Katanga participants, numerical growth of the church is one way of measuring God at work in the partnership. This could be identified as converting/justifying actions of the Spirit and is also in line with missiologies that articulate task of the Church as spreading the message of Christ as Savior and growing numerically by making new disciples. Justifying grace is participatory conversion; it is the result of a conscious action/decision people make, and thus is not passive. There were also portions of responses that pointed to things received through relationships

20. John Enright, interview with the author, January 6, 2016.

with Americans (scholarships, support, etc.). These could be described as sanctifying grace in that the Spirit moved Americans to be loving/generous towards North Katangans. The most prevalent responses, however, were about North Katangans becoming more mature in their understanding of themselves and love of others. This, too, is in the area of sanctifying grace, but can also be identified as prevenient grace in that the Spirit is seen as working to change hearts and minds before persons are aware of their need of it. Thus, as a whole, what was expressed by Katangan participants about how the Holy Spirit is working is consistent with Methodist theology of how God works in the world.

The American responses are more difficult to map onto a traditional Methodist theological construct. Within them are threads of the importance of relationships, thanksgiving for development and relief programs, and an affirmation that North Katagans have become more powerful in the Church. There also is a strong undercurrent of disappointment and doubt in relation to what God is doing in North Katanga and the degree to which the partnership has been an agent of change. This is particularly interesting in that for those living in North Katanga, the narrative is that God is doing great things there. Yet, for American partners, there is amidst the recognition of changes a lack of clarity of what God is doing in Congo.

This is also an issue of different dominant missiologies. For North Katangans, the measurements of God at work focused mostly on church growth and shifts in mentalities. Many of their responses could be categorized under "mission as relationship" (see 2.1.2) or "mission as inreach" (see 2.1.2) in that they celebrate shifts in relationship dynamics (e.g., more church members) and self-understanding (e.g., decolonizing the mind). Americans, however, tend to operate either out of a missiology that focuses on measuring *genuine* repentance and conversions or one that focuses on the ending of suffering through good works/development projects. The more time American participants had spent in North Katanga, the more conflicted they seemed to be about what God is doing through the partnerships. John Enright, for example, had spent much of his time as a missionary in Katanga focusing on church growth/evangelism. In his later years he was known to lament that be believed that most Methodists in Congo were not genuine Christians in that he did not see a conversion of behaviors correlating with numerical growth in the church. Ken Vance noted the difference in results he'd seen in Katanga versus Zambia, citing Zambia's political stability as the cause. Implied in his response (and the responses of certain others) was an unmet expectation that the fruit of God-centered partnerships includes healthy prosperous communities. This view is influenced by the mission as outreach (see 2.1.1) model, where success is measured by quantifiable improvements in the lives of others. In the North Katanga setting, cyclical outbreaks of war and pillaging—which increase and intensify the levels of emotional and physical trauma—have made it difficult to measure improvements in communities. These setbacks to community development can create a theological crisis for those measuring their ministry success using such a framework.

7.1.2 Scriptures

Many of the interview participants were asked to name Scriptures or biblical themes that can be used to discuss the relationship. Most included with their naming of passages and themes a commentary on why they chose them. Below is a sample of the answers I received.

7.1.2.1 NORTH KATANGA RESPONSES

The main scriptural themes that were raised in these responses echo what they emphasized when identifying how God is at work in North Katanga: (1) the call for love, unity, and blessing others, and (2) the command to work and help build the church. For each of these categories, I provide excerpts of responses.

7.1.2.1.1 LOVE, UNITY, AND BLESSING OTHERS

Gertrude Mwadi focused on Christ's saving love for all, the assertion that all are to believe in Him, and that through believing in Christ the relationship between each other is strengthened.

> For me, a favorite is John 3:16. "For God so loved the world." ... Jesus didn't only die for North Katangan people. He didn't die just for Americans. He died for all of us, and through his death there is salvation for you and me. ... We are all invited in the Kingdom of God. First of all, you must believe in Jesus Christ. It is not only Americans who are supposed to believe. Not only North Katangans who are supposed to believe. All of us are to believe in Jesus Christ. When we believe, we are all brothers and sisters in Jesus Christ and we are strengthening the relationship between these two groups and then we are one in Jesus Christ for the building of the kingdom of God.[21] —*Gertrude Mukalay Mwadi*

---

21. Gertrude Mukalay Mwadi, interview with the author, July 14, 2015.

Guy Nyembo Kinkundulu focused on the topic of love and unity. He criticized the absence of foreign missionaries in recent years while celebrating the presence of North Katangans in the USA.

> "Let us be one as Christ and the Father are one." That we can keep this relationship forever. A relationship of understanding, a relationship of exchange; interchange, a relationship of sharing, a relationship of faith, a relationship expressed through love, a relationship expressed through the exchange of experiences. It will be a very good thing.
>
> You notice the office of [GBGM] after a new policy, the missionaries are no longer present in North Katanga where they were. Their absence is a bad thing. . . .
>
> Today, there are Methodist pastors in the United States of North Katanga like Guy Mande [Muyombo], at the Board office. There are the others [for example] John Mutombo, those who are an African presence in America. But, we need the American presence to be able to stay in Africa. In the same way, we want that presence. This unity and this communion and that we can advance in faith in that sense because distance . . . is not good, I will conclude with that.[22] —*Guy Nyembo Kinkundulu*

For Bishop Ntambo, inspiration came from the idea of being a blessing and offering Christ even when one has no material wealth to give to others as well as the biblical teachings about unity.

---

22. Guy Nyembo Kinkundulu, interview with the author, July 15, 2015. Original: "Soyons un comme Christ et son Père sont un. Qu'on puisse garder cette relation pour toujours. Une relation de compréhension, une relation de change; d'inter change, une relation de partage, une relation de foi, une relation qui s'expriment par l'amour, une relation qui s'expriment par des échanges d'expériences. Cela sera une très bonne chose. Vous remarquez les bureau de Board—après une nouvelle politique, les missionnaires ne sont plus présent dans les milieux comme au Northkatanga où ils étaient, leurs absences n'est pas aussi bonne, c'est aussi une mauvaise chose parce que les missions doivent être la pour les cas spéciaux quand cela demande leur présence, là où ils sont valable, l'aviation, a agriculture même dans certains endroits si c'est nécessaire, comme vous là si vous étiez sur place, vous devriez gérer une paroisse, cette différence, cette façon de nous voir, vous dans votre paroisse, et nous la notre, nous travaillons la main dans la main çà allait encore à édifier notre églises. Aujourd'hui, ya des pasteurs Méthodistes aux Etats-Unis du Nord Katanga comme Guy Mande, au bureau des Board il ya les autres—John Mutombo, ceux qui sont la bas, c'est une présence africaine en Amérique. mais nous besoin la présence américaine puissent rester en Afrique, de la même manière, nous voulons cette présence, cette unité et cette communion et qu'on puissent avancer dans la foi dans ce sens là parce que la distance est considérer comme une division c'est pas bon, je vais conclure par ça."

> I like in Genesis 12, where God talked to Abraham, "I will bless you so you can be a blessing." We are born to be a blessing to one another, from individual level to national level.
>
> Second, I like the one in Acts where Peter and John were going to pray, they looked at the man who was asking for money and they said to him "We have no gold, we have no silver, but in the name of Jesus stand up and walk." This man was given Jesus—more than dollar, more than Congolese francs. And with Jesus he was given joy; he was given hope; he was given salvation; he was given grace; he was given love. With Jesus it is all we are looking for. So bringing to us Jesus in Africa—telling us about Jesus—and our people having Jesus—it is a source of hope, a source of peace, a source of forgiveness, a source of everything. Harmony between men and women in the marriage—it is all Jesus.
>
> So, those verses and there are many others: Jesus claiming unity, asking his father to be united, and finally, the LORD's Prayer; I adore it.[23] —*Nkulu Ntanda Ntambo*

Daniel Mumba also focused on the theme of giving to others, and he saw the actions of foreign missionaries as following this teaching.

> Jesus said that the one who gives to another, it is to me that they give. I think this is what the missionary has deeply believed and developed more. Because Jesus said, I was naked and you helped me; I was hungry and you gave me something to eat; I was sick and you helped me with medicine and other things. And anything you have given to a little one, you have given to me. I think this is the passage that the missionaries use. When one talks about the sick, they give to the sick one, but one sees Jesus Christ who said this.[24] —*Daniel Mumba*

23. Nkulu Ntanda Ntambo, interview with the author, July 20, 2015.

24. Daniel Mumba, interview with the author, July 13, 2015. Original: "Jésus a dit c'est lui qui donne à quelqu'un, c'est a moi qu'il a donner. Je pense que c'est ce que les missionaire est voulu beaucoup o bien développent beaucoup plus. Parce que Jesu a dit J'étais nu, et vous m'avez assister; j'avais faim, et vous m'avez donné à mange; j'étais malade, et vous m'avez assister par le medicament o de autre chose. Et quelque chose vous avez donner a un petit, c'est a moi que vous avez donner. Et je pence que c'est le passage que les missionaries utilizent quand on parle de malade, ils donnent a ce malade mais il vois Jesu Christ qui a dit cela."

7.1.2.1.2 Work and Make Disciples

This second category of response, while also implicitly and explicitly addressing the theme of love and generosity to others, focused on an imperative to work and help build the church.

John Maloba touched upon the themes of making disciples, change, hope, working with God, and working despite material poverty.

> There are a lot [of passages]. Matthew 28:19–20: "Go make disciples of all nations." Also, other themes that speak to us about change. . . . We have to change and move on. There is "With God, we have hope," "If we are with God, we accomplish things." . . . Another theme that the bishop preached "Stand up and walk"—Acts 3—"It is He who is in front of the door of the church"; "I have no gold or silver."
>
> "Get up and walk": Walk means to work. We must work hard. . . . When someone works, there must be production. And when someone works a lot, we talk about maintaining productivity. And production is not just spiritual production, there is also material production. Then if you have a lot of people, people will give money and you will buy things and you will also pay the pastor.[25] —*John Maloba*

For Susanne Kisimba, the key theme was the need for more workers to preach the Good News in North Katanga.

> For me, that one from Matthew when Jesus was saying "The harvest is large, but they need more workers." This is my passage from the Bible—Jesus was just working in different villages, preaching the word of God, healing, but when he was working he just saw the crowd and he was feeling pity. . . . It is like those

---

25. Mulume wa Umba John Maloba, interview with the author, July 12, 2015. Original: "Il y a 'en beaucoup. Matthew 28:20: Allez faire de tous l'nations mes disciples Aussi d'autre thème qui nous parlent aussi de changement. Comme la fois passer nous avons parlé de changement . . . nous devons changer et aller d'avant. Il y a Avec Dieu, nous avons l'espoir. Si nous sommes avec dieu, on va faire les exploits . . . Un autre thème que l'évêque a prêche Lève-toi et marche Actes 3 c'est lui qui est devant la porte de l'église Je n'ai d'or ni argent. Lève-toi et marche Marcher signifie travailler—nous devons travailler durement. Quand on dit travailler, le travail doit donner la production. Quand quelqu'un travaille il faut qu'il y a la production. Et quand quelqu'un travaille beaucoup on parle maintenant de la productivité. Et production ce ne pas juste de production spiritual, il y a aussi de production matérielle. Puis que si vous avez beaucoup de gens, les gens vont donner de l'argent et vous allez acheter de choses et vous allez aussi payer le pasteur."

> people, they don't have a shepherd. . . . But the disciples they didn't see. . . .
>
> We need more workers to work for North Katanga. For the people from Africa because among people from North Katanga, there are many problems. We need workers to go to harvest them, to give them to Jesus Christ and the same way to say "Let us go and to preach all over the world of God" I think those are my Scriptures. To say we need people to move, to go to preach, because the harvest is still large.[26] —*Suzanne Kisimba*

Referring to what passages he had often heard used in sermons in North Katanga, Shabana Banza lifted up God's love for the poor and an imperative to literally build churches.

> I know that God wants to help the needy, so God's love is for those needy people, and when we help them fix their problems, fix their trouble, there is much blessing from God. . . .
>
> God also in the Bible wanted people to build his church, like with Solomon; He wanted people to contribute to the building of his church. Nehemiah, for example, is crying because the house of God was destroyed and that the land of his ancestors has been set of fire. So, I think passages like this are most of the time used in church projects.[27] —*Shabana Banza*

Floribert Kora asserted that love is required for us to effectively work for God. He also drew inspiration from a sermon at Annual Conference the previous day which emphasized the need to use the gifts God has given us.

> There is nothing which is bigger than love. As Paul said in 1 Corinthians 13:13, we can do everything, but if we don't have love, all these things that we are doing are nothing. And then it is difficult for us to work for God is we don't have love. If we don't know exactly to support and to understand the need of other people. It is difficult for us to work properly. . . .
>
> As the Bible says, God is working. Last time, yesterday, and today God is working. And maybe tomorrow God will work with people. People are material. And then God is the one who is working with those materials. It is not myself who can work

---

26. Suzanne Kisimba, interview with the author, June 14, 2015.
27. Horace Shabana Banza, interview with the author, July 11, 2015.

> better than another. No, yesterday the preacher was saying that everyone has a gift, but we don't know how to use our gift to the work of God. Most of the time we desire the gift of another person and then leave our gift outside. And then if we knew, we pray, and God help us to understand the meaning of our own gift, that would be able to help us to move toward. And then if we are able to work properly on that side. Even our relationship between US and Congolese, will be able to bring fruit which will be able to build our church from two parties.[28] —*Floribert Mwamba Kora*

This idea that we are commanded to work appeared again in the response from Mpiana Disudiampasu, and an assertion that White people work harder than Black men was made.[29]

> Genesis . . . "Dominate nature." It is a passage that inspires me the development of the world, for me it is a key passage. . . . God put the man in the garden, He told him to keep the garden that is to say, work, do not remain idle, do nothing because the whole garden would be damaged. These gardens are goods that God has put at our disposal to transform our surroundings. . . .
>
> The problem is that: the Bible says that God created man in his image, and the image of God is intelligence. He must use his intelligence to transform the world, and when God created man He told him to dominate nature, to master it. The White man understood that. He transformed the world. Before, it was thought that the White man does not work, but that is lies. The White man works more than the Black man in very difficult conditions. Because of his work, he has mastered and transformed nature. We must use this intelligence to transform our surroundings.
>
> We are responsible ourselves, God says that the man has to work. . . . No one can work without winning some things. We Blacks are lazy. Working, we will transform our nature, our environment. God is with us, we must work.[30] —*Mpiana Disudiampasu*

---

28. Floribert Mwamba, Kora, interview with the author, July 14, 2015.

29. As Mpiana Disudiampasu noted in his interview, he was much influenced by John Enright, who often taught by saying "Africans do [x], but Whites do [y]." It would be interesting (but challenging) to do a study of which North Katangan church leaders were influenced by which missionaries (or no missionary at all) and whether this has had an impact on their views.

30. Mpiana Disudiampasu, interview with the author, July 2015. Original: "Genèse . . . Dominer la nature; maitrisez là . . . C'est un passage qui m'inspire le développement

One of the common threads in these biblical themes and passages is the obligation to take action. The theologies expressed here are not that of a wish-fulfillment god or a prosperity-gospel god. They are also not a salvation-through-works god or a god that can be manipulated by reading aloud certain Scriptures or doing certain rituals. Instead, these responses can be categorized as "mission as relationship" in that they each, to varying degrees, begin with the assumption that we are in a relationship with God and others, and that this relationship demands our collaborative energies.

7.1.2.2 American Responses

The responses from Americans interviewed came at the topic from a different angle. While love and work were still implicitly part of their answers, the general focus was different, with an exploration of issues of unjust suffering and how to inspire people to claim their abilities to be their best.

George Howard pointed to the story of the feeding of the five thousand to speak about the human desire to invest in success—that by doing our best, others are inspired to do the same.

> Feeding of the five thousand. When I first heard that what I interpreted was "Man, if you are going to feed that many people the fish must have been blessed, broken, and turned into the size of whales—how else do you feed so many people?" And what I've come to understand the miracle of that story—it was not the five loaves and two fish, it was that Jesus appealed to the best in everybody that was gathered. When Jesus demonstrated what he did and appealed to the best of them, everybody shared what they had and there was more than enough for all. When we stop

---

du monde, pour moi c'est un passage clé . . . Dieu a mis l'homme dans le jardin, il lui a dit de garder le jardin, c'est à dire travailler, il ne faut pas rester oisif, sans rien faire car tout le jardin serait abimé. Ces jardins sont des biens que Dieu a mis à notre dispositions pour transformer notre entourage . . . Le problème est que: la Bible dit que Dieu a créé l'homme a son image et l'image de Dieu c'est l'intelligence, il doit utiliser son intelligence pour transformer le monde, et quand Dieu a créé l'homme il lui a dit dominer la nature, maitriser là. L'homme blanc a compris cela, il a transformé le monde, avant, on pensait que l'homme blanc ne travaille pas, mais cela se sont des mensonges, l'homme blanc travaille plus que l'homme noir dans des conditions très difficiles mais à cause de son travail, il a maitriséé et transformer la nature, nous devons user de cette intelligence pour transformer notre entourage. Nous sommes nous même responsable, Dieu dit que l'homme doit travailler et Paul dit que si quelqu'un ne travaille qu'il ne lange pas aussi, dieu a déjà béni le travail de l'homme, et personne ne peut travailler sans gagner quelques choses. Nous les noirs, sommes des paresseux, en travaillant, nous allons transformer notre nature, notre environnement. Dieu est avec nous, nous devons travailler."

> looking for some other person or country or structure to provide us with the answers and we start looking at what God has already provided us with, we are blessed and life is transformed.
>
> People want to invest in success. So, when partners see you or me or Ntambo doing the best we can with God is already giving us, they want to join us. They want to give knowledge, or information or other resources to come along and help us. So the feeding of the five thousand holds all of that to me.[31] —George Howard

Neelley Hicks looked to the image of us together being the body of Christ, which transcends notions of being Black or White. She also was inspired by the stories of help coming from unexpected places—that it could be the American on the side of the road rescued by this relationship.

> There are some many different ones that come to mind. I think about the body of Christ which is neither Black nor White . . . it is based on something beyond that . . . so when I sit down at the table with different people I see how we could work together and we could do more than if we simply stayed home . . . the body of Christ wouldn't be complete if we segregated like that.
>
> I also think about the Good Samaritan when I think about the imam and his sons.[32] I think they came rushing to a parade, but my sense is that they would come rushing to someone on the side of the road—and it could very well be the American.[33]
> —Neelley Hicks

Ken Vance noted that biblical stories of unjust suffering, such as found in the book of Job, are metaphors for what people in North Katanga experience. He also expressed a desire for a focus by both Congolese and Americans on the needs of the most vulnerable people, citing Jesus' teaching in Matthew 25.

> There are some cynical ones. One of mine is that the church in North Katanga is Job: one thing after another: famine, disease, sickness. My hope and prayer are that one day that suffering will

---

31. George Howard, interview with the author, January 8, 2016.

32. Referring to a testimony of an imam and his sons helping the North Katanga Conference out of gratitude for what North Katanga leaders had done to help them.

33. Neelley Hicks, interview with the author, January 11, 2016.

> come to an end. Jesus said "I came so that you may have life and have it abundantly" No one in Congo is having abundant life.
>
> I guess for me, Matthew 25: "I was hungry, and you gave me . . . " If we can focus on the least of these—right now the people in the church—the number of widows—I don't know the exact statistic but I'm told around 70 percent of all the UM women are widows, and the way that widows are treated—rubbish, trash, abused by the military and the population as a whole—as Christians we have to take a stand, something has to change. The orphans, the children that are just running around—the street children, the boy soldiers, the girls sold off into prostitution. These are people who have absolutely no control, and these are our brothers and sisters. For us, the church in North America, we need to—and I don't see missionaries going in as the savior—but to somehow empower the church, enable widows, orphans, those that need medical help, to have that—That is my dream, my prayer—that this insanity—again, coming out of fear—we can break through this with the love of God and bring about transformation. It's not happening, and that's where we have to focus.[34] —*Ken Vance*

Bob Walters, whose doctorate work was on identifying and using Scriptures that could help North Katangans process their situation, had much to say on this subject. In his response, he wrestled with the passage about Paul hearing a call to help in Macedonia, Paul's letter to Smyrna telling them that despite their poverty they are rich, the cry of the saints "How Long, Oh Lord?" and the need to act when God answers prayers.

> Well, the passage that I play with a lot is from Acts where Paul has the dream where he is invited to come over to Macedonia to help, and I constantly go back to that struggling "Okay, you've been invited to go over and help. Where is what you are doing helpful? Where is it not?"
>
> So I always struggle with that, but setting that aside, the passage that for twenty-five years now that keeps working is out of the book of Revelation and the letter to the church of Smyrna "I know of your poverty, but you are rich." And the first time I started preaching that, I really felt like a cad—because in the communities I was preaching in, I could buy and sell the whole community with my MasterCard, and I had a low MasterCard limit. And it

---

34. Ken Vance, interview with the author, January 11, 2016.

seemed cruel to say to people in that kind of poverty, that kind of misery, to say, "You are rich." What I would say is "Everything that we need God has already provided." And that did seem callous. And yet, the feedback that I would receive consistently was people would come up to me afterwards and share their dreams and their plans, and they were in agreement. . . .

The community has this "Trust in God" part pretty down pat. It's the roll up the sleeves and get to work part—and they are not lazy—that's not what I mean—you can't be lazy there—it's a lot of hard work just to survive—but in terms of taking on the task of community development . . . and this is something people working out of the charity model will reinforce, "Well God will provide" and so, if you come as a visitor—and you know this—if you come as a visitor with some great gift or something, they may thank you for it, but they really believe that God sent you there to do this, so you are really just an answer to their prayers. This is really just a part of their prayer life and their prayer relationship with God. You didn't cause this; their prayers with God caused this.

One more story illustration. One of the passages we used in the early 1990s when things were scary and bleak and hopeless was—again, out of Revelation—was the prayers of the saints under the altar Rev 6:9–10 "How long, Oh LORD, How long?" . . . And one of the pastors said "Prayer is the answer," and we all just sat there. It was like, "I don't agree with that, but I don't know what to say because that's like Mom and apple pie." How do you say that's not true? So there was this long silence. And then, somebody said "Yes, but, when God answers our prayers, we need to be ready to act." And it turned into a time of confession: how many times our prayers had been answered, and we'd simply moved onto the next prayer. We hadn't acted. . . .

I'm afraid that most of what we do on these church mission trips is not deep enough—these mission trips—and help from general agencies—and help from these big programs—all of those can be helpful if we have as a community had that prayer meeting, that Bible study, where we get that breakthrough: "Okay, we've got to act. Then, these things can help us." But if we haven't done that, then all of these things that are coming to help either are only helpful for a short season or they actually reinforce the brokenness that we are wanting to get on the other side of. That's a sermon.[35] —*Bob Walters*

35. Bob Walters, interview with the author, January 11, 2016.

When Americans were asked to identify Scriptures that could be used to discuss the partnership, the common theme in their answers were passages about suffering: hunger, poverty, affliction, etc. In their responses they spoke and/or wrestled with responding to the needs of those in vulnerable positions. This once again indicates that "mission as outreach" still remains the dominant model in the minds of the Americans interviewed—even though I am convinced based on my conversations with them that most, if explicitly asked to select between "mission as outreach," "mission as partnership," "mission as inreach," or "mission as listening," would respond that they adhere to the "partnership" and/or "listening" models.

7.1.3 Sermon Talking Points

Although asking a person to identify applicable scriptural passage and themes and asking them to offer talking points for a sermon are similar questions that can generate very similar responses, I separated them in this chapter because there were some divergences in the responses, as well as deeper reflections and reprimands. That said, among North Katangans the themes of unity, equality, love, and work remained strong. Their sermon ideas reaffirm my conclusion that, for North Katangan leaders, the *mission as relationship* model dominates, and that this version of the model incorporates a sense of responsibility for action in the relationship. The other reason why I share so many of these responses here—despite their length—is that by doing so I am making a public record of these voices. I hope that other scholars will pull from these interviews in their own work.

Gertrude Mwadi began her sermon outline with the themes of unity and love, and then transitioned into concepts of mutuality and equality in the partnership—helping one another going in both directions, and the importance of visiting one another.

> I can give the example of Paul in the book of Galatians, which is trying to emphasize unity. To emphasize the unity between American and Congolese members—in Christ we are one. There is no men, there is no women, there is no slave. Then I could go far in the same context saying that there is no White, no *Mzungu*, no Black; we are all one. When we are together we can make a difference. Trying to consider someone who is higher and I'm lower—this partnership can help us to strengthen.
>
> Like in Corinthians 13, we have the example of love, of different gifts. So you can be gifted in preaching, and I can be gifted in singing. From what we have also we can make a difference.

> Now the time that I cannot finish something, I can call you as an American; in that context I am seeing you as my sister—I can't do everything—I'm not trying to see you as someone who is more important than me. From what I have, even though I am within the North Katanga area, it is good for me to see you as my sister and friend.
>
> In the same context, you can also learn something from me. That is what togetherness, trying to deepen our friendship—our relationship—within North Katanga. Because today you are in my conference. Tomorrow, I can give myself the example of when I was in America. I was in your church, and I preached. From there also, you are in my conference preaching also. You are learning many things from us. The time we are together, now we are able to learn everything from each other to strengthen that relationship. I am very happy the way we are visiting each other. When we are visiting each other, we are learning. We are also deepening that relationship so we can try to help each other. When we visit each other, we are ready to see the problem we are facing. When you visit me you can see also my problem. And then, when we sit together as a family we can contribute to a solution. We are brothers . . . with the kingdom of God.[36]
> —Gertrude Mukalay Mwadi

For Kabila wa Kubangimayo, it was important to preach on all people belonging to God, and that it was folly to attribute a person's misdeeds to being Black or being from a certain community.

> For example, the passage that Jesus himself said at the well when he found the woman who said to him: "You are Jewish; I am Samaritan. What is the relationship?" But Jesus, the son of God said, "In my father's house, there is no Jew; there is no Samaritan." We are all children of God.
>
> So you ask me my question if I can preach, I can only say, any man, whatever his color, is always a creature of God; we are always brothers. If there is something wrong, do not say, "He did that because he is of such race or he is of such name." It is a fault; it is a mistake of a person; it is only his. I always preached that before God you do not find . . . Blacks or Whites; we always go in the same way. What counts is the faith of everyone. That's what I understand as a message.[37] —Kabila wa Kubangimayo

36. Gertrude Mukalay Mwadi, interview with the author, July 14, 2015.

37. Kabila wa Kubangimayo, interview with the author, July 22, 2015. Original: "Oui, bon, par exemple, nous pouvons ici le passage que jésus lui-même, a dit: au puits:

Joseph Mulongo began with a sermon topic he would like to preach to Americans: Americans and Congolese are called to build the Kingdom of God together, and in this partnership we should consider ourselves as equals. His sermon to North Katangans took a different approach—he emphasized that while they are poor, they are large numerically and have something to contribute to the world. He also rebuked the colonial mindset of waiting for outside help to build churches instead of doing it themselves.

> The relationship between North Katanga and the American Church; we are partners in the construction of the Kingdom of God—the Americans as well as the Congolese—invested with missions of God to make all the nations disciples of the world. This is the first great mission.
>
> The work of American and Congolese missionaries is to build together the Kingdom of God. In this partnership, we must consider ourselves brother, not as bosses, others as workers. When the American church gives money to the African church that does not have means—through us we can go where they cannot reach the Congolese population. To make disciples of Christ, we must be treated as brothers and sisters united by the same mission. Sometimes the boss punishes a worker for his mistakes or the latter gives up his job. This is a subject I would talk to the Americans. . . .
>
> What I can say now, as much as a church called to the transformation of the world, we must first transform ourselves in order to be able to transform others. In this work, as The United Methodist Church in North Katanga is called to work with The United Methodist Church around the world. . . . The people of southern Congo consider themselves better than North Katangans because they [North Katangans] are poor. With our poverty we can bring something to the global church. There are twelve million Methodists, but North Katanga also has a large number. Where there is money. there are not many people. With

---

quand il a trouvé cette femme qui lui disait: Toi tu es juif, moi samaritaine, quelle est la relation, mais jésus, le fils de dieu a dit: chez mon père, il n ya pas de juif, il n y a pas de samaritain, nous sommes tous enfant de Dieu. Alors vous me poser ma question si je peux prêcher, je peux dire seulement, tout homme, quel que soit sa couleur, se sont toujours des créatures de dieu, nous sommes toujours frères, s'il ya quelques chose qui ne va pas, il ne faut pas exagérer de dire, il a fait ça parce qu'il est de tel race ou bien il est de tel nom, ça c'est une faute, c'est une erreur d'une personne, cela n'engage que lui. Sinon moi j'ai toujours prêché que normalement, devant Dieu, un jour, vous ne trouvez des voies de pasteurs, des voies laïques ou bien des noirs ou des blancs, nous entrons toujours par la même voie, ce qui compte c'est la foi de chacun. C'est ce que moi je comprends comme message."

> the contribution of this money, they build the churches; we, we have a lot of people but no money. How to do [this]?
>
> We must banish this spirit of colonization. It is true the first missionaries did a good job; it was full of love—so much so that they spoiled the church. Others build their churches without US support like the Pentecostals. But we remained in the logic of asking everything at the conference to ask the bishop everything.[38] —*Joseph Mulongo*

Nday Bondo saw the example of Paul's relationship with the churches he planted as a good model to look to when discussing what a healthy partnership between Americans and the North Katanga church—Paul planted, but then he left the communities to grow on their own. He stayed in communication, and was even helped by those communities he first helped.

---

38. Joseph Mulongo, interview with the author, July 18, 2015. Original: "La relation entre le nord Katanga et l'église américaine; nous somme partenaire dans la construction du royaume de Dieu, les américains comme les congolais, somme investis de missions de Dieu de faire de par toutes les nations des disciples du monde, c'est la première grande mission. Le travail des missionnaires américains et congolais c'est de construire ensemble le royaume de dieu. Dans ce partenariat, nous devons nous considérer comme frère, non comme des patrons, les autres comme des travailleurs; quand l'église américaine donne l'argent a l'église africaine qui n'a pas de moyens mais par notre biais nous pouvons aller là où ils ne peuvent eux atteindre la population congolaise au nord Katanga. Pour faire des disciples du Christ, nous devons être traités comme frère et sœur unis par une même mission. Parfois le patron punit un travailleur pour ses erreurs ou que ce dernier abandonne son poste. C'est un sujet dont je parlerais avec les américains . . . Ce que je peux dire actuellement, autant qu'église appelé à la transformation du monde, nous devons d'abord nous transformer afin de pouvoir transformer les autres. Dans ce travail, comme l'église méthodiste unie au nord Katanga est appelé à travailler avec l'église méthodiste unie du monde entier, c'est vrai que la majorité (70 pour-cents a 80 pour-cents) de la population du nord Katanga vit dans l'extrême pauvreté mais ne doit pas être une raison pour que les autres soient au-dessus du nord Katanga par exemple. Les gens du sud du Congo les considèrent comme moindre qu'eux car ils sont pauvres, ils roulent dans des voitures, ils ont de bonnes routes, etc. . . . non. Deuxièmement avec notre pauvreté nous pouvons apporter quelques choses à l'église globale. Il y a 12 Millon de membres Méthodistes, mais le Nord Katanga a aussi un grand nombre, là où il ya l'argent il n' ya pas beaucoup de gens, avec la contribution de cet argent, ils construisent les églises, nous, nous avons beaucoup de gens mais pas d'argent ; comment faire? Nous devons bannir cet esprit de colonisation, c'est vrai les premiers missionnaires ont un bon travail, c'est rempli d'amour, a telle point qu'ils ont gâté l'église. D'autres construisent leurs églises sans appuis des USA comme les pentecôtistes. Mais nous nous sommes restés dans la logique de tout demander à la conférence tout demander à l'évêque."

> I would have moved to the Epistles of Paul, to different churches, the way he started churches. He was going to an area, he talked to people, he preached to the people, and then he leaves them but remains in contact with them to share with them their concerns, to assist them in what they are supposed to do, and everything they also share with him the problems that they have, and then they grow.
>
> So the way the church is started is the way I am thinking of this kind of partnership. The American church noticed that we were in need, we needed the gospel and we also need material things to move, and the church came from America to assist us. And [they] should now leave us to grow. "What do you need? Okay, we can assist you. The rest you can do it yourself."
>
> We will move and grow recognizing what our partner is doing and what we are doing because it happened even after a certain time those churches started assisting Paul himself in prison and assisting other communities from their collection, they were collecting something—they send to other churches. We should experience and expect that to happen. The church that we formed, the church we assisted, the church that started with our help, where is it now? What is it doing now? Has it grown? And what is showing that it is grown through what they are doing? So I am seeing the partnership through what Paul did with the Corinthians, the Philippians, the Galatians, and so on—the way he built the church—the way he worked with those people—that's how I see things moving. Instead of saying, "Until I come, you should wait for me to come," and it all depends on Paul. They were put in problems, but they continued with what they had.[39] —*Nday Bondo*

Floribert Kora saw love between groups as the first message to preach. He then tied that to preaching about mission, with the primary mission being to make disciples among all people regardless of differences. All this involved self-sacrifice. Finally, it requires naming wrongs and addressing them with love.

> The first thing, if I want to preach, I need just to preach about love between two parties, and then also I need to preach about missions because the mission started by Jesus, he gave that mission to the apostles, disciples, and then us as pastors we have a

---

39. Nday Bondo, interview with the author, July 14, 2015.

> mission to go and to make effective that relationship between people with any color, race, gender, any discrimination.
> We need to know our people as myself, and then I need also to sacrifice myself to help another which is in need. That is what makes our gospel effective. . . . And then the third things we need to see what was wrong and then to bind and to put love inside. We need to do things which is well in this Christian life.[40]
> —Floribert Mwamba Kora

John Maloba started his sermon talking points on the topic of enemies, and then encouraged the lifting up of what is good—that is, building the Church. He included a reprimand of pastors who abandon North Katanga, especially after they have gone away for higher education. He asserted that God will be faithful to us if we love each other.

> Off the top of my head . . . I can say for example the problem of the enemies. To ask everyone to lift up what is beautiful. . . . To build the church of God. Even ask the pastors who do not want to return that he come as well . . . then they would be trained to come here and build the church of God. To advance the work of God. That's what happens to me. Since God can not abandon us. If we really love each other, God will answer our concerns.[41] —John Maloba

Mary Kabamba preached a connection between work and blessings from God. She also emphasized that hypocrisy will not result in God blessing one's work. This recurring theme in North Katangan responses about the need to work (with the implication that people are not working) raises questions for me. Is it true that North Katangans do not work hard enough, or is this an example internalized racism? Are issues of malnutrition/illness, exhaustion, PTSD, depression, and loss of hope at play? From what I have witnessed over the years, many if not most North Katangans (especially women and girls) engage in hours of intense physical labor everyday just

---

40. Floribert Mwamba Kora, interview with the author, July 14, 2015.

41. Mulume wa Umba John Maloba, interview with the author, July 12, 2015. Original: "Dans le tète, ce qu'arrivent . . . je peux pendre par exemple le problème des ennemies pour demander à tout le monde de s'élevé les beaux . . . Pour construire l'église de Dieu. Même demander aussi aux pasteurs qui ne veulent pas rentrer qu'il se vienne aussi . . . puis qu'ils étaient formés pour rentre ici et construire l'église de Dieu. Faire avancer l'ouvre de Dieu. Ce c'est que m'arrive. Puis que Dieu ne peut pas nous abandonner. Si vraiment on s'aime, Dieu va répondre à nos préoccupations."

to survive (fetching water, harvesting and preparing food, repairing house, etc.). I believe that concentrated research on this question of North Katangan's relationship with the notion and practice of work would contribute much to the conversation.

> In my opinion, God loves everyone, but we know that rewards are always here on earth because God tells us who sows beans harvests beans, and whoever sows peanuts does not harvest beans either. If you have sown badly, you will harvest very badly. If you sowed well, you will harvest well. And you cannot sow corn to harvest beans either! . . . Taking the following case: if I am at school, and I do not read, I would have zero points. That's my harvest! But if I start reading, questioning, examining and applying myself to study, I would always have good marks. . . .
>
> It is like this with God: the one who does not work, has no right to food! The word also tells us, "A man will eat by his sweat, and the woman will bear with pain." This is the Bible that says it, if I am a woman, I know by pregnancy, I would have pains for childbirth from where if I do not work, how would I have money? Money does not fall from the sky if I do not work! And for the little money I earn, I will organize myself for my tithes and offerings. Everything must be well established in all things.
>
> But if you work in hypocrisy, God will not give you everything you are looking for. . . . And hatred and jealousy, cannot be worth a good salary with God. . . . To be faithful to God and to honor all that God recommends in the Bible, it is very simple: it must have faith, patience, gentleness, and good deeds, as Galatians 5:5–25 says . . . to be a good Christian and there will be fruits. But if you work with hypocrisy, you will not know. If you work with begging, you will not be received in the service of God. We must be frank; if it's yes, it's yes, and if it's no, it's no![42]
>
> —*Mary Kabamba (daughter and wife of a pastor)*

42. Mary Kabamba, interview with the author, July 18, 2015. Original: "D'après moi, Dieu aime tout le monde mais nous savons que les récompenses, c'est toujours ici sur terre car dieu nous dit celui qui sème des haricots récolte des haricots, et celui qui sème les arachides ne récolte pas non plus des haricots. Si tu as mal semé, tu vas moissonner très mal. Si tu as bien semé, tu vas bien moissonner. Et tu ne peux pas semer du maïs pour récolter des haricots non plus! Si moi j'ai bien travaillé, c'est suite à des œuvres que j'ai fait que j'aurais les bons points. Prenant le cas suivant: si je suis à l'école et je ne lis pas, j'aurais zéros points, c'est ma récolte! mais je me mets à lire, à faire des interrogations, des examens et que je m'applique pour étudier, j'aurais toujours de bonnes notes, parce que tout travail mérite salaire, sinon une suite d'échecs sans fin. Dieu nous aussi, celui qui ne travaille, n'a pas droit à la nourriture ! la parole nous dit aussi, un homme mangera par sa sueur, et la femme enfantera par des douleurs. Ceci

While most of the American theological responses I included in earlier sections, John Enright's response of the kind of sermon he would preach was by far the most damning of all the responses, and it differed in terms of who he wanted to criticize. While most participants focused their critiques on those of their same nationality (Congolese criticizing Congolese, Americans criticizing Americans), Enright focused on African communities he knew. Instead of reflecting theologically on the nature of the partnership, he reflected on what he thought was most critical to preach in his ministry setting. That said, while Enright was American by parentage and passport, he spent the vast majority of his life (childhood and adulthood) living in Congo and Zambia, and he asserted that he knew the local languages and history better than most Lunda and Luba did. Thus, while by one analytical lens Enright was speaking like a neocolonial missionary, Enright himself did not see it that way. As he had noted that he felt more at home in central Africa than he did in the USA, he saw himself as highly qualified to speak about what he saw as the ugly truths others avoided. This phenomenon of children of American missionaries becoming missionaries themselves in the areas where they were raised creates an additional layer of complication when pondering how one gains the right to harshly criticize a community.

> The big thing . . . is to understand that Jesus Christ has nothing to do with Christianity. Christianity is a structure that evolved long after Jesus. The teachings of Jesus are more correctly called the Reign of God, or in biblical language the Kingdom of God. So for me I'm more interested in the Kingdom of God and anything that talks about it—a world view in which the 7 kingdom principles play out. These are community, servant-hood, focus-on-the-least-of-these, trustee-ship, non-violence, motivation-by-love and unity. Now none of those are inherent

---

c'est la Bible qui le dit, si moi je suis une femme, je sais par la grossesse, j'aurais des douleurs pour l'enfantement d'où si je ne travaille pas comment aurais-je de l'argent? L'argent ne tombe pas du ciel, si je ne travaille pas! et pour le peu d'argent que je gagne, je vais m'organiser pour l'offrande de dieu pour la dime et le manger. Tout doit être bien établi dans toutes choses. Mais si vous travaillez dans l'hypocrisie, Dieu ne va pas vous donner tout ce que vous cherchez. Le problème majeur ici est l'hypocrisie, ne pas être honnête, ne pas être franc, travailler avec des tournures, Dieu n'aime pas ça! Et la haine et la jalousie, ne peuvent valoir un bon salaire avec Dieu—38:14—d'où la persévérance, et être fidèle à Dieu et honorez tout ce que Dieu recommande dans la Bible, c'est très simple, il faut avoir la foi, la patience, la douceur, et les bons actes, comme Galate 5:5–27 qui dit c'est lui qui a la douceur, la patience . . . c'est ça être un bon chrétien et il y aura du fruits. Mais si vous travaillez avec l'hypocrisie, vous ne saurez pas, si vous travaillez avec la mendicité, vous ne serez pas reçu dans le service de dieu; il faut être franc; si c'est oui, c'est oui et si c'est non, c'est non!"

> to Christianity, intrinsic to Christianity, or even necessary to Christianity. They can certainly be found in Christianity, but they are also found in Hinduism, Judaism, Islam, etc. So, for me, I would be very focused and interested in the Bible as it gives us the possibility of a paradigm that correlates to reality.
>
> Now, principle says that if you fight against reality, reality wins everytime. So the challenge is to come up with an understanding of the world which correlates with the way it is. Simplistically, I would say that the teachings of Jesus are that answer sheet, that code. For that reason, there are very few rules; there are simply broad principles that focus on love, community, the least of these, and nonviolence. At any point the principles are violated, and that is imbedded in the culture, then we are going to crash and burn. In Africa tradition, it is the violence against women and children, and this is the antithesis of the kingdom of God.
>
> So, my preaching would be: "We have a chance to look at the answer sheet if we have the courage to do it." And the answer sheet is to stop calling your children black ugly stupid animals: [stop saying] look how fat their noses are; look how ugly they are. Because that is what every Congolese child is told every day of their life. And beating the hell out of your wife is not the Jesus thing to do. Surely you've lived there long enough to know that I'm telling the truth. You cannot believe the level of sexual molestation of small girls. It is virtually universal.[43] —*John Enright*

Enright's assertions throughout his interview, culminating with his theological reflections, raise a number of uncomfortable questions for me: (1) Are his critiques accurate or neocolonial/racist? (2) Could they be both? and (3) If they are accurate, how can an American partner frame such issues (domestic abuse, violence, destructive jealousies, etc.) in her/his own mind such that s/he does not make the (neo)colonial conclusion that s/he is morally or intellectually superior to the local people? To answer this, I return to the discussion in chapter 5—the distinction between trauma and culture. I believe, pragmatically and theologically, that first the American must shift from a narrative of challenging African tradition to participating in the post-trauma recovery process. I also believe that the American must challenge the rose-colored myths about her/his own country—recognizing that sexual assault, racism, child abuse, mass incarceration, and other forms of violence and injustice run rampant in our society—that it is neither accurate nor helpful to compare to our idealized version of America (or even American

---

43. John Enright, interview with the author, January 6, 2016.

Christians) to the exposed realities of Congo. It is, I assert, a form of abuse to preach a message that compares North Katanga's "insides" to America's "outsides."[44] Instead, it would be healthier for Americans to be more honest with themselves and North Katangans about how American society also has and continues to struggle with living into the basic principles of the Kingdom of God. By saying "we too struggle," we shift the conversation from judgement to empathy—from eliciting shame to forging a path to healing. This issue of shame and healing I revisit later in this chapter.

7.1.4 *Other Theological Responses*

As can already be seen in variety of responses thus far, I found that asking participants for their theological reflections was at times like conducting a Rorschach test; it perhaps revealed more about what was on the participant's mind at the time than it directly answered the question of how to reflect theologically on the partnership. That said, each response added value to the overarching conversation on better understanding the context of the interactions. In addition to those already included, there were a handful of responses I wish to highlight that don't fit cleanly in the earlier subsections. This section addresses them.

7.1.4.1 THEOLOGICAL RESPONSE TO HOMOSEXUALITY DEBATES

For the sake of not needlessly stoking the flames of conflict, I deliberately did not ask participants about the homosexuality debates and their recent impact on the dynamics of the partnership. That said, I believe it is appropriate to share the following unsolicited theological reflection, offered by Kabila wa Kubangimayo on how he believed the church should respond. It deserves documenting for multiple reasons, one of which is the type of relationship dynamic existing in the metaphor Kabilia uses.

> I would like to say generally for our Methodist Church, it is the subject of homosexuality; ... it is a movement that is not good. ... In our General Conferences, every four years, we always discuss these things. Even now other countries are beginning to

---

44. This metaphor was taught to me by a friend who counseled me one day when I was comparing where I was in my life to those whose public success triggered in me feelings of jealousy and inadequacy. She said that I was comparing my insides to their outsides. That is, comparing their public persona to my private lived reality. While Enright does not explicitly compare North Katangan behaviors to American behaviors in this transcript excerpt, he was, as discussed in 5.3.1.5, known for contrasting the two, painting the *Mzungu* as the role model.

> accept this. The church must make the effort to pray and preach on these topics. I always remember what Jesus said; that he was a shepherd, a good shepherd. [Being a shepherd] is a difficult job because a sheep is a very complicated animal. It's a beast that gets lost quickly. It is necessary that the shepherd, the pastor go to seek it even in the forest! . . .
>
> Even in conferences, some people say, . . . "They are lost, let's leave them." . . . No, no. Pray. Always go on preaching. Then the sheep is an animal that breaks easily. This animal, which is wounded, is in the forest, you have to go and get it, take it to the village or to the house and look after it. So everywhere, the animals of the world, there is not an animal that has diarrhea like sheep, and it's up to the shepherd to wash it.
>
> So now, a good shepherd, and this sheep that is wounded in the bush, the shepherd must go and take it on his shoulders. Are you ready to bear all the dirt on your shoulders, yes or no? But the Bible of Jesus tells us YES. It is in the same sense as homosexuality. We cannot oppress them, and we cannot accept them to continue with this movement. . . . We must always pray for these people. For our brothers who are swept away by a movement.[45] —*Kabila wa Kubangimayo*

45. Kabila wa Kubangimayo, interview with the author, July 22, 2015. Original: "Je voudrais dire de manière générale pour notre église méthodiste, c'est le sujet de l'homosexualité, ce n'est pas une nouveauté, c'est mouvement qui n'est pas bon. Parfois, dans nos conférences générales, tous les quatre ans, on discute toujours de ces choses-là. Même aujourd'hui d'autres pays commencent à accepter cela, il faut que l'église fasse l'effort nécessaire pour prier et prêcher sur ces sujets. Je me rappelle toujours ce que jésus a dit; qu'il était berger, un bon berger, alors que nous faisons l'analyse du berger, c'est un travail un peu difficile parce qu'une brebis est un animal très compliqué, c'est une bête qui se perd rapidement, il faut que berger, le pasteur aille la chercher même dans le foret, il doit y ailler! Mais alors un mauvais berger se dit: ah. . . . Cela n'est pas bien. Même dans les conférences, certains disent: . . . Ce sont des perdus, laissons les . . . non, non, prions, continuons toujours à prêcher. Alors la brebis est un animal qui se casse facilement. Cet animal qui est blessé, est dans le foret, il faut aller le chercher et le prendre, l'amener au village ou bien a la maison et la soigner, alors partout, les bêtes du monde, il n'y a pas un animal qui a de la diarrhée comme le mouton et c'est au berger de la laver. Alors maintenant, un bon berger, et ce mouton qui s'est fracturé en brousse, il faut que le berger aille le prendre et le mettre sur ses épaules. Est-ce que vous êtes prêt à supporter toutes ses saletés sur vos épaules, oui ou non? Mais la Bible de par Jésus nous dit Oui, c'est dans le même sens que l'homosexualité, nous ne pouvons pas les refouler et nous ne pouvons pas non plus les accepter à continuer avec ce mouvement. Voilà position comme pasteur Kabila. Nous devons toujours prier pour ces gens là. Pour nos frères qui sont emportés par un mouvement."

While the dominant narrative in North Katanga is that homosexuality does not exist there, the debates in The UMC on the denominational level have inserted all General Conference delegates into the conflict. For Kabila, American United Methodists who have affirmed homosexuality are not enemies or demons. They are not powerful forces attacking Congo. Instead, they are wounded and filthy sheep that he, as a shepherd, is called to seek out and carry home. In this metaphor, he is the one with moral and intellectual superiority, and those [predominantly Americans] in the church who affirm homosexuality are the primitive animals that require him to go try to save.

Regardless of one's personal views on human sexuality, it cannot be denied that one of the results of these debates in The UMC is that African UMC leaders are becoming more vocal in their challenging assumptions that American United Methodists are their superiors in terms of biblical interpretation and moral behavior. Thus, one of the silver linings from these debates is that they have accelerated the pace of decolonization. The debate has had a galvanizing effect on African bishops and other leaders. While there is diversity of opinion among the African UMC bishops and delegates to Africa-wide gatherings, there has been a marked increase in joint public statements issued by African UMC leaders. Implicit (and at times explicit) in all of these is the assertion that African church leaders have confidence in their own ability to read and interpret Scripture and to discern what is and isn't sinful.[46] The days when American UMC leadership could manipulate and/or speak condescendingly to African UMC bishops without fear of political blowback have ended.

7.1.4.2 Decolonizing Prayer

In his interview, Shabana Banza raised the subject of how North Katangans and Americans should pray and how to be open with one another. His commentary raised for me important questions that I had not previously considered: (1) What is the role of prayer in healthy mission partnerships? (2) How can we decolonize our prayers? (3) How can prayer decolonize us?

> When we pray we should be very honest—asking forgiveness for what God wanted us to do, but, in fact, we did not do. I think we need also to open a dialogue. We need sitting together, the North Katangana and the Americans. We need to sit together

---

46. E.g., Mafunda, "Commentary"; Jusu, "African Bishops Reaffirm Stance."

> and see where we are coming from, where we are, and where we are going. It is very important.
>
> And I think in such dialogs it is better to include all the categories, because sometimes I see that we are not reaching the appropriate people. I can see those low people are not involved, yet for any mission to succeed you should start by the very low class. So that is where the problem dwells, and that is where the reality is.
>
> We need that, and in that dialogue we should be clear, we should be open to say all the problems. We should be open to reveal all that is destroying this relationship, this partnership. We have to find out what is now going on and then get a way to an adapted leadership. We cannot create a very good model of development without understanding the right people. Sometimes we understand the people, but these people are not the right people to exhume all the problems. If I was to be the doctor of getting solutions, if I was going to lead such a dialogue, this is what I should say. We should be open. We should say all the problems.
>
> The Americans have to understand the culture where they come to. Because you know the problem with the Africans is that the very important values of the society are kept hidden. There were many practices of healing, but they could not reveal their ways. Our ancestors were not revealing to even their own children. And when they died, we were even proud to say that when an old person dies it is like a library which has been destroyed. We should be proud of that? We shouldn't. We have been losing all of this because we are not open. I don't think keeping secret all things you know is a value for the community. There are some things we can keep secretly, but other things, why? This is what I'm not happy with. We have to be open, what has been wrong, what we have to do, so that we can go further. But if we are not open with one another, I am not sure we will be able to do something for this conference.[47] —*Shabana Banza*

In his reflection Shabana highlighted the importance of full honesty, open dialogue, and asking forgiveness—both in our prayers and in our relationships with each other. What Shabana described here encompasses the models of "mission as relationship," "mission as inreach," and "mission as listening and prophetic dialogue." As J. N. J. Kritzinger pointed out to me, what Shabana described is "a kind of 'truth and reconciliation' process to own our joint failures from the past, to confess them to each other and

---

47. Horace Shabana Banza, interview with the author, July 11, 2015.

to God, to receive forgiveness jointly, and to recommit ourselves to God's mission. It is an important dimension of the way forward, without merely 'moving on' from the colonial past."[48]

Truth and reconciliation work understands that a healthy relationship/partnership cannot be built upon shameful secrets, lies, and unacknowledged injuries. Confession, deep listening, and forgiveness are required to move forward. This is true in our relationship with God, ourselves, and others. This is especially true in the work of decolonizing relationships. Thus, when we pray as individuals and as partners, our prayers are not simply another area that we must decolonize, they are a powerful access point to a decolonized relationship.

7.1.4.3 Bumuntu, Patronage, and True Mutuality in Partnership

North Katanga's new UMC bishop, Mande Muyombo, had much to say on what he identified as the theological groundings for healthy partnerships. In this interview excerpt (recorded a year before his election while he was living in the USA and working as a director at GBGM), he emphasized the importance of self-emptying and equality. He noted that a positive change is occurring, and then talked about the vital importance of dignity (*bumuntu*) in a relationship. With the concept of *bumuntu* being strongly valued in Luba tradition, it makes sense that the quality of relationships is stressed in the theological reflections given by North Katangans in their interviews.

> Yes, I think that there are significant biblical and theological grounds to this [study]. This takes me back to the concept of creation—being created in the image or likeness of God. If we are of the understanding that mission is God's mission and this God who created all of us in his image, in his likeness, then in the best practices of mission, we are invited to approach mission while we look at each other with dignity as equal partners who have been created in God's likeness and God's image.
>
> Remember that in the past local people were looked at as not as partners in mission but as objects of mission. I'll give an example: we did have in the past some issues in the health sector where old equipment that was not working in the US were now being dumped and put in containers and being sent to some of our areas, and they've never worked. That kind of relationship considered people as objects of mission to whom

48. J. N. J. Kritzinger, email with the author.

> every object could be thrown at. But today the concept has changed. We partners often say "What are the needs in the health area?" The local people make their own decision. They know where to get what they need.
>
> So the theology of creation and the doctrine of God vis-à-vis mission—*Mission Dei*—is a powerful one. And I also see it, in a sense, as a partnership. If you look at Philippines 2 . . . in the partnership in this case of mutuality, there has to be space for emptying ourselves—and giving space for listening and learning opportunities for best practices so we can allow God's glory to shine in our partnerships. I think mission will be energized when on both sides there is this notion of self-emptying—or what we call kenosis. That will be God's time to create with us and to create the energy that is needed in our mission relationship and mission partnership.
>
> Let me go further: in North Katanga, you have the Luba people. Taylor, one thing that a Luba person values is the notion of dignity. You can be an administer in the government; you can have all the money that you have; a Luba person can tell you, "You don't feed me." A Luba person is a very proud person. That is why when you cross the line of the Luba, they've been known as warriors. They fight for their dignity. The concept of dignity in the Luba culture is known as bumuntu. A Luba person values their dignity—the bumuntu. If a mission relationship effects the dignity of the people, they will be the last ones to accept that mission. So that, from an anthropological/cultural concept that is also relevant in the theological and biblical understanding—that the notion of bumuntu—dignity—is paramount among the Luba people. So we encourage partners that they are dealing with a culture that values dignity.[49] —*Mande Muyombo*

As it was discussed in section 3.2.2, this understanding of the importance of bumuntu among Luba people is critical in understanding relational dynamics. As has been explained to me, dignity is lost by failure to provide for or protect one's family. This sort of failure is for many seen as much more shameful than acts committed in attempts to save face (e.g., theft/embezzlement, telling lies, etc.). While the same could be said in much of American society, in North Katanga these pressures are intensified by the levels of poverty and the continued dominance of the patronage system,

---

49. Mande Muyombo, interview with the author, January 2016.

where the "have-nots" acquire resources by shaming the "haves" (that is, threatening their dignity) into distributing their wealth.

The idea that Congo is composed of collective societies and the USA is an individual society is over-simplistic. While much has been written about American individualism,[50] expressions such as "family comes first" or "blood is thicker than water" are still commonly used in the USA, and the pressure and desire to be loyal one's family and/or community remains. Cultural differences, then, are more a matter of degree (e.g., How far would you go to protect family members, even if they have committed a crime?), a matter of economic context (most Americans—especially those involved in mission partnerships—aren't faced with the pressure to steal to feed their family), and a matter of how one's family/community is defined.

While in theory a patronage system can be a healthy wealth distribution system, it is extremely difficult to function in a large population, and I know of no modern examples of where it works effectively. Partnership as having the marks of true mutuality found in beginning of Philippians 2 (e.g., compassion, humility, valuing others more than self/self-emptying) stands as an alternative to colonial and patronage relationships. It replaces such imbalances of respect and power with a fuller understanding of *bumuntu*—that is, dignity through recognizing our divine worth and equality through Christ.

Thus, I see the concept of *bumuntu* as a profoundly biblical one—the idea of our worth/dignity coming from our relationship with the entire family—that is, the family of God, who are called to serve as citizens of the Kingdom of God. This is at the foundational-level of my theological understanding of a decolonized mission partnership.

This vision of partnership forces us to also theologically wrestle with the question of acting as and/or seeking a patron. As noted in section 6.1.1, Jesus offered two responses to patronage: "You don't need to seek a patron" and "God is the only good patron." Being siblings in Christ's Kingdom, we are not to act as the patrons of others. For me, this is clear. This is what true partnership and mutuality in mission means.

7.2 WESLEYAN THEOLOGY

The UMC looks to the life, teachings and other writings of John and Charles Wesley as our guide in what it means to be Methodists. And, in many ways, The UMC in North Katanga has retained the Wesley brothers' practices better than The UMC in the USA, especially when it comes to the spiritual disciplines of accountability groups and service to the community (e.g.,

---

50. E.g., Putnam, *Bowling Alone*.

Methodist schools, hospitals, feeding programs, orphan care, laity visitations, etc.). This is, in part, due to the contextual similarities between the early days of Methodism and the current political-economic context in Congo. When Methodism first began in industrial Britain, the government there did not provide schools, health care or any form of state-sponsored humanitarian assistance to the general public. Wesleyan missiology was formed in that context, and thus the discipleship methodology the Wesleys practiced and taught was systematically designed to address both physical survival needs (e.g., education, healthcare, housing for orphans, etc.) and the emotional/spiritual need for love and connection (e.g., visiting widows and those in prison). Because North Katanga also lacks adequate state-sponsored social services, traditional Wesleyan Christian praxis continues to be a highly effective and appropriate methodical response to the issues facing the communities there. This extends even to the large role of hymn-writing and singing in Methodism, which serves as a tool of community-building, emotional processing, and theological education—especially in settings where books are scarce and expensive.

In contrast, in the USA these forms of discipleship gradually fell out of practice as the perception became that general education, healthcare and social services were the domain of the government and private sector.[51] As American civil society began to look more to the government and businesses to provide for physical and emotional needs, mainline churches in America lost much of the role they once had in public life (and, not coincidentally, began to decrease numerically). These changes in American government/society and the loss of many of the Wesleyan missiological disciplines left Methodism in America without a clearly articulated and taught contextually appropriate Christian praxis for discipleship in today's USA. While this thesis is not explicitly on the topic of articulating such a missiology, the discussions within these chapters can function as the building blocks for it.

One could raise the question of whether by using the life and teachings of a colonial-period *Mzungu* as a guide to how to be Methodist, North Katangan Methodism's praxis is inextricably rooted in colonialism. I believe that while (neo)colonial-period missionaries infused colonialism into the relationship dynamic, Methodist praxis as modeled by Wesley is not inherently colonial. In fact, since the Wesley brothers focused heavily on ministry with those who had been marginalized inside British society (e.g., the working poor)—inviting them into full membership in the Methodist

---

51. Many United Methodist congregations in the USA continue to manage food pantries, charity thrift shops, Christmas toy and coat drives, and similar programs for vulnerable persons in their geographic area, but the days of owning hospitals, schools, and other large-scale operations are almost entirely over.

movement—their missiology was not confined to the mission as outreach model (despite it gradually morphing into that in American Methodism as Americans focused on the social services aspects of Methodist praxis while neglecting the full incorporation of vulnerable persons into their community); it encompassed mission as relationship and mission as inreach in that the quality of relationships built in those early Methodist class meetings had a transformative and liberating impact on those in them. This same praxis, which has already been embraced by North Katangan leaders, has imbedded into it blueprints for decolonization (e.g., egalitarianism, mutuality, accountability groups, trust/respect-building disciplines, etc.). Thus, when we reflect specifically on the decolonization of the mission partnership between North Katangan and American United Methodists, we should explore what Methodist theology and traditions can contribute to the conversation.

7.2.1 Grace

John Wesley's teachings on God's grace are arguably the foundation of what it means to be Methodist. His published sermon "Free Grace" is considered by historians as the point in his ministry where Wesley publicly rejected the doctrine of predestination. Wesley writes that "the grace or love of God, whence cometh our salvation, is free in all and free for all."[52] Among his itemized objections to the idea that God's grace is predestined for some and not others (and that there is no way to be completely certain which you are) is that such a doctrine "tends to destroy Christian holiness, happiness, and good works."[53]

For Wesley, God's love is for all, and we have the choice to accept or reject it. His writings about the role of God's grace in the process of salvation—especially those about the works of the Holy Spirit, justification and Christian perfection—are still emphasized in courses on Methodist theology. Methodists affirm that there are three kinds of grace from God: prevenient, justifying and sanctifying. God's prevenient grace is at work in our lives before we realize we need it. Through the movement of the Holy Spirit, we discover that we are imperfect and in desperate need of forgiveness. Looking back on our lives, it often becomes apparent where the Spirit acted to lead us toward God.

God's act of justifying grace is experienced once we repent of our past sins and cling to God. Through justifying grace, we are assured that we are loved and forgiven. For some, this transforming experience occurs so quickly and powerfully that they always remember that moment when they

---

52. Wesley, "Free Grace," 50.
53. Wesley, "Free Grace," 54.

were born again in Christ. For others, justifying grace is a gradual transformation while confidence in their salvation is slowly built.

Finally, sanctifying grace is the Divine's continual presence in our lives, perfecting us in love so that we may better serve the One who saves us. In this process of becoming sanctified/perfected, we manifest more and more joy and good works. These good works are not done in attempts to be saved but out of thanksgiving for the love and forgiveness one has already received. Even today, when United Methodist pastors are ordained, included in the ritual questions asked in the ceremony used throughout the denomination is whether s/he expects to be made perfect in love in this life. The candidate is expected to respond that with God's help, s/he will.

As I touched upon in section 2.1, a false dichotomy has been created in The UMC with the debate over whether the Church's primary mission is to "make disciples" or "transform the world." In the USA, there is an extremely high correlation between which of these two options one choses and where one stands on debates about human sexuality.[54] As discussed in section 4.3.1.1, this same dividing line appeared (and continues) decades ago in the debates about whether missionaries and mission initiatives should focus on converting souls and numerically growing the Church or serving struggling communities and addressing their physical needs. To the outrage of the "traditional" caucuses, when given the choice of which to prioritize, North Katangan leadership (as well as other historically missionary-receiving conferences), chose funding and staff for medical and economic development initiatives over receiving missionaries who focused on conversion ministries. Thus, to assume with the impending ruptures in the denomination that North Katanga and other African conferences will/should naturally continue its mission partnerships with the traditional branch and reject future partnerships with the progressives is to assume that North Katanga's official stance on human sexuality[55] trumps all other areas of shared mission, both in Congo and the USA (e.g., immigration justice, interfaith dialogues, etc.). While the taboo about homosexuality in North Katanga

---

54. This assertion is based both on my observations of individuals over the years as well as where the official caucuses stand on these issues. These same dividing lines even can be seen in which American political party one supports. Both in national government politics and denominational politics, the wedge is deep, and the fracture is growing.

55. The challenges North Katanga currently faces in the area of human sexuality and the rights of women and children (sexual assault, domestic violence, child marriages, debates on polygamy, etc.) are a topic worthy of devoting much research. My clergy colleague Lana Robyne hopes to soon do her doctorate research on the issues of sexism and abuse North Katanga UMC women in leadership positions (including clergy wives) face.

is indeed so strong as to potentially result in hostile rejection among its members of any suggestion to become mission partners with a Reconciling[56] United Methodist congregation or entity, I would not completely rule out the possibility of such partnerships in the future. In fact, over the years numerous progressive American and Swiss United Methodists have worked in and with North Katanga and are remembered with appreciation. The difference going forward is that the global-border-crossing of social media and communication platforms has meant that it is now relatively easy for foreign mission partners to be "outed" in North Katanga as someone who supports the full inclusion of LGBTQ persons in church leadership. Till now, the only bashlash I have seen such outings create is when rivals within the conference use a colleague's known ties to progressives as political ammunition to discredit and gain power.

As I see it, the Methodist understanding of justification and sanctification makes the "evangelism" versus "good works" debate a false alternative. It is the Holy Spirit who works in our hearts—both leading us to repentance and on the path to perfect love. The process of making a disciple—that transition from repentance to perfect love—is the same process that produces good works and the transformation of the world.

The Methodist teachings on grace and the work of reconciliation and peace-building are interconnected. One example of this can be seen in Bishop Mande's paper "Theological Responses to the Mai-Mai Conflict," which looks at the challenges of reintegrating Mai-Mai militants into Congolese society and the church. In it, Mande identifies the concepts of grace, justice, and forgiveness as the necessary ingredients for true reconciliation. In doing so, he emphasizes that grace cannot be a cheap grace, for that leads to a sort of reconciliation that does not last. Instead, "grace must be seen in the light of justice and forgiveness."[57] The same can be said about the process of decolonizing partnerships.

For me personally, and for the decolonizing partnership process, it is very important that Methodism teaches that our ultimate goal as followers of Christ is to become perfected in love. This journey towards sanctification requires self-transformation (*mission as inreach*) through confession and repentance as well as transformation of the quality of one's relationship with God and others (*mission as relationship*) through genuine listening (*mission as listening*), acts of compassion and justice (*mission as outreach* done in conjunction with *mission as relationship*), and respect-filled communication

---

56. Reconciling is the chosen label for United Methodist congregations that support same-sex marriage and "practicing" LGBTQ clergy.

57. Muyombo, "Theological Responses," 31.

(*mission as prophetic dialogue*). All of theses aspects of mission have their role to play in Christian discipleship; the key is that we do not treat them as either-or methods but as needing one another to be fruitful, just as we as the body of Christ need one another.

7.2.2 Money

The topic of money, which is both a social construct and a tool of exchange, is filled with strife. A lack or loss of money and the fear of a lack of money can create suffering and conflict. The possession of money can create jealousy and resentment, driving a relational wedge between "haves" and "have-nots." The pursuit of money can lead to greed and neglect of relationships. All obsessive thinking about money can undermine one's relationship with God and others. This is, I believe, why both Jesus and John Wesley spoke often on the topic.

In John Wesley's often-quoted sermon, "The Use of Money," he states that it is not money itself that is the problem; it is those who use it. Therefore, he provides guidelines for the use of money. First, he says, one should "gain all you can"[58] of it, but he stipulates that one must gain without causing harm or injustice to one's self or others in any way. Second, he says, one must save all one can. He condemns the spending of money for gluttonous or vain/prideful purposes and insists upon buying only what is truly necessary for one's survival.[59] He also advises against bequeathing one's money to one's children, saying that would set a trap for them to live a frivolous and vain life.[60] Instead, "having first gained all you can, and secondly saved all you can, give all you can."[61] Wesley lists in order of importance who should receive the benefits of the money one has saved. First, one should take care of one's self (but only what is needed for health and strength). Then, one's spouse, children, and any other members or employees of the household to the same degree. If funds remain, one should "do good to them that are of the household of faith," and if there are still additional funds, "as you have opportunity, do good unto all men [sic]."[62]

As can be surmised from Wesley's list, many of the people hearing this sermon would not have had much if any funds left after taking care of the basic needs of those living under their roof. However, some were relatively wealthy. The amount of time Wesley devotes in the sermon to describing and

---

58. Wesley, "Use of Money," 350.
59. Wesley, "Use of Money," 353.
60. Wesley, "Use of Money," 354.
61. Wesley, "Use of Money," 355.
62. Wesley, "Use of Money," 355.

admonishing methods of gaining wealth that are harmful or abusive compared to the time given in the sermon to methods of distribution of funds outside of the household shows that he was more concerned with persuading persons to do *economic justice* (e.g., paying workers fairly, creating safe working conditions, not preying on the vulnerable with false promises, etc.) than he was with praising persons for sharing their wealth with the brothers and sisters in their household of faith or with humanity in general.

This aspect of economic justice is an important point that tends to be overlooked when Methodists preach "Gain all you can; save all you can; give all you can." I believe it also provides an opening for shifting the conversation about missional giving. For the average Methodist in the pews in the USA, *mission partnership* means giving money to help sisters and brothers in the faith in a difficult ministry setting. The language used on the American end of Methodist partnerships tends to be about sharing money one has left over after taking care of the needs of one's family and local congregation. It is not uncommon for there to be speeches about how one could give-up non-essential spending habits (e.g., a cup of coffee or eating out) in order to afford to increase one's giving to mission programs. Yet, outside of some social-justice focused congregations, there is not much said from the pulpit about how the methods we employ to acquire wealth harm our mission partners. While the complex web of multinational corporations, government economic policies, and mutual fund retirement savings plans make it nearly impossible to not financially benefit from harm/injustice done to others, that does not give us permission to not wrestle with it as a community of faith. I am cautiously optimistic that this is beginning to happen—at least in areas where an easy corrective action can be presented to the congregation. One example of this is the growing popularity of fair-trade products (e.g., coffee and chocolate) used and promoted by congregations seeking to be more ethical in their spending habits.

In the context of the decolonization process of the American-North Katangan UM partnership, shifting the conversation narratives from being about benevolently helping the poor to being about economic justice is an important first step. Talking about the massive flows of wealth (e.g., rubber, copper, cobalt, coltan) from Congo to the USA—so that partnership conversations are held in the context of recognizing what Katanga has already given (without consent) to build America's wealth (including our ability to buy affordable laptops and smartphones)[63]—is an essential part of moving from a neocolonial charity model to a partnership of equals. In this way, sending

---

63. See Browning, "Where Apple Gets the Tantalum"; Kinniburgh, "Beyond Conflict Minerals."

money is no longer seen an act of charity on the part of Americans; it is an act of repentance and the first steps towards restitution. When American partners start thinking in these terms, then they can begin to explore other ways to stop the injustices they are benefitting from—such as advocating for laws and policies that would require manufacturers to better track their supply chains and mandate that the bulk of mining profits are used to pay fair wages and fund community infrastructure projects.

While in his sermon Wesley referred specifically to the problems created by the practice of inheritance and/or unethically acquired wealth, he was pointing to a larger issue: money can become a curse rather than a blessing. This continues to be a praxis challenge, and is addressed in a growing number of books about church mission. Most books I have found about the issues that arise when money is given to alleviate the symptoms of poverty focus on pragmatic strategies for tackling problems without going so far as to say that aid itself is the problem. Dambisa Moyo's *Dead Aid* and Robert Lupton's *Charity Detox* are two significant exceptions. Moyo argues that "aid is not benign—it's malignant. No longer part of the potential solution, it's part of the problem—in fact aid *is* the problem."[64] Using her expertise in economics, she details all the ways in which aid money given both by foreign governments and non-profit organizations such as churches hurts instead of helps struggling countries and communities. This does not mean that all outside financial infusions are bad, though. Moyo strongly supports foreign direct investment (FDI)—that is, creating business that operate for profit and that hire locally. Lupton, who writes primarily for church audiences, also agrees that the dominant models for helping are ineffective at solving poverty (see quote in 2.1.1.2) and sees ethical FDI as the solution for those who truly care about results. Lupton raises the question of what the goals of international mission trips/partnerships are:

> Compassion fatigue has brought us to the moment of truth. Are these efforts really about poverty alleviation? Or are they primarily about community building? Both goals are legitimate, I suppose. But when prosperous Americans have the capacity and connections to create businesses that lift people out of a life of grinding poverty, I find it difficult to understand how we can be satisfied doing "relational" ministry built on an artificial economy that offers no way for the poor to rise above survival. My hope is to discover ways to accomplish both—affirm respect for the indigenous culture while building a profitable business.[65]

64. Moyo, *Dead Aid*, 47.
65. Lupton, *Charity Detox*, 41.

For Lupton, when economically prosperous Americans engage in *mission as relationship* in such a way that does not result in them leveraging their connections/privileges to create pathways to prosperity for their mission partners, such a relationship is meaningless. For him, genuine mission partnerships involve investing in a relationship with the goal of economic prosperity (not simply survival incomes) for all. What Lupton describes is a variation of the practices of the early Church as described in Acts (e.g., Acts 2:44–45; 4:32, 34–35). The key difference is that, instead of wealthy Christians giving up their wealth by selling and distributing it to those in the fellowship, Lupton argues that wealthy Christians should leverage their wealth and privileges to help their mission partner to also become wealthy. Is such an understanding compatible with Methodist praxis concerning the use of money? Setting aside the debate on what constitutes modest living, it is clearly Methodist to gain all the money we can (by ethical means), and thus it follows that it is good to assist others in doing so. The key contextual difference between the money ethics of some in the early Church and those of Methodism is that Methodists do not base their financial decisions on the assumption that Christ will return soon, and thus, we promote tithes and offerings but do not advise members to give away all of their money and possessions, since this could cause one to become destitute. In fact, one of the ritual questions asked in the ordination service is whether one has substantial financial debt.

The key aspects of money ethics that I believe transcend socio-economic contexts are the mandate to do no harm and to redistribute the flow of wealth (which can include creating new streams of revenue) so that everyone has enough. In the following section, I explore the relationship context in which such a praxis must exist in order to for a mission partnership to be truly decolonized.

7.2.3 Partnership as Presence and Connection

Connectionalism, itineration and a ministry of presence are at the historic foundations of Methodism. While in the USA and North Katanga clergy itineration is not as frequent as it was in the early days of Methodism, there remains structurally (through oversight, share resources, and regular gatherings at the district, conference, jurisdiction, and denominational levels) and culturally (especially among the clergy) an understanding of being an interconnected church. Even today, The UMC's official website names "connectional" as one of the distinctive characteristics of the denomination.[66]

---

66. "Who We Are."

To varying degrees, presence is still a practiced discipline of discipleship in Methodism. I believe a revival and re-examination of this praxis is merited—especially in the context of mission partnerships. In John Wesley's sermon, "On Visiting the Sick," Wesley addresses the importance in Christian praxis of visitations to the homes and neighborhoods of the poor and marginalized. He writes:

> One great reason why the rich, in general, have so little sympathy for the poor, is, because they so seldom visit them.... "Indeed, Sir," said person of large substance, "I am a very compassionate man. But, to tell you the truth, I do not know anybody in the world that is in want." How did this come to pass? Why, he took good care to keep out of their way; and if he fell upon any of them unawares "he passed over on the other side."[67]

As discussed in the book *Friendship at the Margins*, it was not simply the disciplines Wesley instituted about visiting vulnerable and marginalized persons that addressed the relational disconnect between "haves" and "have-nots"; the class meeting system itself built boundary-crossing relationships: "The small group structure of the early Methodist communities made it much more likely that people from different social backgrounds would get to know each other and understand and address one another's circumstances."[68] Through this praxis of regular meeting together and visiting one another, early Methodists were able to not simply *do for* others but to *meet with* and support their friends. Wesley's understanding of the value of presence and connection shaped all levels of Methodist praxis—from the class meeting to circuit riders (i.e., itinerant clergy who visited on a rotation Methodist communities around a region) to annual and general conferences. Underneath the pragmatic aspects of presence and itineration fueling the growth of the movement was the theological foundations of relationship.

7.2.3.1 The Trinity and Overcoming Isolation

Wesleyan teaching, and The UMC today, affirms the doctrine of the Trinity as expressed in the Nicene Creed. My personal understanding of the Trinity and the missiological implications of this belief has been heavily influenced by the concept of perichoresis—the relationship of the three persons of the triune God—as well as Samuel Wells's theological writings on isolation and Christian ethics.

---

67. Wesley, "On Visiting the Sick."
68. Heuertz and Pohl, *Friendship at the Margins*, 63.

Perichoresis focuses on the aspect of mutual interpenetration. Jurgen Moltmann writes, "If God is 'all in all,' then fellowship in God and fellowship in the world are no longer something separate or antithetical."[69] The perichoresis has also been described as a divine round dance. This metaphor—especially as it is articulated by Elizabeth Johnson[70]—resonates with me not simply because of my love of ballroom dance but because the image of a harmonious interconnected collaboration—many elements becoming one organism—speaks to connectional Methodist theology I was raised in. Participating in the Mission of God is like joining a communal dance.

The image of *Missio Dei* as an invitation to a collaborative dance can be a helpful tool in envisioning a healthy mission partnership with North Katangans and Americans. To dance well together requires attunement to one another; it involves trust, joy, vulnerability, cooperation, communication, and improvisation. Dancing together encompassing the values of presence, visitation, and connection. Through this divine dance we experience at-one-ment. This is a beautiful image of partnership in mission.

In her essay "Partnership in Mission: An Appraisal of the Partnership of Women and Men," Isabel Apawo Phiri expresses similar ideas about the missiological implications of affirming the Trinity, especially how this applies of mission partnerships:

> First, there is the theological affirmation that the Triune God is partnership based . . . the foundation of partnership is the model provided by the drama of the incarnation of Jesus Christ. God with us. . . . The second theological affirmation for partnership in mission is based on God inviting humanity to partnership through the incarnation of Jesus Christ. . . . [The third affirmation] states that humanity . . . is invited by God to be in partnership with the Triune God and with each other. . . . The fourth . . . is the sharing in a common project. This project is sharing the Gospel of Jesus Christ as a part of partnership in mission.[71]

What exactly does it mean to share the Gospel of Christ as partners in mission? Christian ethicist Samuel Wells has heavily influenced my thoughts on this topic as well. His books—such as *Improvisation*; *God's Companions*; *Living Without Enemies*; and *A Nazareth Manifesto*—collectively form a blueprint of how Christians are called to be in relationship with others in the

---

69. Moltmann, *Coming of God*, 278.

70. "If God is dancing, why not step out to the contagious rhythms of salsa, merengue, calypso, swing, reggae or to the intricate a-rhythmic patterns of modern dance?" (Johnson, *Quest*, 214).

71. Phiri, "Partnership in Mission," 67–68.

world. I assert that this blueprint can aid in decolonizing mission partnerships by shifting what we see as the primary issue to address together the ways in which we interact with one another. Wells argues that the "conventional way of 'doing good' is based on a false premise"[72] because the fundamental problem of the human condition in not mortality (as most believe) but isolation. According to Wells, when we think in terms of mission as addressing issues of mortality (e.g., hunger, sickness, physical safety) we use metaphors of deficit, whereas with isolation (e.g., loneliness, abandonment, disconnection, being forgotten or rejected) one can speak in terms of dislocation—of disconnection. Our efforts to do good often cause harm because we fail to prioritize human connection and dignity over assisting with material needs. As Wells asserts, "Those initiatives in mission that generally begin with a deficit notion of poverty, and assume the human predicament is mortality and limitation, have a tendency of actually increasing isolation."[73] Wells repeatedly emphasizes the importance of responding to isolation by *being with* in Christian theology and praxis. He gives both modern pragmatic examples as well as the example set by Jesus himself: "Before Jesus ever got into *working with* and *working for*, he spent thirty years in Nazareth *being with* us, setting aside plans and strategies, and experiencing in his own body not just the exile and oppression of the children of Israel living under the Romans but also the joy and sorrow of family and community life."[74]

Wells's missiological writings are synergistic with the Wesleyan teachings that the ultimate goal in a Christian's life is not justification (salvation from condemnation) but sanctification (perfection in love of God and God's creation). In both, discipleship is about the quality of relationship one has with others. Thus, our mission as Christians can be expressed as ending isolation (i.e., at-one-ment), and the purpose of our partnerships is the same.

7.2.3.2 Intimacy and Salvation

I believe that one reason that Christians with socio-economic privilege tend to gravitate to mission programs that ask them to donate money, material objects, or labor (e.g., painting a house, serving food, etc.) is that doing so temporarily alleviates complex feelings of guilt without the messiness or shame-triggers that come with entering into relationships with persons they have been conditioned to view as the objects of their generosity. There are legitimate reasons to feel anxious about boundary-crossing partnerships. There are fears about being asked to give more of one's time and resources

---

72. Wells, *Nazareth Manifesto*, 33.
73. Wells, *Nazareth Manifesto*, 46.
74. Wells and Owen, *Living Without Enemies*, 42.

than one is willing to give (i.e., guilt), about saying or doing the wrong thing (i.e., shame), or, as a relatively privileged person, about being viewed in ways that don't match one's chosen persona (again, shame).

Underneath this intimacy avoidance behavior is the assumption that "the poor/marginalized" need our help, but we are better off without them. Much has been written and preached about God's preferential option for the poor—but little, if anything, has been said in the pulpits of mainstream churches in the USA about the role marginalized persons play in the salvation of the privileged. And while it is common for Americans to return from mission trips saying that they feel they received more from the journey than they gave, rarely do they realize that they've stumbled onto the truth. Wells asserts, "You are not the answer to their [the marginalized's] prayer. They are the answer to yours. You are searching for a salvation only they can bring."[75] In his revisiting of the parable of the Good Samaritan, Wells writes that the socio-economically privileged are neither the Samaritan nor the religious authorities who walk by. Instead they/we are the one in the gutter. We are the ones benefiting from unjust governments and laws. We are the ones whose consumption patterns fuel wars, labor abuses, and ecological disasters. As Wells confesses about himself, "By any fair account of judgement day, I am going to be in big trouble."[76] Thus:

> We are the needy ones. We long for relationship, we long for forgiveness, we long for reconciliation, we long for eternal life. And we would be happy to accept these things from the priest or the Levite. These are people who seem like ourselves, people from our own social background. They have security. They have social esteem. They have resources. But the story is telling us that those people cannot help us.[77]

In Jesus' parable, salvation instead comes from a Samaritan—a marginalized person who shows compassion—who sacrifices his own clothing and financial resources to heal a stranger who might not even love him back in return. Such an expression of selfless love is rarely seen in "respectable" society, but it is often practiced by persons of goodwill who know what it feels like to be beaten and robbed. Once socio-economically privileged Christians grasp that they themselves are the ones who need saved—that they suffer from isolation from the Kingdom of God, then they can begin to push past their fears and seek to build intimate relationships. By *intimacy* I am referring to trust, empathy, presence, and communication. When there

---

75. Wells, *Nazareth Manifesto*, 96.
76. Wells, *Nazareth Manifesto*, 94.
77. Wells, *Nazareth Manifesto*, 93.

is trust and empathy in a conversation, guilt and shame dissipate. Even when mistakes are made, they can be forgiven. As Lillian Roybal Rose writes in "Healing from Racism," "Intimacy is the ability to relate to another person with authenticity and genuineness, without pretense, without posturing. If there's intimacy, we can make politically incorrect mistakes. If there's intimacy, when you make that mistake—and you will—or when I make that mistake-and I will-it will determine if we blow each other out of the water for it, or if we hang in there as allies trying to reach understanding, and working toward a common good."[78]

The theologies of atonement (i.e., salvation), intimacy and boundary-crossing relationships are interconnected, and they are all part of a theology of healing together: healing from guilt, healing from shame, healing from grief and trauma, and healing from hate. The following section explores mission partnerships as spiritually healing together.

7.3 HEALING TOGETHER

The question of how to decolonize mission partnerships is also the question of how to heal individually and collectively. Instead of attempting to ignore or bury the pain we carry, we can face it together, and, by doing so, discover a new possibility. Roybal Rose, who spent most of her life as a social justice/anti-racism activist and conflict-resolution facilitator, testifies that "On the other side of your pain, on the other side of your grief, on the other side of your rage, on the other side of your exhaustion, lies the creative alternative. And it will be healing, it will be spiritual, it will be humane, and it will be right. It will change the system deep in its roots. The system will go back to the earth, it will go back to the spirits-and it will be lasting."[79]

Grieving together—reaching out to one another in love—is the key to unlocking the path to decolonizing and/or healing relationships. It is through intimacy, not power struggles, that unjust systems are truly transformed. Intimacy is a powerful force; it can accomplish what traditional power struggles cannot. "During most of my life . . . I felt that if oppressed people could just get the power, things would get better. Shifting the power, flipping the power, is not really changing things systematically. What it does is reenact dehumanization. One of the most powerful things we can do to heal from racism is to let go of the rage and reach for the intimacy."[80] What Roybal Rose expresses in secular language can also be expressed through atonement theologies—the belief that it is through an act of love,

78. Rose, "Healing from Racism," 17.
79. Rose, "Healing from Racism," 17.
80. Rose, "Healing from Racism" 17.

presence, vulnerability, and forgiveness that we are reconciled with God and one another. The following sections explore the praxis of reconciling and healing together.

7.3.1 Shame and Atonement

One of the powers of atonement is that it takes away shame and isolation, allowing for healthy relationships to grow in their place. In a chapter titled "Removing Alienating Shame," Joel Green and Mark Baker discuss and reflect theologically on a phone interview they had in 1999 with Norman Kraus, a missionary serving in Japan. In Japan, the traditional Western missionary explanation of why Jesus died (i.e., penal substitution: to pay for our sins) did not make sense to the persons Kraus spoke with. Kraus concluded the reason for this was that Japan is a shame-based culture whereas most North Americans live in predominantly guilt-based cultures. This difference results in different concepts of justice.[81]

Upon reflection on these differences, Kraus created a chart that compares the nature of guilt versus shame, and his distinctions add more layers to the discussion above (see 5.4). Kraus describes shame as a "focus on the self" and guilt as a "focus on the act." Shame is a "failure to meet self-expectations," while guilt is an "offense against legal expectations." While both can create feelings of fear and anger, shame has more of an element of embarrassment and social alienation. Thus, the remedies to shame and guilt are not the same. Guilt can be solved through "restitution," "penalty," or "justification," whereas "identification and communication" and "love banishes shame."[82]

Green, Baker, and Kraus argue that the issue of shame and atonement is very much present in the Bible, and it is logical that it would be because shame was a major issue in that period as well; it is Western theologians who have failed to see and articulate how the cross addresses both shame and guilt.

As has been repeatedly discussed, shame—feeling inadequate/unworthy and falling short of the community's ideals—can be a barrier to healthy relationships. While the problem of guilt can potentially be rectified by accepting a punishment or replacing what was broken/lost/stolen, "shame cannot be eased by punishment or expiated through substitutionary compensation or retaliation."[83] The cross, however, can not only be understood as Christ accepting our punishment but as Christ experiencing public humiliation—shame—as an act of solidarity and love. Through his humiliation

---

81. Green and Baker, *Recovering the Scandal of the Cross*, 155.
82. Green and Baker, *Recovering the Scandal of the Cross*, 156.
83. Green and Baker, *Recovering the Scandal of the Cross*, 158.

on the cross Christ exposes false shame (i.e., perverted social rules and norms) for what it is and "breaks its power to instill fear."[84] Through the power of the crucifixion, "God removes the alienation of shame through love"[85] and thus creates the possibility of reconciliation and full inclusion.

Thus far, I have focused on shame in terms of self-loathing and/or losing face in public. As Taylor Burton-Edwards[86] notes, historically, shame was primarily understood as being about one's status relative to others in society.

> The idea of "being ashamed of" in the ancient world meant to treat another disdainfully, as if they were of lower status than you, not worthy of your attention.
>
> When Paul says he is not ashamed of the gospel, this has nothing to do with brashness or bravado. He is first acknowledging "the world" may very well view a crucified man as one who had been thoroughly and irretrievably shamed in the ancient sense. Paul says, No . . . this is the very power of God to bring about salvation. Paul upends the world's reading of what is shameful as God in the incarnation, ministry, crucifixion, and resurrection of Jesus was upending sin and death. I am not ashamed of the gospel means, indeed, I feel proper shame in the face of its majesty, revealed at manger, mountain, cross, and empty tomb.[87]

Shame can be healthy when it is not about focusing on how wretched we are as imperfect humans but rather about how awesome God is compared to us. In a healthy (and decolonized) partnership, we view ourselves as having equal status to one another; it is God who infinity outranks us.

As discussed in chapter 5, the problems of unhealthy guilt and shame exist both in Katanga and the USA, but one could make the argument that public shaming is felt and feared more intensely in Katanga due not simply to internalized racism or the *bumuntu* concept of dignity but because of how hard it is to provide for and protect one's household and how dependent one is on public honor to survive.[88] The understanding Kraus describes

---

84. Green and Baker, *Recovering the Scandal of the Cross*, 166.

85. Green and Baker, *Recovering the Scandal of the Cross*, 167.

86. Taylor Burton-Edwards is The UMC's Board of Discipleship's former director of worship resources. He continues writing as "Liturgy Man" for their blog, *Equipping Disciples*.

87. Taylor Burton-Edwards, Facebook comment.

88. Classic American novels such as *The Scarlet Letter* give evidence that American society was more shame-based before its changing economic structures allowed for one to more easily survive without public approval.

of the cross as having the power to remove shame and reconcile us is a very powerful statement of faith that I believe is an essential ingredient in removing the dynamic of shame from mission partnerships.

7.3.2 Power in the Blood

In many anglophone Protestant hymns, including classic ones found in The UMC hymnal, the blood of Jesus is celebrated for its power to wash away sin and restore right relationship with God. Such imagery is especially popular in African American Gospel music and vocalized prayers. There is even a practice of praying for someone or something to be "covered in the blood of Jesus," which is meant to express a desire have divine protection—like the story of the Passover in Egypt. Such language, while having solid biblical roots, is not commonly used these days (outside of certain hymns) in White United Methodist congregations, however. I suspect that this, too, is related to the guilt versus shame conversation, and it would explain what appears to be a correlation between the popularity of discussions of Christ's blood and the degree to which one is living in a shame-based community.

As Green and Baker reflected after having read the autobiography of Mennonite Bishop Nelson Kisare, traditional rituals involving blood sacrifice can play an atoning role for an individual and community. Thus, in the case of where Kisare served in Tanzania, "the concept of the cleaning and reconciling power of Jesus' death on the cross was easily understood by the people because of the role blood sacrifice had played in the traditional religion and culture of the predominant tribe-the Luo."[89] Kisare's community practiced the tradition of requiring someone who had been expelled for an egregious act to, after an extended period (even decades) of social ostracization, ritually sacrifice a sheep, confess his/her sins, and be covered in the blood and juices of the lamb to become symbolically cleansed and reconciled with the community. Kisare pointed out that this tradition has strong similarities to the understanding of Jesus reconciling humanity through his blood sacrifice. Green and Baker emphasize that atonement understood this way is not about blood sacrifice as a payment to God. Instead, it is "a way of removing a barrier or curse—a cleansing of the consequences of an evil action."[90]

Understood through the lens of the problem of shame preventing healthy partnerships, I believe that the language of Christ's blood washing away our inadequacies and transforming us into new people can be an extremely effective approach (especially in North Katanga) to the pastoral work of psychologically overcoming the burdens of shame (both private

---

89. Green and Baker, *Recovering the Scandal of the Cross*, 188.
90. Green and Baker, *Recovering the Scandal of the Cross*, 190.

and public) which are exacerbated by the legacy of mental colonization and economic divisions.

Kisare's example also serves as a reminder that, in the spiritual work of healing relationships, we must be aware of the role of beliefs that pre-date the arrival of Christian missionaries. From my observations and interviews over the years, I have concluded that when Luba and Lunda people become Christian, they often layer Christianity onto their existing beliefs about the spiritual/supernatural world. For example, most continue to believe that others have the ability to place supernatural curses on them through the use of witchcraft. At the same time, Christ—and Christ's blood—is claimed as the ultimate protection from such curses. Some Methodist preachers challenge the presumed power of witchdoctors and fetishes. Two sermons I heard in 2010 by Lunda[91] UM preachers living in Lusaka, Zambia, highlight the theological struggles found in reconciling Christianity with traditional beliefs of this region of Africa. One sermon focused on the story in Mark 5 of the hemorrhaging woman. The preacher emphasized that the woman had wasted all her money on traditional healers—just as people do today—yet they were impotent; it was only through Jesus that she was healed. Another sermon was on David refusing to wear heavy armor when going to battle Goliath. The armor was compared to the fetishes often worn these days—not only are they not helpful, they weigh people down spiritually.

While some Americans would raise their eyebrows at the suggestion, I believe that the richness and keen awareness of the spiritual forces of wickedness (be they literal or metaphorical) and the rituals and debates created to exorcise and/or challenge the validity of such powers can act as useful tools in the wholistic work of reconciling peoples in conflict.

7.3.3 *Transforming Together: Scripture as Freirian Code*

While the previous conversations in this chapter have said much about the theological concepts about healing, reconciliation, and right relationship, more needs to be explored in the pragmatic realm of application. For this, I turn to the work of community transformation practitioners—especially those who have been influenced by the work of Paulo Freire.

In her essay "Healing from Racism," Lillian Roybal Rose cites the works of Brazilian educator and writer Paulo Freire as having provided her "language for the behavior of oppressed groups." In *Pedagogy of the Oppressed*, Freire discusses how an outsider to a community can act as a catalyst for

---

91. I am fairly certain they were both Lunda, although one might have been Luba. Unfortunately, I have forgotten the names of who was preaching that day in those congregations; their sermon points stuck with me.

liberating thinking by identifying and reflecting back to the community through a code (that is, an analogous story or image), its generative themes (i.e., the topics that trigger strong emotions and passionate conversations), and creating a space for the community to wrestle with those issues so that the community itself takes ownership of them and formulates a positive plan of action. Just as Freire's books, especially those later in his career, were heavily influenced by the postcolonial author Franz Fanon, Freire's writings and pedagogical models inspired other writers and teachers—such that many of those who follow Freirean models learned them second- or thirdhand through books and seminars such as Anne Hope and Sally Timmel's *Training for Transformation: A Handbook for Community Workers*;[92] Global Health Action's *Transformation for Health* trainings; and Clemens Sedmak's *Doing Local Theology, a Guide for Artisans of a New Humanity*.[93]

Applying Freire's model to the task of decolonizing North Katanga's mission partnerships, one could begin with the generative theme of the topic of *Mzungu*, which I identify as a generative theme because of the energy the topic brought into the interviews with each North Katangan participant. Pinpointing the applicable generative theme for American partners is more difficult for me; perhaps because it sometimes requires an outsider to identify our own blind spots. Once the themes have been identified, we search for appropriate codes. In the case of decolonizing mission partnerships, I suggest that there are many biblical passages that would serve this purpose well.

My proposal to use Scripture in this way was inspired by Bob Walters, who built upon Freirean models in his work in the North Katanga region of DR Congo over the past twenty years. His DMin in Practical Theology dissertation, "Scripture as a Tool of Community Development," focuses on how leading Freirian-inspired Bible studies that strategically use scriptural passages that reflect back to the community its generative themes can be used as a catalyst for transformed thinking and action. Walters notes that Musa Dube's book *Postcolonial Feminist Interpretation of the Bible* also presents scriptural passages in the same way that Freire describes codes: ways that reflect a generative theme back to the community without explicitly naming that theme. In his field research, Walters presented to North Katangan United Methodist church leaders passages from Revelation—2:9 ("I know of your poverty, but you are rich"); 4:1–8:1 (the cry of "How long?" from the saints under the altar); 12 (the woman, her child, and the dragon); and 17–22 (the two cities). Walters documents how he used the Freirean process in presenting these codes and the changes both in context and responses

---

92. Hope and Timmel, *Training for Transformation*.
93. Sedmak, *Doing Local Theology*.

that he noted when he returned to the region six years later and presented the same scriptural passages.

The Freirean process requires the outsider (e.g., a partner) to first listen deeply and then reflect back what s/he is hearing, recognizing that s/he may not have heard correctly. (If this is the case, the code does not generate conversations and the outsider simply needs to listen better—and build more trust so that s/he is allowed to hear—before trying again.) The outsider does not take the stance of a person of superior intellect or knowledge in this dynamic. Instead, the partner takes a stance of humility, respect, and patience, and s/he understands that the community is not only the true expert on its problems; it is also the most qualified to address them (and, in fact, is the only group capable of bringing lasting change).

7.3.3.1 Partner: Friend or Therapist?

Despite having been heavily indoctrinated into the Freirean approach to community development and ways in which Scriptures can be used as codes in it, I have never to this point been comfortable using it in my interactions with my American or North Katangan friends. The reason for this, I suspect, is that implicit in the model as I was taught it is an element of professional emotional detachment—similar to the relational dynamics which are considered appropriate between a therapist and her/his client(s), or a pastor and a member of her/his congregation. In both of those examples, while there is deep listening, trust, and hopefully healing and growth on the part of the one(s) being heard, there is a professional taboo for the relationship to have a vulnerability balance; a therapist or pastor can be friendly with those s/he serves, but not truly friends in the sense of a two-way relationship between equals.

Does this mean that the Frierian model is incompatible with a faith-based partnership? Not necessarily. A partnership between communities (such as a conference to conference partnership) can encompass persons of many vocations and skill sets. This can include a church leader from one conference inviting a person from another who is skilled in therapy and/or counseling to come and play that role in a given setting or with a selected group. It is also possible for a friend to play more than one role in one's life. When there is sufficient trust and respect, one can request that a friend temporarily shift modes of being: for example, pastor A can say to pastor B: "I could use some counseling right now. Could you put on your clergy hat for me for a moment?" while on another day, pastor B could make the same request. There is within such a friendship an understanding that each person is highly capable *and* each has something the other needs. As Samuel Wells expresses it, "A community seeking regeneration has already within it most of what it needs for its own transformation.... No individual has everything they need: the wonder of being with is for the relationship to elicit surprising surpluses to meet its more obvious deficits.... We do not have about our person ... all the answers, all resources."[94]

Wells's commentaries on how to be with one another provide a corrective layer to the Freirean approach as it is typically expressed. For Wells, the attitude or agenda we bring into a *being with* relationship "does not start with a problem—or, if it does, the problem lies with ourselves, rather than with the person in whom we perceive scarcity." We sit with the other not to solve their problem—"we do so because we want to receive the wealth of wisdom, humanity, and grace that God has to give us through them."[95]

One might rightly ask if, by engaging in mission partnerships with the conscious agenda of receiving from the other, one risks exploiting them. This, I believe, is why there must be an element of exchange—of giving and receiving with an attitude of gratitude and abundance. In such a context, the practice of using Scripture as Freirean code becomes friends studying and wrestling with biblical passages together—praying together, healing together, learning from one another, and discerning God's missional call together.

---

94. Wells, *Nazareth Manifesto*, 29.
95. Wells, *Nazareth Manifesto*, 29.

8

Mission Partners Moving Forward

8.1 FURTHER RESEARCH

Despite having spent the past five years proactively engrossed in seeking a deeper understanding of the dynamics and trajectory of the relationships between American and North Katangan United Methodist leadership, I feel as though I have barely scratched the surface of all that could be said and explored on the topic. My hope is that scholars reading this thesis will be inspired to delve into the numerous important areas of inquiry that I glanced over. Some of the opportunities for further research this thesis identified are:

- The possible role of mission partnerships in reconciliation and trauma recovery (see esp. 5.1.3; 7.3).

- The dynamics of guilt (including White Guilt) and shame (including internalized racism) on mission partnerships (see esp. 5.4; 7.3.1), including questions surrounding shame-based conversation taboos (see 6.2.3).

- The role of women in mission partnerships and the potential impact of increasing women's authority to lead collaborative initiatives and opportunities to interact across socio-economic and linguistic divides (see esp. introduction to chapter 6).

- The challenges North Katanga currently faces in the area of human sexuality and the rights of women and children (sexual assault, domestic violence, child marriages, debates on polygamy, etc.). This also includes issues of sexism and abuse North Katanga UMC women in leadership positions—including clergy wives—face (See esp. Enright interview in 7.1.3). What role could mission partnerships play in addressing these challenges? Can the practice of deep listening be transformative in this context? What could be the impact of older American clergywomen sharing their experiences of discrimination as well as the challenges women face in America?

- The costs and benefits of short-term partnerships (e.g., short-term visitors/volunteers that do not return or stay in contact)—In particular, whether healthy decolonized mission partnerships can involve both long-term international partners *and* fair-weather financiers (see 6.3.2.3).
- The impact the North Katanga diaspora is having on the perceptions and interactions between Americans and North Katangans as well as the impact of their appointments in the USA on Americans, North Katangans, and others (see 6.5).
- The experiences of Third Culture North Katangans who have lived and/or studied abroad when they attempt to return and engage in ministry in their home conference (see 4.1.1, esp. note 24).
- The role of internet access and modern communication tools (e.g., smart phones, WhatsApp, etc.) on the decolonization process (see 6.5).
- How mission partnerships can respond to burnout and despair among church leaders (see 6.6.2).
- The impact of mission partnerships on the theologies of partners (see 7.1.1.2).
- The theology, ethics, and practices surrounding the concept of work, job responsibilities, and stewardship in North Katanga (see 7.1.3).

8.2 MOVING FORWARD

Human relationships are complex and often messy. When persons of differing socio-economic situations and cultures attempt to collaborate as the body of Christ in the world, disagreements, misunderstandings, and challenges are certain to occur. Our personal and collective traumas, yearnings, egos, and biases make us troubled people reaching out to troubled people. That does not mean, however, that such efforts to connect are in vain or that we cannot grow stronger and wiser together. Instead, it is in this striving to unite—to move forward together—that the Kin-dom of God is found. In the words of Albert Einstein, "It is the same with people as it is with riding a bike. Only when moving can one comfortably maintain one's balance."[1]

I believe that the issues of assumed superiority/inferiority, wealth gaps, violence, racism, gender, and sexuality are intimately intertwined—that we cannot untangle one thread without addressing the others. Truly decolonizing our mission partnerships requires us all to dig deep within ourselves—to question everything society has taught us to be true about us and the "other."

As we wrestle together with these issues, we should incorporate and hold in tension the various models of mission that have been explored, especially: mission as inreach, mission as relationship, and mission as listening and prophetic dialogue. We will also need to explore what *being with* means in the age of highspeed internet, smartphones, and affordable video chats. To what degree can we effectively be with each other without physically being in one another's sanctuaries, kitchens, and hospital rooms? Such questions are to be embraced not as problems but as opportunities to become something new together.

This thesis has been a journey for me personally, moving me forward into a healthier understanding of my place and role as an American ordained elder in the North Katanga Conference. It has helped me put the story of The UMC's North Katanga partnership into the larger context of mission history in the denomination as well as the Church and world in general; it has helped me find the words to articulate my critiques and my hopes for mission partnerships, and it has forced me to listen better to the experiences and wisdom of my colleagues. I pray that the lessons from this journey will make me a better pastor, teacher, and friend.

---

1. Einstein, "Life Is Like Riding a Bicycle."

Epilogue: When a Missionary Dies

In July 2017, the Rev. Dr. "Biking Bob" Walters, my father, died unexpectedly of a coronary blockage while on a bike ride near his home in Indiana. He had spent much of the last quarter-century of his life traveling back and forth to Katanga and was well known to many church leaders and rural communities there since his preferred method of visitation was by bicycle. While most of these years he came in the capacity of an unpaid itinerant pastor, he was viewed as a missionary. The outpouring of love and condolences my family received was overwhelming. Numerous Congolese friends shared that they and their neighbors had stayed up all night weeping over his death. The following July, I escorted my mother to the remote town of Mulongo in North Katanga, where a memorial service and funeral (we brought a tiny urn containing some of his remains) had been organized. To her amazement, two bishops, the regional traditional chief, and the vice-governor flew in to offer words at the service. Even the vice-commander of the region's Mai-Mai militia had traveled far to pay her respects. A full-sized casket had been purchased for the urn, and uniformed scouts paraded it through town with a marching band and color guard behind them. The route from the airstrip to the church to the burial site was packed with people waving flags that had been specially printed with Walters's image on them. When we finally reached the selected hill, we were both shocked to find that a mausoleum in the form of a paillote[1] had been constructed as his final resting place, and across from it, the ground had been prepared for the construction of a church named in his memory.

On December 26, 2017, there was yet another unexpected death of a well-known American missionary to the region. John Enright was killed in a road accident near his home in northern Zambia. His widow and family also received an outpouring of condolences, and his funeral was also a major event in the region, with various church and government dignitaries in attendance.

---

1. A gazebo-like structure.

I am told that even Bishop Ntambo, who had not been on speaking terms with Enright for many years, wept upon learning of his death.

I lack the data to know how these two funerals compared to others given for foreign missionaries (especially United Methodist ones) in the region over the years. While I know that, just in the USA, motivations for attending a funeral and speaking well about the dead are complex, I am convinced that in both funerals there was an outpouring of a genuine sense of loss and grief. Part of this grief was about the loss of the specific individual and part was about the loss of what the individual represented—a sense of connection to the outside world, a safety net, or source of hope. Part of a funeral's function is to honor the dead, and part is to affirm and strengthen connections with the loved ones of the deceased. In the year since my father's death, I have been inundated with messages from Congolese young people saying that my father was like a father to them.[2] I have lost track of how many people I have reassured that although my father has died, they are still in the hearts and prayers of my family.

Walters and Enright, while both White American United Methodist men, were very different people in terms of their personalities, theologies, and missiologies. And yet, when their deaths came in 2017, the communities who claimed them as their missionaries gave each a hero's funeral. I share the accounts of these two funerals to illustrate that, despite the complexities and conflicts that arise in the relationships between American missionaries and Katangan church leaders, missionaries who demonstrate with their actions a long-term commitment to *be with* the people and know their realities are wanted and appreciated. We may at times be a dysfunctional family, but ultimately, we are family.

---

2. He had become a father-figure to a number of people, especially orphaned youth and young adults over the years.

APPENDIX

Intro Letter, Consent Form, and Interview Schedule

Introductory Letter

Department of Christian Spirituality, Church History and Missiology

> University of South Africa
> PO Box 392
> UNISA
> 0003

> March 2015

As supervisor of the doctoral research project of Taylor Denyer, I hereby affirm that she is a bona fide postgraduate student of the University of South Africa, who is doing a research project entitled:

Decolonizing Partnerships: Evolving mission collaboration between United Methodists in North Katanga and the USA.

In her research she will be studying the changing mission relationship between The United Methodist Church's (UMC) North Katanga Conference and UMC agencies, conferences and congregations in the United States of America. I commend her to you, with the request that you assist her in pursuing this important research topic.

Her mailing address is 6030 Algiers Place Dulles, VA 20189 and she can be contacted at (+213) 0770-105-404 (cell phone) or taylor.denyer@gmail.com (email).

If you have any questions about this research project, you are welcome to contact me at the departmental address above. My email address is kritzjnj@unisa.ac.za

Yours sincerely,
JNJ Kritzinger, DTh supervisor

INFORMED CONSENT LETTER

I, the undersigned, hereby give consent that Taylor Denyer, a Doctor of Theology student at the University of South Africa, may use the information that I supplied to her in an interview for her doctoral thesis. I declare the following:

Statement	Agree	Do not agree
1. I have been informed by the researcher of the objectives of the intended research	☐	☐
2. The researcher supplied to me her name, address and contact details as well as the details of her research supervisor	☐	☐
3. I was informed why I was selected as an informant for the research project	☐	☐
4. I give this consent willingly, under no coercion and without inducement	☐	☐
5. I received satisfactory answers to any questions that I had about the research	☐	☐
6. I was informed of the estimated time that the interview would take	☐	☐
7. I retain the right to refrain from answering any questions posed by the researcher	☐	☐
8. I agree that the interview may be recorded by means of an electronic device	☐	☐
9. I agree that the researcher may quote my views in her thesis and in any subsequent publications that may flow from it	☐	☐
10. I require that she should present to me (for my approval) the record that she made of the interview(s), before including it in his thesis	☐	☐
11. I agree that she may refer to me by name when quoting my views in her thesis and possible subsequent publications	☐	☐
12. I accept that he will store the record of my interview(s) safely and that she will destroy it no later than two years after her thesis has been accepted	☐	☐
13. I understand this information and its implications	☐	☐
14. I understand that I may withdraw this consent at any time in writing, without needing to give reasons	☐	☐

Full names: _____

Place: _____ Date: _____

Signature: _____

INTERVIEW SCHEDULE

The following questions formed the overall structure for each interview.

Actions and Agency: What mission initiatives involving North Katanga and the USA has the person been involved in (particularly since the 1990s, but background context is also good to know)? What was done? Who else was involved? How was the work and the decision-making power distributed (Who decided what was to be done? Who contributed resources? Who did the hands-on work? Who supervised?) What other mission initiatives were going on at that time? [Be sure to suggest reflection on both mission in DRC and in the USA/denominational level if interviewee does not raise it by end of this interview section.]

Context, Scrutiny and Reflexivity:* What was the local context of the initiatives discussed? What was going on at the time socially/politically? Looking back, what wise choices or mistakes were made? What has been learned? What has been gained/lost over time in this relationship? What have we failed to learn? If you were teaching a class on the history of the mission relationship between North Katangan and American United Methodists, what social critiques would you make? What are the things that the other agents do not understand about this mission context that you wish you could help them understand? What would you like to see change?

Theological Reflection and Spirituality: Where is the Spirit of God in all of this? What scripture passages or beliefs about God have inspired or sustained the mission initiatives over time? Where is the Spirit leading?

*As noted in the thesis, after noticing in an early interview that raising the subject of *Mzungu* changed the energy levels of the responses, I began to include a question about the meaning of the word Mzungu and its impact on the partnership over time.

Bibliography

"2020 General Conference Delegate Distribution by Annual Conference Now Available." The UMC (January 26, 2018). http://www.umc.org/who-we-are/2020-general-conference-delegate-distribution-by-annual-conference-now-avai.

"About the Advance." The UMC. http://www.umcmission.org/Give-to-Mission/The-Advance.

Accapadi, Mamta Motwani. "When White Women Cry: How White Women's Tears Oppress Women of Color." *College Student Affairs Journal* 26 (2007) 208–15. http://files.eric.ed.gov/fulltext/EJ899418.pdf.

Adichie, Chimanmanda Ngozi. *Americanah*. New York: Random, 2013.

Adkins, Bonnie Totten. "Heirs of God in Mission: Africa Church Growth and Development." NWO (May/June 1994) 8–10.

"African United Methodists Strengthen Refugee Work." UMN (September 16, 1994).

Ammons, Edsel, and John Murdock. "Health and Welfare Ministries Program Department." NWO (May 1987) 31–32.

Anderson, David. "Conservatives in the 10-Million Member United Methodist Church took . . . " UPI (May 18, 1983). https://www.upi.com/Archives/1983/05/18/Conservatives-in-the-10-million-member-United-Methodist-Church-took/1531422078400/?spt=su.

Andrews, Becca. "The Methodist Church May Split over LGBT Issues. Meet the Lesbian Bishop Caught in the Middle." *Mother Jones* (August 29, 2016). http://www.motherjones.com/politics/2016/08/gay-bishop-divide-united-methodist-church.

Apte, Mahadev. "Language in Sociocultural Context." In vol. 4 of *The Encyclopedia of Language and Linguistics*, edited by R. E. Asher, 2000–2010. Oxford: Pergamon, 1994.

Ault, James, dir. *African Christianity Rising*. DVD. Northhampton, MA: James Ault Productions, 2013.

Backstein, Karen. *The Blind Men and the Elephant*. New York: Scholastic, 1992.

Balmer, Randall. "The Real Origins of the Religious Right." *Politico Magazine* (May 27, 2014). https://www.politico.com/magazine/story/2014/05/religious-right-real-origins-107133?o=0.

Bibliography

Banister, Doug. "Rethinking the $3,000 Mission Trip." *Christianity Today* (July 23, 2013). http://www.christianitytoday.com/thisisourcity/7thcity/rethinking-3000-missions-trip.html?start=1.

Barber, Benjamin. "Jihad vs McWorld." *The Atlantic* (March 1992). https://www.theatlantic.com/magazine/archive/1992/03/jihad-vs-mcworld/303882.

Barnes, Jonathan. "Partnership in Christian Mission: A History of the Protestant Missionary Movement." PhD diss., University of KwaZulu-Natal, 2010.

Barnett, Errol. "The Fashion Cult Cut from a Different Cloth." *CNN* (December 8, 2015). https://www.cnn.com/2012/11/09/world/africa/congo-sapeur-fashion/index.html.

Bauman, Zygmunt. *Postmodern Ethics*. Oxford: Blackwell, 1993.

Bender, Jeremy. "Ranked: The World's Strongest Militaries." *Business Insider* (October 3, 2015). http://www.businessinsider.com/these-are-the-worlds-20-strongest-militaries-ranked-2015-9.

Bevans, Stephen B., and Roger Schoeder. *Constants in Context: Theology of Mission for Today*. Maryknoll, NY: Orbis, 2004.

"Bishop Asks for Medical Teams to Africa." UMN (August 5, 1994).

"Bishop Fama Onema." The UMC. http://www.umc.org/bishops/fama-onema.

"Bishops in Congo See Progress There." UMN (September 12, 1997).

Bloom, Linda. "Most Missionaries Return to Congo." UMN (November 6, 1997).

———. "Zairian Bishops Express Confidence in Church Future." UMN (May 19, 1997).

"Board Addresses Mid-East, Africa Concerns." UMN (April 1, 1993).

Bortolot, Alexander Ives. "Kingdoms of the Savanna: The Luba and Lunda Empires." http://www.metmuseum.org/toah/hd/luba/hd_luba.htm.

Bosch, David. *Transforming Mission*. Maryknoll, NY: Orbis, 1991.

Bouma-Prediger, Steven, and Brian Walsh. *Beyond Homelessness: Christian Faith in a Culture of Displacement*. Grand Rapids: Eerdmans, 2008.

Boyette, Keith. "WCA Launches Mission Fund for Threatened Global Ministries." *WCA* (May 17, 2019). https://wesleyancovenant.org/2019/05/16/wca-launches-mission-fund-for-threatened-global-ministries.

Brinton, Howard. "A Panorama of Church Development, Vitality, and Growth in Zaire, Africa." NWO (March 1979) 22.

Brown Taylor, Barbara. *Learning to Walk in the Dark*. New York: Harper Collins, 2014.

Brown, Brené. "Listening to Shame." *TED Talk* (March 2012). https://www.ted.com/talks/brene_brown_listening_to_shame.

———. *Men, Women, and Worthiness: The Experience of Shame and the Power of Being Enough*. Boulder, CO: Sounds True, 2012. Audiobook.

Browning, Lynnley. "Where Apple Gets the Tantalum for Your iPhone." *Newsweek* (February 4, 2015). https://www.newsweek.com/2015/02/13/where-apple-gets-tantalum-your-iphone-304351.html.

Brueggemann, Walter. *The Prophetic Imagination*. 2nd ed. Minneapolis: Fortress, 2001.

Buechner, Frederick *Wishful Thinking: A Seeker's ABC*. SanFranciso: HarperOne 1993.

Bumuntu Peace Institute. "Bumuntu Peace Institute." Dialogue Institute. http://dialogueinstitute.org/bpi.

Burton, Hettie H. *My Black Daughters*. London: Assemblies of God, 1949.

Butler, Joey. "50 Years On, Central Jurisdiction's Shadow Looms." UMNS (April 18, 2018). http://www.umc.org/news-and-media/50-years-on-central-jurisdictions-shadow-looms.

Caldwell, Neil. "Court Defers East Africa Financial Dispute." UMNS (October 29, 2012). http://www.umc.org/news-and-media/blogs-commentaries/post/court-defers-east-africa-financial-dispute.

Carcaño, Minerva. "Bishop Carcaño on the Good and Bad of GC2012." *United Methodist Reporter* (May 17, 2012). http://unitedmethodistreporter.com/2012/05/17/bishop-carcano-on-the-good-and-bad-of-gc2012.

Case, Riley. "The Integrity of Missions." *Good News Magazine* (May 23, 2017). goodnewsmag.org/2017/05/the-integrity-of-missions.

"Celebrating Bishop Ntambo." Tanenbaum Center (November 17, 2010). https://tanenbaum.org/blog/2010/11/celebrating-bishop-ntambo.

A Centenary Survey of Methodist Episcopal Missions. New York: Joint Centenary Committee, Methodist Episcopal Church, 1919.

Chali, Kalaba. "UMC Nairobi Meeting: Purely Neo-Colonialism Cooked in Religion." Reconciling Ministries Network (September 5, 2018). https://rmnetwork.org/umc-nairobi-meeting-purely-neo-colonialism-cooked-in-religion.

Che-Mponda, Chemi. "The Meaning of the Word *Mzungu*—Meaning of Mzungu." *Swahili Time* (blog) (February 5, 2013). http://swahilitime.blogspot.com/2013/02/the-meaning-of-word-Mzungu-maana-ya.html.

Chen, Kuam-Hsing. "The Decolonization Question." In *Trajectories: Inter-Asia Cultural Studies,* edited by Kuan Hsing Chen, 1–46. London: Routledge, 1998.

"Church World Service Sends United Methodists to Rwanda." UMN (December 9, 1994).

"Church in Zaire Reported Thriving." UMN (June 7, 1991).

Clarke, Sathianathan. "Postcolonial Voices in Biblical Interpretations and Theology." Class Handout. Wesley Theological Seminary, Washington DC, September 11, 2006.

"Clergy: Should Ministers Be Draft-Exempt?" *Time* (April 7, 1967). http://content.time.com/time/magazine/article/0,9171,843549,00.html.

Cleveland, Christena. "How to Be Last: Towards a Practical Theology for Privileged People." *Christena Cleveland* (blog) (December 2016). www.christenacleveland.com/blog/2016/12/new-series-how-to-be-last-a-practical-theology-for-privileged-people.

Cole, Charles. *Christian Mission in the Third Millennium*. New York: GBGM, 2004.

Cole, Teju. "The White Savior Industrial Complex." *The Atlantic* (March 2012). http://www.theatlantic.com/international/archive/2012/03/the-white-savior-industrial-complex/254843.

Congo Mission Conference of the Methodist Episcopal Church: Journals of the Eleventh, Twelfth, Thirteenth, and Fourteenth Sessions. n.p.: 1928–1931. https://divdl.library.yale.edu/divinitycontent/dayrep/Methodist%20Episcopal%20Church.%20Congo%20Mission%201928-1931%20v11-14.pdf.

"Connexio." http://www.connexio.ch/en/about-us.html.

Corbett, Steve. *When Helping Hurts: How to Alleviate Poverty Without Hurting the Poor and Yourself*. Chicago: Moody, 2009.

Couture, Pamela. *We Are Not All Victims: Local Peacebuilding in the Democratic Republic of Congo*. International Practical Theology 18. Zurich: Lit Verlag, 2016.

Cunha, Darlena. "This Is What Happened When I Drove My Mercedes to Pick Up Food Stamps." *The Washington Post* (July 8, 2014). https://www.washingtonpost.com/posteverything/wp/2014/07/08/this-is-what-happened-when-i-drove-my-mercedes-to-pick-up-food-stamps/?utm_term=.d9f909d218f0.

"Defining Culture." https://www.peacecorps.gov/educators/resources/defining-culture.
"Delegation Visits African Refugee Camps." UMN (August 26, 1994).
"Democratic Republic of Congo Profile-Timeline." *BBC News* (December 6, 2017). http://www.bbc.com/news/world-africa-13286306.
Denyer, Taylor. "Africa, Reconciling Ministries, and The United Methodist Church." *United Methodist Insight* (September 13, 2013). http://um-insight.net/perspectives/africa-reconciling-umc.
"Derald Wing Sue." *Psychology Today*. https://www.psychologytoday.com/experts/derald-wing-sue-phd.
Dharmaraj, Glory, and Jacob Dharmaraj. *Mutuality in Mission: A Theological Principle for the Twenty-First Century*. New York: GBGM/The UMC, 2001.
DiAngelo, Robin. "White Fragility: Why It's So Hard to Talk to White People About Racism." *The Good Men Project* (April 9, 2015). https://goodmenproject.com/featured-content/white-fragility-why-its-so-hard-to-talk-to-white-people-about-racism-twlm.
Dias, Elizabeth. "'We Are Not Going Anywhere': Progressive Methodists Vow to Fight Ban on Gay Clergy." *New York Times* (March 1, 2019). https://www.nytimes.com/2019/03/01/us/united-methodist-church-gay-clergy-ban.html.
Dodge, Ralph E. *The Revolutionary Bishop Who Saw God at Work in Africa*. Reprint, Tucson, AZ: Wheatmark, 2009.
———. *The Unpopular Missionary*. Westwood, NJ: Fleming H. Revell, 1964.
"Dr. Glen Eschtruth Slain in Zaire." NWO (July/August 1977) 50.
"DRCongo Provinces Named." Wikimedia Commons. https://commons.wikimedia.org/wiki/File:DRCongo_provinces_named.png#file.
Dube, Musa W. *Other Ways of Reading: African Women and the Bible*. Geneva: WCC, 2001.
———. *Postcolonial Feminist Interpretations of the Bible*. Saint Louis: Chalice, 2000.
DuVernay, Ava, dir. *13th*. Los Gatos, CA: Netflix, 2016.
Edgerton, Robert. *The Troubled Heart of Africa: A History of Congo*. New York: St. Martin's, 2002.
Einstein, Albert. "Life Is Like Riding a Bicycle. To Keep Your Balance You Must Keep Moving." Letter to Eduard Einstein (February 5, 1930). Translated by Barbara Wolff. https://quoteinvestigator.com/2015/06/28/bicycle.
Elliott, Dorinda. "Giving Back: A Special Report on Volunteer Vacations." *Conde Nast Traveler* (January 15, 2013). https://www.cntraveler.com/stories/2013-01-15/volunteer-vacations-rewards-risks.
Fanon, Frantz. *Black Skin, White Masks*. Translated by Richard Philcox. New York: Grove, 1952.
———. *The Wretched of the Earth*. Translated by Richard Philcox. New York: Grove, 1963.
"First Medical Team Goes to Help African Refugees." UMN (September 2, 1994).
"Food Shortages Reported in Zaire." UMN (December 6, 1991).
Freire, Paulo. *Pedagogy of the Oppressed*. New York: Continuum, 1970.
"Frequently Asked Questions About the Council of Bishops." The UMC. http://www.umc.org/who-we-are/frequently-asked-questions-about-the-council-of-bishops.
Friedman, Thomas L. *Thank You for Being Late: An Optimist's Guide to Thriving in the Age of Accelerations*. New York: Macmillan, 2016. Audiobook.
"Friendly Planet Missiology." www.friendlyplanetmissiology.org.

Friesen, Gary Randall. "The Long-Term Impact of Short-Term Missions on the Beliefs, Attitudes and Behaviors of Young Adults." DTh thesis, University of South Africa, 2004.

"Funeral for John Enright." Facebook video, 1:54:18 (January 1, 2018). https://www.facebook.com/KafakumbaZambia/videos/1536407639776603.

Garrison, Lloyd. "28 More White Hostages Found Slain in Stanleyville." *New York Times* (November 28, 1964). https://www.nytimes.com/1964/11/28/28-more-white-hostages-found-slain-in-stanleyville.html.

The General Commission on Race and Religion (GCORR). *Vital Conversations on Race, Culture, and Justice: Series 1 and 2.* n.p.: The UMC, 2016. https://www.gcorr.org/series.

Gilbert, Kathy. "Pastors Bike Through Congo to Bring Hope." UMNS (November 3, 2010). http://archives.gcah.org/xmlui/bitstream/handle/10516/2189/8853523.htm?sequence=3.

———. "Western Jurisdiction Elects Openly Gay United Methodist Bishop." UMNS (July 15, 2016). http://www.umc.org/news-and-media/western-jurisdiction-elects-openly-gay-united-methodist-bishop.

Gipe, Emily. "Adventures of a Missionary Kid in Africa." NWO (September/October 1998) 22–23.

Gipe, Beth, and Emily Gipe. "Christmas in Congo." NWO (November/December 1998) 18–19.

Green, Joel B., and Mark D. Baker. *Recovering the Scandal of the Cross: Atonement in the New Testament and Contemporary Contexts.* Downers Grove, IL: InterVarsity, 2000.

Hahn, Heather. "Agency Urges Withholding Funds from East Africa." The UMC (May 21, 2015). http://www.umc.org/news-and-media/agency-urges-withholding-funds-from-east-africa.

Haller, Scot. "Africa's Sick and Hungry Kids are All in the Family for Actress Sally Struthers." *People* (April 18, 1983). http://people.com/archive/africas-sick-and-hungry-kids-are-all-in-the-family-for-actress-sally-struthers-vol-19-no-15.

Harman, Robert J. *From Missions to Mission: The History of Mission of The United Methodist Church, 1968–2000.* New York: GBGM, 2005.

Hartzler, Omar Lee. "Zaire After Twenty-One Years." NWO (January 1982) 13–18.

Heuertz, Christopher, and Christine Pohl. *Friendship at the Margins: Discovering Mutuality in Service and Mission.* Downers Grove, IL: InterVarsity, 2010.

"History of The United Methodist Church in Africa." The UMC. http://www.umc.org/who-we-are/history-of-the-united-methodist-church-in-africa.

Hochschild, Adam. *King Leopold's Ghost: A Story of Greed, Terror, and Heroism in Colonial Africa.* New York: Mariner, 1999.

Holley, Peter. "Republican Lawmaker Wants to Ban Welfare Recipients from Buying Steak and Lobster." *Washington Post* (February 23, 2016). https://www.washingtonpost.com/news/wonk/wp/2016/02/23/republican-lawmaker-wants-to-ban-welfare-recipients-from-buying-steak-and-lobster/?utm_term=.9b61e50133c2.

"Homes of Zaire Bishops, Missionaries Looted." UMNS (February 5, 1993).

"Homosexuality: Full Book of Discipline Statements." The UMC. http://www.umc.org/what-we-believe/homosexuality-full-book-of-discipline-statements.

Hoover, Jeffrey. "Big Men, Wealth in People, and Religious Change Methodism in the Rural Katanga Copperbelt Hinterland." Paper presented at the University of Leiden African Studies Centre, Leiden, November 28–29, 2013.

———. "La construction de la Wallace Memorial Church (1922–1932)." In *Lubumbashi, Cent Ans D'histoire*, edited by Maurice Amuri Mpala-Lutebele, 183–98. Paris: L'Harmattan, 2013.

———. "Sipilingas: Intra-regional African initiatives and the United Methodist Church in Katanga and Zambia, 1910–1945." In *The Objects of Life in Central Africa: The History of Consumption and Social Change, 1840–1980*, edited by Richard Ross et al., 67–91. Leiden/Boston: Brill, 2013.

Hoover, Jeffrey, et al. *L'Église Méthodiste-Unie au Katanga: Hier, Aujourd'hui, Demain.* Likasi: Presses de l'Université Méthodiste au Katanga Mulungwishi, 2010.

Hope, Anne, and Sally Timmel. *Training for Transformation: A Handbook for Community Workers*. Gweru, Zimbabwe: Mambo, 1984.

House, Christie. "House Notes: Caring for Mothers, Samuteb Hospital." Ministry With the Poor. http://www.ministrywith.org/blog/view/27.

"How Are Local Church Apportionments Figured?" The UMC. http://www.umc.org/what-we-believe/how-are-local-church-apportionments-figured.

Howell, Brian M. *Short-Term Mission: An Ethnography of Christian Travel Narrative and Experience*. Downers Grove, IL: Intervarsity, 2012.

Howell, Leon. *Methodism at Risk: A Wake-Up Call*. Kingston, NY: Information Project for United Methodists, 2003.

Illich, Ivan. "To Hell with Good Intentions." Paper presented at Conference on InterAmerican Student Projects, Cuernavaca, Mexico, April 20, 1968.

Ingleby, Jonathan. *Beyond Empire: Postcolonialism and Mission in a Global Context*. Keynes, Buckinghamshire: AuthorHouse, 2010.

"International Strife Addressed by Bishops." UMN (November 22, 1991).

Israel, Jeff. "African Civilizations Map Pre-Colonial." Wikimedia Commons. https://commons.wikimedia.org/wiki/File:African-civilizations-map-pre-colonial.svg.

Jackson, Henry F. "Zaire: How Poverty in the Midst of Plenty Challenges United States Policy." NWO (October 1983) 8–11.

Johnson, Elizabeth. *Quest for the Living God: Mapping Frontiers in the Theology of God*. New York: Continuum, 2007.

Journal of the 1948 General Conference of The Methodist Church. Nashville: Methodist, 1948.

Journal of the Second and Third Sessions: Congo Mission Conference. Bristol: Musgrove, 1919.

Judge, Monique. "White Fragility Leads to White Violence: Why Conversations About Race with White People Fall Apart." *The Root* (January 15, 2017). http://www.theroot.com/white-fragility-leads-to-white-violence-why-conversati-1791233086.

Jusu, Phileas. "African Bishops Reaffirm Stance on Marriage, Vow to Maintain Unity." UMNS (September 24, 2018).

Kazadi, Betty. "When You Are in Christ, You Become a New Creature." Facebook (May 29, 2017). https://www.facebook.com/bkazadi1.

Kelly, Sean. *America's Tyrant: The CIA and Mobutu of Zaire: How the United States Put Mobutu in Power, Protected Him from His Enemies, Helped Him Become One of the Richest Men in the World, and Lived to Regret It*. Washington, DC: American University Press, 1993.

Kemper, Thomas. "How Mission Sustains the Church: An Appreciation of New World Outlook." NWO (July 2018) 6–10. https://www.mtnskyumc.org/newsdetail/how-mission-sustains-the-church-an-appreciation-of-new-world-outlook-11606515.
Kendi, Ibram. *How to Be an Anti-Racist*. New York: Random, 2019.
"Kingdom of Lunda." Wikipedia. https://en.wikipedia.org/wiki/Kingdom_of_Lunda.
Kinniburgh, Colin. "Beyond Conflict Minerals: The Congo's Resource Curse Lives On." *Dissent* (Spring 2014). https://www.dissentmagazine.org/article/beyond-conflict-minerals-the-congos-resource-curse-lives-on.
Kliff, Sarah. "How Abortion Became a Political Litmus Test." *Washington Post* (October 24, 2011). https://www.washingtonpost.com/blogs/ezra-klein/post/how-abortion-became-a-political-litmus-test/2011/10/24/gIQAwOdOCM_blog.html?utm_term=.7ae1dec90ba5.
Knutson, Phillip James. "Partnership in Mission: Mismeeting in Jesus' Name?" DTh diss., University of the Western Cape, 1998.
Kritzinger, J. N. J. "Faith to Faith. Missiology as Encounterology." *Verbum et Ecclesia* 29 (2008) 764–90.
———. "Interreligious Dialogue: Problems and Perspectives: A Christian Theological Approach." *Scriptura* 60 (1997) 47–62.
———. *Tutorial Letter: Research Proposal Module for the DTh in Missiology*. Pretoria: UNISA, 2013.
Kritzinger, J. N. J., and Willem Saayman. *David J. Bosch: Prophetic Integrity, Cruciform Praxis*. Pietermaritzburg: Cluster, 2011.
Kurewa, John Wesley Zwomunondiita. *An African Pilgrimage on Evangelism: A Historical Study of the Various Approaches to Evangelism in Africa 100–2000 CE*. Africa Ministry Series. Nashville: Discipleship Resources International, 2011.
———. *Preaching and Cultural Identity: Proclaiming the Gospel in Africa*. Nashville: Abington, 2000.
Lederleitner, Mary. *Cross-Cultural Partnerships: Navigating the Complexities of Money and Mission*. Downers Grove, IL: InterVarsity, 2010.
Leedy, Paul D., and Jeanne Ellis Ormrod. *Practical Research: Planning and Design*. 8th ed. Upper Saddle River, NJ: Pearson Prentice Hall, 2005.
Lerrigo, Charles. "Mutuality in Mission." NWO (April 1984) 20–25.
Livermore, David. *Serving with Eyes Wide Open: Doing Short-Term Missions with Cultural Intelligence*. Grand Rapids: Baker, 2013.
Lovell, Bill. *100th Anniversary of the Methodist Church in Central Congo 1912–2013*. www.scribd.com/doc/167701380/100th-Anniversary-of-United-Methodism-in-Central-Congo-1912-Present.
Luhahi, Lahi. "Africa: Making Mission Happen at Home." NWO (May/June 1994) 4–6.
"Lunda Empire." Wikimedia Commons. https://commons.wikimedia.org/wiki/File:Lunda_Empire.png.
Lupton, Robert D. *Charity Detox: What Charity Would Look Like If We Cared About Results*. New York: HarperOne, 2015.
———. *Toxic Charity: How Churches and Charities Hurt Those They Help and How to Reverse It*. New York: HarperOne, 2011.
Mafunda, Simon. "Commentary: African Delegates Informed, Ready for GC2019." UMNS (September 26, 2018).
Makarechi, Kia. "What the Data Really Says about Police and Racial Bias." *Vanity Fair* (July 14, 2016). http://www.vanityfair.com/news/2016/07/data-police-racial-bias.

"March Opposes Zaire Violence." UMN (March 6, 1992).
Mason, J. *Qualitative Researching*, 2nd ed. London: Sage, 2002.
Maxwell, David. "Freed Slaves, Missionaries, and Respectability: The Expansion of the Christian Frontier from Angola to Belgian Congo." *The Journal of African History* 54 (2013) 79–102.
———. "The Soul of the Luba: W. F. P. Burton, Missionary Ethnography, and Belgian Colonial Science." *History and Anthropology* 19 (2008) 325–51.
Mbembe, Achille. *On the Postcolony*. Berkeley: University of California Press, 2001.
McAnally, Thomas S. "Make Noise—Bishop Asks United Methodists in Zaire." UMNS (May 24, 1991).
"Meet the Peacemakers: Bishop Ntambo Nkulu Ntanda." https://tanenbaum.org/peacemakers-in-action-network/meet-the-peacemakers/bishop-ntambo-nkulu-ntanda.
Memmi, Albert. *The Colonizer and the Colonized*. Boston: Beacon, 1965.
The Methodist Episcopal Church. *The Christian Advocate* (February 17, 1949).
Metzl, Jonathan M. "When the Shooter is White: The Racial Motivations Behind the 'Lone Wolf' Label." *Washington Post* (October 6, 2017). https://www.washingtonpost.com/news/made-by-history/wp/2017/10/06/when-the-shooter-is-white/?utm_term=.35182d3cd6bd.
"Mission is More Than a Two-Way Street." NWO (May 1989) 10–13.
"Mission Memo: Changes in Congo." NWO (November/December 1997) 19.
"Mission Memos: Deaths." NWO (November/December 1998) 27.
"Mission Memo: Moratorium." NWO (December 1975) 2.
"Mission Memo: Zaire." NWO (July/August 1977) 3.
"Mission Memo: Zaire." NWO (September 1977) 3.
"Mission Memo: Zaire." NWO (December 1977) 6.
"Mission Memo: Zaire." NWO (July/August 1978) 4.
"Mission Memo: Zaire." NWO (January 1979) 3.
"Mission Memo: Zaire." NWO (March 1979) 6.
"Mission Memo: Zaire." NWO (May 1979) 3.
"Mission Memo: Zaire." NWO (January 1981) 3.
"Missionaries Leave Zaire." UMNS (October 4, 1991).
"Missionaries Move out of Congo as Fighting Rages." UMNS (August 21, 1998).
"Missionaries Safe in Wave of Looting in Zaire." UMNS (September 27, 1991).
"Missionary Injured." NWO (May 1985) 6.
Moltmann, Jurgen. *The Coming of God: Christian Eschatology*. Minneapolis: First Fortress, 2004.
Montgomery, Richard. "Disclosing Murder or Suicide When Selling a Home." *Green Bay Gazette* (July 23, 2015). http://www.greenbaypressgazette.com/story/money/2015/07/23/disclosing-murder-suicide-selling-home/30526789.
Montgomery-Fate, Tom. *Beyond the White Noise: Mission in a Multicultural World*. St. Louis: Chalice, 1997.
Mooney, Chris. "Across America, Whites Are Biased and They Don't Even Know It." *Washington Post* (December 8, 2014). https://www.washingtonpost.com/news/wonk/wp/2014/12/08/across-america-whites-are-biased-and-they-dont-even-know-it/?utm_term=.79c450e37a12.
Moyo, Dambisa. *Dead Aid: Why Aid Is Not Working and How There Is a Better Way for Africa*. New York: Farrar, Straus and Giroux, 2009.

Mungazi, Dickson A. *In the Footsteps of the Masters: Desmond M. Tutu and Abel T. Muzorewa*. Westport, CT: Praeger, 2000.
Munza, Kasongo. *A Letter to Africa About Africa*. Johannesburg: Trans World Radio, 2008.
Mutombo, Nkulu-N'Sengha. "Baluba." In *Encyclopedia of African Religion*, edited by Molefi Asante and Ama Mazama, 97–100. Thousand Oaks, CA: Sage, 2009.
———. "Bumuntu." In *Encyclopedia of African Religion*, edited by Molefi Asante and Ama Mazama, 142–47. Thousand Oaks, CA: Sage, 2009.
———. "Bumuntu Memory and Authentic Personhood: An African Art of Becoming Humane." In *Memory and the Narrative Imagination in the African and Diaspora Experience*, edited by Tom Spencer-Walters, 295–336. Troy, MI: Bedford, 2011.
Muyombo, Mande. "Episcopal Installation." Speech delivered at Episcopal installation, Kamina, DR Congo, May 28, 2017.
———. "Theological Responses to the Mai-Mai Conflict." *Journal of Pastoral Theology* 17 (2007) 27–35.
Muzorewa, Abel. "Letter to Marshall Murphree." (July 5, 1973).
Myers, Bryant. *Walking With the Poor: Principles and Practices of Transformational Development*. Maryknoll, NY: Orbis, 2011.
Navarro, Nelson A. "The Flying Methodists of Zaire." NWO (September 1985) 13.
Nelson Enright, Kenneth. "Foreword." In *A Deep Gladness: Stories from the Lives of Ken and Lorraine Enright*, by Gina Riendeau, n.p. Indianapolis: Dog Ear, 2013.
"Nelson Navarro Memoir to Launch January 16 at Philippine Center." *The FilAm* (January 7, 2014). http://thefilam.net/archives/13558.
"News in Brief." UMN (September 11, 1992).
"News in Brief." UMN (October 2, 1992).
"News in Brief." UMN (October 30, 1992).
"News in Brief." UMN (December 16, 1994).
"News in Brief." UMN (January 16, 1995).
"News in Brief." UMN (February 10, 1995).
"News in Brief." UMN (April 28, 1995).
"News in Brief." UMN (June 16, 1995).
"News in Brief." UMN (September 1, 1995).
"News in Brief." UMN (September 8, 1995).
"News in Brief." UMN (December 1, 1995).
"News in Brief." UMN (December 8, 1995).
"News in Brief." UMN (February 2, 1996).
"News in Brief." UMN (May 10, 1996).
"News in Brief." UMN (September 27, 1996).
"News in Brief." UMN (October 25, 1996).
"News in Brief." UMN (November 1, 1996).
"News in Brief." UMN (November 8, 1996).
"News in Brief." UMN (November 15, 1996).
"News in Brief." UMN (November 22, 1996).
"News in Brief." UMN (December 13, 1996).
"News in Brief." UMN (February 14, 1997).
"News in Brief." UMN (February 21, 1997).
"News in Brief." UMN (March 14, 1997).
"News in Brief." UMN (March 28, 1997).

"News in Brief." UMN (May 16, 1997).
"News in Brief." UMN (May 19, 1997).
"News in Brief." UMN (May 23, 1997).
"News in Brief." UMN (September 12, 1997).
"News in Brief." UMN (November 14, 1997).
"News in Brief." UMN (September 11, 1998).
Ngandu, Kahakatshi Basua. *Contextual Evangelism of The United Methodist Church in Bemba Culture: A Missiological Perspective.* PhD diss., UNISA, October 2017.
Ngoy, Nelson K. "Paradigm Shift in Twenty-First Century Mission in Post-Colonial Africa: Rethinking the Future of The United Methodist Church in Light of Emerging Challenges." Unpublished draft of talk given at the UMC's Bicentennial Mission Conference, Atlanta, GA, April 2019.
Nhiwatiwa, Eben K. *Preaching in the African Context: Why We Preach.* Africa Ministry Series. South Africa: Shumani/Discipleship Resources International, 2012.
Nkonge, Jean-Marie. *An Examination of the Development of Christian Worship in the Southern Congo Methodist Church with a View to Promoting a Relevant and Indigenous Form of Worship.* PhD diss., Rhodes University, August 2000.
Nooter Roberts, Mary. "The King is a Woman: Shaping Power in Luba Royal Arts." *African Arts* 46 (2013) 68–81.
Norwood, Frederick A. *The Story of American Methodism.* Nashville: Abingdon, 1974.
Nzongola-Ntalaja, George. *The Congo: From Leopold to Kabila: A People's History.* New York: Zed, 2001.
"Oppression Seen as Opening Doors for Church." UMN (August 14, 1992).
Persons, David, and Lori Persons. "July News Centennial." *Congo Missions—Mulungwishi* (blog) (July 31, 2010). http://umccongo.blogspot.com/2010/07/july-news-centennial.html.
———. "Seminary." *Congo Missions—Mulungwishi* (blog). http://umccongo.blogspot.com/p/methodist-seminary.html.
———. "Women's School." *Congo Missions—Mulungwishi* (blog). http://umccongo.blogspot.com/p/womens-school.html.
Phiri, Isabel Apawo. "Partnership in Mission: An Appraisal of the Partnership of Women and Men." In *Postcolonial Mission: Power and Partnership in World Christianity*, edited by Desmond van der Water, 452–65. Upland, CA: Sopher, 2011.
Pollock, David C., and Ruth van Reken. *Third Culture Kids: The Experience of Growing Up Among Worlds.* London: Nicholas Brealey, 2001.
"President's Report." *Daily Journal of The United Methodist Board of Missions* (September 5–9, 1968).
Putnam, Robert D. *Bowling Alone: The Collapse and Revival of American Community.* New York: Simon & Schuster, 2000.
"Radi-Aid; Africa for Norway." https://www.radiaid.com.
"Radi-Aid Awards." Rusty Radiator. http://www.rustyradiator.com.
Reefe, Thomas Q. *The Rainbow and the Kings: A History of the Luba Empire to 1891.* Berkeley: University of California Press, 1981.
"Refugee Work Exhilarating but Hard." UMN (September 30, 1994).
"Report of the Africa Bishops Consultation, Salisbury, Rhodesia." In *Daily Journal*, October 10–18, World Division Minutes, Appendix G, 484. New York: GBGM, 1974.

Richards, Randolph, and Branson O'Brien. *Misreading Scripture with Western Eyes: Removing Cultural Blinders to Better Understand the Bible*. Downers Grove, IL: InterVarsity, 2012.

Rieger, Joerg. "Theology and Mission Between Neocolonialism and Postcolonialism." *Mission Studies: Journal of the International Association for Mission Studies* 21 (2004) 201–27.

Riendeau, Gina. *A Deep Gladness: Stories from the Lives of Ken and Lorraine Enright*. Indianapolis: Dog Ear, 2013.

Robb, James. "Missions Derailed: A Special Report on the UM General Board of Global Ministries." *Good News Magazine* (May/June 1983).

Robert, Dana. "History Lessons for Methodism in Mission." NWO (May/June 1999) 5–9.

———. *Joy to the World: Mission in the Age of Global Christianity: A Mission Study for 2010 and 2011*. New York: Women's Division, GBGM, 2010.

———. "Springer, Helen Emily [Chapman] Rasmussen (1868–1946)." http://www.bu.edu/missiology/missionary-biography/r-s/springer-helen-emily-chapman-rasmussen-1868-1946.

Rose, Lillian Roybal. "Healing from Racism: Cross-Cultural Leadership Teaching for the Multicultural Future." *Winds of Change* (Spring 1995) 14–17. www.roybalrose.com/healing.pdf.

Rothman, Joshua. "The Meaning of 'Culture.'" *New Yorker* (December 26, 2014). https://www.newyorker.com/books/joshua-rothman/meaning-culture.

Sano, Roy, and Peggy Billings. "World Program Division: Boldly into the Future of Mission." NWO (May 1987) 6–11.

Sarantakos, S. *Social Research*. 4th ed. Houndmills, Basingstoke: Palgrave Macmillan, 2013.

Sartre, Jean Paul. "Introduction." In *The Colonizer and the Colonized*, by Albert Memmi, xxi–xxix. Boston: Beacon, 1965.

Schutz, Chris Kinyon. "Oklahoma Church Sends Bibles to Congo." UMNS (January 11, 2012).

Sedmak, Clemens. *Doing Local Theology: A Guide for Artisans of a New Humanity*. Maryknoll, NY: Orbis, 2002.

Shearer, Lee. "Bishop Issues Call for Tolerance as Methodist Conference Opens in Atlanta." *OnlineAthens* (June 13, 2017). https://www.onlineathens.com/local-news/2017-06-13/bishop-issues-call-tolerance-methodist-conference-opens-athens.

Scherer, James. *Gospel, Church, and Kingdom: Comparative Studies in World Mission Theology*. Minneapolis: Augsburg, 1987.

———. *Missionary Go Home!: A Reappraisal of the Christian World Mission Today—Its Basis, Philosophy, Program, Problems, and Outlook for the Future*. Englewood Cliffs, NJ: Prentice Hall, 1964.

Scott, James C. *Domination and the Arts of Resistance: Hidden Transcripts*. New Haven, CT: Yale University Press, 1990.

Smith, Jeremy. "Hacking Christianity." *Hacking Christianity* (blog). http://hackingchristianity.net.

———. "Schism." *Hacking Christianity* (blog). http://hackingchristianity.net/umc/schism.

———. "UMC Schismatics Are Now in Plain View . . . but Why?" *Hacking Christianity* (blog) (March 19, 2018). http://hackingchristianity.net/2018/03/umc-schismatics-are-now-in-plain-view-but-why.html.

Springer, John McKendree. *Pioneering in the Congo.* New York: Katanga, 1916. https://archive.org/details/pioneeringincongoospririch.

———. "Work in Lunda." Paper presented at West Central Africa Mission Conference, MEC, Tenth Session, Quiongua, Angola, August 1913.

Stearns, Jason. *Dancing in the Glory of Monsters: The Collapse of the Congo and the Great War of Africa.* New York: Public Affairs, 2011.

Sue, Derald Wing, et al. "Racial Microaggressions in Everyday Life: Implications for Clinical Practice." *American Psychologist* 62.4 (2007) 271–86.

Tanton, Tim. "Bishops' Appeal Changes Lives in Africa." UMNS (June 1, 2003).

Tatum, Beverly Daniel. *Why Are All the Black Kids Sitting Together in the Cafeteria? And Other Conversations About Race.* Rev. ed. New York: Basic, 1997.

Tempels, Placide. *Bantu Philosophy.* Translated by Colin King. Reprint, Orlando: HBC, 2010.

Tharps, Lori L. "The Case of Black With a Capital B." *New York Times* (November 18, 2014). https://www.nytimes.com/2014/11/19/opinion/the-case-for-black-with-a-capital-b.html.

Thiong'o, Ngũgĩ wa. *Decolonizing the Mind: The Politics of Language in African Literature.* Nairobi: East African Educational, 2005.

"Timeline: Sixty Years of Sharing Through The Advance." The UMC. http://www.umcmission.org/Give-to-Mission/About-the-Advance/Timeline.

Tlostanova, Madina, and Walter Mignolo. *Learning to Unlearn: Decolonial Reflections from Eurasia and the Americas.* Columbus: Ohio State University Press, 2012.

Totolo, Edoardo. "Coltan and Conflict in the DRC." https://reliefweb.int/report/democratic-republic-congo/Coltan-and-conflict-drc.

"UM Missionary Tells of Trial in Kolwezi." NWO (July/August 1978) 43.

UN Security Council. "Report of the Panel of Experts on the Illegal Exploitation of Natural Resources and Other Forms of Wealth of DR Congo." https://reliefweb.int/report/democratic-republic-congo/report-panel-experts-illegal-exploitation-natural-resources-and-.

"The United Methodist Church in Senegal." NWO (September/October 1998) 27.

"United Methodist Church Structure in Africa: Zaire." NWO (May/June 1994) 28.

"United Methodists Dispatch Second Team to Zaire." UMN (September 30, 1994).

"United Methodist Teams Work in Zaire Refugee Camps." UMN (January 16, 1995).

"United States Urged to Cut Ties with Zaire." UMN (April 3, 1992).

"Upheaval in Zaire Featured on TV Series." UMN (October 25, 1991).

"US Should Act Immediately to End Wars in Africa: Bishops." UMN (November 13, 1998).

Uzukwu, Elochukwu E. *A Listening Church: Autonomy and Communion in African Churches.* Maryknoll, NY: Orbis, 1996.

Verkuyl, Johannes. *Contemporary Missiology: An Introduction.* Grand Rapids: Eerdmans, 1978.

Walters, Bob. *The Last Missionary.* Indianapolis: Dog Ear, 2016.

Wan, Enoch. *Diaspora Missiology.* Portland: Institute of Diaspora Studies, 2011.

Water, Desmond van der. "Council for World Mission: A Case Study and Critical Appraisal of Postcolonial Partnership in Mission." In *Postcolonial Mission: Power and Partnership in World Christianity*, edited by Desmond van der Water, 33–60. Upland, CA: Sopher, 2011.

Webster, Paul, and Roxanne Webster. "Improving Agriculture and Family Health." NWO (July/August 1998) 44.

Wellman, David. *Portraits of White Racism*. 2nd ed. Cambridge: Cambridge University Press, 1993.

Wells, Samuel. *God's Companions: Reimagining Christian Ethics*. Oxford: Blackwell, 2006.

———. *Improvisation*. Grand Rapids: Brazos, 2004.

———. *A Nazareth Manifesto: Being with God*. Oxford: Wiley Blackwell, 2015.

———. "Rethinking Service." *The Cresset* 76 (2013) 6–14. http://thecresset.org/2013/Easter/Wells_E2013.html.

Wells, Samuel, and Marcia Owen. *Living Without Enemies: Being Present in the Midst of Violence*. Downers Grove, IL: InterVarsity, 2011.

Wesley, John. "Free Grace." In *John Wesley's Sermons: An Anthology*, edited by Albert Outler and Richard Heitzenrater, 49–60. Nashville: Abingdon, 1991.

———. "On Visiting the Sick (Sermon 98)." The UMC. https://www.umcmission.org/Find-Resources/John-Wesley-Sermons/Sermon-98-On-Visiting-the-Sick

———. "The Scriptural Way of Salvation." In *John Wesley's Sermons: An Anthology*, edited by Albert Outler and Richard Heitzenrater, 371–80. Nashville: Abingdon, 1991.

———. "The Use of Money." In *John Wesley's Sermons: An Anthology*, edited by Albert Outler and Richard Heitzenrater, 347–58. Nashville: Abingdon, 1991.

"Wesleyan Covenant Association." https://www.wesleyancovenant.org.

White, Deborah. "Leaders Remember Central Jurisdiction's Dissolution." UMNS (April 27, 2008). http://www.umc.org/news-and-media/leaders-remember-central-jurisdictions-dissolution.

"White Noise." *Merriam-Webster*. https://www.merriam-webster.com/dictionary/white%20noise.

Whitworth, David Martin. "Missio Dei and the Means of Grace." PhD diss., University of Manchester, 2012.

"Who We Are." The UMC. http://www.umc.org/who-we-are.

Wilkinson, Brenda. "A Panel of Witnesses." NWO (September/October 1997) 12–15.

Wilson, Anne. "Long Distance Trade and the Luba Lumami Empire." *The Journal of African History* 13 (1972) 575–89.

"World Division." NWO (April 4, 1981) 14.

Worrall, Emily. "Barbie Savior." https://www.instagram.com/barbiesavior/?hl=en.

Wright, Jamie. *The Very Worst Missionary: A Memoir or Whatever*. New York: Convergent, 2017.

Young, Robert J. C. "Sartre: The African Philosopher." In *Colonialism and Neocolonialism*, by John Paul Sartre, viii–xix. London: Routledge Classics, 2001.

"Zaire: African Evangelism." NWO (June 1977) 42.

www.ingramcontent.com/pod-product-compliance
Lightning Source LLC
Chambersburg PA
CBHW071150300426
44113CB00009B/1153